CCCC

Bibliography of Composition and Rhetoric

1991

Gail E. Hawisher
Cynthia L. Selfe
Editors

Sibylle Gruber
William J. Williamson
Associate Editors

Conference on College Composition and Communication, A Conference of the National Council of Teachers of English

Southern Illinois University Press
Carbondale and Edwardsville

Printed in the United States of America
Production supervised by Natalia Nadraga

ISSN 1046–0675
ISBN 0-8093-1892-X
ISBN 0-8093-1893-8 (pbk.)

The paper used in this publication meets the minimum requirements of American National Standard for Information Sciences—Permanence of Paper for Printed Library Materials, ANSI Z39.48-1984. ∞

This volume is dedicated, with much love and respect, to Erika Lindemann, founder of the *CCCC Bibliography of Composition and Rhetoric*. As founder of the *CCCC Bibliography,* Professor Lindemann has provided the entire profession with a way to see itself and trace its emerging history as a field of study. She has also shown her many colleagues how they might locate their own contributions within the larger professional conversation, while at the same time providing her fellow editors with an exemplary role model.

Contents

Preface ix
Gail E. Hawisher
Cynthia L. Selfe

Guidelines for Users of the *CCCC Bibliography* xi
Erika Lindemann

Contributing Bibliographers xv

Journal Abbreviations xvii

Abbreviations in Entries xxi

1. Bibliographies and Checklists 1

2. Theory and Research 4
Entries that discuss concepts or hypotheses, that explain how people learn, that describe fields or general methodologies, that examine historical developments, that review previous explanations of a subject, or that advance conclusions drawn from empirical evidence.
2.1 Rhetorical Theory, Discourse Theory, and Composing 4
2.2 Rhetorical History 26
2.3 Political, Religious, and Judicial Rhetoric 32
2.4 Computer and Literacy Studies 46
2.5 Advertising, Public Relations, and Business 63
2.6 Literature, Film, and Theater 68
2.7 Reading 74
2.8 Linguistics, Grammatical Theory, and Semantics 78
2.9 Psychology 90

2.10 Education 97
2.11 Journalism, Publishing, Television, and Radio 99
2.12 Philosophy 103
2.13 Science and Medicine 105
2.14 Cross-Disciplinary Studies 108
2.15 Other 110

3. Teacher Education, Administration, and Social Roles **112**

Entries that discuss the education of teachers, that examine administrative or personnel policies and procedures, that describe services supporting classroom instruction, or that treat relations between educational institutions and the larger society.

3.1 Teacher Education 112
3.2 Administration 115
3.3 Support Services 118
3.4 Role in Society 123
3.5 Other 125

4. Curriculum **126**

Entries that explain teaching methods, that describe courses or units of instruction, or that combine theory with practice in a specific subject area or skill.

4.1 General Discussions 126
4.2 Higher Education 138
  4.2.1 Developmental Writing 138
  4.2.2 First-Year College Composition 140
  4.2.3 Advanced Composition 143
  4.2.4 Business Communication 143
  4.2.5 Scientific and Technical Communication 148
  4.2.6 Writing in Literature Courses 155
  4.2.7 Communication in Other Disciplines 156
4.3 Adult and Graduate Education 160
4.4 English as a Second Language 162
4.5 Research and Study Skills 167
4.6 Other 168

5. Testing, Measurement, and Evaluation **170**

Entries that examine ways to assess students' work, that describe statistical or analytical techniques to measure or evaluate teaching and learning, or that discuss appropriate criteria for and uses of tests, scales, or other instruments.

5.1 Evaluation of Students 170
5.2 Evaluation of Teachers 174
5.3 Evaluation of Programs 175
5.4 Other 176

Subject Index **179**

Name Index **185**

Preface

Gail E. Hawisher
Cynthia L. Selfe

As new editors of the *CCCC Bibliography of Composition and Rhetoric*, we are pleased to take on the important task of ensuring that the *Bibliography* continues as the only annual and comprehensive scholarly resource available to scholars and teachers in composition and rhetoric: this 1991 volume cites 1925 titles that, with few exceptions, were published during the 1991 calendar year.

We should add a few words about the goals we have identified for the *CCCC Bibliography* project this year. Under Erika Lindemann's capable editorship, the *Bibliography* became a key tool for scholars and teachers and a productive influence on the profession. To continue the fine tradition that Lindemann has established, we adopted three preliminary goals for the tenure of our editorship; these are listed below. We ask that you review these goals and write to us about your response. We always welcome suggestions for improving the *Bibliography*—both as a scholarly tool for colleagues and as a record of our profession's interests and direction over time. We suspect that our goals will change, not only as we learn more about editing the *Bibliography* but also as the profession itself responds to the demands of society's renewed interest in composition and rhetoric. Our initial goals, however, are as follows:

- to master the process of producing a first-rate *CCCC Bibliography* for 1991;
- to increase CCCC members' involvement;
- to improve the accessibility of the entries in the *Bibliography*.

For the first year of our editorship we have directed our energies at the first goal. Dividing the many tasks between two institutions, finding new software to accomplish the tasks, and assembling a capable staff have occupied much of our time. With the help of good bibliographic and word-processing software and with the many advantages provided through e-mail, we are now able to send formatted files back and forth between the two schools as easily as—if not easier than—we can communicate through the telephone. Without the new capabilities that e-mail provides, we doubt that we could have edited the *Bibliography* in a timely fashion. But without Bill Williamson of Michigan Tech University and Sibylle Gruber of the University of Illinois at Urbana-Champaign, we *know* that we could not have accomplished the task. Their innovative ideas and tireless work have made the process of moving the *Bibliography* from the University of North Carolina, Chapel Hill, to the University of Illinois at Urbana-Champaign, and Michigan Tech workable. Certainly, this task would have been much more difficult and much less fun without the two of them.

Our second goal—to increase CCCC members' involvement with the *Bibliography*—had already received a great deal of attention during Erika Lindemann's tenure. And, as a result of a call for suggestions that Rick Gebhardt kindly featured for us in last October's issue of *College Composition and Communication*, we have had many letters, e-mail messages, and telephone calls, ranging from colleagues' suggesting editorial improvements, to their adding periodicals and publishers, and to their volunteering as contributing bibliographers. All these suggestions have helped us make what we hope are improvements to the 1991 edition. This year 171 contributing bibliographers have annotated 1925 entries, and we are grateful for their participation and their many excellent suggestions. We have also appreciated colleagues' requesting that their university libraries purchase the *Bibliography* so that the resource is available to as many teachers, researchers, and graduate students who are interested in composition and rhetoric as is possible.

Our third goal—making the entries more easily accessible to our readers—has been more elusive. For this first year as new editors, we decided to use the system now in place for indexing and categorizing the entries and to solicit suggestions from our readers and colleagues for the next edition. The one change we have made is to make sure that the authors listed in the author index for edited collections will appear in the annotation as well. At this point, we do not plan to annotate the individual chapters, because we do not always have access to the books themselves. But the authors will be listed so that readers are not left wondering why a particular book has been attributed to an author whose name fails to appear anywhere in the entry. With the help of our colleague, Michael Pemberton, we have also experimented with ways in which the *CCCC Bibliography* might be offered to readers in electronic form. Many of the problems of accessing the entries disappear when users can search electronically for authors, titles, and keywords. Such improvements can only increase the usefulness of the publication, and these are all projects needing attention as we move steadily toward making the *Bibliography* "reader-friendly" and available to all who desire it.

As this edition of the *CCCC Bibliography on Composition and Rhetoric* goes to press, we would like to thank the many contributing bibliographers for their conscientious and valuable work. We are also grateful to the CCCC officers, the CCCC Executive Committee members, and Miles Myers and Deborah Fox of the NCTE Headquarters staff for the excellent advice and support they have provided during our first year. We thank too the staff at Southern Illinois University Press for putting up with our many phone calls and questions about how to publish and market the *Bibliography* successfully. Teresa Bertram, the secretary to the Center for Writing Studies of the University of Illinois at Urbana-Champaign, has also been invaluable to the project. We are exceedingly sorry to be losing Kenney Withers to retirement and thank him too for listening to and advising us this past winter. And, finally, we thank Erika Lindemann for never being more than an e-mail message away. Her support continues to be essential for the success of the *CCCC Bibliography*.

Guidelines for Users of the CCCC *Bibliography*

Erika Lindemann

The *CCCC Bibliography of Composition and Rhetoric,* published by the Conference on College Composition and Communication, offers teachers and researchers an annual classified listing of scholarship on written English and its teaching. The bibliography lists each work only once, but it descriptively annotates all citations, cross-references them when appropriate, and indexes all authors and editors. A group of contributing bibliographers, listed on pages xv to xvi, prepared the citations and annotations for all entries appearing in this volume.

SCOPE OF THE BIBLIOGRAPHY

The *CCCC Bibliography* includes works that treat written communication (whether the writing people do is in English or some other language), the processes whereby human beings compose and understand written messages, and methods of teaching people to communicate effectively in writing. The *Bibliography* lists entries in five major categories (see the Contents for a more complete description of these categories):

Section 1. Bibliographies and Checklists
Section 2. Theory and Research
Section 3. Teacher Education, Administration, and Social Roles
Section 4. Curriculum
Section 5. Testing, Measurement, and Evaluation

The *Bibliography* makes few restrictions on the format, medium, or purpose of the works it includes, so long as the subject of the work falls into one of the five categories described in the preceding list. It lists only published works: books, articles, monographs, published collections (of essays, conference presentations, or working papers), bibliographies and other reference works, films, microforms, videotapes, and sound recordings. It includes citations for unpublished doctoral dissertations appearing in *Dissertation Abstracts International*. It also includes review articles that discuss several works, define movements or trends, or survey an individual's contribution to the discipline. It excludes masters theses, textbooks, computer software, book reviews, and works written in a language other than English.

SOURCES

The *CCCC Bibliography* cites works from four major sources.

Periodicals. Journals publishing articles on composition and its teaching are the source for approximately 1000 entries. Each journal is identified by an abbreviation; an alphabetical list of journal abbreviations begins on page xvii. With few exceptions, the contributing bibliographers preparing entries for journal articles examined the material firsthand.

Publishers. A second source of materials are commercial publishers and university presses. These publishers, whose participation in the bibliography project is voluntary, provided contributing bibliographers with written information for the books listed in this volume. Often, contributing bibliographers were unable to examine books firsthand and had to rely on these materials for their entries.

This volume also includes scholarly essay collections, books that bring together essays, articles, or papers by several authors. The *Bibliography* annotates these collections, but does not annotate each essay. All authors contributing to the collection are included in the annotation and listed in the Name Index.

Dissertation Abstracts International (DAI). DAI represents a third source for citations. Not all degree-granting institutions list their unpublished doctoral dissertations in *DAI*, and as a rule, the contributing bibliographers have not examined these dissertations firsthand. The citations in this volume serve only to direct readers to abstracts in *DAI*. Users will want to consult the *DAI* abstracts for additional information, including who supervised the degree candidate's work and which institution granted the degree.

Resources in Education (RIE). A fourth source of materials in the *CCCC Bibliography* is the Educational Resources Information Center (ERIC), a federally funded document retrieval system coordinated by sixteen clearinghouses.

ERIC indexes its materials in two reference works. Journal articles appear in *Cumulative Index to Journals in Education (CIJE). Resources in Education (RIE)*, on the other hand, indexes documents in the ERIC microfiche collection, available in 2600 regional libraries or directly from ERIC. These documents, frequently published elsewhere, include government documents, research and project reports, bibliographies, and conference papers. Documents indexed in *RIE* receive a six-digit "ED" number (for example, ERIC ED 305 701) and are cross-referenced under various subject headings or "descriptors."

Some documents may be listed in *RIE* and may become available through ERIC several years after they were written. For convenience and to ensure comprehensiveness, the *CCCC Bibliography* reports ERIC documents cited in *RIE* during the years covered in the current volume; that is, this volume cites ERIC documents listed in *RIE* in 1991, even though the works themselves may have an earlier "date of publication." Also as a convenience, each ERIC entry includes the six-digit "ED" number.

Contributing bibliographers working with ERIC materials have developed the following criteria for determining what documents to include in this volume:

Substantiveness. Substantive documents of general value to college composition teachers and researchers are included. Representative publications are curriculum guides, federal government final reports, and technical reports from various publication series, such as those published, for example, by the Center for the Study of Writing and the Center for the Study of Reading.

Relevance. Documents that seem to represent concerns of high interest to researchers are included. The topics of functional literacy, computers and literacy, and revision, for example, represent concerns of greater relevance than the teaching of handwriting.

Inclusiveness. All papers on composition and rhetoric available in ERIC and delivered at the annual meetings of the Conference on College Composition and Communication (CCCC) and the National Council of Teachers of English (NCTE—Fall and Spring conventions) are included. Papers delivered at other regional and national meetings—for example, meetings of the American Educational Research Association (AERA), the International Reading Association (IRA), and the Modern Language Association (MLA)—are selected for inclusion on the basis of their substantiveness and relevance.

Reference value. Items for which the ERIC microfiche system might provide unique access are included. Representative of entries meeting this criterion would be books or collections of articles no longer available from their original publishers.

Alternate access. Many professional organizations regularly make copies of book and monograph publications available as ERIC microfiche. And many papers presented as reports or conference talks and available in ERIC are later published as monographs or as articles in journals. When such information is available, the entry in this volume will include ERIC ED numbers to indicate an alternate source of access to the document. However, users of this volume should keep in mind that, although a book in ERIC reflects the exact contents of the published work, an article in ERIC is a manuscript that may see substantial revision before it is published.

The following criteria determine which items cited in *RIE* are excluded from this volume:

Communication theory. ERIC documents broadly concerned with human communication or with language study in general, rather than with college composition and rhetoric, are routinely excluded.

Local interest. ERIC documents concerned with composition and rhetoric but judged to be primarily of local interest are excluded. For example, this volume omits annual evaluation reports of writing programs in local schools.

Availability. Publications of commercial publishers and other organizations that are listed in *RIE* and assigned an ERIC ED number but are not available through the ERIC microfiche system are omitted.

Users of the *CCCC Bibliography* may wish to supplement this resource by consulting *RIE* or various computer-assisted retrieval systems that access ERIC documents. Copies of most documents indexed in *RIE* can be purchased in paper or microform from the ERIC system. ERIC clearinghouses also make available free or inexpensive guides to special topics of interest to rhetoric and composition teachers and researchers. Order forms and current addresses for these clearinghouses appear at the back of each monthly issue of *RIE*.

A few entries in this volume show publication dates earlier than 1991. By and large, these materials have two sources. They represent articles published in 1991 but appearing in journals showing earlier volume numbers, or they represent materials accessioned by ERIC clearinghouses in 1991 but originally published earlier.

The items listed in the annual bibliography are not housed in any single location or owned by any single individual. The *CCCC Bibliography* lists and describes these materials but does not provide users of the bibliography any additional means of retrieving them. However, librarians can be extremely helpful in finding copies of particular works to examine firsthand. Some materials may be available through interlibrary loan, OCLC and on-line catalogues, ERIC and other information retrieval systems, or state and university libraries. To locate materials cited in this volume, ask your librarian for help.

CONTRIBUTING BIBLIOGRAPHERS

The reliability and usefulness of these annual volumes depend primarily on a large group of contributing bibliographers. Contributing bibliographers accept responsibility for compiling accurate entries in their areas of expertise, for preparing brief, descriptive annotations for each entry, for determining where each entry will appear within one of the five sections of the *Bibliography*, for cross-referencing entries when appropriate, and for submitting completed entries by a specified deadline.

To ensure consistency, contributing bibliographers receive a *Handbook for Contributing Bibliographers* to guide them in their work and fill out a printed form for each entry. Contributing bibliographers agree to serve a three-year term and, thereafter, may request reappointment for another two-year term. In return for their valuable service to the profession, they receive a copy of each annual volume they have had a substantial hand in preparing. Graduate students, teachers, researchers, or other individuals who wish to become contributing bibliographers may write to the editors.

ANNOTATIONS

Annotations accompany all entries in this volume. They describe the document's contents and are intended to help users determine the document's usefulness. Annotations are brief and, insofar as the English language allows, are meant to be descriptive, not evaluative. They explain what the work is about but leave readers free to judge for themselves the work's merits. Most annotations fall into one of three categories: they present the document's thesis, main argument, or major research finding; they describe the work's major organizational divisions; or they indicate the purpose or scope of the work.

CROSS-REFERENCES AND INDEXES

This volume cites and annotates each document only once, in one of the five major sections of the *Bibliography*. Every entry, however, receives an "entry number" so that cross-references to other sections are possible. Cross-references are necessary because much scholarship in composition and rhetoric is interdisciplinary. Cross-references appear as a listing of entry numbers preceded by "*See also*," found at the end of each subsection of the *Bibliography*.

The Subject Index lists most of the topics discussed in the works cited in this volume. Consulting the Subject Index may help users locate sections and subsections of the *Bibliography* that contain large numbers of entries addressing the same topic.

The Name Index lists all authors, editors, and contributors to publications cited in this volume.

Contributing Bibliographers

Val Abordonado
Elizabeth H. Addison
Jim Addison
Clara Alexander
J. D. Applen
Ken Autrey
Linda Bannister
Pat Belanoff
Kathleen Bell
Carole Bencich
Deborah A. Bertsch
Pam Besser
Renee Betz
Laurel Black
Virginia A. Book
Diana Bowling
Lady Falls Brown
Mary Louise Buley-Meissner
Kathryn M. Burton
Daniel J. Callahan
Barbara Cambridge
John Centers-Zapico
Gregory Clark
Irene Lurkis Clark
John Clifford
Joseph Colavito
Leni Cook
Amanda Inskip Corcoran
Bill Costanzo
Rick Cypert
Donald A. Daiker
Thomas E. Dasher
Dwight Davidson
Kenneth W. Davis
Bonnie Devet
William M. Dodd
Robert Donahoo
Mary Bradstreet Donnelly
Ray Drake
Suellynn Duffey
Ann Duin
Elizabeth Ervin
Chuck Etheridge
Timothy J. Evans
Marissa Farnum
Andrea Fishman
Janis Forman
Judith Fuego
Richard Fulkerson
T. Clifford Gardiner
Greg Glau
Joan I. Glazer
Judith Goleman
Gwendolyn Gong
Alice A. Goodwin
Perry M. Gordon
Jonathan Gotsick
Patricia Goubil-Gambrell
Barbara Griffin
C. W. Griffin
Stephen Hahn
Liz Hamp-Lyons
Kathy Haney
Jim Hanlon
Meaghan Hanrahan
Kristine Hansen
Sarah E. Harrold
Patrick Hartwell
Gary Layne Hatch
Malcolm Hayward
Nancy Hayward
Cozette K. Heller
Marguerite H. Helmers
Alexandra R. Henry
Doug Hesse

John Heyda
Dona Hickey
Dixie Elise Hickman
Betsy Hilbert
Elizabeth Hodges
Elizabeth A. Hoger
Deborah H. Holdstein
Sylvia A. Holladay
Elizabeth Huettman
Rebecca Innocent
Kimberly L. Jacobs
Dee James
Jack Jobst
Patricia Kedzerski
Deborah Kehoe
Joyce Kinkead
James Kinney
Mike Klein
Renee Kupperman
Elizabeth Larsen
Richard Larson
Janice M. Lauer
Mary Lay
Cynthia Lewiecki-Wilson
Erika Lindemann
Maggy Lindgren
Kim Lovejoy
Marilyn Luecke
Donald A. McAndrew
Sandra J. McBride
Allison McCormack
Dana Gulling Mead
Vincent P. Mikkelson
Corinne L. Miller
Charles Moran
Max Morenberg
Sandy Murphy
Debra J. Nash
Michele Noel
Ed Nolte
Terence Odlin
Jeanne Olson
Suzanne C. Padgett
Peggy Parris
Barry Pegg
Michael A. Pemberton
Elizabeth F. Penfield
Virginia Perdue
Virginia G. Polanski
James Postema
John W. Presley
P. W. Ranieri
D. R. Ransdell
Tom Reigstad
Valerie Reimers
Duane Roen
Audrey J. Roth
Diana Royer
Marsha Ryan
Phyllis M. Ryder
Sara L. Sanders
Lew Sayers, Jr.
Judith Scheffler
Erica Scott
Ed Sears
Dennis Selder
Cynthia M. Sheard
Barbara M. Sitko
Betsy Smith
Elizabeth Overman Smith
Penelope Smith
Susan R. Smith
James Strickland
Patricia Sullivan
Dan J. Tannacito
Josephine K. Tarvers
Nathaniel Teich
Patricia Terry
Freddy Thomas
Charlotte Thralls
Myron Tuman
Lisa Tyler
Elizabeth Vander Lei
Billie J. Wahlstrom
Cynthia Walker
Deborah Walker
Keith Walters
Virginia K. Wasserman
Robert H. Weiss
Edwina Welton
Jacqueline Wheeler
David E. Wilson
Shannon Wilson
J. Randal Woodland
Kathleen Blake Yancey
George Xu

Journal Abbreviations

Contributing bibliographers reviewed the journals listed below in preparing entries for this volume. Entries for journal articles cited in this volume will include an abbreviation identifying the journal or serial in which it was published.

A&EQ	Anthropology and Education Quarterly
AA	American Anthropologist
AAF	Adult Assessment Forum
AAHE	AAHE Bulletin
ACEN	Assembly for Computers in English Newsletter
ADEB	Association of Departments of English Bulletin, the
AdEd	Adult Education
AdLBEd	Adult Literacy and Basic Education
AERJ	American Educational Research Journal
AJS	American Journal of Semiotics
AM	Academic Medicine
AmE	American Ethnologist
AmP	American Psychologist
Annals	Annals of the American Academy of Political and Social Sciences
ArEB	Arizona English Bulletin
Arg	Argumentation
AS	American Speech
ASch	The American Scholar
B&L	Brain and Language
BABC	Bulletin of the Association for Business Communication
Boundary	Boundary 2: A Journal of Postmodern Literature and Culture
C&C	Computers and Composition
C&I	Cognition and Instruction
CACJ	Computer-Assisted Composition Journal
CalE	California English
CALS	Carleton Papers in Applied Language Studies
CCC	College Composition and Communication
CCR	Community College Review
CCrit	Cultural Critique
CE	College English
CEA	CEA Critic

CEAF CEA Forum
CHE Chronicle of Higher Education
CHum Computers and Humanities
CJL Canadian Journal of Linguistics
CLAJ College Language Association Journal
Cognition Cognition
CollL College Literature
CollM Collegiate Microcomputer
CollT College Teaching
CEd Communication Education
ComM Communication Monographs
CompC Composition Chronicle
CompEd Computers and Education
CompQ Composition Quarterly
ComQ Communication Quarterly
ComR Communication Research
ComS Communication Studies
CPsy Cognitive Psychology
CritI Critical Inquiry
CSc Cognitive Science
CSSJ Central States Speech Journal

D&S Discourse and Society
Daedalus Daedalus: Journal of the American Academy of Arts and Sciences
DAI Dissertation Abstracts International
DP Developmental Psychology
DPr Discourse Processes

EdEPA Educational Evaluation and Policy Analysis
EdM Educational Measurement: Issues and Practice
EdPsy Educational Psychologist
EdTech Educational Technology
EEd English Education
EES Explorations in Ethnic Studies
EJ English Journal
ELTJ English Language Teaching Journal
ELQ English Leadership Quarterly
EnEd Engineering Education
EngR English Record
EnT English Today
EQ English Quarterly
ESP English for Specific Purposes
ET English in Texas
ETC ETC.: A Review of General Semantics
ExEx Exercise Exchange

FEN Freshman English News
FLA Foreign Language Annals
Focuses Focuses
FSt Feminist Studies

GaR Georgia Review

HCI Human-Computer Interaction
HCR Human Communication Research
HD Human Development
HER Harvard Education Review
HT History Teacher
Hypermedia Hypermedia

IDJ Information Design Journal
IEEE IEEE Transactions on Professional Communication
IL Informal Logic
IlEB Illinois English Bulletin
IndE Indiana English
Intelligence Intelligence
IPM Information Processing and Management
IRAL International Review of Applied Linguistics in Language Teaching
Issues Issues in Writing

JAC Journal of Advanced Composition
JAF Journal of American Folklore
JBC Journal of Business Communication
JBS Journal of Black Studies
JBTC Iowa State Journal of Business and Technical Communication
JBW Journal of Basic Writing
JC Journal of Communication
JCBI Journal of Computer-Based Instruction
JCE Journal of Chemical Education
JCS Journal of Curriculum Studies
JCST Journal of College Science Teaching

JDEd	Journal of Developmental Education
JEd	Journal of Education
JEdM	Journal of Educational Measurement
JEdPsy	Journal of Educational Psychology
JEdR	Journal of Educational Research
JEngL	Journal of English Linguistics
JEPG	Journal of Experimental Psychology: General
JEPH	Journal of Experimental Psychology: Human Perception and Performance
JEPL	Journal of Experimental Psychology: Learning, Memory, Cognition
JFR	Journal of Folklore Research
JGE	JGE: The Journal of General Education
JL	Journal of Linguistics
JLD	Journal of Learning Disabilities
JMEd	Journal of Medical Education
JMemC	Journal of Memory and Cognition: Learning, Memory, Cognition
JMemL	Journal of Memory and Language
JNT	Journal of Narrative Technique
JOC	Journal of Organizational Computing
JourEd	Journalism Educator
JPsy	Journal of Psychology
JPsyR	Journal of Psycholinguistic Research
JR	Journal of Reading
JRB	JRB: Journal of Reading Behavior: A Journal of Literacy
JRDEd	Journal of Research and Development in Education
JT	Journal of Thought
JTEd	Journal of Teacher Education
JTW	Journal of Teaching Writing
JTWC	Journal of Technical Writing and Communication
Lang&S	Language and Style
L&E	Linguistics and Education: An International Research Journal
L&M	Literature and Medicine
L&S	Language and Speech
Language	Language
LangS	Language Sciences
LangT	Language Testing
Leaflet	The Leaflet
Learning	Learning
Linguistics	Linguistics
LSoc	Language in Society
M&C	Memory and Cognition
M&M	Media and Methods
MCQ	Managment and Communication Quarterly
MEd	Medical Education
MissQ	Mississippi Quarterly
MLJ	The Modern Language Journal
MLQ	Modern Language Quarterly
MLS	Modern Language Studies
MSE	Massachusetts Studies in English
MT	Mathematics Teacher
Multimedia	Multimedia
NYRB	The New York Review of Books
OralHR	Oral History Review
P&L	Philosophy and Literature
P&R	Philosophy and Rhetoric
PC	The Professional Communicator
Perspectives	Perspectives
PhiDK	Phi Delta Kappan
PhS	Philosophical Studies
PMLA	Publication of the Modern Language Association
PMS	Perceptual and Motor Skills
PPR	Philosophy and Phenomenological Research
PoT	Poetics Today
PR	Partisan Review
Pre/Text	Pre/Text
PsychologR	Psychological Review
PsyT	Psychology Today
QJS	Quarterly Journal of Speech
QNWP/CSW	The Quarterly for the National Writing Project and the Center for the Study of Writing

QRD	Quarterly Review of Doublespeak
R&W	Reading and Writing: An Interdisciplinary Journal
Raritan	Raritan
Reader	Reader
RER	Review of Educational Research
Rhetorica	Rhetorica
RIE	Resources in Education
RMR	Rocky Mountain Review of Language and Literature
RR	Rhetoric Review
RRQ	Reading Research Quarterly
RSQ	Rhetoric Society Quaretерly
RTDE	Research and Teaching in Developmental Education
RTE	Research in the Teaching of English
SAF	Studies in American Fiction
ScAm	Scientific American
SCJ	Southern Communication Journal
SCL	Studies in Canadian Literature
ScT	Science Teacher
SFS	Science Fiction Studies
Signs	Signs
SLang	Studies in Language
SNNTS	Studies in the Novel
StHum	Studies in the Humanities
Style	Style
SubStance	SubStance
TC	Technical Communication
TCQ	Technical Communication Quarterly
TECFORS	TECFORS
TESOLQ	Teachers of English of Speakers of Other Languages Quarterly
TETYC	Teaching English in the Two-Year College
TEXT	TEXT: An Interdisciplinaly Journal for the Study of Discourse
TWM	Teachers and Writers Magazine
TWT	The Technical Writing Teacher
UEJ	Utah English Journal
V&R	Visions and Revisions
VLang	Visible Language
WAC	Writing across the Curriculum
WC	Written Communication
WCJ	Writing Center Journal
WE	Writing on the Edge
WI	The Writing Instructor
WJSC	Western Journal of Speech Communication
WLN	The Writing Lab Newsletter
WLWE	World Literature Written in English
WN	The Writing Notebook
WPA	Journal of the Council of Writing Program Administrators
Writer	The Writer
WS	Women's Studies

Abbreviations in Entries

AAUP	American Association of University Professors
ASL	American Sign Language
CAI	Computer-Assisted Instruction
EFL	English as a Foreign Language
ASL	American Sign Language
CCCC	Conference on College Composition and Communication
CLAST	College Level Academic Skills Test
ELT	English Language Teaching
ERA	Equal Rights Amendment
ERP	Event-Related Brain Potentials
ESL	English as a Second Language
ERIC/FLL	ERIC Clearinghouse on Language and Linguistics
ERIC/RCS	ERIC Clearinghouse on Reading and Communication Skills
FMG	Foreign Medical Graduates
FPT	Five-Paragraph-Theme
LC MARC	Library of Congress Machine Readable Catalog
MLA	Modern Language Association
NCTE	National Council of Teachers of English
NYPL	New York Public Library
OCLC	Online Computer Library Center
PEPI	Projective English Placement Instrument
PS	Philosophical Spacing
STM	Short Term Memory
TASP	Toll Alternative Studies Program
TOEFL	Test of English as a Foreign Language
TSE	Test of Spoken English
WAC	Writing across the Curriculum
WM	Working Memory

CCCC

Bibliography of Composition and Rhetoric

1991

1

Bibliographies and Checklists

1 BIBLIOGRAPHIES AND CHECKLISTS

1. Baer, E. Kristina, and Daisy E. Shenholm. *Leo Spitzer on Language and Literature: A Descriptive Bibliography*. New York: MLA Publications, 1991. 172 pages

   Provides a comprehensive overview of Spitzer's publications. Subjects treated include etymology, grammar, lexicology, literary criticism and theory, morphology, semantics, statistics, and syntax. Languages addressed are Basque, Catalan, English, French, German, Italian, Latin, Portuguese, Provençal, Romanian, and Spanish.

2. Belanger, Kelly, Heather Brodie Graves, Andrea Lunsford, Melanie Boyd, Diane Chambers, Marcia Dickson, Patricia Kedzerski, Carrie Shively Leverenz, Veronica Lopez, Margaret Gentry Neff, Kari Schneider, Sarah Sloane, and Tracy Vezdos. "Gender and Writing: Biblio(bio)graphical Stories." *RSQ* 20 (Fall 1990): 367–402.

   Annotated bibliography of works on gender and writing, interspersed with excerpts from the authors' journals.

3. *Bibliographic Guide to Conference Publications: 1990*. G. K. Hall Bibliographic Guides. Boston, MA: G. K. Hall and Company, 1991. 1354 pages

   Lists conference publications catalogued during the year by the Research Libraries of the NYPL, with additional entries from LC MARC tapes. Annually indexes some 26,000 private and government conference publications, including proceedings, reports of conferences, and collections of papers. Covers all disciplines, countries, and languages.

4. *Bibliographic Guide to Education: 1990*. G. K. Hall Bibliographic Guides. Boston, MA: G. K. Hall and Company, 1991. 625 pages

   Lists material recorded on the OCLC tapes of the Columbia University Teachers College during the year, with additional entries from the NYPL for selected publications.

Covers all aspects of education. Supplements the 1970 *Dictionary Catalog of the Teachers College Library*.

5. Bizzell, Patricia, and Bruce Herzberg. *The Bedford Bibliography for Teachers of Writing*. New York: Bedford Books, 1991. 90 pages

Annotates 386 books, articles, and other resources grouped under the following headings: resources, history and theory, composing processes, curriculum development, writing programs, and related fields. Includes a brief history of rhetoric and composition, an author index, and a catalog of composition books published by Bedford Books.

6. Craig, John S. "Approaches to Usability Testing and Design Strategies: An Annotated Bibliography." *TC* 38 (April 1991): 190–196.

Annotates document usability sources in such categories as user-testing strategies, field testing, and improving document design.

7. Donawerth, Jane. "Bibliography of Women and the History of Rhetorical Theory to 1900." *RSQ* 20 (Fall 1990): 403–414.

Offers a bibliography divided into primary and secondary works.

8. Durst, Russell K., and James D. Marshall. "Annotated Bibliography of Research in the Teaching of English." *RTE* 25 (December 1991): 497–509.

Annotates selected 1990 and 1991 dissertations and articles in major composition and rhetoric journals. Organized into the areas of writing, language, literature, and teacher education.

9. Ehrlich, Heyward. "An Interdisciplinary Bibliography for Computers and the Humanities Courses." *CHum* 25 (October 1991): 315–326.

Lists and describes current textbooks, anthologies, individual works, and critical studies that deal with computers and their relationship to humans.

10. Foxworthy, Deb J. "The Process of Revision." *CompC* 4 (September 1991): 6–7.

Presents a nine-item annotated bibliography on teaching revision.

11. Frankinburger, Patricia. "An Annotated Bibliography of the Literature Dealing with the Effects of Student Attitude and Teacher Behaviors on Writing Apprehension and Composition." Indiana University at South Bend. 1991. ERIC ED 333 482. 45 pages

Contains an introduction, 27 annotations (1976–1990), a summary, conclusions, and recommendations.

12. Greene, Beth G. "Writing the Research Paper." *CompC* 4 (April 1991): 8–9.

Provides a seven-item annotated bibliography of ERIC documents on teaching research papers.

13. Harner, James L. *MLA Directory of Scholarly Presses in Language and Literature*. New York: MLA Publications, 1991. 300 pages

Describes the fields of interest, submission requirements, contract provisions, and editorial procedures of publishers of book-length literary and linguistic studies. Includes entries on 284 publishers from 31 countries.

14. Horner, Winifred Bryan. "Nineteenth-Century Rhetoric at the Universities of Aberdeen and St. Andrews with an Annotated Bibliography of Archival Materials." *RSQ* 20 (Summer 1992): 287–299.

A brief history of northern Scottish universities, a bibliography organized by college, and a chronology with notes on conditions of materials make up the substance of this text.

15. Hutton, Clark. "A Selected Annotated Bibliography on Using Computers to Teach Technical and Business Writing (1984–1990)." *TWT* 18 (Fall 1991): 223–235.

Covers past research, effects of computers on student attitudes, the use of word processors, collaborative writing, and text analysis software.

16. Lutz, William. "Keeping Up with Your Reading" *QRD* 17 (January 1991): 8–9.

Provides annotated bibliography of five recent books related to doublespeak.

17. Marinara, Martha. "Bibliography of Recent Writing Center Scholarship (April 1990–March 1991)." *WCJ* 12 (Fall 1991): 105–111.

Presents a bibliography concerning writing centers from *Writing Lab Newsletter*, *The Writing Center Journal*, *Freshman English News*, and *Writing Program Administration*.

18. *MLA Directory of Periodicals: A Guide to Journals and Series in Languages and Literatures*. New York: MLA Publications, 1990–1991. 772 pages

Contains information about journals and series indexed in the *MLA International Bibliography*. Includes addresses, prices, and submissions requirements. Presents four indexes: subject matter, editorial personnel, sponsoring organizations, and the languages in which articles and monographs are published. An appendix lists journals with author-anonymous submissions policies.

19. National Clearinghouse on Literacy Education. "Dialogue Journal Bibliography: Published Books, Articles, Reports and Dissertations about Dialogue Journal Research and Use." ERIC/FLL 1991. ERIC ED 333 722. 11 pages

Provides a 90-item bibliography about dialogue journal research and use.

20. "Publications of George Yoos." *RSQ* 20 (Fall 1990): 361–363.

Presents a bibliography of George Yoos's publications.

21. Robinson-Armstrong, Abbie. "Academic Journals: Annotated Bibliography." EDRS. 1991. ERIC ED 329 977. 10 pages

Summarizes 16 articles (1975–1988) which provide practical information on using student journals.

22. Sensebaugh, Roger. "Assessing Writing Using Portfolios." *CompC* 4 (November 1991): 8–9.

Presents a seven-item annotated bibliography of articles on portfolio assessment.

23. Shires, Nancy Patterson. "Teaching Writing in College Chemistry." *JCE* 68 (June 1991): 494–495.

Presents an annotated bibliography that helps college chemistry faculty who are interested in teaching writing skills.

24. Tovey, Janice. "Using Visual Theory in the Creation of Résumés: A Bibliography." *BABC* 54 (September 1991): 97–99.

Annotated bibliography covers résumé research and instruction, rhetorical issues, and visual theory and graphic design.

25. Wolff, William C. "Annotated Bibliography of Scholarship on Writing Centers and Related Topics, 1990–1991." *Focuses* 4 (Summer 1991): 24–74.

Annually listed entries include books, collected essays, and journal articles.

See also 599, 1165, 1866

2

Theory and Research

2.1 RHETORICAL THEORY, DISCOURSE THEORY, AND COMPOSING

26. Aber, John. "The Technical, the Practical, and the Emancipatory: A Habermasian View of Composition Pedagogy." *JTW* 10 (Fall/Winter 1991): 123–136.

Warns against confusing cognitive, practical, and emancipatory interests in teaching. Recommends writing tasks that correspond to the three interests.

27. Afokpa, Kodjo. "Greeting Performance in Eveland: Ethnographic Approach and Cultural Analysis with a Historical Survey of Folklore Scholarship in French West Africa." *DAI* 51 (June 1991): 4237A.

Suggests some practical ways to approach the study of oral genres.

28. Allen, Julia M. *Rhetorics of Resistance.* Boston, MA: CCCC, March 1991. ERIC ED 332 207. 15 pages

Argues that feminist discourse requires a critical rhetoric.

29. Alves, Julio. "The Social Construction of Subjectivity through Narrative Discourse: The Case of Urban Working-Class, Portuguese Boys." *DAI* 52 (July 1991): 149A.

Observes narratives in classroom, playground, and community. Concludes that children's narratives are not innocent, but are ideologically constructed.

30. Angert, Marlene Rubin. "An Analysis of the Treatment of Females in Basal Reading Textbooks." *DAI* 51 (February 1991): 2690A.

Analyzes old and current texts of basal readers from four publishers. Finds that more positive portrayals of females have been implemented in later texts, including greater representation as main characters in stories and a demonstration of problem-solving skill.

31. Arrington, Phillip. "The Agony over What 'Composition Research' Means." *JAC* 11 (Fall 1991): 377–393.

Provides an agonistic history of the term "composition research"; concludes that the term can have several meanings.

32. Autrey, Ken. "Toward a Rhetoric of Journal Writing." *RR* 10 (Fall 1991): 74–89.

Describes the history and rhetoric of commonplace books, diaries, and traditional student journals; advocates problematizing the genre for more effective use in first-year college composition studies.

33. Ayim, Maryann. "Dominance and Affiliation: Paradigms in Conflict." *IL* 13 (Spring 1991): 79–88.

Points out that gender patterns in speech styles show both (male) dominant confrontational and (female) affiliative nurturing styles. Argues that the latter are superior and should be taught.

34. Ball, Carolyn C. "Having the Right Kind of Life: The Production of "Experience" in and through Composition Instruction." *DAI* 52 (November 1991): 1667A.

Investigates the student population of the 1890s and 1970s and examines the production of self-expressive writing practices by students who have been designated as "other."

35. Bannister, Linda. *The Feminine Rhetorics of Janet Emig and Andrea Lunsford*. Boston, MA: CCCC, March 1991. ERIC ED 328 918. 14 pages

Shows how Emig and Lunsford reinvented a feminist rhetorical tradition of process, integration, community, and collaboration.

36. Battenfeld, Mary. "Writing on a Battlefield: Women and Documentary Discourse in the 1930s." *DAI* 51 (May 1991): 3795A.

Describes, defines, and analyzes American women's documentary discourse of the 1930s.

37. Bazerman, Charles. "Book Review: The Second Stage in Writing across the Curriculum." *CE* 53 (February 1991): 209–212.

Reviews four books that investigate the roles of written language in the real worlds of the classroom and beyond.

38. Bazerman, Charles, and James Paradis, eds. *Textual Dynamics of the Professions: Historical and Contemporary Studies of Writing in Professional Communities*. Madison, WI: University of Wisconsin Press, 1991. 416 pages

Fifteen essays examine the effects of texts on professional practices. Includes case studies, student papers, medieval letters, and product instructions. The book is also an introduction to studies of rhetoric, writing theory, and the sociology of knowledge.

Essayists: John Ackerman, Charles Bazerman, Carol Berkenkotter, Amy J. Devitt, Stephen Doheny-Farina, Jeanne Fahnestock, Barbara A. Fennell, Cheryl Geisler, Carl G. Herndl, Thomas N. Huckin, Lucille Parkinson McCarthy, Carolyn R. Miller, Greg Myers, James Paradis, Les Perelman, Robert A. Shwegler, Marie Secor, Linda K. Shamoon, Ann Harleman Stewart, Gail Stygall, James P. Zappen.

39. Beckelman, Dana. "Sex, Lies, and Microcassette Tapes: Jane Gallop Reads Writing and Other (Inter) Views." *FEN* 19 (Spring 1991): 2–10.

Presents a transcript of a conversation between Gallop and the author about the rhetoric in her feminism and her views on writing and teaching.

40. Belanoff, Pat, Peter Elbow, and Sheryl I. Fontaine, eds. *Nothing Begins with "N": New Investigations of Free Writing*. Carbondale, IL: Southern Illinois University Press, 1991. 345 pages

Sixteen essays, diverse in focus, methodology, and point of view, provide a theoretical underpinning for the practice of freewriting.

Essayists: Sheryl I. Fontaine, Pat Belanoff, Richard H. Haswell, Lynn Hammond, Joy Marsella, Thomas L. Hilgers, Diana

George, Art Young, Anne E. Mullin, Barbara W. Cheshire, James W. Pennebaker, Ken MacRorie, Peter Elbow, Robert Whitney, Karen Ferro, Chris Anderson, Burton Hatlen, Sheridan Blau.

41. Berthoff, Ann. *Richards on Rhetoric: Selected Essays (1929–1974)*. New York: Oxford University Press, 1990. 320 pages

Focuses on Richards' discussion of literacy, his critique of positivist linguistics, his explorations of C. S. Pierce's semiotics, and his theory of translation, which led to his analysis of the structure and foundation of metaphor and his formulation of reader-response theory.

42. Berthoff, Ann E. "Rhetoric as Hermeneutic." *CCC* 42 (October 1991): 279–287.

Proposes "supplementing Saussure's dyadic semiology with Peirce's triadic semiotics" to form a basis for reconceiving "rhetoric as a hermeneutical enterprise."

43. Bishop, Walton Burrell. "Cognitive Cybernetics and Human Communication: The Regulatory Effects of Prior Knowledge." *DAI* 52 (August 1991): 326A.

Measures the effectiveness of human communication using a new theory; includes an experiment designed to test the theory.

44. Bishop, Wendy. *Reliable and Valid Stories?—Turning Ethnographic Data into Narratives*. Boston, MA: CCCC, March 1991. ERIC ED 331 048. 16 pages

Calls for more discussion of the process of "writing up" ethnographic research, specifically in the field of writing research.

45. Boggs, William. "A Comment on 'Writing as Collaboration' [*CE* 51 (December 1989)]." *CE* 53 (February 1991): 227–229.

Argues that Reither and Vipond's article is self-serving and does not advance the pedagogy of composition.

46. Bowers, Roger. "Verbal Behavior in the Language Teaching Classroom (Volumes I–III)." *DAI* 52 (August 1991): 524A.

Presents an empirical study of the dialogue between teacher and student without presupposing a theoretical position.

47. Boyd, Richard. "Imitate Me; Don't Imitate Me: Mimetics of David Bartholomae's 'Inventing the University.' " *JAC* 11 (Fall 1991): 335–345.

Points out weaknesses in Bartholomae's essay; suggests that the theories of Rene Girard are more beneficial to the writing instructor.

48. Brent, Doug. "Young, Becker and Pike's 'Rogerian' Rhetoric: A Twenty-Year Reassessment." *CE* 53 (April 1991): 452–466.

Suggests that "Rogerian" rhetoric can provide a useful rhetorical focus if it takes a more social approach to invention and a less dichotomous approach to evaluation.

49. Briggs, John C. "Peter Elbow, Kenneth Burke, and the Idea of Magic." *JAC* 11 (Fall 1991): 363–375.

Reviews Elbow's and Burke's discussions of rhetorical magic, showing how each points out serious contradictions in both authors' work.

50. Brown, David Donald. "Ricoeur's Narrative Methodology and the Interpretation of Life History Texts." *DAI* 51 (January 1991): 2540A.

Explores the relevance of Ricoeur's philosophy and inquiry into time and narration, including narrative identity, for sociological inquiry.

51. Brown, Stuart Cameron. "I. A. Richards' New Rhetoric: Metaphor and 'Ethos.' " *DAI* 51 (February 1991): 2562A.

Claims that Richards should be more fully recognized as an important infuence in modern rhetorical theory.

52. Brummett, Barry. *Rhetorical Dimensions of Popular Culture*. Tuscaloosa, AL: University of Alabama Press, 1991. 220 pages

Treats rhetoric as the social function that influences and manages meaning; discusses such aspects of culture as television programs, science fiction, horror films, and urban race relations.

53. Bruner, Jerome. "The Narrative Construction of Reality." *CritI* 18 (Autumn 1991): 1–21.

Presents thoughts on the subject of how narrative organizes human experience.

54. Bryan, Alvenice H. "Cohesion Analysis of the Speaking and Writing of Four Black College Students." *DAI* 51 (February 1991): 2616A.

Results indicate that texts were cohesive but not coherent. In rank order, readability variables included subject, age, sex, and placement on standardized tests.

55. Burbules, Nicholas C., and Suzanne Rice. "Dialogue across Differences: Continuing the Conversation." *HER* 61 (November 1991): 393–416.

Asks whether dialogue across differences is worthwhile, even possible; examines varieties of dialogic exchange; calls for a rethinking of dialogue along modernist principles.

56. Burns, Richard A. "Texas Prison Folklore." *DAI* 52 (July 1991): 262A.

Focuses on form, function, and meaning of folklore to the inhabitants of a Texas prison farm.

57. Bybee, Michael D. "Abduction and Rhetorical Theory." *P&R* 24 (Winter 1991): 281–300.

Describes and distinguishes abduction, shows its rhetorical force, and offers implications for discourse theory.

58. Calleros, Margie. "Emergent Literacy: The Development of Early Writers." *DAI* 51 (February 1991): 2664A.

Examines data relevant to the developmental writing stages of early writing; emphasizes audience, purpose, and meaning.

59. Canapa, Sally Ann. "Reclaiming I. A. Richards: Method and Imagination for Basic Writers." *DAI* 51 (April 1991): 3348A.

Based on Richards, this study provides a theoretical base and a pedagogical instrument that is responsive to the needs of basic writers.

60. Carroll, Jeffrey. "Giving and Taking: A Note on Ownership." *WI* 11 (Fall 1991): 17–22.

Discusses the incompatibility of emphasizing ownership of text; encourages collaboration and co-authorship at the same time.

61. Castle, Terry. "Contagious Folly: *An Adventure* and Its Skeptics." *CritI* 17 (Summer 1991): 741–772.

Argues that detailed presentation of scholarly evidence when writing of encounters with strange phenomena does not always result in credibility when common-sense beliefs are involved.

62. *CCCC Luncheon: Speaker, Paule Marshall; Annual Convention 1990*. [audiocassette]. Urbana, IL: NCTE, 1991.

Marshall describes "mother poets" who influenced her writing, giving her a sense of context and experience to draw from in her creative writing.

63. Chambers, Simone Evelyn. "Discourse and Procedural Ethics." *DAI* 51 (February 1991): 2857A.

Argues that Jurgen Habermas's discourse model of procedural ethics is superior to earlier theories.

64. Cixous, Helene. *"Coming to Writing" and Other Essays*. Cambridge, MA: Harvard University Press, 1991. 214 pages

Explores the problems of a "feminine" mode of writing, basing her method on the premise that differences between the sexes—viewed as a paradigm for all difference—manifest themselves in texts.

65. Clark, Gregory, and Stephen Doheny-Farina. "Response to Lunsford/Ede and Jarratt

[*WC* 8 (January 1991)]." *WC* 8 (January 1991): 120–124.

Addressing issues raised by Lunsford and Ede and by Jarratt, Clark and Doheny-Farina discuss the nature of theory building in rhetoric through qualitative case studies.

66. Clark, Suzanne. "Discipline and Resistance: The Subjects of Writing and the Discourses of Instruction." *CollL* 18 (June 1991): 119–134.

Argues that poststructuralist pedagogy must address the cultural situation in the American classroom and help students deal with issues of "authority and resistance."

67. Clifford, John. "The Neopragmatic Scene of Theory and Practice." *RR* 10 (Fall 1991): 100–107.

Advocates a neopragmatic approach for composition classes; wants to move beyond an emphasis on rhetorical skills by including social and ethical issues in reading and writing.

68. Clifford, John. "Toward a Productive Crisis: A Response to Gayatri Spivak [*JAC* 10 (1990)]." *JAC* 11 (Winter 1991): 191–196.

Praises Spivak's postmodernism.

69. Cole, Caroline. " 'Oh Wise Women of the Stalls. . . .' " *D&S* 2 (October 1991): 401–411.

Examines graffiti from women's lavatory walls to identify ways in which women communicate to each other.

70. Cooper, Marilyn M. "Dueling with Dualism: A Response to Interviews with Mary Field Belenky and Gayatri Spivak [*JAC* 9 (1989)]." *JAC* 11 (Winter 1991): 179–185.

Argues that male/female and social/cognitive dualisms in interviews cannot be dealt with by pretending that they do not exist. Points out that cognitive/social dualism is valuable for research.

71. Corder, Jim W. "Academic Jargon and Soul-Searching Drivel." *RR* 9 (Spring 1991): 314–326.

Identifies distinctions between academic and personal writing styles. Calls on composition teachers to use both, ask "essayist" questions, and look at "particulars."

72. Coupland, Justine, Nikolas Coupland, Howard Giles, and Karen Henwood. "Formulating Age: Dimensions of Age Identity in Elderly Talk." *DPr* 14 (January–March 1991): 87–106.

Authors argue that elderly people in Wales reveal their condition through implicit and explicit mentions of the circumstances in which they find themselves.

73. Cullum, Charles. *Collaborative Learning, Phase Two: Experimental Research*. Boston, MA: CCCC, March 1991. ERIC ED 332 216. 39 pages

Reports results of an experimental study of the effect of collaborative learning on word- and sentence-level writing. Shows that the greatest impact appears to be on sentence length, voice, and the verb "to be."

74. Cummings, Mary-Ellen. "The Rhetoric of Scapegoating." *DAI* 51 (March 1991): 3053A.

Confronts the growing tension between rhetoric and poetics in English departments through scapegoating discussions by Burke and Derrida.

75. Currie, Gregory. "Text without Context: Some Errors of Stanley Fish." *P&L* 15 (October 1991): 212–228.

Critiques Fish's brand of relativism implicit in his concept of "interpretive communities." Aims "to defend the idea of literal meaning."

76. Dasenbrock, Reed Way. "Do We Write the Text We Read?" *CE* 53 (January 1991): 7–18.

Critiques the "conceptual relativism" of Stanley Fish and Barbara Herrnstein Smith, arguing that Donald Davidson's "radical interpretation" offers a more satisfactory account of why interpretations differ.

77. Dautermann, Jennie Parsons. "Writing at *Good Hope* Hospital: A Study of Negotiated Discourse in the Workplace." *DAI* 52 (December 1991): 2123A.

This two-year observation of a department of nursing examines how negotiated discourse prompts change within the hospital.

78. Davis, Kevin. "The Personal and Social Changes First-Year Writers Encounter when Entering the Academic Discourse Community: Two Case Studies." *ET* 22 (Spring 1991): 6–10.

Discusses the adjustments to college that two students underwent. Uses phenomenological and case study research philosophies.

79. Davis, Lloyd Benjamin. "Guides and Disguise: Rhetoric and Characterization in the Renaissance." *DAI* 52 (August 1991): 545A.

Argues that the Renaissance discourse of disguise unveils the rhetorical and dramatistic processes of selfhood, saying in effect, "I speak therefore I am not."

80. De Beaugrande, Robert. "Language and the Facilitation of Authority: The Discourse of Noam Chomsky." *JAC* 11 (Fall 1991): 425–442.

Applies discourse analysis to Chomsky's interview with the *Journal of Advanced Composition*.

81. DeGroot, Elizabeth J. "A Reconceptualization of the Enthymeme from a Feminist Perspective." *DAI* 52 (July 1991): 20A.

Finds that a feminist conception of the enthymeme includes relational subject matter, a developmental process of caring, and contextual and connected knowledge expressions.

82. DeKlerk, Vivian. "Expletives: Men Only?" *ComM* 58 (June 1991): 156–169.

Examines the relationship between social power and the use of expletives.

83. Derewianka, Beverly. *Exploring How Texts Work*. Portsmouth, NH: PETA, 1991. 88 pages

Considers how different texts—grouped under headings such as instructions, narratives, and information reports—achieve their purposes.

84. Diekema, David Anthony. "Social Status and the Rhetoric of Debate: The Case of *Ad Hominem* Arguments." *DAI* 52 (September 1991): 737A.

Finds that *ad hominem* arguments are only effective in equal status groups, not in low- or high-status groups.

85. Dillon, George L. *Contending Rhetorics: Writing in Academic Disciplines*. Bloomington, IN: Indiana University Press, 1991. 192 pages

Analyzes academic discourse in relation to practical, everyday writing and defends its perceived difficulty and difference.

86. Droge, Edward F., Jr. "How College Students Revise in Response to Written Peer Review Exclusive of Oral Components." *DAI* 52 (December 1991): 2002A.

Characterizes the written peer review method of writing and provides insights into the connection between written peer comments and the revision made in the response.

87. Duncan, Ralph Randolph. "Panel Analysis: A Critical Method for Analyzing the Rhetoric of Comic Book Form." *DAI* 51 (June 1991): 3942A.

Uses the three components of panel analysis—historical context, micro analysis, and macro analysis—to explore how the form of the comic book medium communicates content.

88. Ebert, Teresa L. "The 'Difference' of Postmodern Feminism." *CE* 53 (December 1991): 886–904.

Offers a political rewriting of feminism and discusses the emergence of a theory and critical practice that the author calls "postmodern materialist feminism."

89. Eggers, Ellen Kahan. "Temporal Anaphora in Discourse." *DAI* 51 (March 1991): 3055 A.

Applies discourse representation theory to languages with complex temporal situations in order to understand how content determines the temporal structure of discourse.

90. Elbow, Peter. "Reflections of Academic Discourse: How It Relates to Freshmen and Colleagues." *CE* 53 (February 1991): 135–153.

Argues that first-year college students should learn academic discourse as only one of many discourses because academic discourse leads to indirectness and detachment.

91. Elbow, Peter. "Some Thoughts on *Expressive Discourse*: A Review Essay." *JAC* 11 (Winter 1991): 83–93.

Reviews and meditates on Jeanette Harris's book and the terms "*expressive*" *discourse, theory,* and *pedagogy*.

92. Ellis, Donald G. *From Language to Communication*. Hillsdale, NJ: Lawrence Erlbaum Associates, 1991. 300 pages

Introduces students to key topics such as discourse, coherence, language and mind, history of language, and communication codes.

93. el-Sakran, Tharwat Mohemed el-Sayed. "Footnotes in Academic Written Discourse: A Formal and Functional Analysis." *DAI* 52 (September 1991): 897A.

Concludes that using footnotes is a compensatory strategy to overcome excess/lack of information.

94. Elsley, Judith Helen. "The Semiotics of Quilting: Discourse of the Marginalized." *DAI* 51 (January 1991): 2379A.

Uses process of quilting as a paradigm for women's search for voice; shows how the paradigm can demonstrate marginalized voices in other texts.

95. Enos, Theresa. "Reports of the 'Author's' Death May Be Greatly Exaggerated but the 'Writer' Lives on in the Text." *RSQ* 20 (Fall 1990): 339–348.

Explains areas of agreement between contemporary rhetoric and poststructuralist theory, most notably on the status of the writer as ethos active in the text.

96. Erlwein, Bradley Raymond. "Using Rhetorical Canons as a Heuristic in Natural Language Processing Systems." *DAI* 52 (October 1991): 2136B.

Describes a prototype program that argues for preexistent forms that serve as templates for organizing ideas within a discourse.

97. Farrell, Thomas B. "Inventing Rhetorical Culture: Some Issues of Theory and Practice." *RSQ* 21 (Winter 1991): 17–25.

Argues that criticism should connect and interpret theory and practice; in doing so, it will reveal normative qualities intrinsic to the rhetorical tradition.

98. Farrell, Thomas B. "Practicing the Arts of Rhetoric: Tradition and Invention." *P&R* 24 (1991): 183–212.

Reappraises the rhetorical tradition and demonstrates how the practice of rhetoric makes reflection and invention possible.

99. Ferriss, Suzanne E. "Post-Revolutionary Letters." *DAI* 51 (March 1991): 3064A.

Applies historical and post-structuralist theories to reveal writers' ambivalence about whether their revolutionary rhetoric was corrupted for political ends.

100. Flannery, Kathryn T. "Composing and the Question of Agency." *CE* 53 (October 1991): 701–713.

Reviews books by Marilyn Cooper and Michael Holzman, Patricia Donahue and Ellen Quandahl, Susan Miller, Donald M. Murray, and Marilyn S. Sternglass.

101. Fleckenstein, Kristie S. "Defining Affect in Relation to Cognition: A Response to Susan

McLeod [*JAC* 11 (Winter 1991)]." *JAC* 11 (Fall 1991): 447–453.

Questions McLeod's intensity-stability continuum definition of affect; recommends an alternative which interweaves affect and cognition.

102. Fleckenstein, Kristie S. "Inner Sight: Imagery and Emotion in Writing Engagement." *TETYC* 18 (October 1991): 210–216.

Indicates that students who can produce mental imagery are also inclined toward emotional involvement with their writing.

103. Flood, James, Julie Jenson, Diane Lapp, and James R. Squire, eds. *Handbook of Research on Teaching the English Language Arts*. New York: MacMillan, 1991. 888 pages

Presents 70 essays grouped into six sections: theoretical bases for English language arts teaching, methods of research on English language arts teaching, research on language learners, environments for English language arts teaching, research on teaching specific aspects of the English language arts curriculum, and the shaping of the English language arts.
Essayists: Merlin C. Wittrock, Rita S. Brause, John S. Mayher, Elizabeth Sulzby, Carole Cox, Robert J. Marzano, George Hillocks, Jr., James F. Baumann, James L. Kinneavy, Nancy L. Roser, Dianne L. Monson, Alan C. Purves, Gay Su Pinnell, Jana M. Mason, Kathryn H. Au, Diane Lapp, Anne Haas Dyson, Richard E. Hodges, Jane Hansen, Mary K. Healy, Julie Jensen, Janice Dole, Lee Galda, Bernice E. Cullinan, Bertram Bruce, Arthur N. Applebee, James W. Ney, Michael Smith, Edward J. Kameenui, Miriam G. Martinez, Robert E. Probst, Sam L. Sebasta, Leslie Mandel Morrow, Angela M. Jaggar, Patricia A. Herman, James Flood, Thomas G. Devine, Sarah Warshauer Freedman, Betty Jane Wagner, Donald H. Graves, Mary A. Barr, James Moffett.

104. Flynn, Elizabeth A. "Politicizing the Composing Process and Women's Ways of Interacting: A Response to 'A Conversation with Mary Belenky' [*JAC* 9 (1989)]." *JAC* 11 (Winter 1991): 173–178.

Praises Evelyn Ashton-Jones and Dene Kay Thomas's interview with Belenky. Expands on the idea of politicizing writing through women's intellectual development. Argues that the picture of women as cooperative should be modified by research.

105. Foertsch, Mary Mae. "The Rhetoric of Feminist Object Relations Psychoanalysis: Chodorow, Greek Myth, and the U. S. Women's Movement." *DAI* 52 (October 1991): 1130A.

Advocates using a different critical approach to examining Chodorow's work, thus revealing greater contributions to the women's movement.

106. Frodesen, Jan Marie. "Aspects of Coherence in Writing Assessment Context: Linguistic and Rhetorical Features of Native and Nonnative English Essays." *DAI* 52 (July 1991): 150A.

Examines aspects of coherence in 100 essays written by native and nonnative English students.

107. Fulmer, Hal W., and Carl L. Kell. "A Sense of Place, A Spirit of Adventure: Implications for the Study of Regional Rhetoric." *RSQ* 20 (Summer 1990): 225–232.

Uses myths of the American South and West to establish the existence of regional rhetorics, to explain a method of analysis, and to speculate about implications.

108. Gibian, Jill L. "Three Ways of Rewriting a Text: Parody, Translation, and Criticism in the Latin American Model: A Sociocultural Analysis." *DAI* 51 (May 1991): 3733A.

Uses postmodern theories of textual production to examine how the three "metatexts" involve critical acts of interpretation with literary and political implications.

109. Gilbert, Pam. "From Voice to Text: Reconsidering Writing and Reading in the English Classroom." *EEd* 23 (December 1991): 195–211.

Evaluates assumptions that have been created and supported by authorities to explain the link between the production of written text and the concept of voice.

110. Gold, Ruby. "Answering Machine Talk." *DPr* 14 (April–June 1991): 243–260.

Argues that responding to taped answering machines constitutes a distinct kind of discourse in which speakers combine elements of spoken and written language to create a "dialogue."

111. Greenberg, Karen Joy, and Brenda Dervin. *Conversations on Communication Ethics*. Communication and Information Science. Norwood, NJ: Ablex, 1990. 188 pages

Nine essays discuss historic, individual, and social systems of account-making. The book surveys existent Western concepts of ethics, weighing the role of ethics in contemporary communication. It also examines how individuals make sense of communication norms, values, and virtues and how people make meaning collectively.
Essayists: J. Vernon Jensen, Kenneth E. Andersen, Vernon E. Cronen, Ronald C. Arnett, Frederick J. Antczak, Karen Joy Greenberg, Josina M. Makau, J. Michael Sproule, Robert A. White, Samuel M. Edelman.

112. Greenberg, Ruth B. "A Contextual Study of Coauthoring in Medical Writing: Two Cases of Neophyte Academic Physicians." *DAI* 52 (December 1991): 2123A.

Concludes that revision and collaborative work improve the composition process. Points out benefits of direct social interaction with writing teachers.

113. Greene, Stuart. "Writing from Sources: Authority in Text and Task." *DAI* 52 (August 1991): 450A.

Proposes to increase understanding of how different writing-to-learn tasks invite and authorize the way students construct meaning in writing from sources.

114. Gronbeck, Bruce E., Thomas J. Farrell, and Paul A. Soukup, eds. *Media, Consciousness, and Culture: Explorations of Walter Ong's Thought*. Newbury Park, CA: Sage Publications, 1991. 296 pages

Presents the readers with 15 essays exploring Ong's impact on rhetoric and modern thought.
Essayists: Ruth El Saffar, Richard Leo Enos, John M. Ackerman, Thomas J. Farrell, Bruce E. Gronbeck, David Heckel, William J. Kennedy, Philip Leith, Anthony J. Palmeri, David Payne, Dennis P. Seimff, Roger Silverstone, Annabelle Sreherny-Mohmmadi, C. Jan Swearingen, Noel Valis.

115. Grunst, Robert C. *Situating "Egocentric Language" in the Teaching of Composition: Piaget, Britton, and Merleau-Ponty*. Boston, MA: CCCC, March 1991. ERIC ED 331 051. 12 pages

Compares Piaget's devaluation of egocentric language to Britton's and Merleau-Ponty's recognition that adults need access to a range of languages.

116. Halasek, Evonne Kay. "Toward a Dialogic Rhetoric: Mikhail Bakhtin and Social Writing Theory." *DAI* 51 (April 1991): 3397A.

Investigates Bartholomae, Kinneavy, and others through the lens of Bakhtin's sociocultural theory to construct a dialogic pedagogy that addresses social issues.

117. Hambrick, Mary Margaret. "The Language of Peace: A Burkean Analysis of the Peace Rhetoric of William Sloane Coffin." *DAI* 52 (October 1991): 1130A.

Analyzes the rhetoric of peace through the perspective of the motives of language.

118. Hampton, Rosemary E. "The Rhetorical and Metaphorical Nature of Graphics and Visual Schemata." *RSQ* 20 (Fall 1990): 347–356.

Argues that composition classes should teach that visual schemata and graphics are rhetorical and metaphorical.

119. Hare, Victoria Chou, and Denise A. Fitzsimmons. "The Influence of Interpretive Communities on Use of Content and Procedural Knowledge in a Writing Task." *WC* 8 (July 1991): 348–378.

Contrasts responses of four experimental groups to the task of writing the discussion section for a research article with focus on transfer of discourse conventions.

120. Harkin, Patricia. "Hyperscholarship and the Curriculum." *RR* 10 (Fall 1991): 108–117.

Calls for the use of history and foregrounding of conflict in a reformed curriculum which enables students to examine purpose and context of composition studies.

121. Harkin, Patricia, and John Schilb, eds. *Contending with Words: Composition and Rhetoric in a Postmodern Age*. New York: Modern Language Association Publications, 1991. 242 pages

Reviews the present disciplinary impulses of composition studies and looks at transforming the composition course from a "service" component of the curriculum to a locus of intellectual activity concerned with various aspects of postmodern thought: feminism, neo-Marxist theories, the historiography of Michel Foucault, and cultural criticism.

Essayists: Patricia Harkin, John Schilb, Don H. Bialostosky, William A. Covino, John Clifford, Patricia Bizzell, Bruce Herzberg, Lynn Worsham, Susan C. Jarratt, Victor J. Vitanza, Sharon Crowley, James J. Sosnoski.

122. Haswell, Richard H. *Gaining Ground in College Writing*. Dallas, TX: Southern Methodist University Press, 1991. 352 pages

Examines how teachers, students, researchers, and theorists view and experience growth in writing. Points out that a constructivist approach revises central concerns such as gender, error, production rate, use of models, and remediation for teachers of composition and rhetoric.

123. Hatch, Gary. *Reviving the Rodential Model for Composition: Robert Zoellner's Alternative to Flower and Hayes*. Boston, MA: CCCC, March 1991. ERIC ED 333 458. 13 pages

Argues for rejecting the assumption that writing is thinking; turns to Zoellner's behavioral theory of writing as signifying act.

124. Hayes, John R. "Peeking Out from Under the Blinders: Some Factors We Shouldn't Forget in Studying Writing (Occasional Paper No. 3)." Center for the Study of Writing, 1991. ERIC ED 334 587. 21 pages

Offers a personal list of six factors—of task, skills, and context—often overlooked in writing research.

125. Heine, Patricia Jean. "Writers Supporting Writers." *DAI* 52 (September 1991): 791A.

Shows that writers interact frequently in a process writing environment.

126. Heller, Carol. "An Interview with Linda Flower." *QNWP/CSW* 13 (Winter 1991): 3–5, 28–30.

Reflects on composing, research, classroom teaching, teacher-research collaboratives, and community literacy projects.

127. Herndl, Carl G. "Writing Ethnography: Representation, Rhetoric, and Institutional Practice." *CE* 53 (March 1991): 320–332.

Discusses ethnography as a textual process that is both communally maintained rhetoric and institutional practice.

128. Himley, Margaret. *Shared Territory: Understanding Children's Writing as Works*. New York: Oxford University Press, 1991. 240 pages

Draws on theories of Mikhail Bakhtin and Patricia Carini to study the development of children's early written language.

129. Holbrook, Sue Ellen. "Women's Work: The Feminizing of Composition." *RR* 9 (Spring 1991): 201–229.

Delineates from a historical perspective the link between the "inferior" status of women and the "unprestigeous" status of composition teachers in the academy.

130. Houston, Marsha, and Cheris Kramarae. "Speaking from Silence: Methods of Silencing and of Resistance." *D&S* 2 (October 1991): 387–399.

Describes ways in which male-dominated society has prevented women from speaking out; suggests the means by which women have begun to overcome this silence.

131. Huettman, Elizabeth. "Writing for the Unknown Reader: An Ethnographic Case Study in a Business Setting." *DAI* 52 (July 1991): 154A.

Presents a thirty-month case study of a business writer as she writes one feasibility report.

132. Hunter, Susan. "A Woman's Place Is in the Composition Classroom: Pedagogy, Gender, and Difference." *RR* 9 (Spring 1991): 230–245.

Examines a feminist composition classroom populated by "privileged" science and engineering students. Asserts that all feminist classrooms should be sites of "conversations about difference."

133. Hurlbert, C. Mark, and Michael Blitz, eds. *Composition and Resistance*. Portsmouth, NH: Boynton/Cook, 1991. 178 pages

Analyzes the economic, social, political, and practical aspects of teaching writing; each essay exposes unexamined beliefs and practices.

Essayists: James Berlin, Miriam T. Chaplin, Judith Fetterly, Jeff Golub, Joseph Harris, C. Mark Hurlbert, Michael Blitz, C. H. Knoblauch, Nancy Mack, Stephen M. North, Louann Reid, Cecilia Rodriguez Milanes, Jay Rosen, Donna Singleton, James Sledd, Kurt Spellmeyer, J. Elspeth Stuckey, Marian Yee, James Thomas Zebroski.

134. Ingham, Zita. "Reading and Writing a Landscape: A Rhetoric of Southwest Desert Literature." *DAI* 52 (September 1991): 917A.

Discusses rhetorical aspects of the experiences and the representation of the American desert using a transactional model of reading and writing.

135. Ingham, Zita, and Peter Wild. "The Preface as Illumination: The Curious (If Not Tricky) Case of John C. Van Dyke's *The Desert*." *RR* 9 (Spring 1991): 328–339.

Reviews Van Dyke's *The Desert* in comparison to composition studies and discusses how nonfiction should be used with teaching composition.

136. Jacques, Francis. *Difference and Subjectivity*. New Haven, CT: Yale University Press, 1991. 384 pages

Develops a new relational model of the subject defined in the course of communication with others.

137. Jamieson, Sandra. "Rereading 'Readers': The Use of Textbook Readers in the Teaching of College-Level Composition." *DAI* 52 (October 1991): 1239A.

Contrasts the selection of topics chosen by minorities and women to those chosen by white males.

138. Jarratt, Susan C. "Comments on Clark and Doheny-Farina [*WC* 8 (January 1991)]." *WC* 8 (January 1991): 117–120.

Suggests that Clark and Doheny-Farina might profitably have analyzed more explicitly the analytical framework and assumptions they made in their article.

139. Johnstone, Henry W., Jr. "Rhetoric as a Wedge: A Reformation." *RSQ* 20 (Fall 1990): 333–338.

Elaborates on a defintion of rhetoric as a 'wedge' that forces a gap between subject and object.

140. Jost, Walter. "Teaching the Topics: Character, Rhetoric, and Liberal Education." *RSQ* 21 (Winter 1991): 1–16.

Uses the work of Wayne Booth to argue that inductive mastery of special topics (*eide*) is the heart of rhetorical invention and liberal education.

141. Judd, David Thomas. "An Examination of the Influence of Writing upon Thinking." *DAI* 51 (March 1991): 2971A.

Examines the influence of writing upon thinking from a naturalistic perspective using three participants.

142. Karlson, Kathy J. "Writing Training: Collaboration between Academy and Government Agency." *TC* 38 (November 1991): 493–497.

Offers background on General Accounting Office (GAO) and its concern with writing and research. Describes benefits to GAO and academic consultants.

143. Keith, Philip. "A Reexamination of George Yoos's 'Role-Identity in Reading and Writing.'" *RSQ* 20 (Fall 1990): 357–360.

Illustrates how Yoos's multiple-reflexive reading and writing model can be used in teaching and reflecting on teaching and writing.

144. Kemmy, Anne M. "From Practice to Theory: The Evolution of Rhetorical Stasis and Its Implications for Discourse and for Teaching Writing." *DAI* 51 (February 1991): 2727A.

Suggests that approaching stasis as principle rather than system makes for more effective writing instruction.

145. Kent, Thomas. "On the Very Idea of a Discourse Community." *CCC* 42 (December 1991): 425–445.

Uses the philosophical "externalism" of Donald Davidson to "offer an alternative to social constructionism that rejects essentialism, endorses anti-foundationalism, but refutes charges of relativism and skepticism."

146. Kent, Thomas. "Talking Differently: A Response to Gayatri Chakravorty Spivak [*JAC* 10 (1990)]." *JAC* 11 (Winter 1991): 185–191.

Praises Spivak's interview with *JAC* for her talking as a Derridean externalist rather than an internalist.

147. Kienpointer, Manfred. "Rhetoric and Argumentation—Relativism and beyond." *P&R* 24 (1991): 43–53.

Argues that rhetorical relativism is a fruitful instrument for dealing with disagreement in society.

148. King, Debra W. "Just Can't Find the Words: How Expression Is Achieved." *P&R* 24 (1991): 54–72.

Points out that the written word can express human emotions and sensations if we search for a supplement that is only felt or heard.

149. Kirsch, Gesa. "Writing Up and Down the Social Ladder: A Study of Experienced Writers Composing for Contrasting Audiences." *RTE* 25 (February 1991): 33–53.

Presents a study that uses protocol analysis to explore how writing instructors at large public universities compose differently for incoming first-year college students and faculty committees.

150. Kissling, Elizabeth Arveda. "Street Harassment: The Language of Sexual Terrorism." *D&S* 2 (October 1991): 451–460.

Analyzes the ways in which men oppress women by addressing sexual remarks in public to women they do not know.

151. Knowles-Borishade, Adetokunbo F. "Paradigm for Classical African Narrative: Instrument for a Scientific Revolution." *JBS* 21 (June 1991): 488–500.

Develops paradigm for analyzing "Afrocentric discourse" as a corrective to Western rhetorical standards for critical analysis.

152. Kraemer, Don. "Abstracting the Bodies of/in Academic Discourse." *RR* 10 (Fall 1991): 52–69.

Discusses his ambivalence about assimilating students into the academic discourse community. Argues for heterogeneous discourse that incorporates "writing the body" as well as abstraction.

153. Krasick, Carole Linda. "A Descriptive Study: How Themes Emerge and Are Transmitted in a Temporary Society." *DAI* 52 (August 1991): 475A.

Examines how ideas and themes are initiated and then transmitted through society.

154. Krol, Tineke F. "Women Talk about Talk at Work." *D&S* 2 (October 1991): 461–476.

Investigates the gendered rhetoric used by working-class women on the job.

155. Kuzmic, Jeffrey J. "Toward a Practice Informed Theory of Critical Pedagogy: Individualism, Community, and Democratic Schooling." *DAI* 52 (August 1991): 411A.

Argues for a closer union and dialogue between critical and feminist theory to serve as a basis for developing a "practice informed" theory of critical pedagogy.

156. Lassner, Phyllis. "Bridging Composition and Women's Studies: The Work of Ann E. Berthoff and Suzanne K. Langer." *JTW* 10 (Spring/Summer 1991): 21–37.

Analyzes how Berthoff and Langer advocate the interplay of subjective experience and separate reality, especially through metaphor.

157. Leggo, Carl. "Questions I Need to Ask Before I Advise My Students to Write in Their Own Voices." *RR* 10 (Fall 1991): 143–151.

Establishes the sense of a writer's unique voice and poses an extended list of specific questions directed toward understanding issues of "voice."

158. Leki, Ilona. "Twenty-Five Years of Contrastive Rhetoric: Text Analysis and Writing Pedagogies." *TESOLQ* 25 (Spring 1991): 123–143.

Reviews contrastive rhetoric research (1966–1991), discusses relation to process pedagogy, and presents additional pedagogical implications.

159. Lindemann, Erika, and Gary Tate, eds. *An Introduction to Composition Studies*. New York: Oxford University Press, 1991. 208 pages

Nine essays introduce the nonspecialist to composition studies, discussing the nature of the field, the relationship between composition and rhetoric and between theory and practice, the history of the discipline, its bibliographic sources and problems, its methods of research, the teaching of writing, and the politics of the profession. *Essayists:* Andrea L. Lunsford, John T. Gage, Charles I. Schuster, Robert J. Connors, Patrick Scott, Lillian Bridwell-Bowles, Lisa Ede, James F. Slevin, Charles Moran.

160. Littlewood, Derek G. "The Signification of Speech and Writing in the Work of Charles Dickens." *DAI* 52 (July 1991): 4132A.

Draws upon Bakhtin and Derrida to conclude that Dickens observed the transition from oral to literate culture.

161. Logan, Brian S. "The Structure of Design Problems." *DAI* 51 (March 1991): 2901A.

Examines the interrelationships between problem criteria which ultimately determine the solution to a design composition problem.

162. Lu, Hsiao-peng. "The Order of Narrative Discourse: Problems in Chinese Historiography and Fiction." *DAI* 51 (May 1991): 3733A.

Argues that the close interrelationships between forms of Chinese discourse make it difficult to apply Western discourse theories to Chinese texts.

163. Lunsford, Andrea A., and Lisa Ede. "Comments on Clark and Doheny-Farina [*WC* 8 (January 1991)]." *WC* 8 (January 1991): 114–117.

Using Burke, Lunsford and Ede problematize the "compelling" dichotomies set out by Clark and Doheny-Farina.

164. Lux, Paul A. "Discourse Styles of Anglo- and Latin-American College Student Writers." *DAI* 52 (December 1991): 2128A.

Analyzes 158 essays written by four groups of student writers. Supports the contrastive rhetoric hypothesis.

165. Macaruso, Victor Maurice. "Taking Risks and Empowerment: Three Case Studies." *DAI* 52 (November 1991): 1669A.

Looks at the linguistic, social, and political risks that three nontraditional women took as they became empowered in a conversation-based composition classroom.

166. Martin, James E. *Contrastive Rhetoric: Implications of a Revised Approach to Rhetoric*. 1991. ERIC ED 329 118. 16 pages

Discusses recent research suggesting that analysis of pragmatic differences across languages are more fruitful than examining only formal differences.

167. Marting, Janet. "Writers on Writing: Self-Assessment Strategies for Student Essays." *TETYC* 18 (May 1991): 128–132.

Presents students' responses to a series of questions about their writing strategies.

168. McAndrew, Donald A. *Ecofeminism and the Teaching of Writing*. Boston, MA: CCCC, March 1991. ERIC ED 333 452. 8 pages

Claims that parallels to ecofeminism are seen in the writing workshop, recent theoretical understandings of text/reader/writer, research methodology, and classroom practices.

169. McCreight, Thomas Dean. "Rhetorical Strategies and Word Choices in Apuleius' 'Apology.'" *DAI* 52 (November 1991): 1737A.

Considers strategies of persuasion in the "Apology." Appendixes document first- or only-time usage of Latin words in speech.

170. McLeod, Susan H. "The Affective Domain and the Writing Process: Working Definitions." *JAC* 11 (Winter 1991): 95–105.

Argues that since writing processes involve cognition and affect, key-term definitions, informed by current thought, are useful; defines "affect," "emotion," "attitude," "anxiety," "belief," "motivation."

171. McLeod, Susan H. "Reply to Kristie Fleckenstein [*JAC* 11 (Fall 1991)]." *JAC* 11 (Fall 1991): 453–454.

Finds Fleckenstein's comments thought-provoking, in regard to the "relationship of affect and schema theory" and in her criticism of Louise Rosenblatt.

172. Mettauer, Patrice A. "Gender Differences in the Affect of Communication Behavior on Self-Perceptions of Power in Conflict Interaction." *DAI* 52 (November 1991): 1573A.

Generates a theory about the relationship between self-perception, power, gender and communication behavior in conflict.

173. Mill, Michael. *The Cultural Politics of Expression: A Qualified Critique of Freewriting*. Boston, MA: CCCC, March 1991. ERIC ED 332 198. 13 pages

Presents a political interpretation of the culture of freewriting.

174. Motley, Michael T. "How One May Not Communicate: A Reply to Andersen." *ComS* 42 (Winter 1991): 326–339.

Demonstrates that common postulates contradict the notion that all perception is communication.

175. Mueller-Lust, Rachel A. G., and Raymond W. Gibbs, Jr. "Inferring the Interpretation of Attributive and Referential Definite Descriptions." *DPr* 14 (April–June 1991): 107–131.

Argues that context helps readers distinguish statements of criteria from references to individuals as in "The woman who can sing this song will get the job."

176. Nash, Jane Gradwohl. "Writing from Sources: A Structure-Mapping Model." *DAI* 51 (May 1991): 5617B.

Argues that an essay is influenced by the order in which sources are read and by the way they are organized.

177. Nass, Clifford, and Byron Reeves. "Combining, Distinguishing, and Generating Theories of Communication: A Domain of Analysis Framework." *ComR* 18 (April 1991): 240–261.

Replaces notions of level in organizing themes for communication research with domains and justifies their use in theory and data collection.

178. Nealy, Constance Jean. "A Study of Two Instructional Methods—Process and Product—in Improving the Writing Ability of Selected College Freshmen." *DAI* 51 (March 1991): 2973A.

Determines the difference in the effect of a process- versus product-oriented method for improving writing in first-year college students. Points out that statistically significant findings slightly favored the process-oriented method.

179. Nespor, Jan, and Liz Barber. "The Rhetorical Construction of 'The Teacher.' " *HER* 61 (November 1991): 417–433.

Examines rhetorical strategies that a widely cited article employs in constructing "the teacher" as the object of the study; calls for more "critical literacy" among readers and writers of research texts.

180. Newkirk, Thomas. "Barrett Wendell's Theory of Discourse." *RR* 10 (Fall 1991): 20–31.

Discusses Wendall's unfinished composition text as a contrast to his earlier *English Composition*; addresses the inadequacies of modal systems.

181. Nordling, John G. "Indirect Discourse and Rhetorical Strategies in Caesar's 'Bellum Gallicum' and 'Bellum Civile.' " *DAI* 52 (November 1991): 1737A.

Argues for "discourse continuum" as a defining principle to investigate levels of discourse.

182. Nordquist, Richard F. "Voices of the Modern Essay." *DAI* 52 (September 1991): 919A.

Considers the authorial voice of twentieth-century American essays and argues that the character of the essayist is a textual construct.

183. Nystrand, Martin, and Jeffrey Wiemelt. "When Is a Text Explicit? Formalist and Dialogical Conceptions." *TEXT* 11 (1991): 25–41.

Explores opposing notions of meaning; concludes that textual meaning reflects "the negotiated interests and purposes of both writer and reader."

184. Olson, Gary, and Lester Faigley. "Language, Politics, and Composition: A Conversation with Noam Chomsky." *JAC* 11 (Winter 1991): 1–35.

Chomsky defends innate structure of language, feminism, Freire, and Plato's method of thought. Criticizes Kuhn, Derrida, and social constructionism.

185. Olson, Gary A. "The Role of Theory in Composition Scholarship." *FEN* 19 (Fall 1991): 4–5.

Argues that theory is the "heart of the mind" of composition studies and is "what makes rhetoric and composition more than a service provider."

185. Olson, Gary A. "The Social Scientist as Author: Clifford Geertz on Ethnography and Social Construction." *JAC* 11 (Fall 1991): 245–268.

An interview with Geertz explores the application of anthropological modes of inquiry to composition.

187. Olson, Gary A., and Irene Gale, eds. *(Inter)views: Cross-Disciplinary Perspectives on Rhetoric and Literacy*. Carbondale, IL: Southern Illinois University Press, 1991. 288 pages

Contains interviews with Belenky, Chomsky, Derrida, Freire, Geertz, Rorty, and Spivak, followed by essay responses from scholars in rhetoric and composition.

Essayists: Gary A. Olson, Irene Gale, David Bleich, Evelyn Ashton-Jones, Dene Kay Thomas, Elizabeth A. Flynn, Marilyn M. Cooper, Lester Faigley, James Sledd, Robert de Beaugrande, Sharon Crowley, Jasper Neel, James A. Berlin, C. H. Knoblauch, Linda Brodkey, Lisa Ede, Kenneth A. Bruffee, John Schilb, Phillip Sipiora, Janet Atwill, John Clifford, Thomas Kent, Andrea A. Lunsford.

188. Oravec, Christine. "The Ideological Significance of Discursive Form: A Response to Solomon and Perkins." *ComS* 42 (Winter 1991): 383–391.

Suggests acknowledging the ideological qualities of form; juxtaposes theory with analysis, history with subjectivity, and language with practice.

189. Osborn, Susan. "Revision/Re-Vision: A Feminist Writing Class." *RR* 9 (Spring 1991): 258–273.

Describes revision/re-vision as a way to understand gender construction through language and to know ourselves as both readers and writers.

190. Ostrander, Tammy M. "Confrontation Rhetoric of Selected Native American Tribes: A Genre Study." *DAI* 51 (May 1991): 3559A.

Identifies techniques—ethical appeals and metaphors, examples authorized by the Great Spirit, proposals of unification and action—as features of this rhetoric.

191. Page, Miriam D. "The Anthropologist as Essayist." *DAI* 51 (June 1991): 4173A.

Studies the Montaignean essay; emphasizes its role in twentieth-century sociocultural anthropology.

192. Pemberton, Michael A. "Graven Images: The Epistemology of Cognitive Composing Process Models." *DAI* 51 (May 1991): 3719A.

Discusses the integration of "global," "developmental," and "linguistic" composing models.

193. Perkins, Sally J. "The Myth of the Matriarchy: Annulling Patriarchy through the Regeneration of Time." *ComS* 42 (Winter 1991): 371–382.

Applies Eliade's theory of origin myths to two feminist rhetorical texts.

194. Perry, Patricia Harris. "Transformations of Consciousness and Knowledge-Making about Writing: The Philosophies of Paulo Freire and Peter Elbow." *DAI* 52 (October 1991): 1251A.

Argues for a reassessment of Elbow and Freire in composition instruction, noting their affinity for the Socratic method and dialogism.

195. Petraglia, Joseph. "Interrupting the Conversation: The Constructionist Dialogue in Composition." *JAC* 11 (Winter 1991): 37–55.

Identifies four key assertions of social constructionism and subjects each to interdisciplinary critique.

196. Phelps, Louise Wetherbee. "Practical Wisdom and the Geography of Knowledge in Composition." *CE* 53 (December 1991): 863–885.

Revises and extends Stephen North's concept of lore, charts a speculative geography of knowledge in composition, and discusses the contributions of practical wisdom to theory.

197. Pollock, Della, and J. Robert Cox. "Historicizing 'Reason': Critical Theory, Practice, and Post Modernity." *ComM* 58 (June 1991): 170–178.

Discusses critical theory as an attempt to respond to the postmodern.

198. Pratt, Michael W., and Susan L. Robins. "That's the Way It Was: Age Differences in the Structure and Quality of Adults' Personal Narratives." *DPr* 14 (January–March 1991): 73–85.

Points out that adult raters of varying ages judged the narratives of older adults more favorably.

199. Pullman, George L. "Interpretive Rhetoric: Politics and the Attribution of Meaning." *DAI* 52 (August 1991): 346A.

Concludes that the study of meaning must account for the socio-rhetorical conditions that influence interpretation.

200. Putnam, Linda L., Shirley A. Van Hoeven, and Connie A. Bullis. "The Role of Rituals and Fantasy Themes in Teachers' Bargaining." *WJSC* 55 (Winter 1991): 85–103.

Applies symbolic convergence theory to collective bargaining as a social construction of reality.

201. Pytlik, Betty P. "Teaching the Teaching of Composition: Evolving Theories." *WI* 11 (Fall 1991): 39–50.

Uses a case study to generalize about how new writing teachers develop and enact their own theories about writing and teaching.

202. Quigley, Rooke Lee. "The Use of Rhetorical Strategies in the Formation of Consensus: A Dramatistic Analysis of a Decision-Making Process." *DAI* 51 (May 1991): 3560A.

Examines rhetorical strategies in the discourse of a small decision making group that reached consensus on a difficult policy issue.

203. Reed, Janine. "How Notions of Self Shape Goals and Practices in Two Views of Expressive Writing." *DAI* 51 (May 1991): 3647A.

Discusses the difference between an "authenticity" orientation to expressive writing and a "generativity" orientation; explores how it operates in the writing process.

204. Reimers, Valerie Ann. "Abstraction and Abstract Thinking: Definitions in Composition Studies." *DAI* 52 (September 1991): 830A.

Explores the meanings of the terms "abstraction" and "abstract thinking" in composition classrooms, literacy-orality studies, and composition theory.

205. Reither, James A., and Douglas Vipond. "James A. Reither and Douglas Vipond Respond [to Boggs, *CE* 53 (February 1991)]." *CE* 53 (February 1991): 229.

Authors ask if self-serving writing is necessarily invalid.

206. Reynolds, Nedra. "Textual Rhetorics and *Textual Carnivals*: Susan Miller and the 'Subjects' of Rhetoric and Composition." *JTW* 10 (Fall/Winter 1991): 255–268.

Recommends Miller's *Textual Carnivals* and *Rescuing the Subject* as original and stimulating works for rethinking theory and practice.

207. Risjord, Mark Winden. "Semantics, Culture and Rationality: Toward an Epistemology of Ethnography." *DAI* 51 (April 1991): 3432A.

Argues that a coherence based conceptualization of the epistemology of ethnography is more satisfactory than the neorationalist alternative.

208. Rivers, Thomas R. *Accommodating Virtue: Weak and Strong Discourse*. Boston, MA: CCCC, March 1991. ERIC ED 331 067. 12 pages

Draws lines of congruence between ethical and rhetorical traditions, suggesting implications for a pedagogy of virture and character.

209. Roberts, Patricia. "Habermas' Varieties of Communicative Action: Controversy without Combat." *JAC* 11 (Fall 1991): 409–424.

Suggests that Habermas's theories will assist the composition instructor in teaching persuasive writing and will provide empowerment to students.

210. Root, Robert L., Jr. *Working at Writing: Columnists and Critics of Composing*. Carbondale, IL: Southern Illinois University Press, 1991. 258 pages

Examines the composing processes of seven expository writers who regularly come up on deadlines. Contains a discussion of writing, a collection of interviews, and an anthology of nonfiction prose.

211. Roulis, Eleni. "The Relative Effect of a Gender-Linked Language Effect and a Sex Role Stereotype Effect on Readers' Responses to Male and Female Argumentative-Persuasive Writing." *DAI* 52 (November 1991): 1670A.

Finds that female writers are rated higher than male writers on aesthetic quality, socio-intellectual, and cooperative factors.

212. Royer, Daniel J. "New Challenges to Epistemic Rhetoric." *RR* 9 (Spring 1991): 282–297.

Clarifies the presuppositions of objectivists and relativists. Suggests that New Realism may reconcile existing polarity; encourages rhetorical theorists to consider this alternative.

213. Rudinow, Joel. "Argument-Appreciation/Argument-Criticism: The 'Aesthetics' of Informal Logic." *IL* 13 (Spring 1991): 89–97.

Explores the analogy between argument criticism and art criticism; argues that it helps resolve problems central to normative theories of argument.

214. Rudnick, Kenneth Joseph. "Charles Sanders Peirce on the Cognitive Given." *DAI* 52 (August 1991): 565A.

Examines the cognitional theory of Charles Sanders Peirce; concludes that Peirce developed a nontraditional alternative form of foundationalism.

215. Runciman, Lex. "Fun?" *CE* 53 (February 1991): 156–162.

Argues that instructors need to help students find enjoyment and satisfaction in the writing process.

216. Ryan, Howard S. "The Whys of Teaching Composition: Social Visions." *FEN* 19 (Fall 1991): 9–17.

Provides a taxonomy of goals and implied social visions in composition that includes five models: utility, individual growth, individual mobility, collaborative growth, and collective empowerment.

217. Schenck, Mary Jane. "Nothing Is Simple as ABC." *JTW* 10 (Spring/Summer 1991): 95–105.

Critiques Ivan Illich's and Barry Sanders' *ABC: The Alphabetization of the Popular Mind* because of their assumptions about illiteracy and the relationship between orality and writing.

218. Schilb, John. "What's at Stake in the Conflict between 'Theory' and 'Practice' in Composition." *RR* 10 (Fall 1991): 91–97.

Discusses paradoxes and conflicts in contemporary theory and practice, problems of opposition between theory and practice, and the need for an exchange of ideas.

219. Schriver, Karen A. "Plain Language for Expert or Lay Audiences: Designing Text Using Protocol-Aided Revision (Technical Report No. 46)." Center for the Study of Writing, 1991. ERIC ED 334 583. 46 pages

Offers two protocol-aided case studies of text revision; notes the role of visuals in text comprehension.

220. Scott, Joan M. "The Evidence of Experience." *CritI* 17 (Summer 1991): 773–797.

Argues against the foundational concept of experience. Offers instead a consideration of experience as a culturally determined category.

221. Sebastian, Daniel. "Ethic-Centered Composition: A Course Design." *DAI* 51 (April 1991): 3347A.

Argues that composition courses should focus more attention on the ethical dimension since a review of rhetoric indicates that the ultimate aims of writing are ethical in character.

222. Segal, Erwin M., Judith F. Duchan, and Paula J. Scott. "The Role of Interclausal Connectives in Narrative Structuring: Evidence from Adults' Interpretations of Simple Stories." *DPr* 14 (January–March 1991): 27–54.

Argues that connectives help to signal the continuity or discontinuity in readers' mental representations of narratives. Points out that the connectives "and" and "then" signal differing degrees of continuity.

223. Seitz, James. "Composition's Misunderstanding of Metaphor." *CCC* 42 (October 1991): 288–298.

Critiques approaches which teach metaphor only as something to be used, thereby ignoring "how metaphor inevitably shapes, enables, and constrains discourse."

224. Seitz, James E. "Metaphors for Reading: A Study in the Rhetoric of Reflexive Figures." *DAI* 51 (February 1991): 2727A.

Explores the transaction between theories of reading in terms of a "suggestive rhetoric" of mutual clarification.

225. Shapiro, Michael A. "Memory and Decision Processes in the Construction of Social Reality." *ComR* 18 (February 1991): 3–24.

Argues that a person must determine the usefulness of memories when constructing social reality. Points out the relevance of perceived communication sources.

226. Simons, Elizabeth Radin. "Students' Spontaneous Joking in an Urban Classroom." *DAI* 51 (March 1991): 3179A.

Finds that student joke-making in class is not oppositional, but is related to classroom involvement and control.

227. Simons, Herbert W. "On the Rhetoric of Social Movements, Historical Movements, and 'Top-Down' Movements: A Commentary." *ComS* 42 (Spring 1991): 94–101.

Proposes a modified definition of 'social movement' that retains centrality of the institutionalization variable in rhetorical analysis.

228. Sledd, James. "Response to 'Language, Politics, and Composition: A Conversation with Noam Chomsky' [*JAC* 11 (Fall 1991)]" *JAC* 11 (Fall 1991): 443–446.

Criticizes Olson and Faigley's interview of Chomsky, citing poor questions as well as a lack of opportunity for full development of responses and rebuttals.

229. Smagorinsky, Peter. "The Writer's Knowledge and the Writing Process: A Protocol Analysis." *RTE* 25 (October 1991): 339–364.

Differentiates three instructional treatments (study of models, instruction in task-specific procedures, instruction in general composing procedures) and compares their effects on students' writing processes.

230. Smit, David W. "The Rhetorical Method of Ludwig Wittgenstein." *RR* 10 (Fall 1991): 31–51.

Holds that Wittgenstein's practice can be a corrective to arguments over interpretive strategies. Claims, however, that our "understanding will always be partial, fragmented, undetermined."

231. Smith, Barbara Herrnstein. "Belief and Resistance: A Symmetrical Account." *CritI* 18 (Autumn 1991): 125–139.

Explores the relationship between belief and evidence and the implications for persuasive discourse.

232. Smudde, Peter. "A Practical Model of the Document-Development Process." *TC* 38 (August 1991): 316–323.

Studies the process by which documents in nonacademic settings are generated.

233. Snyder, Leslie B. "Modeling Dynamic Communication Processes with Event History Analysis." *ComR* 18 (August 1991): 464–486.

Teaches event history analysis as a communication research technique for measuring quantitative changes to a person, relationship, or organization.

234. Sperling, Melanie. "Dialogues of Deliberation: Conversation in the Teacher-Student Writing Conference." *WC* 8 (April 1991): 131–162.

Using discourse analysis, the study examines the influence of teacher/student conversations on student texts.

235. Spitzberg, Brian H., and Claire C. Brunner. "Toward a Theoretical Integration of Context and Competence Inference Research." *WJSC* 55 (Winter 1991): 28–46.

Presents and tests a set of propositions regarding the nature of social contexts and communication competence.

236. Spivey, Nancy Nelson. "The Shaping of Meaning: Options in Writing the Comparison." *RTE* 25 (December 1991): 390–418.

Finds that students organize comparisons primarily by aspect and object and select content that is symmetrical and available for both objects being compared.

237. Sternberg, Robert J., and Todd I. Lubart. "An Investment Theory of Creativity and Its Development." *HD* 34 (January/February 1991): 1–31.

Presents tests and describes an investment theory of creativity based on the following elements: intellectual processes, knowledge, intellectual style, personality, motivation, and environmental context.

238. Stewart, John. "A Postmodern Look at Traditional Communication Postulates." *WJSC* 55 (Fall 1991): 354–379.

Summarizes postmodernism as an alternative to four traditional postulates; suggests how reexamination might affect communication research and teaching.

239. Stewart, Susan. *Crimes of Writing: Problems in the Containment of Representation*. New York: Oxford University Press, 1991. 368 pages

Explores the symbolic texture of cultural life. Explains authorship and text by focusing on graffiti, pornography, forgery, and literary imposture. Shows how law is implicated in and threatened by "the containment of representation."

240. Strong, Michael, and Asa DeMatteo. "The Effects on Metalinguistic Awareness of an Experimental Bilingual Program for Deaf Children." *L&E* 2 (Winter 1991): 345–364.

Students asked to tell stories in both ESL and signed English increased metacognitive skills while children in a nonbilingual control group did not.

241. Sullivan, Patricia A. "Writing in the Graduate Curriculum: Literary Criticism as Composition." *JAC* 11 (Fall 1991): 283–300.

Indicates that the shift from "text-oriented" to "reader-oriented" theory is not accompanied by a "text-oriented" to "writer-oriented" shift in pedagogy.

242. Susman, Linda Santarelli. "Pragmatic Performance and Reflections of Competence." *DAI* 51 (February 1991): 2730A.

Concludes that acceptable pragmatic performance indicates native language ability.

243. Sweigart, William. "Classroom Talk, Knowledge Development, and Writing." *RTE* 25 (December 1991): 469–496.

Finds that student-led, small-group discussion is significantly more effective than lecture or class discussion in improving students' knowledge as they prepared to write; suggests that it leads to higher quality essays.

244. Tedesco, Janis. "Women's Ways of Knowing/Women's Ways of Composing." *RR* 9 (Spring 1991): 246–256.

Examines gender in the models of Perry and Belenky; suggests a combination of these different, but important tools to discover the mysteries of the writing process.

245. Tirone, Patricia L. "The Structure of Directionless Talk: The Interactional Management of Equality and Hierarchy in the Discourse of a School Staff Meeting." *DAI* 51 (January 1991): 2199A.

Presents an ethnographic study of the impact of differing achievement values on dialogue among ESL teaching staff.

246. Tobin, Lad. "Writing Relationships: Reading Students, Reading Ourselves." *DAI* 52 (November 1991): 1671A.

Argues that context in composition is primarily determined by interpersonal, classroom relationships between students and teachers, students and other students, and teachers and other teachers.

247. Touchton, Judith G., and Lynne Davis. *Fact Book on Women in Higher Education.* New York: American Council on Education, 1991. 289 pages

Collects data on female administrators, faculty members, students, staff members, and trustees.

248. Tracy, Karen, ed. *Understanding Face-to-Face Interaction: Issues Linking Goals and Discourse.* Hillsdale, NJ: Lawrence Erlbaum Associates, 1991. 224 pages

Examines the thinking and rhetorical strategies involved in human communication by discussing discourse-goal linkages in specific face-to-face encounters, as well as in more general theoretical dilemmas.
Essayists: K. Tracy, R. Penman. S. Jacobs, S. Jackson, S. Stearns, B. Hall, N. R. Buttny, J. R. Cohen, N. Coupland, J. Coupland, H. Giles, K. Henwood, W. K. Rawlins, J. B. Bavelas, B. J. O'Keefe, J. Mandelbaum, A. Pomerantz, R. E. Sanders, G. J. Shepherd, E. W. Rothenbuhler.

249. Trout, Robert Edwin. "Episodic Analogy: An Approach to Analogical Problem-Solving." *DAI* 52 (November 1991): 2655B.

Describes a method for solving new problems by analogy with old problem-solving experiences and demonstrates the importance of knowing a problem's domain to its solution.

250. Trufant, Laurel Warren. "Metaphors in the Construction of Theory: Ramus, Peirce and the American Mind." *DAI* 52 (August 1991): 661A.

Argues for the mutual impenetration of logical, legal and scientific metaphors; attempts to determine their role in the construction of American ideology.

251. Turow, Joseph. "The Challenge of Inference in Interinstitutional Research on Mass Communication." *ComR* 18 (April 1991): 222–239.

Suggests that notions of "storytelling" and cognitive aesthetics are ways to deal with the ambiguities of interinstitutional research.

252. Varnhagen, Connie K. "Text Relations and Recall for Expository Prose." *DPr* 14 (October–December 1991): 399–422.

Compares three approaches to textual analysis: content structure, causal relations, and argument repetition. The first two identified recall differences among subjects of varying ages.

253. Walberg, Herbert J, and Corinna A. Ethington. "Correlates of Writing Performance and Interest: A U.S. National Assessment." *JEdR* 84 (March/April 1991): 198–203.

Correlation to nine "productivity factors" confirm previous findings, but to a lesser degree. Argues that writing performance was much less predictable than writing motivation.

254. Wallace, David L. "From Intention to Text: Developing, Implementing, and Judging Intention in Writing." *DAI* 52 (October 1991): 1242A.

Finds that the effectiveness of initial intentions is related to the effectiveness of the finished text.

255. Wallace, Wanda T., and David C. Rubin. "Characteristics and Constraints in Ballads and Their Effects on Memory." *DPr* 14 (April–June 1991): 181–202.

Argues that meter, imagery, and other characteristics aid singers in accurately remembering ballads that they have only heard once or twice.

256. Walsh, Christine M. "The Degree of Congruence among Writing Teachers' Writing,

Thinking and Teaching." *DAI* 51 (April 1991): 3352A.

Findings suggest a considerable degree of congruence among writing teachers' metacognitive awareness, theoretical orientations, and pedagogical practices during writing and instruction.

257. Walzer, Arthur E. "The Meanings of 'Purpose.'" *RR* 10 (Fall 1991): 118–129.

Discusses two understandings of purpose—unique or conventional—as found in different textbooks. Concludes this difference relates to different views in the teaching of writing.

258. Wershoven, Carol. "Personal Writing in the Composition Class: When the Personal Is Dangerously Political." *WI* 11 (Fall 1991): 31–37.

Argues that using personal writing as a replacement for academic writing will not empower students to challenge the academy's discourse community.

259. Whipple, Robert Dale, Jr. "Socratic Method and Writing Instruction." *DAI* 51 (May 1991): 3657A.

Describes the Socratic method and analyzes its use in three modern rhetorics.

260. Whitney, Paul, Bill G. Ritchie, and Matthew B. Clark. "Working-Memory Capacity and the Use of Elaborative Inferences in Text Comprehension." *DPr* 14 (April–June 1991): 133–145.

Argues that individual differences in memory capacity correlate with differences in the textual details interpreted. Points out that readers with low memory span tend to eschew open-ended interpretations.

261. Williams, David Cratis. "Toward Kenneth Burke's Philosophy of Rhetoric: An Intellectual History, 1897–1935." *DAI* 52 (August 1991): 348A.

Analyzes the relationship between Burke's early personal and professional lives and their effect on his theories of symbolic action.

262. Winders, James A. "Writers, Bodies, Subjects: Conflicts in Postmodern Writing Theories." *WI* 11 (Fall 1991): 7–16.

Describes contradictions in the use of postmodern theory as a tool for emancipatory pedagogy.

263. Winterowd, Ross. "A Philosophy of Composition." *RR* 9 (Spring 1991): 340–348.

Supports the New Rhetoricians' view that writing is a way of doing something rather than a way of making/finding something, as romantic idealists believe.

264. Wiwcharuk, Tom. "The Resolution Function of Argument." *DAI* 51 (March 1991): 3106A.

Examines the three functions of argument and concludes that the resolution function best accounts for the complexity of argumentative behavior.

265. Worley, Demetrice Anntia. "Visual and Verbal Transactions: The Effect of Visual Imagery Training on the Writing of College Students." *DAI* 51 (March 1991): 3006A.

Investigates the effect of visual imagery training on college students' use of detailed information and problem solving in written texts and the overall quality of written texts.

266. "Writing (Special Collection No. 5)." ERIC/RCS, 1991. ERIC ED 334 604. 69 pages

Gathers five research reports (ERIC digests) and nine research summaries (ERIC FAST Bibs) on the teaching of writing, along with information on using the ERIC system.

267. Youmans, Madeleine, and Constance A. Gergen. "Theories of Writing." *WI* 11 (Fall 1991): 3–5.

Argues for theory-driven writing instruction to keep teachers aware of their power to empower or oppress.

268. Zani, Bruna, Maria Grazia Carelli, Beatrice Benelli, and Elvira Cicognani. "Communicative Skills in Childhood: The Case of Twins." *DPr* 14 (July–September 1991): 339–356.

Supports earlier characterization of gender differences in verbal conflict, with boys' disputes tending to be more competitive and girls' more collaborative.

269. Zhao, Shanyang. "Rhetoric as Praxis: An Alternative to the Epistemic Approach." *P&R* 24 (1991): 255–266.

Examines some "major problems" in epistemic rhetoric and proposes an "alternative approach" which aims to preserve the "rational core" while avoiding problems of epistemic rhetoric.

2.2 RHETORICAL HISTORY

270. Adamson, David McLaren. "Eighteenth-Century Rhetorics and Rhetafictions." *DAI* 52 (December 1991): 2146A.

Urges the reconsideration of eighteenth-century rhetoric. Examines three texts to restore the performative aspects of rhetoric.

271. Allison, Alida Louise. "Eurydice: The Lost Voice." *DAI* 51 (January 1991): 2371A.

Argues that Eurydice represents the marginal position due to her lack of power; points out that her voice explains much about the status and stereotyping of women.

272. Ansani, Antonella. "Imago Magi: Magic and Rhetoric in the Italian Renaissance." *DAI* 52 (August 1991): 557A.

Examines magic and its relation to rhetoric in the writings of Giovanni Pico della Mirandola and Ludovico Ariosto.

273. Aristotle. *On Rhetoric: A Theory of Civic Discourse*. Translated by George A. Kennedy. New York: Oxford University Press, 1991. 335 pages

Provides a translation, with commentary, of Aristotle's treatise on the art of persuasion.

274. Ashcroft, Joseph Gerard. "The Fertility of the Word: The Impact of the Development of Writing on the Hierarchy of Deities in Early Mesopotamian and Mediterranean Cultures." *DAI* 51 (June 1991): 3940A.

Based on a combination of media ecology and social constructivism, suggests that with the development of a writing system, goddess-worship transformed to god-worship.

275. Baym, Nina. "Between Enlightenment and Victorian: Toward a Narrative of American Women Writers Writing History." *CritI* 18 (Autumn 1991): 22–41.

Shows that writing history was a woman's writing practice in America in the eighteenth and nineteenth centuries.

276. Benardete, Seth. *The Rhetoric of Morality and Philosophy*. Chicago, IL: University of Chicago Press, 1991. 215 pages

Links *Gorgias*, a dialogue about the rhetoric of morality, and *Phaedrus*, a discourse about genuine rhetoric, to demonstrate that Plato constructed a complete psychology, giving morality and eros a place in the human soul.

277. Bennett, Beth S. "The Rhetoric of Martianus Capella and Anselm de Desate in the Tradition of Menippean Satire." *P&R* 24 (1991): 128–142.

Demonstrates the continued use of Menippean satire beyond the Middle Ages; argues that this genre provides access to the rhetorical practices of different ages.

278. Benoit, William L. "Isocrates and Aristotle on Rhetoric." *RSQ* 20 (Summer 1990): 251–260.

Argues that both men agreed on the function of rhetoric and the shortcomings of sophists but disagreed on rhetoric as epistemic and on the nature of ethos.

279. Benoit, William L. "Isocrates and Plato on Rhetoric and Rhetorical Education." *RSQ* 21 (Winter 1991): 60–71.

Finds considerable similarities and important differences in Isocrates' and Plato's views on the sophists, the nature of rhetoric, and rhetorical education.

280. Biesecker, Susan L. "Rhetorical Discourse and the Constitution of the Subject: Prodicus' *The Choice of Heracles*." *Arg* 5 (May 1991): 159–169.

Argues that Prodicus's text reshapes narrative form and articulates a different notion of human subjectivity and thus "registers a resistance to pre-Sophistic morality."

281. Biester, James Paul. "Strange and Admirable: Style and Wonder in the Seventeenth Century." *DAI* 51 (February 1991): 2750A.

Notes that stylistic strategies like rough brevity and embellished metaphors in lyric poems created a rhetoric of wonder highly valued in Renaissance culture.

282. Branciforte, Suzanne. "*Ars Poetica Rei Publicae*: The Herald of the Florentine Signoria." *DAI* 51 (February 1991): 2731A.

Analyzes historical aspects of the post of the herald, his public position, and the relation of his civic and literary functions.

283. Brasington, Bruce Clark. "The Prologue to the 'Decretum' and 'Panormia' of Ivo of Chartres: An Eleventh-Century Treatise on Ecclesiastical Jurisprudence." *DAI* 51 (January 1991): 2487A.

Analyzes Ivo's treatise on legal theory to show his pastoral orientation.

284. Bullock, Richard, John Trimbur, and Charles Schuster, eds. *The Politics of Writing Instruction: Postsecondary*. Portsmouth, NH: Boynton/Cook, 1991. 332 pages

Discusses the political implications of a full range of issues in composition studies from feminist theory and history of composition to basic writing and assessment.

Essayists: Richard Ohmann, J. F. Slevin, J. A. Berlin, S. Miller, R. J. Connors, C. I. Schuster, B. Herzberg, T. Newkirk, E. A. Flynn, L. W. Phelps, T. R. Donavan, T. Fulwiler, R. Bullock, R. A. Schwegler, S. Wall, N. Coles, V. Villanueva, Jr., A. R. Gere, J. Trimbur, M. Holzman.

285. Carter, Michael F. "The Ritual Functions of Epideictic Rhetoric: The Case of Socrates' Funeral Oration." *Rhetorica* 9 (Summer 1991): 209–232.

Explains some ritual functions of epideictic rhetoric: leads to extraordinary knowledge, generates a sense of community, and offers a means of guiding behavior.

286. Cohen, Elizabeh S. "'Courtesans' and 'Whores': Words and Behavior in Roman Streets." *WS* 19 (1991): 201–208.

Analyzes the ambivalent treatment of female prostitutes in Renaissance culture and art.

287. Cole, Lucinda. "Sympathy, Gender, and the Writing of Value in Late Eighteenth-Century English Letters." *DAI* 51 (March 1991): 3080A.

Presents a feminist study of how sympathy operates as an alternative discourse to male-dominated systems of values and produces a different version of community.

288. Corbeill, Anthony Thrower. "Political Humor in the Late Roman Republic: Romans Defining Themselves." *DAI* 51 (March 1991): 3053A.

Analyzes the persuasiveness of the *ad hominem* attacks in the late Roman Republic.

289. Daston, Lorraine. "Marvelous Facts and Miraculous Evidence in Early Modern Europe." *CritI* 18 (Autumn 1991): 93–124.

Considers the historical development of what constitutes a fact, a sign, and evidence with particular attention paid to preternatural phenomena.

290. Davis, Gregson. *Polyhymnia: The Rhetoric of Horatian Lyric Discourse*. Berkeley,

CA: University of California Press, 1991. 293 pages

Discusses four rhetorical strategies in the Roman poet's odes.

291. During, Simon. "Writing Outside the Book." *CCrit* (Fall 1990): 129–160.

Discusses how social forces determine what is written. Focuses on the history of periodical literature.

292. Eliades, Savvas Jack. "Plato's Theory of Forms." *DAI* 52 (August 1991): 562A.

Examines Plato's Theory of Forms from different perspectives and claims there is unity of thought concerning the Forms.

293. Enos, Richard Leo. "Socrates Questions Gorgias: The Rhetorical Vector of Plato's 'Gorgias.'" *Arg* 5 (February 1991): 5–15.

Argues that Plato's "Gorgias," a dialogue lauding dialectic over rhetoric, uses a question-and-answer format as a heuristic of argument.

294. Eskenasy, Pauline Ellen. "Antony of Tagrit's Rhetoric Book One: Introduction, Partial Translation, and Commentary." *DAI* 52 (September 1991): 936A.

Translates Tagrit's book. Provides background materials, possible sources, parallels, connections, suggestions for further research, and an outline and charts of the structure and contents of the book.

295. Falzer, Paul R. "On Behalf of Skeptical Rhetoric" *P&R* 24 (1991): 238–254.

Discusses rhetoric's place in the skeptical tradition, the move toward consensus and social knowledge, and the relationship of rhetoric to philosophy.

296. Farrell, Edmund J. "What is English?" *JTW* 10 (Fall/Winter 1991): 111–122.

Presents an historical view of literature and writing. Predicts continuing inclusion of print literature, writing in various modes for different purposes, and change.

297. Gleason, Maud Worcester. "Embodying the Rhetoric of Manhood: Self-Presentation in the Second Sophistic." *DAI* 52 (October 1991): 1316A.

Considers the rhetorical techniques deployed by Polemo and Fovorinus. Claims that rhetorical training was training in male deportment.

298. Glover, Carl W. "Kairos and Composition: Modern Perspectives on an Ancient Idea." *DAI* 52 (September 1991): 895A.

Traces the history of Kairos through Greek and the Old Testament. Suggests that changing audience demands should be considered diachronically.

299. Halford, Donna Allard. "A Rhetorical Legacy: The Art of Memory's Place in Literature and Semiotics." *DAI* 52 (August 1991): 547A.

This historical survey demonstrates that the classical art of memory remains a useful rhetorical device.

300. Halm, Ben Burnaby. "Theatre and Ideology: The Question of Theatre in Human Self-and-World Representations." *DAI* 51 (June 1991): 3958A.

Examines Plato's dismissal of poetry and theatre in favor of philosophy, then examines Aristotle's, Bacon's, and Nietzsche's amplifications and modifications of this view.

301. Harvill, Jerry G. "Aristotle's Concept of Ethos as Ground for a Modern Ethics of Communication." *DAI* 52 (July 1991): 21A.

Contrasts the ancient meaning of ethos as moral character with the modern conception of ethos as image of credibility.

302. Henry, David, and Richard J. Jensen. "Social Movement Criticism and the Renaissance of Public Address." *ComS* 42 (Spring 1991): 83–93.

Situates the critical analysis of social movements within the public address tradition.

303. Herbert, Christopher. *Culture and Anomie: Ethnographic Imagination in the Nineteenth Century*. Chicago, IL: University of Chicago Press, 1991. 312 pages

Researches the historical emergence of the modern idea of culture; provides an extended critical analysis of the perplexities and suppressed associations underlying exploitation in the nineteenth century.

304. Innes, D. C. "Gorgias, Antiphin, and Sophistopolis." *Arg* 5 (May 1991): 221–231.

Analyzes the use of declamation and the timeless city of "Sophistopolis" in fifth-century writings such as Antiphon's *Tetralogies* and Gorgias's *Helen* and *Palamedes*.

305. Isenberg, Nancy Gale. " 'Coequality of the Sexes': The Feminist Discourse of the Antebellum Women's Rights Movement in America." *DAI* 51 (March 1991): 3001A.

Examines political, legal, and religious discourses of the antebellum women's rights movement. Bases her investigation on proceedings of conventions, reform periodicals, religious tracts, church records, and manuscripts.

306. Jacob, Bernard E. "Finding a Place for Rhetoric: Aristotle's Rhetorical Art in Its Philosophical Context." *DAI* 52 (December 1991): 2165A.

Places Aristotle's rhetorical art in its proper context; finds that his rhetoric is dynamic, emphasizing both the plausible and the ethical.

307. Jarratt, Susan C. *Rereading the Sophists: Classical Rhetoric Reconfigured*. Carbondale, IL: Southern Illinois University Press, 1991. 181 pages

Argues that the first sophists—not Aristotle and Plato—are the most significant classical voices on rhetoric.

308. Johnson, Nan. *Nineteenth-Century Rhetoric in North America*. Carbondale, IL: Southern Illinois University Press, 1991. 320 pages

Argues that nineteenth-century rhetoric was primarily synthetic, derived from a combination of classical elements and eighteenth-century belletristic and epistemological approaches to theory and practice.

309. Kastely, James L. "In Defense of Plato's *Gorgias*." *PMLA* 106 (January 1991): 96–109.

Argues for a reading of the *Gorgias* that treats rhetoric as a way of opening oneself to critical, dialectical refutation.

310. Lawrence, LeeAnn Michelle. "The Teaching of Rhetoric and Composition in Nineteenth-Century Women's Colleges." *DAI* 51 (February 1991): 2660A.

Explores the ways in which ninteenth-century college women resolved problems of learning to communicate in a traditionally male academic discipline.

311. Levine, Robert. "Prudentius' Romanus: The Rhetorician as Hero, Martyr, Satirist, and Saint." *Rhetorica* 9 (Winter 1991): 5–38.

Argues that *Peristephanon* shows Christian martyrs defeating pagan gods by dying with joy, fortitude, sense of play, and disturbing loquacity.

312. Liu, Yameng. "Aristotle and the Stasis Theory: A Reexamination." *RSQ* 21 (Winter 1991): 53–59.

Argues that despite claims that Aristotle espoused an early theory of stasis, he deliberately marginalized stasis theory.

313. McComiskey, Bruce. *Plato's Critique of Rhetoric in "Gorgias" (447a–466a): Epistemology, Methodology, and the Lyotardian Differend*. Boston, MA: CCCC, March 1991. ERIC ED 333 462. 14 pages

Argues that Plato misrepresents Gorgias's epistemology and that Plato's claims against Gorgias and rhetoric are mere fiction created to control the differend between Socrates and Gorgias.

314. Miller, Thomas. "The Formation of College English: A Survey of the Archives of

Eighteenth-Century Rhetorical Theory and Practice." *RSQ* 20 (Summer 1990): 261–286.

Research on institutionalized discourse in England, Ireland, Scotland, and America reveals that College English began in the eighteenth century; suggests resources for more archival research.

315. Miller, Thomas P. "Treating Professional Writing as Social Praxis." *JAC* 11 (Winter 1991): 57–72.

Stresses that classical rhetoric did not use theory and practice as binary opposites but *theoria*, *praxis*, and *techne*. Argues that professional writing should be taught as social praxis.

316. Moore, Dennis Duane. "More Letters from the American Farmer: An Edition of Unpublished and Uncollected Essays in English by J. Hector St. John de Crevecoeur." *DAI* 51 (January 1991): 2381A.

Brings together published and previously unpublished essays; standardizes spelling. Includes omitted passages to show Crevecoeur's revising strategies.

317. Moye, Richard Hamilton. " 'Clio's Fictions' and the Case of Walter Pater: Narrative Form and Historical Understanding, Ancient Models and Modern Constructions." *DAI* 52 (August 1991): 550A.

Examines the relation between the construction of history and the function of narrative in ordering and giving meaning to experience; focuses on Walter Pater.

318. Nelms, Ralph Gerald. "A Case History Approach to Composition Studies: Edward P. J. Corbett and Janet Emig." *DAI* 51 (April 1991): 3350A.

Illuminates aspects of composition studies during the post-WWII period through case studies of Corbett and Emig.

319. Norton, Mary Fenton. "The Rhetoric of Qualifications: John Milton's Prose Tracts." *DAI* 51 (January 1991): 2387A.

Notes that the rhetorical strategies Milton used to communicate qualifications position him in the Aristotelian and Augustinian rhetorical traditions.

320. Osborne, Kelly Thomas. "The 'Peri Demosthenous' of Didymos Grammatikos." *DAI* 52 (August 1991): 529A.

Presents an historical, rhetorical, and etymological commentary of Didymos' writings.

321. Persak, Christine. "Rhetoric in Praise of Silence: The Ideology of Carlyle's Paradox." *RSQ* 21 (Winter 1991): 38–52.

Points out that Carlyle's voluminous publication belies his advocacy of silence, grounded in Platonic logocentrism, but is consistent with the prophets' role to reveal the truth they intuit.

322. Porter, Frank Lee. "Sophistic Rhetoric: The Language of Power and Play in a Democratic Setting." *DAI* 51 (May 1991): 3727A.

Reassesses the writings of the elder Sophists regarding the humanistic belief that discourse is essential to a democratic society.

323. Potkay, Adam Stanley. "The Ideal of Eloquence in the Age of Hume." *DAI* 51 (January 1991): 2387A.

Argues that despite the scientific outlook of Enlightenment, eloquence still aided perception and language was not de-mythologized.

324. Poulakos, John. "New Idioms for Sophistical Rhetoric." *Arg* 5 (May 1991): 109–115.

Reviews the history of approaches to Sophistical rhetoric.

325. Purcell, William M. "*Identitas*, *Similitudo*, and *Contrarietas* in Gervasius of Melkley's *Ars Poetica*: A *Stasis* of Style." *Rhetorica* 9 (Winter 1991): 67–91.

Argues that the work restructures stylistic devices into a compositional stasis system that fuses invention and style.

326. Ragland, Cynthia Lee. "The Rhetoric of Anticipation: The Development of the Unwritten Constitution of American Literature in the 1790s." *DAI* 52 (November 1991): 1749A.

Concludes that the Constitution's rhetoric of anticipation, which employs the metaphors of yellow fever, Indians, and Algerian pirates, allowed the country to justify aggression and expansion.

327. Rajan, Gita. "*Ecriture Feminine* as Autobiography in Walter Pater." *DAI* 51 (January 1991): 2387A.

Analyzes the semiotics of Pater's writing to suggest that his intertextuality illustrates marginalization and voices a radical response to Victorian ideology.

328. Round, Phillip H. "Scientific Americans: Natural History and the Rhetoric of National Identity, 1630–1862." *DAI* 51 (May 1991): 3747A.

Argues that the rhetoric of scientific inquiry as adapted by Thoreau became a political tool and shaper of national identity.

329. Russell, David R. *Writing in the Academic Disciplines, 1870–1990: A Curricular History*. Carbondale, IL: Southern Illinois University Press, 1991. 400 pages

Presents a history of cross-curricular writing instruction outside the scope of general composition courses.

330. Schiappa, Edward. *Protagoras and Logos: A Study in Greek Philosophy and Rhetoric*. Studies in Rhetoric/Communication. Columbia, SC: University of South Carolina Press, 1991. 256 pages

Synthesizes the contributions and rhetoric of one of the earliest and most prominent Sophists. Focuses on Protagoras's surviving words to argue that he influenced Plato and Aristotle and that he was the first rhetorical theorist.

331. Schiappa, Edward. "Sophistic Rhetoric: Oasis or Mirage?" *RR* 10 (Fall 1991): 5–18.

Discusses the difficulties of defining "sophistic rhetoric"; suggests that the traditional grouping of "Sophists" is too problematic. Claims that it is a "construct we can do without."

332. Scott, Izadora. *Controversies over the Imitation of Cicero in the Renaissance*. 2d ed. Davis, CA: Hermagoras Press, 1991. 271 pages

Originally published in 1910, this is a classic survey of humanists' debates over the role of Cicero's prose style in education and in literature. It includes translations of letters between Pietro Bembo and Gianfrancesco Pico (*On Imitation*) and a translation of Desiderius Erasmus's *The Ciceronian* (Ciceronianus).

333. Seltzer, Amy. "Erasmus, for the Sake of Argument." *DAI* 51 (March 1991): 3053A.

Presents a rhetorical analysis of three works that addresses concerns about audience in biography, formalist theory, and theology.

334. Shaw, Clara Seiler. "Aspects of the Narrating Voice in Herodotus." *DAI* 51 (February 1991): 2733A.

Identifies the elements of Herodotus's narrative technique that give rise to divergent assessments of his abilities.

335. Simmons, Lovie Sue. "A Critique of the Stereotype of Current-Traditional Rhetoric: Invention in Writing Instruction at Harvard, 1875–1900." *DAI* 52 (October 1991): 1241A.

Analyzes the forces shaping the institutional attitudes toward invention as an element of writing.

336. Sloane, Thomas O. "Schoolbooks and Rhetoric: Erasmus' *Copia*." *Rhetorica* 9 (Spring 1991): 113–129.

Argues that Erasmian copiousness centers in a rhetorical *inventio* that is more complex and functional than its stylistic lessons.

337. Spence, Sarah. *Rhetorics of Reason and Desire: Virgil, Augustine, and the Troubadours*. Ithaca, NY: Cornell University Press, 1988. 192 pages

Examines the transformation of Ciceronian rhetoric in Virgil's *Aeneid*, St. Augustine's *Confessions* and *On Christian Doctrine*, and works by medieval troubadours.

338. Sutherland, Christine Mason. "Reforms of Style: St. Augustine and the Seventeenth Century." *RSQ* 21 (Winter 1991): 26–37.

Argues that in their disdain for "the grand style" of *copia* and ornament, Bacon, Glanvill and Spat echo Augustine, the similarities arising from common rhetorical situations.

339. Sutton, Jane. "Rereading Sophistical Arguments: A Political Intervention." *Arg* 5 (May 1991): 141–157.

Argues that Aristotle's categories of oratory are not useful in judging the methods of Sophistical rhetoric; reevaluates the Sophistical argumentative method as a political practice.

340. Tebeaux, Elizabeth. "Ramus, Visual Rhetoric, and the Emergence of Page Design in Medical Writing of the English Renaissance: Tracking the Evolution of Readable Documents." *WC* 8 (October 1991): 411–445.

Argues that Ramus's "visual dialectic" influenced the page layout of Renaissance texts in medicine and other fields, beginning a practice that continues today.

341. Tulin, Alexander. "Plato's 'Euthyphro.'" *DAI* 52 (October 1991): 1317A. Analyzes the use of indirect argument in the dialogue of "Euthyphro."

342. Vitanza, Victor J. "'Some More' Notes, toward a 'Third' Sophistic." *Arg* 5 (May 1991): 117–139.

Argues that there is a third sophistic represented by Gorgias, Friedrich Nietzsche, Jean-Francois Lyotard, Michel Foucault, Jacques Lacan, and Paul de Man.

343. Welch, Kathleen E. *The Contemporary Reception of Classical Rhetoric: Appropriations of Ancient Discourse*. Hillsdale, NJ: Lawrence Erlbaum Associates, 1990. 186 pages

Discusses the adaptability of classical rhetoric to new language situations affected by political, cultural, and linguistic changes.

344. Whitson, Steve Earl. "Nineteenth-Century Interpretations of the Greek Sophists." *DAI* 52 (August 1991): 566A.

Uses works by Hegel, Grote, Zeller, and Nietzsche to examine four major nineteenth-century receptions of the Greek Sophists.

345. Winner, Emmanuel John. "The Language of Despair: Hegelian Rhetoric in an Early Text by Paul de Man." *DAI* 51 (May 1991): 3740A.

Reveals a totalitarian view of history in the dialogic of de Man's "The Temptation of Permanence."

346. Woods, Marjorie Curry. "A Medieval Rhetoric Goes to School—and to the University: The Commentaries on the *Poetria nova*." *Rhetorica* 9 (Winter 1991): 55–65.

Explains three types of commentary on *Poetria nova*: textual, considering it exemplary and identifying rhetoric and poetic; theoretical, criticizing it and noting differences between rhetoric and poetic; and finally, a combination of the two types.

347. Young, Richard. "Working on the Margin: Rhetorical Studies and the New Self-Consciousness." *RSQ* 20 (Fall 1990): 325–332.

Presents a perspective on the development of the new rhetoric in the 1960s; calls it an enterprise more "ecumenical" than the present state of rhetoric and composition.

See also 723, 1550

2.3 POLITICAL, RELIGIOUS, AND JUDICIAL RHETORIC

348. Agar, Michael. "Writing Left in America." *DPr* 14 (April–June 1991): 261–276.

Argues that an essay on poverty in America fails in its purpose because it does not correctly assess the role of gender and ethnicity in political discourse.

349. Al-Osaimi, Mohammed 'Abd Al-Moshen. "The Persuasion of King Faisal Ibn 'Abd Al-'Aziz: A Case Study in Contemporary Islamic Oratory." *DAI* 52 (August 1991): 342A.

Finds Faisal's strategies different from Aristotle's due to an equal use of all modes of proof, reliance on the Qur'anic authority, and use of silence.

350. Aune, James Arnt. "Burke's Palimpset: Rereading *Permanence and Change*." *ComS* 42 (Fall 1991): 234–237.

Argues that the two different versions of *Permanence and Change* reveal three different Burkes—pragmatic Marxist, neoconservative critic of Marxism, and unrepentent left liberal.

351. Ayers, Cathy Fallon. "The Rhetorical Expression of Authority through Religious, Civil Rights, and Political Terministic Screens: Strategic Choices of Jesse Jackson's 1984 and 1988 Presidential Campaigns." *DAI* 52 (September 1991): 737A.

Concludes that Jackson's influence in the political arena is based partially on his attempt to reintroduce morality and ethics into politics.

352. Bart, John A. "The Rhetorical Constraints of American Anarchism: 1880–1920." *DAI* 51 (May 1991): 3557A.

Examines the rhetoric of Emma Goldman and Voltairine de Cleyre; argues that it is based on the value of the free individual.

353. Bartlet, Andrew Hugh. "Style and Structure in Prophetic Rhetoric: Isaiah 2–12." *DAI* 52 (September 1991): 935A.

Develops a method of poetic analysis of Isaiah as an example of prophetic rhetoric.

354. Benoit, William L. "Argumentation in *Miranda v. Arizona*." *ComS* 42 (Summer 1991): 129–140.

Describes and evaluates discourse advanced in briefs and oral arguments by attorneys and the role of the Supreme Court in decision making.

355. Benoit, William L., Paul Gullifor, and Daniel A. Panici. "President Reagan's Defensive Discourse on the Iran-Contra Affair." *ComS* 42 (Fall 1991): 272–294.

Analyzes Reagan's rhetorical efforts to maintain his positive image during crises.

356. Bernabo, Lawrance Mark. "The Scopes Myth: The Scopes Trial in Rhetorical Perspective." *DAI* 52 (September 1991): 737A.

Argues that the alterations and omissions in the Scopes trial lead to the myth we associate with it.

357. Bosmajian, Haig. "Celebrating the Bicentennial of the Bill of Rights." *WJSC* 55 (Fall 1991): 305–318.

Discusses recent erosion in the freedom of speech under the First Amendment.

358. Bostdorff, Denise M. "Vice-Presidential Comedy and the Traditional Female Role: An Examination of the Rhetorical Characteristics of the Vice Presidency." *WJSC* 55 (Winter 1991): 1–27.

Analyzes public talk by and about those who run for vice-presidential office.

359. Buchanan, Ronald Thomas. "Broadcast Evangelism: The Rhetorical Nature of the Televised Sermon Text in the Mid–1980s." *DAI* 51 (January 1991): 2188A.

Using Edward P. J. Corbett's methodology, Buchanan examines the rhetorical features of seven television preachers.

360. Burkholder, Thomas R. "Symbolic Martyrdom: The Ultimate Apology." *SCJ* 56 (Summer 1991): 289–297.

Suggests that early characterizations of "scaffold confessions" and "martyrdom speeches" as a discrete genre of discourse should be recast as a distinctive subgenre of *apologia*.

361. Burks, Don M. "Kenneth Burke: The Agro-Bohemian 'Marxoid.' " *ComS* 42 (Fall 1991): 219–233.

Focuses on Burke's views of communism, capitalism, and consumerism.

362. Bury, Mary J. "A Rhetorical Analysis of Selected Speeches of the Reverend Jerry Falwell." *DAI* 51 (January 1991): 2197A.

Uses Burke's dramatistic pentad to examine 14 sermons and finds an emphasis on the elements of act, agency, and agent.

363. Campbell, Lauren D. "A Burkean Conceptual Analysis of the American Presidential, Selected Reagan Administration, and Selected Print Media Response to Muammar El-Qaddafi: 1981–1986." *DAI* 52 (August 1991): 343A.

Examines the effects of language usage and dramatistic themes of hierarchy, guilt, victimization, and redemption in Qaddafi's public presentations.

364. Carroll, Rebecca. "A Rhetorical Biography of Harry J. Anslinger, Commissioner of the Federal Bureau of Narcotics, 1930–1962." *DAI* 52 (November 1991): 1569A.

Explores Anslinger's use of authority to shape a national attitude against drug trafficking and to emphasize punishment over production.

365. Carter, Hodding III. "A Confederacy of Liars, Guarded by a Yawning Watchdog." *QRD* 18 (October 1991): 5–6.

Cites numerous examples of lies by government officials to demonstrate media's lack of interest in sustained coverage and erosion of public confidence.

366. Christiansen, Adrienne Elizabeth. "Persuasion and Technology: A Rhetorical Criticism of New Direct Mail Appeals." *DAI* 51 (March 1991): 2922A.

Discusses the rhetorical functions of direct mail in the New Right social movement; concludes that direct mail helps find supporters and funds.

367. Classen, C. Joachim. "The Speeches in the Courts of Law: A Three-Cornered Dialogue." *Rhetorica* 9 (Summer 1991): 195–207.

Analyzes a pair of speeches by Demosthenus and Aeschines to illustrate a form of dialogue between two parties in a court of law.

368. Condit, Celeste Michelle, and John Louis Lucaites. "The Rhetoric of Equality and the Expatriation of African-Americans, 1776–1826." *ComS* 42 (Spring 1991): 1–21.

Argues that the discursive structure of the commitment to equality did not guarantee emancipation but partially led to the colonization of free blacks.

369. Conroy, Sarah Booth. "How to Avoid Those Fighting Words." *QRD* 18 (October 1991): 9–10.

Cites multiple contemporary and historical U. S. and foreign euphemisms associated with war.

370. Daniel, Brian Lewis. "A Quantitative Assessment of Elements of a Leadership Construct Based on a Burkean Analysis of 11 Presidential Inaugural Addresses." *DAI* 51 (March 1991): 2923A.

Studies the "worldviews" of presidential addresses and concludes that the views of Presidents Truman through Bush have been comprehensive and consistent.

371. Darsey, James. "From 'Gay Is Good' to the Scourge of AIDS: The Evolution of Gay Liberation Rhetoric, 1977–1990." *ComS* 42 (Spring 1991): 43–66.

Examines the conceptual framework, the relationship between catalytic events and rhetorical movements, and the efficacy of the catalytic model.

372. Davis, Woody Lynn. "Beyond the Personal Pronoun: Gender Schemas and Perceptions of Christians and Their Messages." *DAI* 52 (November 1991): 1570A.

Studies the relationship between gender, men's participation in church activities, and messages containing "feminine" Christian themes.

373. Depoe, Stephen P. "Space and the 1960 Presidential Campaign: Kennedy, Nixon, and 'Public Time.'" *WJSC* 55 (Spring 1991): 215–233.

Analyzes temporal visions to enhance understanding of how time functions in political campaign discourse.

374. Dey, Jim. "'Chain' Letter 'Very Effective' for RNC." *QRD* 18 (October 1991): 11–12.

Reports that mailing from Republican National Committee included a sample letter to the editor supporting the Gulf War that people sent in as their own.

375. Dobkin, Bethami A. "Tales of Terror: News Coverage of Terrorism and the Construction of Public Crises." *DAI* 51 (May 1991): 3557A.

Analyzes relationships between media portrayals and official United States policy statements; concludes that the media escalates the significance of discrete terrorist acts.

376. Dombrowski, Paul M. "Existential Psychology in the Rhetoric of Martin Luther King, Jr." *DAI* 51 (May 1991): 3557A.

Finds that Irvin Yalom's psychology yields new insights into King's psychology.

377. Donnelly, Nadine M. "Discord and Harmony: Rhetorical Images of Women Religious." *DAI* 51 (June 1991): 4160A.

Analyzes various discourses, including Mother Theresa's and the Dominican Adrian Sisters', to see if women's position in the Roman Catholic Church is moving away from patriarchal control.

378. Dorsey, Francis E. "A Rhetoric of Values: An Afrocentric Analysis of Marcus Garvey's Convention Speeches, 1921–1924." *DAI* 51 (March 1991): 2923A.

Claims that "Afrocentricity" must be employed by white and black scholars when analyzing African rhetors in order to eliminate the use of racist language.

379. Dow, Bonnie J. "The 'Womanhood' Rationale in the Woman Suffrage Rhetoric of Frances E. Willard." *SCJ* 56 (Summer 1991): 298–307.

Examines Willard's success through strategic use of euphemism and metaphor and the implications for later feminist action.

380. Farrell, James M. "*Pro Militibus Oratio*: John Adams's Imitation of Cicero in the Boston Massacre Trial." *Rhetorica* 9 (Summer 1991): 233–249.

Analyzes John Adams's possible use of Cicero's rhetorical strategies in *De Inventione*, *Pro Roscio*, and *Pro Milone*.

381. Fineman, Martha Albertson. *The Illusion of Equality: The Rhetoric and Reality of Divorce Reform*. Chicago, IL: University of Chicago Press, 1991. 240 pages

Argues that divorce reforms are only successful on a symbolic level and do not aid women and children. Focuses on the symbols of the reform and the language used by reformers.

382. Frank, Robert L. "Reason and Religion in *Rerum Novarum*." *SCJ* 56 (Summer 1991): 257–267.

Examines the 1891 encyclical that forged an "antecedent genre" setting the terms for a century of Catholic rhetoric on social justice.

383. Goldfarb, Jeffrey C. *The Cynical Society: The Culture of Politics and the Politics of Culture in American Life*. Chicago, IL: University of Chicago Press, 1991. 216 pages

Explores how cynicism manifests itself and how it undermines our capacity to think critically about society's strengths and weaknesses. Demonstrates how cynical explanation and manipulation are substituted for reasoning and debate.

384. Goode, Gloria D. "Preachers of the Word and Singers of the Gospel: The Ministry and

Women among Nineteenth-Century African-Americans." *DAI* 51 (June 1991): 4165A.

Examines the religious traditions of African-American women in the North who as preachers told their stories in spiritiual autobiographies during the nineteenth century.

385. Gordon, Jon Clair. "International Political Cartoons as Rhetoric: A Content Analysis." *DAI* 51 (January 1991): 2184A.

Attempts to formulate a theory of the rhetoric of political caricature.

386. Gray, Chris Hables. "Computers as Weapons and Metaphors: The U. S. Military, 1940–1990 and Postmodern War." *DAI* 52 (December 1991): 2255A.

Points out how the discourse of war reflects the military's commitment to computing, especially to artificial intelligence.

387. Griffin, Robert J., Dayle H. Molen, Clay Schoenfeld, James F. Scotton, David Cassady, Bruce Garrison, Thomas Heuterman, Freda McVay, Robert Meier, and Kenneth Rystrom. *Interpreting Public Issues*. Ames, IA: Iowa State University Press, 1991. 458 pages

Identifies public issues, the collection and collation of information, the selection of story material, and the clear and balanced presentation of all sides of an issue.

388. Grindstaff, Roy A. "The Institutionalization of Aimee Semple McPherson: A Study in the Rhetoric of Social Intervention." *DAI* 51 (January 1991): 2198A.

Uses social intervention model of rhetorical invention to examine symbol usage in ideology, interpersonal relationships, and intrapersonal needs.

389. Halford, Sarah A. "A Change of Style: The Question of 'Feminist Discourse' in the Writing of Naomi Goldenberg, Demaris Wehr, and Julia Kristena." *DAI* 51 (June 1991): 4302A.

Focuses on the problematic interpretation of irony in feminist theological and psychological discourse.

390. Halkowski, Timothy Robert. "Hearing Talk: The Social Organization of a Congressional Hearing." *DAI* 51 (March 1991): 3225A.

Studies the rules of vocal and nonvocal interaction that regulate the Congressional hearing as a speech exchange system.

391. Hambrick, Mary M. "The Language of Peace: A Burkean Analysis of the Peace Rhetoric of William Sloane Coffin, Jr." *DAI* 52 (October 1991): 1130A.

Uses the dramatistic pentad to examine linguistic motives and finds the dominant relationship to be between agent and scene.

392. Harvey, David R. "A Rhetorical Analysis of the Nuclear Debate 1945–1988." *DAI* 51 (April 1991): 3403A.

Representative speeches from American politicians and anti-nuclear activists reveal the rhetorical strategies that competing discourse communities use to advance leadership positions.

393. Haynes, Douglas. *Rhetoric and Ritual in Colonial India: The Shaping of a Public Culture in Surat City, 1852–1928*. Berkeley, CA: University of California Press, 1991. 374 pages

Describes how Surat's Indian elite appropriated the political rhetoric of their British rulers, a linguistic borrowing that shaped ideas of justice and authority.

394. Heilke, Thomas Wolfgang. "Friedrich Nietzsche's Political Education: The Foundation for an Aesthetic State." *DAI* 52 (August 1991): 665A.

Argues that Nietzsche had a vision of an aesthetic state as the best political regime, developing a new kind of political education to serve the regime.

395. Hinds, Lynn Boyd, and Theodore Otto Windt, Jr. *The Cold War as Rhetoric: The*

Beginnings, 1945–1950. New York: Praeger Publishers, 1991. 304 pages

Discusses the role of American political rhetoric in creating the domestic and international reality of the cold war.

396. Hirschman, Albert O. *The Rhetoric of Reaction: Perversity, Futility, Jeopardy*. Cambridge, MA: Harvard University Press, 1991. 197 pages

Explores the world of reactionary rhetoric in which conservative public figures, thinkers, and polemicists have been arguing against progressive agendas and reforms for the past 200 years.

397. Hirst, Russel K. "Rhetorical Invention in the Conservative Tradition in American Protestant Homiletic Theory, 1850–1900." *DAI* 52 (August 1991): 344A.

Examines the use of classical techniques and finds invention focused on synthesis of classical rhetoric, Christian ideologies, and views of the nature and function of language.

398. Hogan, J. Michael, and Leroy Dorsey. "Public Opinion and the Nuclear Freeze: The Rhetoric of Popular Sovereignty in Foreign Policy Debate." *WJSC* 55 (Fall 1991): 319–338.

Examines the role of rhetorically mediated public opinion in the congressional debate of 1982 to 1983.

399. Hupka, John Paul. "The Effects of Psycholinguistic Factors on Attitudes toward Nuclear Weapons." *DAI* 52 (August 1991): 1063B.

Argues that semantic meanings associated with the names of nuclear weapons significantly influence attitudes toward those weapons; points out that findings are important for propaganda studies.

400. Ishak, Zuraidi B. "The Rhetoric of Racial Harmony: An Analysis of Presidential Addresses of Three Multiracial Leaders of the Alliance Party on the Issues of Racial Harmony and Independence of Malaya, 1955–1957." *DAI* 52 (November 1991): 1571A.

Examines the fantasy themes of Tengku Abdul Rahman, Tan Cheng Lock, and V. T. Sambanthan and finds that they advance a conservative vision of unity in diversity.

401. Jenefsky, Cindy. "Confronting Male Power with Integrity: Andrea Dworkin's Rhetoric, Art and Politics." *DAI* 51 (March 1991): 2925A.

Demonstrates that Dworkin's "artistry is fundamental to her feminist politics."

402. Jenkins, Keith B. "The Rhetoric of Gospel Song: A Content Analysis of the Lyrics of Andre Crouch." *DAI* 51 (June 1991): 3955A.

Uses Knupp's analysis of protest and labor movement songs to examine Crouch's music; finds that the lyrics focus on individual spiritual growth.

403. Johnston, Theodore E. "A Persuasive Plenty: 'Copia' in the English Renaissance Parliament." *DAI* 52 (July 1991): 21A.

Analyzes the theory and practice of amplification and stylistic fullness by examining speeches concerning the fate of Mary Queen of Scots.

404. Juster, Susan Mary. "Sinners and Saints: The Evangelical Construction of Gender and Authority in New England, 1740–1830." *DAI* 51 (January 1991): 2498A.

Studies the relationship between language and power in a variety of texts; notes that the evangelical community was committed to sexual equality in language.

405. Kalb, Milton Larry. "A Study of Ong's Psychodynamics in Ephesians." *DAI* 52 (November 1991): 1572A.

Studies Paul's letter by using grammatical analysis and concludes that four of Ong's nine psychodynamic characteristics can be found in the letter.

406. Kelman, Mark. "Reasonable Evidence of Reasonableness." *CritI* 17 (Summer 1991): 798–817.

Argues that preparation of the legal defense of a murderer can be influenced by either conservative or liberal sympathies.

407. Kennedy, Rodney. "The Epistemic Power of Metaphor: A Rhetorical Model for Homiletics." *DAI* 52 (September 1991): 738A.

Offers a deconstruction of classical homiletics via Foucault's theories and concludes by detailing a "rhetoric of folly."

408. Kern, Kathi L. "Rereading Eve: Elizabeth Cady Stanton and *The Women's Bible*, 1885–1896." *WS* 19 (1991): 371–383.

Discusses the controversy, within the women's suffrage movement, surrounding Stanton's "collection of feminist commentaries" on biblical passages published in two volumes in 1895 and 1898.

409. Kiewe, Amos, and Davis W. Houck. *A Shining City on a Hill: Ronald Reagan's Economic Rhetoric, 1951–1989*. New York: Praeger Publishers, 1991. 264 pages

Analyzes Reagan's speeches on economic issues since his years as president of the Screen Actors Guild.

410. Kinsley, Michael. "A Citizen's Guide to Judicial Buzzwords." *QRD* 17 (July 1991): 10–11.

Lists and defines 13 buzzwords associated with Supreme Court nominations.

411. Klope, David C. "The Rhetorical Constitution of the Creationist Movement." *DAI* 52 (December 1991): 1942A.

Identifies the creationist movement as a world movement of conservative Protestants articulating a worldview with transcendent and material dimensions that is not an immediate threat to secular science and education.

412. Krug, Linda T. *Presidential Perspectives on Space Exploration: Guiding Metaphors from Eisenhower to Bush*. New York: Praeger Publishers, 1991. 160 pages

Links shifts in public support for the space program to the metaphors presidents have used to describe space efforts.

413. Lanoue, David J., and Peter R. Schrott. *The Joint Press Conference: The History, Impact, and Prospects of American Presidential Debates*. New York: Greenwood Press, 1991. 192 pages

Argues that previous scholars have understated the effects of presidential-campaign debates on American voting behavior.

414. Lee, Ronald E. "The Rhetorical Construction of Time in Martin Luther King Jr.'s 'Letter from Birmingham Jail.' " *SCJ* 56 (Summer 1991): 279–288.

Offers an explanation of the ideological heritage that temporally unifies the discourse.

415. Leeman, Richard W. *The Rhetoric of Terrorism and Counterterrorism*. Contributions to the Study of Mass Media and Communication, vol. 29. New York: Greenwood Press, 1991. 217 pages

Analyzes possible discursive responses to terrorism, prescribing "democratic rhetoric" as the most strategic counterterrorist response available.

416. Leland, Christopher M. "Narrative Functionality: A Description, Analysis, and Comparison of Political Campaign Narrative Elements." *DAI* 52 (December 1991): 1942A.

Examines political media coverage and political advertising in the 1990 gubernatorial campaigns in Arkansas, Oklahoma, and Texas.

417. Lempereur, Alain. "Logic of Rhetoric in Law?" *Arg* 5 (August 1991): 283–297.

Examines the nature of legal reasoning; questions whether this reasoning belongs to logic or to rhetoric. Proposes an interrogative rhetoric as an alternative to argumentation.

418. Leroux, Neil R. "Style in Rhetorical Criticism." *DAI* 51 (June 1991): 3956A.

Uses a three-fold conceptual scheme of focus, presence and communion, based on the notions of Burke and Perelman, to analyze the eight Wittenberg sermons.

419. Lester, Charles Emory. "A Rhetorical Analysis of the Unification Church in America between 1970 and 1980." *DAI* 51 (February 1991): 2564A.

Analyzes several speeches made by Sun Myung Moon in the early seventies and offers some explanations for why the church continues to flourish.

420. Lewis, Bernard. *The Political Religion of Islam*. Chicago, IL.: University of Chicago Press, 1991. 168 pages

Describes the development from the time of the Prophet to the present. Analyzes documents that clarify perception, discussion, and practice of the politics in the Islamic world.

421. Liljestrand, Petra. "Rhetoric and Reason: Donor Insemination Politics in Sweden." *DAI* 51 (February 1991): 2879A.

Analyzes policy documents, newspaper articles, and interviews; explains the passage of the 1984 legislation regulating donor insemination.

422. Lillie, Richard George. "Obscenity Law: Politics, Morality, Free Speech, and the Struggle to Define Obscenity." *DAI* 51 (January 1991): 2501A.

Presents a history of the changing legal definition of obscenity and examines reasons for the changes.

423. Mack, Phyllis. "Teaching about Gender and Spirituality in Early English Quakerism." *WS* 19 (1991): 223–237.

Discusses the ways in which the spiritual rhetoric of Quakerism transcends gender roles as illustrated by the life and work of Elizabeth Hoofton.

424. Mackey-Kallis, Susan. "Spectator Desire and Narrative Closure: The Reagan 18-Minute Political Film." *SCJ* 56 (Summer 1991): 308–314.

Investigates the narrative logics that preceded Reagan's acceptance speech at the 1984 Republican National Convention.

425. Mackey-Kallis, Susan, and Dan F. Hahn. "Questions of Public Will and Private Action: The Power of the Negative in the Reagan's 'Just Say No' Morality Campaign." *ComQ* 39 (Winter 1991): 1–17.

Uses Kenneth Burke to describe how rhetorically the Reagan administration advocated private solutions to public problems and reasserted authority in problem definition.

426. Marchio, James David. "Rhetoric and Reality: The Eisenhower Administration and Unrest in Eastern Europe, 1953–1959." *DAI* 51 (January 1991): 2499A.

Uses recently declassified materials to analyze U.S. policy. Finds Eisenhower's policies more coherent than previously thought but flawed in conception and implementation.

427. Martycz, Virginia K. "Identification as Process: A Rhetorical Study of Three Televangelists as Social Intervenors." *DAI* 52 (November 1991): 1573A.

Uses Brown's model of social intervention to examine differences in the rhetoric of Jim Bakker, Jimmy Swaggart, and Pat Robertson.

428. McCabe-Juhnke, John E. "Narrative and Everyday Experience: Performance Process in the Storytelling of the Swiss Volhynina Mennonites." *DAI* 51 (June 1991): 3956A.

Uses interviews and observation to examine how narrative performance is both sustained and shaped by the social and cultural norms of this mutually supportive community.

429. McEvoy, Sebastian T. "Issues in Common Law Pleading and Ancient Rhetoric." *Arg* 5 (August 1991): 245–261.

Analyzes the differences between concepts of "issue" and "status"; contends that the respective functions of pleadings and invention account for most of the differences.

430. McFarland, Michael W. " 'Remembering Zion'—Demythologizing Mythic Appeals in Public Discourse: With a Case Study on the Self-Justificatory Rhetoric of the Sanctuary Movement of the 1980s." *DAI* 52 (August 1991): 345A.

Uses the methodology of Rudof Bultmann and finds myths to be transhistorical and process-oriented.

431. McGaw, Dickinson. "Governing Metaphors: The War on Drugs." *The American Journal of Semiotics* 8 (1991): 53–74.

Analyzes the war metaphor in Bush's war-on-drugs speech and its power to shape and guide policy.

432. Mechling, Elizabeth Walker, and Jay Mechling. "The Campaign for Civil Defense and the Struggle to Naturalize the Bomb." *WJSC* 55 (Spring 1991): 105–133.

Presents a socio-rhetorical analysis of the American public debate over civil defense from the late 1940s through the early 1960s.

433. Medhurst, Martin J., Robert L. Ivie, Philip Wander, and Robert L. Scott. *Cold War Rhetoric: Strategy, Metaphor, and Ideology*. Westport, CT: Greenwood, 1991. 240 pages

Includes rhetorical critique on speeches by Presidents Eisenhower and Kennedy, the Murrow-McCarthy confrontation on CBS, the speeches and writings of peace advocates, and recurring themes of unAmericanism as expressed in various media throughout the Cold War years. The authors use a strategic, metaphorical, and ideological approach to rhetorical criticism.

434. Mesfer, Al Beshr. "An Analytical and Descriptive Study of a Communication Campaign against Drugs in Saudi Arabia." *DAI* 51 (February 1991): 2556A.

Identifies strategies and weaknesses of the campaign; proposes a model for a more effective campaign.

435. Mesner, David Earl. "The Rhetoric of Citations: Paul's Use of Scripture in Romans 9 (Volumes I and II)." *DAI* 52 (November 1991): 1775A.

Analyzes scripture citations in Romans 9 to determine their rhetorical function within the text of Paul's argument.

436. Metcalf, Eric Nelson. "In the Snows of New Hampshire: Rhetorical Constructions of the Political Arena in the 1988 Primary." *DAI* 52 (August 1991): 345A.

Explores how candidates interact with the citizenry through mass media.

437. Meyers, Joyce S. "Communications Law Developments." *PC* 11 (February/March 1991): 20–22.

Reviews recent court decisions concerning confidentiality of sources and First Amendment rights.

438. Meyers, Joyce S. "Supreme Court Defines Limits." *PC* 11 (Winter 1991): 24–26.

Reviews two recent Supreme Court decisions on First Amendment issues: confidentiality of sources and the use of altered or fabricated quotations.

439. Meyers, Robin R. "Preaching as Self-Persuasion: A New Metaphor for the Rhetoric of Faith." *DAI* 52 (December 1991): 1943A.

Explores the role of listeners in preaching and advocating; emphasizes what they do with the sermonized message.

440. Miller, Rita Maria. "Media Constructions of Gender in the 1984 Presidential Campaign: A Rhetorical Perspective." *DAI* 52 (August 1991): 345A.

Uses Burke's cluster criticism to study gender construction; concludes that when women enter presidential politics they must balance feminine and masculine characteristics.

441. Moore, Mark P. "A Rhetorical Criticism of Political Myths: From Goldwater Legend to Reagan Mystique." *ComS* 42 (Fall 1991): 295–308.

Describes a model of political myth based on form and function.

442. Mullen, William L. "The Polemical Sermons of John Chrysostom against the Judaizers: A Dramatistic Analysis." *DAI* 51 (May 1991): 3559A.

Explores the use of the Representative Anecdote to promote the concept of struggle through military, medical, and legal metaphors.

443. Murrain, Ethel P. "The Mississippi Man and His Message: A Rhetorical Analysis of the Cultural Themes in the Oratory of Medgar Wiley Evers, 1957–1963." *DAI* 51 (January 1991): 2199A.

Uses Molefi Aasante's model of black cultural themes to examine 33 speeches for thematic content concerning civil rights and racial conflict.

444. Nelson, Elizabeth Jean. " 'Nothing Ever Goes Well Enough': Mussoloni and the Rhetoric of Perpetual Struggle." *ComS* 42 (Spring 1991): 22–42.

Examines the rhetorical process as it functions in a successful social movement.

445. Ober, Josiah. *Mass and Elite in Democratic Athens: Rhetoric, Ideology, and the Power of the People*. Princeton, NJ: Princeton University Press, 1991. 408 pages

Analyzes the nature of communication between elite and nonelite citizens in Athens with a focus on the role of political and legal rhetoric.

446. Olmsted, Wendy Raudenbush. "The Uses of Rhetoric: Indeterminacy in Legal Reasoning, Practical Thinking, and the Interpretation of Literary Figures." *P&R* 24 (1991): 1–24.

Argues that rhetoric functions between the impossible alternatives of objectivity and indeterminacy by adapting rules to the particularities of situation and action.

447. Orlinsky, Harry M., and Robert G. Bratcher. *A History of Bible Translation and the North American Contribution*. Atlanta, GA: Scholars Press, 1991. 376 pages

Traces the history of biblical translations from 200 B.C. to the present.

448. Owen, Diana. *Media Messages in American Presidential Elections*. Westport, CT: Greenwood, 1991. 198 pages

Investigates the way people process media messages during campaigns. Examines the role of ads, news stories, poll results, and debates and compares four message categories to determine their relative importance to voters. Bases her study on surveys done during the 1984 and 1988 Presidential campaigns.

449. Pauley, Matthew Alfred. "I Do Solemnly Swear: The President's Constitutional Oath—What It Means, Why It Matters." *DAI* 51 (January 1991): 2506A.

Uses Nixon's and Johnson's oaths to analyze the potential of presidential power in worldwide matters; shows how presidents rely on oaths to establish power.

450. Peirce, Roberta. "The Rhetoric of Hymn Texts: A Feminist Perspective." *DAI* 51 (February 1991): 2732A.

Argues that even though many hymn texts have been changed to eliminate male exclusivity, their basic metaphor system still supports patriarchal structures and male dominance.

451. Pfau, Michael, and Jong Geun Kang. "The Impact of Relational Messages on Candidate Influence in Televised Political Debates." *ComS* 42 (Summer 1991): 114–128.

Explores relationships among verbal messages, visual messages, and production techniques.

452. Pimple, Kenneth D. "Speech and Moral Character: A Study of Selected Preachers in Nineteenth-Century American Literature." *DAI* 52 (December 1991): 2240A.

Applies methodologies of folklore and ethnography of speaking to analyze the relationship between moral character and fictive dialogue.

453. Pogoloff, Stephen Mark. "Logos and Sophia: The Rhetorical Situation of I Corinthians 1–4 in the Light of Greco-Roman Rhetoric." *DAI* 52 (August 1991): 576A.

Attempts to determine the rhetorical situation for I Corinthians 1–4 and reconstructs, through an historically informed narrative, Paul's letter-writing situation.

454. Polle, Sig T. "The Nonviolent Rhetoric of Martin Luther King, Jr." *DAI* 51 (May 1991): 3560A.

Uses a historical-critical approach and functionalist movement methodology to examine the dynamics of social change in Martin Luther King's ideology and speech.

455. Popkin, Samuel L. *The Reasoning Voter: Communication and Persuasion in Presidential Campaigns*. Chicago, IL: University of Chicago Press, 1991. 272 pages

Presents a model of the way voters sort through commercials and sound bites to choose a candidate. Argues that campaigns do not matter.

456. Possin, Kevin. "Ethical Argumentation." *JTWC* 21 (1991): 65–72.

Challenges a legalistic model for ethical argumentation and proposes that argument from analogy works better for discovering and presenting well-defended ethical positions.

457. Prott, Lyndel V. "Argumentation in International Law." *Arg* 5 (August 1991): 299–310.

Contends that modern international law depends on persuasive discourse for justifying state actions, negotiating and interpreting treaties, and justifying international judicial decisions.

458. Purvis-Smith, Virginia Louise. "Women and Rhetoric: Composing Text, Self, and Professional Authority." *DAI* 52 (September 1991): 829A.

Studies eight protestant clergywomen to find out if language discourse fashioned by men can be used by women.

459. Raheim, Salome. "Empowerment and the Discourse of Social Movements," *DAI* 51 (June 1991): 3957A.

Examines Jesse Jackson's discourse of rainbow politics; finds that it fosters the empowerment of movement members.

460. Rao, Arati. "The Feminist Concept of Connectedness: The Different Voice and Its Implications for Political Theory." *DAI* 52 (August 1991): 667A.

Examines the implications of the concept of connectedness for political theory; bases study on Carol Gilligan's work on the moral development of women.

461. Rice, Donald Everett. "The Rhetorical Uses of the Authorizing Figure: Fidel Castro and Jose Marti." *DAI* 51 (March 1991): 2926A.

Discusses the ways in which leaders use the past to justify their present actions by looking at Castro's uses of Marti.

462. Rieke, Richard D. "The Judicial Dialogue." *Arg* 5 (February 1991): 39–55.

Argues that judges focus on judicial decisions and their justification to disguise their engagement "in a continuing and evolving dialogue to structure their normative universe."

463. Rigsby, Enrique DuBois. "A Rhetorical Clash with Established Order: An Analysis of Protest Strategies and Perceptions of Media Responses, Birmingham, 1963." *DAI* 51 (May 1991): 3560A.

Explores the rhetorical strategies used by civil rights workers during the Birmingham protests of 1963 based on the principles of Robert Cathcart.

464. Roach, Timothy L. "Rhetoric and Dialectic of Reformation Anglican Homiletics." *DAI* 51 (February 1991): 2732A.

Differentiates between rhetorical and dialectical situations according to Fish and Moffett. Concludes that dialectical situations allow students greater control over texts.

465. Ruberstein, Diane. *What's Left? The Ecole Normale Superieure and the Right.* Madison, WI: University of Wisconsin Press, 1991. 232 pages

Argues against myths about politics and writing and redefines the terms. The book constitutes a work of theory that allows its empirical research to reread its theoretical texts.

466. Schiappa, Edward, and Mary F. Keehner. "The 'Lost' Passages of Kenneth Burke's *Permanence and Change*." *ComS* 42 (Fall 1991): 191–198.

Identifies changes from the original to current editions to transform *Performance and Change* from a timely socialist treatise to a more timeless theoretical text.

467. Schollmeier, Paul. "Practical Intuition and Rhetorical Example." *P&R* 24 (1991): 95–104.

Argues that Aristotle's analysis of example provides a model for the discussion of social and political policies.

468. Schreffler, Peter Hans. "Caught between Two Worlds: The Spiritual Predicament and Rhetorical Ambivalence of Garrison Keillor." *DAI* 52 (September 1991): 921A.

Studies the rhetorical appeal of four Keillor works; concludes that they do not serve as a clear and consistent witness to the Christian faith.

469. Sens, Alexander. "Not I, but the Law: Juridical and Legislative Language in Aristophanes' 'Eccesiazusae' " *DAI* 52 (November 1991): 1738A.

Explores the audience's awareness of the legal terminology and its effects on the humor of the play.

470. Seward, Linda G. "The Equal Rights Amendment Campaign in Indiana: A Study of Ideas and Arguments." *DAI* 52 (December 1991): 1943A.

Examines the structure and substance of arguments supporting and opposing ERA debate; compares ideas about ERA with those about women's suffrage.

471. Shaw, Charles Stewart. "The Speeches of Micah: A Rhetorical-Historical Analysis." *DAI* 51 (April 1991): 3436A.

Investigates six distinct discourses in Micah, analyzing the persuasive goals of the speakers.

472. Short, Brant. "Earth First! and the Rhetoric of Moral Confrontation." *ComS* 42 (Summer 1991): 172–188.

Analyzes the function of agitative rhetoric in the context of the contemporary environmental movement.

473. Slagell, Amy R. "Anatomy of a Masterpiece: A Close Textual Analysis of Abraham Lincoln's Second Inaugural Address." *ComS* 42 (Summer 1991): 155–171.

Examines Lincoln's rhetorical techniques in relation to ideas and their development.

474. Smith, Craig R., and Paul H. Arntson. "Identification in Interpersonal Relationships: One Foundation of Creativity." *SCJ* 57 (Fall 1991): 61–72.

Argues that Burkean theory of indentification de-emphasizes interpersonal and subjective conceptions of communication.

475. Smith, Frances Lee. "Gender and the Framing of Exegetical Authority in Sermon Performances." *DAI* 51 (May 1991): 3728A.

Compares strategies used by men and women for presenting themselves as textual authorities to determine how gender differences are reflected in performance.

476. Snowball, David. *Continuity and Change in the Rhetoric of the Moral Majority*. New York: Praeger, 1991. 181 pages

Examines the life, rhetoric, and demise of the Moral Majority. Bases arguments on research conducted with primary sources and interviews with insiders; concludes that core of agenda did not change over time, although style of argument became more mature. Shows that critics of the Moral Majority respond to their own stereotypes of fundamentalists, not to what the organization actually did.

477. Sobnosky, Matthew J. "A Critical Rhetorical Analysis of Three Responses to White Supremacy." *DAI* 52 (August 1991): 347A.

Examines ideological commitments underlying the discourse of the Anti-Defamation League of B'nai B'rith, the Southern Poverty Law Center, and the Center for Democratic Renewal.

478. Sobota, Katharina. "System and Flexibility in Law." *Arg* 5 (August 1991): 275–282.

Argues that the Mainz school, founded by Theodor Viehweg, sees legal rhetoric as a flexible system rather than "volatile, arbitrary, and void of any system."

479. Solomon, Martha. "Autobiographies as Rhetorical Narratives: Elizabeth Cady Stanton and Anna Howard Shaw as 'New Women.' " *ComS* 42 (Winter 1991): 354–370.

Suggests that autobiographies can complement and supplement formal public arguments for a movement in distinctive ways.

480. Steward, Charles J. "The Ego Function of Protest Songs: An Application of Gregg's Theory of Protest Rhetoric." *ComS* 42 (Fall 1991): 240–253.

Concludes that protestors have difficulty making the transition from a self-image of victim to one of power, worth, and virtue.

481. Sun, Hsiao-yu Janet. "Originary Paradox: Authorial Identity in Contemporary Theoretical, Legal, and Literary Discourses." *DAI* 51 (May 1991): 3735A.

Examines the discrepancy regarding the nature of authorship in the three forms of discourse. Concludes that authorship is a paradoxical concept.

482. Sutherland, Christine Mason. "Outside the Rhetorical Tradition: Mary Astell's Advice to Women in Seventeenth-Century England." *Rhetorica* 9 (Spring 1991): 147–163.

Explains that Astell shows women that their education in Christian morality helps train them in the arts of speaking and writing.

483. Suwarno, Peter. "The Rhetoric of Unity and Freedom: Burkean Analysis of Soekarno's Selected Writings, 1926–1933." *DAI* 52 (November 1991): 1573A.

Identifies association and disassociation among the following terms: *labeling, scapegoating, manipulating myths,* and *puppeteering* as frequently used strategies in Soekarno's writings.

484. Takayama, Machiko. "Poetic Language in Nineteenth-Century Mormonism: A Study of Semiotic Phenomenology in Communication and Culture." *DAI* 52 (November 1991): 1574A.

Uses Derrida's theories to demonstrate that Joseph Smith, the church's founder, should be considered primarily a poet.

485. Taylor, Bryan C. "Remembering Los Alamos: Culture and the Nuclear Weapons Organization." *DAI* 52 (August 1991): 347A.

Uses postmodern and poststructural language theories to examine the representation of wartime atomic bomb construction through autobiography, biography, novels, and films.

486. Taylor, Larissa Juliet. "Preaching in Late Medieval and Early Reformation France." *DAI* 51 (February 1991): 2843A.

Examines techniques that Catholic preachers used to remain faithful to their theology while countering the "Protestant threat."

487. "The Tyndall Report." *QRD* 18 (October 1991): 9.

Describes monthly newsletter that measures exact time networks devoted to news stories and features thereby highlighting the national agenda.

488. Thibeaux, Evelyn Rose. "The Narrative Rhetoric of Luke 7: 36–50: A Study of Context, Text, and Interpretation." *DAI* 51 (January 1991): 2411A.

Studies Luke 7:36–50 and explains the text as an historical and theological document using narrative for rhetorical purposes.

489. Thomas, Brook. "Reflections on the Law and Literature Revival." *CritI* 17 (Spring 1991): 510–539.

Explores relationship between literary theory and legal rhetoric.

490. Todd, Judith A. "Can Their Voices Be Heard? Narratives about Women in Samuel 16 through 1 Kings 2." *DAI* 51 (January 1991): 2452A.

Combines rhetorical, literary, and social-scientific approaches to stories of women's roles in biblical agrarian society.

491. Trebing, James D. "Socially Constructed Realities and the Rhetoric of the Palestine National Movement in the United States: An Interpretive Analysis of an Attempted Transformation of a Universe of Discourse." *DAI* 51 (June 1991): 3958.

Analyzes the historical and rhetorical context of the movement, using Ting-Toomey's intercultural perspective; finds it a reactive response to an external threat.

492. Trooien, Roberta Peirce. "The Rhetoric of Hymn Texts: A Feminist Perspective." *DAI* 51 (February 1991): 2732A.

An examination of hymnals from four denominations reveals that attempts to eliminate sexist language and references are superficial and inconsistent.

"The Tyndall Report," *see* 487

493. Verlinden, Jay G. "Burkean Identification in Conservative Christian and Feminist Antipornography Rhetoric." *DAI* 52 (September 1991): 739.

Studies the language used by these two groups; points out that they cannot be considered a unified rhetorical community.

494. Walsh, Rosemary E. "Resumption and Burden of Proof in Situations of Crisis: The Muscle Shoals Debates, 1897–1933." *DAI* 51 (May 1991): 3561A.

Examines Richard Whately's theory of argumentation, concluding that presumption and proof are determined by the decision-making audience within a particular context.

495. Wander, Philip C. "At the Ideological Front." *ComS* 42 (Fall 1991): 199–218.

Examines the critical culture of the 1930s and Kenneth Burke's place in it.

496. Weber, Janet M. " 'Please Call Me Catherine. Oh Sister I Couldn't': Approaches to the Study of Insider-Outsider Boundary Constitution, Boundary Maintenance." *DAI* 51 (January 1991): 2534A.

Explores how spoken and written discourse make evident the borders of a woman's religious order.

497. Wiesner, Marcus. "Mario M. Cuomo Decides to Run: The Construction of a Political Self." *D&S* 2 (January 1991): 85–104.

Analyzes Cuomo's diary as private narrative and as public discourse, the rhetoric of which was intended to create a political impression.

498. Willhite, R. Keith. "Audience Relevance and Rhetorical Argumentation in Expository Preaching: A Historical-Critical Comparative Analysis of Selected Sermons of John F. MacArthur, Jr. and Charles Swindoll." *DAI* 51 (March 1991): 2928A.

Argues that these two preachers have varying ideas related to expository preaching and the needs of their listeners.

499. Williams, Mary R. "A Reconceptualization of Protest Rhetoric: Characteristics of

Quilts as Protest." *DAI* 51 (May 1991): 3561A.

Examines four quilts to determine the alternative rhetorical strategies used by women to communicate dissatisfaction with the status quo.

500. Willis, Clyde Edward. "The Hermeneutics in Judicial Decision-Making." *DAI* 52 (December 1991): 2261A.

Contrasts three approaches to legal texts: formalism, subjectivism, and Llewellyn's *Common Law Tradition* as refined by Gadamer's philosophical hermeneutics.

501. Wilson, Paula. "Hubert Humphrey's Civil Rights Rhetoric: 1948–1964." *DAI* 52 (July 1991): 23A.

Uses Burke's notion of hierarchy to examine persuasive strategies; finds an emphasis on themes of guilt, purification, and redemption.

502. Wright, Alan. "The Idea of Political Communication." *DAI* 51 (March 1991): 3213A.

Examines the four modes of communicative activity relevant to politics, namely, judging, deliberating, choosing, and arguing.

503. Zorn, Jeff. "Demonizing in the Gulf War: Reading the Archetypes." *EJ* 80 (September 1991): 44–46.

Urges English teachers to recognize the powerful effects of propaganda.

2.4 COMPUTER AND LITERACY STUDIES

504. Andersen, Wallis May. "Computerized Invention for Composition: An Update and Review." *C&C* 9 (November 1991): 25–38.

Surveys existing invention and planning programs. Sees possibilities for teacher-developed hypertext programs.

505. Bacig, Thomas D., Robert A. Evans, and Donald W. Larmouth. "Computer-Assisted Instruction in Critical Thinking and Writing: A Process/Model Approach." *RTE* 25 (October 1991): 365–382.

Study compares pencil-and-paper and computer-assisted versions of a process/model approach to teaching writing.

506. Barker, Thomas T., ed. *Perspectives on Software Design*. Technical Communication Series. Amityville, NY: Baywood Publishing, 1991. 294 pages

Chapters represent various perspectives on writing software documentation: education and research, the influence of cognitive science, design issues, and innovations in management, quality improvement, and online documentation.

Essayists: Henrietta N. Shirk, Cynthia L. Selfe, Jay Lieberman, Paula Bell, Joe Chew, Andrew Oram, Nancy E. Cohen, D. Michael Willoughby, Doann Houghton-Alico, Helen D. Klein, Scott E. Hubbard, Roger A. Grice, Lenore S. Ridgeway, Marlene C. Semple, Bruno Petrauskas, Thomas T. Barker.

507. Barton, David, and Roz Ivanic, eds. *Writing in the Community*. Newbury Park, CA: Sage Publications, 1991. 320 pages

Contends that literacy is a component of everyday life. Examines writing practices outside of educational settings; focuses on the way communities define, value, and use writing. Explores sociocultural, historical, linguistic, and ethnographic approaches to literacy.

Essayists: D. Barton, A. R. Fishman, C. Klassen, S. Padmore, U. Howard, G. T. Gregory, J. C. Street, B. V. Street, S. Gardener, R. Ivanic, W. Moss.

508. Batschelet, Margaret. "Computers and Basic Writing Students: Where We Are and Where We're Going." *ACE Newsletter* 7 (Spring 1991): 1, 3.

Finds that computers improve basic writers' attitudes toward writing.

509. Beder, Hal. *Adult Literacy: Issues for Policy and Practice*. Malabar, FL: Krieger, 1991. 182 pages

Identifies policy issues raised by research on adult literacy; recommends solutions. Examines adult literacy from the perspective of the learners. Focuses attention on low literate adults.

510. Bell, Martha Clark. "A Comparative Study of Error in Compositions by First-Year College Students Using Handwriting and Word Processing." *DAI* 52 (November 1991): 1729A.

Analyzes punctuation, one-word errors, sentence structure, consistency, and spelling; concludes that word processing does not affect overall frequency of errors.

511. Bikai-Nyunai, Victor-Janvier. "Cognitive Styles Match and Mismatch in Autotutorial Computer-Based Instruction: Effects of Paired Learning on Flowcharting Achievement by Individuals." *DAI* 52 (July 1991): 8A.

Confirms that "group composition based upon cognitive style is determinate factor in learning."

512. Bizzell, Patricia. "Professing Literacy: A Review Essay." *JAC* 11 (Fall 1991): 315–322.

Reviews recent "proliferation" of texts on literacy to determine why and how this "flexible" concept is being employed by postsecondary writing teachers.

513. Black, Kathleen. "How Students See Their Writing: A Visual Representation of Literacy." *JR* 35 (November 1991): 206–214.

This study reveals that 187 first-year college students who were taught using visual representation did not internalize elements of the writing process.

514. Boiarsky, Carolyn. "Fluency, Fluidity, and Word Processing." *JAC* 11 (Winter 1991): 123–133.

A survey of 2300 students at Illinois State shows that composition taught with word processing increases fluency and fluidity but does not improve writing quality.

515. Bolter, Jay David. *Writing Space*. Hillsdale, NJ: Lawrence Erlbaum Associates, 1991. 272 pages

Maintains that the concept of hypertext has far-reaching implications in the fields of human and artificial intelligence, cognitive science, philosophy, semiotics, and literary theory. The software *Writing Space: A Hypertext* is available as an accompaniment to the book.

516. Boren Gilkenson, Francine Rose. "Adult Literacy: Case Studies of Adults Attending Literacy Classes." *DAI* 51 (May 1991): 3598A.

Describes and analyzes the uses of literacy at school, home, and work of two working adults labeled functionally illiterate.

517. Brand, Alice G. "Introducing Computers into the Composition Class: Students' Self-Report." *CompC* 4 (December 1991): 4–6.

Points out that a survey of first-year college students at one campus indicated that basic writers used computers more than average writers.

518. Brent, Doug. "Computer-Assisted Commenting and Theories of Writing Response." *WI* 10 (Winter 1991): 103–110.

Describes limitations of current responding software as "electronic rubber-stamping"; suggests using macros to supplement an individual word-processing response.

519. Brown, Rexford G. "Schooling and Thoughtfulness." *JBW* 10 (Spring 1991): 3–15.

Presents the keynote address given at the 1989 conference of the National Testing Network in Writing; promotes "literacy of thoughtfulness" characterized by critical and creative thinking; presents the author's related research.

520. Brown, Rexford G. *Schools of Thought: How the Politics of Literacy Shape Thinking in the Classroom*. San Francisco, CA: Jossey-Bass Publishers, 1991. 240 pages

Shows how policies that set basic minimum learning standards limit teachers to lecture-and-drill exercises, thereby fostering complacency and low expectations in the classroom. Demonstrates how policies that harnass students' natural curiosity encourage conversation, stimulate inquiry, and promote trust and collaboration between students and teachers.

521. Bruffee, Kenneth A., and Kathleen M. Blair. "Two Comments on 'Computer Conferences and Learning: Authority, Resistance, and Internally Persuasive Discourse' [*CE* 52 (December 1990)]." *CE* 53 (December 1991): 950–953.

Authors discuss and criticize Marilyn M. Cooper's and Cynthia L. Selfe's perception of teachers' authority in conferencing and in other types of collaborative learning.

522. Bushman, Donald E. "New Revision Exercises for the Computer-Assisted Composition Classroom." *ExEx* 36 (Spring 1991): 28–29.

Uses editorial essays from *USA Today* to teach revision.

523. Butler, Sidney J., and Roy Bentley. *Literacy through Lifewriting: The Foundations of Growth in Engagement*. Norwich, England: International Conference of Language and Literacy, April 1991. ERIC ED 329 980. 23 pages

Discusses how growth into literacy occurs most effectively with the engagement of the learner. Reports that life writing is a most powerful medium.

524. Cangarajah, Athelstan Suresh. "Negotiating Competing Discourses and Identities: A Sociolinguistic Analysis of Challenges in Academic Writing for Minority Students." *DAI* 51 (April 1991): 3398A.

Argues that African-American students must negotiate conventions that contrast with those of their own discourse communities in order to acquire academic literacy.

525. Carey, John. "Plato at the Keyboard: Telecommunications Technology and Education Policy." *Annals* 514 (March 1991): 11–21.

Argues that the role of telecommunications in education and economic development will be essential during the next century.

526. Cavalier, Todd, and Ravinder Chandhok. "Graphic Design for a Collaborative Workstation: Columns for Commenting and Annotation." *IDJ* 6 (1991): 187–198.

Describes an experimental on-line environment for collaborative writing by using a visual interface and a prep editor.

527. Caverly, David C., and Bill Broderick. "Techtalk: Learning through Hypermedia." *JDEd* 14 (Spring 1991): 38–39.

Argues that the use of hypermedia facilitates instruction in developmental writing, reading, and critical thinking.

528. Cawsey, Alison. "Generating Explanatory Discourse: A Plan-Based, Interactive Approach." *DAI* 51 (May 1991): 5422B.

Describes a computer model of explanatory discourse and suggests a practical approach to generating complex explanations in tutorial help systems.

529. Chase, Sharon. "The Corporate Illiterates: The Hidden Illiterates of Silicon Valley." *BABC* 54 (December 1991): 31–35.

Discusses the problem of poor writing skills among young employees and job applicants.

530. Clark, Suzanne. "Review: Literacy and Teaching: In Search of a 'Language of Possibility.' " *CE* 53 (February 1991): 213–221.

Reviews books that investigate students and teachers as subjects of literacy and examines resistance to literacy from students and the dominant culture.

531. Clarke, Christopher Thomas. "Rationale and Development of a Scale to Measure Computer-Mediated Communication Apprehension." *DAI* 52 (October 1991): 1129A.

Studies the tendency to feel anxious when using or expecting to use computers for communication.

532. Clay, Marie M. *Becoming Literate: The Construction of Inner Control*. Portsmouth, NH: Heinemann, 1991. 372 pages

Argues that all successful readers and writers develop a deep command of literacy regardless of how they are taught.

533. Cochran-Smith, Marilyn, Cynthia L. Paris, and Jessica L. Kahn. *Learning to Write Differently: Beginning Writers and Word Processing*. Norwood, NJ: Ablex, 1991. 336 pages

Teachers used word processors with beginning writers. Working with this teaching medium shaped their understanding and changed their perspectives of the writing and learning process.

534. "Colleges Are Urged to Help High Schools Extend Computer Use." *CHE* 38 (28 December 1991): A21, A24.

Harvey Weiner, academic dean at CUNY, points out in an address to the association for managers of information technology (CAUSE) that computer use would help eliminate remedial programs in college.

535. "Computer Notes." *CHE* 37 (17 April 1991): A19.

Ronald T. Kellogg, University of Missouri at Rolla, concludes from a study of 100 students that word processors change the process but do not improve writing skills.

536. Cooper, Marilyn M. " 'We Don't Belong Here, Do We?' A Response to *Lives on the Boundary* and *The Violence of Literacy*." *WCJ* 12 (Fall 1991): 48–62.

Argues that literacy is not an inherent value. Points out that limiting through schooling effectively restricts access to power, creating class differences.

537. Crook, Charles. "Computers in the Zone of Proximal Development: Implications for Evaluation." *CompEd* 17 (1991): 81–91.

Argues from a cultural psychology stance for a better evaluation of computer-based learning, especially for "teacher-driven integrative activity."

538. Crosby, Arthur. "The Mississippi Literacy Assessment (SSRC Report 91–1)." Mississippi Governor's Office for Literacy. 1991. ERIC ED 284. n.p.

Reports survey data on the literacy proficiencies of the adult population.

539. D'Souza, Patricia Veasey. "The Use of Electronic Mail as Instructional Aid: An Exploratory Study." *JCBI* 18 (Summer 1991): 106–110.

Finds significant differences in four performance scores favoring students receiving assignments through mail as opposed to traditional handouts.

540. Daly, Bonita Law. "The Effects of Computer-Mediated Communication on Inductive Learning by Groups." *DAI* 51 (June 1991): 3936A.

Determines that computer-mediated communication is more time-consuming and less satisfactory compared to face-to-face discussion.

541. Damarin, Suzanne K. "Computers, Education, and Issues of Gender." *JT* 25 (Spring/Summer 1991): 81–98.

Analyzes artificial intelligence and computer use from a feminist perspective such as patriarchal world views and masculine notions of normal and normative.

542. Davis, Ruth A. "A Comparison of the Reading and Writing Performance of Children in a Whole Language Prefirst-Grade Class and a Modified Traditional First-Grade Class." *DAI* 52 (September 1991): 861A.

Studies the differences in literacy development among five sets of students in the two classes.

543. Dobberstein, Michael. "Managing the Technology in a Desktop Publishing Course." *JBTC* 5 (April 1991): 200–207.

Describes pedagogical and technological dimensions of teaching a desktop publishing course.

544. Dobrin, David. "Alphabetic Software Manuals: Notes and Comments." *TC* 38 (February 1991): 89–100.

Offers six reasons and four steps for producing an alphabetic manual.

545. Downing, Joseph G. "A Study of the Relationships between Literacy Levels and Institutional Behaviors of Incarcerated Male Felons." *DAI* 51 (February 1991): 2882A.

Concludes that literacy education leads to a decrease in unacceptable institutional behaviors; recommends that correctional departments develop more resources to support and nurture educational programs.

546. Du Bartell, Deborah Ann. "Language, Technology and the Communications Network: An Assessment of the Relationships between Speech and Writing." *DAI* 52 (July 1991): 149A.

Argues that new media does not displace written language and literacy.

547. Dubrovsky, Vitaly J., Sara Kiesler, and Beheruz N. Sethna. "The Equalization Phenomenon: Status Effects in Computer-Mediated and Face-to-Face Decision-Making Groups." *HCI* 6 (Spring 1991): 119–146.

Authors compare face-to-face and e-mail decision-making groups whose members differed in social status. They argue that status and expertise inequalities in participation were reduced with e-mail.

548. Duin, Ann Hill. "Computer-Supported Collaborative Writing: The Workplace and the Writing Classroom." *JBTC* 5 (April 1991): 123–150.

Examines software appropriate to computer-supported collaborative writing in business and technical writing course.

549. Ede, Lisa. "Literacy in Theory and Practice: One Class's Efforts to Bridge the Gap." *FEN* 19 (Spring 1991): 22–23, 26.

Describes a course titled "Composition, Literature, and Literacy" in which the author discovered the need to emphasize conflicts between theory and practice.

550. Edwards, Bruce L. "How Computers Change Things: Literacy and the Digitized Word." *WI* 10 (Winter 1991): 68–76.

Claims that digitized textuality closely parallels oral tradition. Electronic texts reflect the flexibility and power of oral words yet can become fixed, stored, and transmitted in print.

551. Eldred, Janet Carey. "Narratives of Socialization: Literacy in the Short Story." *CE* 53 (October 1991): 686–700.

Demonstrates how reading fiction for literacy issues, particularly collisions between competing discourse communities, enables fusion of critical theory with composition and literacy studies.

552. Eldred, Janet M. "Pedagogy in the Computer-Networked Classroom." *C&C* 8 (April 1991): 47–61.

Concludes that networking will only be useful in composition classrooms if the technology is fully and carefully integrated into class plans.

553. Falk, Dennis R., and Helen L. Carlson. "Evaluating the Effectiveness of Multimedia Applications in Human Service and Teacher Education." *Multimedia Review* 2 (Fall 1991): 12–17.

Reports on 20 studies of nine videodisc applications that incorporate numerous instructional techniques and multimedia.

554. Feldman, Tony. "Human Perspectives in Multimedia." *Multimedia Review* 2 (Winter 1991): 56–61.

Reviews commercial influence in multimedia development; argues for more "heart and mind" in such development.

555. Fitzgerald, Sharyn. "A Comment on *College English* [*CE* 52 (March 1990)]." *CE* 53 (February 1991): 223–224.

Argues for less jargon and simpler language in journal articles.

556. Freer, Kevin Joseph. "The Value of Literacy for the Rural Elderly: A Naturalistic Study." *DAI* 51 (March 1991): 2957A.

Explores the contextual nature of literacy among low-literate elderly persons living in rural North Florida; shows what they perceive as their literacy needs and interests.

557. Frese, Michael, Felix Brodbeck, Torsten Heinbokel, Christina Mooser, Erik Schleiffenbaum, and Petra Thiemann. "Errors in Training Computer Skills: On the Positive Function of Errors." *HCI* 6 (Winter 1991): 77–93.

Argues that errors can have a positive function. Points out that groups given error-training showed higher scores on tests.

558. Gardiner, Ellen F. "Ideologies, Technologies, and Teaching." *JTW* 10 (Fall/Winter 1991): 241–253.

Reviews *Evolving Perspectives on Computers and Composition Studies*, edited by Gail Hawisher and Cynthia Selfe, and *The English Classroom in the Computer Age*, edited by William Wresch.

559. Gerrard, Lisa. "Computers and Compositionists: A View from the Floating Bottom." *C&C* 8 (April 1991): 5–15.

Explores how the English teaching profession perceives computer and composition specialists; shows why many composition teachers do not have time to explore computer applications.

560. Gibson, Martin L. *Editing in the Electronic Era*. 3rd ed. Ames, IA: Iowa State University Press, 1991. 320 pages

Includes a new chapter on layout and new material on economical writing. Emphasizes editing on electronic equipment. Includes headline writing.

561. Gillespie, Marilyn Kay. "Becoming Authors: The Social Context of Writing and Local Publishing by Adult Beginning Readers." *DAI* 52 (December 1991): 1983A.

Gathers information about the history of writing and publishing by adult beginning readers and studies the experiences of authors in three literacy programs.

562. Gilstrap, Tracy A. "Collaborative Computer-Assisted Composition Classrooms: The Solution to the Classical Problems." *CACJ* 5 (Spring 1991): 52–53.

Argues that peer collaboration using computers provides the dialectic that Plato considered missing in writing.

563. Girelli, Alan. "Aspects Groupware, Intertextuality and the Collaborative Process in a Freshman Writing Classroom." *CompC* 4 (November 1991): 13–14.

Explains a project on intertextuality and group editing conducted through networking software.

564. Gowen, Sheryl Greenwood. " 'Eyes on a Different Prize': A Critical Ethnography of a Workplace Literacy Program." *DAI* 51 (March 1991): 2957A–2958A.

Shows that literacy educators need to mediate between employer-employee literacy needs when minority differences exist.

565. Graeber, Janet Miller. "The Effects of Planning and Writing Environment on the Quality of Expository Essays Written by Seventh-Grade Catholic School Girls." *DAI* 51 (January 1991): 2352A.

Explores the effects of pencil-and-paper, fixed computer, and flexible computer environments. Finds that writing ability has an important effect on essay quality.

566. Graubard, Stephen R, ed. *Literacy: An Overview by 14 Experts*. New York: Noonday Press, 1991. 288 pages

Twelve articles, originally published in the Spring 1990 issue of *Daedalus*, survey the history and scope of literacy and numeracy. The authors examine the complex social, economic, political, and cultural issues that underlie problems of illiteracy.

Essayists: Jerome Bruner, Daniel P. Resnick, Leon Botstein, Mihaly Csikszentmihalyi, Lauren B. Resnick, Bonnie B. Armbruster, Lynn Arthur Steen, David Hawkins, William Damon, Howard Gardner, John U. Ogbu, Richard C. Anderson, Mary Roe, Benson R. Snyder.

567. Gribbons, William M. "Visual Literacy in Corporate Communication: Some Implications for Information Design." *IEEE* 34 (March 1991): 42–50.

Presents a model for the design of information products, including the perceived significance of a range of visual elements.

568. Grudin, Jonathan. "Systematic Sources of Suboptimal Interface Design in Large Product Development Organizations." *HCI* 6 (Spring 1991): 147–196.

Describes contextual forces in large organizations that block user involvement in the iterative design of software products.

569. Guindon, Raymonde. "Users Request Help from Advisory Systems with Simple and Restricted Language: Effects of Real-Time Constraints and Limited Shared Context." *HCI* 6 (Winter 1991): 47–75.

Presents users' requests for help from what they believe is a computerized advisor. Results show that users request help with simple, restricted language.

570. Guthrie, John T., Tracy Britten, and K. Georgene Barker. "Roles of Document Structure, Cognitive Strategy, and Awareness in Searching for Information." *RRQ* 26 (1991): 300–324.

Presents two studies in which college students searched the same information base on computer in three formats: table, directory, and prose.

571. Guthrie, John T., William D. Schafer, and Susan R. Hutchinson. "Relations of Document Literacy and Prose Literacy to Occupational and Societal Characteristics of Young Black and White Adults." *RRQ* 26 (1991): 30–48.

Using data from the 1986 National Assessment for Educational Progress, researchers conclude both are directly related to the occupations and participation in society.

572. Halio, Marcia Peoples. "On Being Famous." *CompC* 3 (January 1991): 4–6.

A personal narrative characterizes the responses to the author's *Academic Computing* article favoring IBM over Macintosh computers.

573. Hall, Susan, and Palmer Hall. *Between Schools: Inter-Classroom Collaboration*. Old Westbury, NY: Conference on Computers and English, April 1991. ERIC ED 333 481. 15 pages

Discusses the benefits and problems of students on two campuses using telecommunications software and e-mail to exchange comments on their papers.

574. Halverson, John. "Olson on Literacy." *LSoc* 20 (December 1991): 619–640.

Argues against David Olson's thesis that literacy has caused a significant alteration of human condition.

575. Harrington, Susan Marie. "Women, Literacy, and Intellectual Culture in Anglo-Saxon England." *DAI* 52 (July 1991): 147A.

This sociolinguistic study argues that literate Anglo-Saxon culture included women as well as men.

576. Harris, R. Allen. "A Do-It-Yourself Usability Kit." *JTWC* 21 (1991): 351–368.

Presents practical guidelines for conducting small-scale usability study; includes discussion of preparing task lists, recruiting participants, conducting the study, and analyzing the data.

577. Harris, William V. *Ancient Literacy*. Cambridge, MA: Harvard University Press, 1991. 408 pages

Provides a general survey of literacy in classical antiquity. Challenges the view that most of the population of Athens could read.

578. Hartman, Geoffrey H. *Minor Prophecies: The Literary Essay in the Culture Wars*. Cambridge, MA: Harvard University Press, 1991. 252 pages

First presents an account of the culture of criticism in the last 100 years. Then widens the focus to provide a picture of the critical essay from 1700 to the present to show that a major change in style took place after 1950. Shows developments that have disrupted the friendship and conversational style.

579. Hartmann, Karen, Christine M. Neuwirth, Sara Kiesler, Lee Sproull, Cynthia Cochran, Michael Palmquist, and David Zubrow. "Patterns of Social Interaction and Learning to Write: Some Effects of Network Technologies." *WC* 8 (January 1991): 79–113.

Compares patterns of teacher/student and student/students interaction in traditional and networked writing classrooms.

580. Hawisher, Gail E., and Michael A. Pemberton. "The Case for Teacher as Researcher in Computers and Composition Studies." *WI* 10 (Winter 1991): 77–88.

Offers research suggestions to discover the role(s) of computers in the writing classroom.

581. Hawisher, Gail E., and Cynthia L. Selfe. "The Rhetoric of Technology and the Electronic Writing Class." *CCC* 42 (February 1991): 55–65.

Calls for the rhetoric of technology to include a "critical perspective on the problematic aspects of computer use."

582. Hawisher, Gail E., and Cynthia L. Selfe, eds. *Evolving Perspectives on Computers and Composition Studies: Questions for the 1990s*. Advances in Computers and Composition Studies. Urbana, IL, and Houghton, MI: National Council of Teachers of English and *Computers and Composition* Press, 1991. 384 pages

Collection seeks to "set an agenda of scholarship and research for the next decade" in the area of computers and composition by offering broad outlines of important areas needing research and reflection. Essay topics include ideology and technology in writing instruction, hypertext possibilities, feminism and computers, and politics of technology.

Essayists: Janis Forman, Mary Louise Gomez, Andrea W. Herrman, Emily Jessup, Nancy Kaplan, Kathleen Kiefer, Elizabeth Klem, Charles Moran, John McDaid, Stuart Moulthrop, Ruth Ray, Elen Barton, Donald Ross, Henrietta Nickels Shirk, Catherine F. Smith, James Strickland, Patricia Sullivan.

583. Henley, Jessie L. "The Effects of Writing and Word Processing on Vocabulary and Reading Comprehension of At-Risk College Freshmen." *DAI* 52 (October 1991): 1274A.

Points out that word processing facilitates the reading comprehension of students; suggests that word processors should be used more frequently.

584. Hiebert, Elfrieda H., ed. *Literacy for a Diverse Society: Perspectives, Practices, and Policies*. New York: Teachers College Press, 1991. 328 pages

Presents issues of multicultural education at all levels from a constructive perspective.

Essayists: Richard L. Allington, Arthur N. Applebee, Rexford Brown, Robert Calfee, Nancy L. Commins, Katherine Cutts-Dougherty, Yvonne Marie David, Patricia A. Edwards, Margaret A. Eisenhart, Carol Emmer, Frederick Erickson, Charles W. Fisher, Janet S. Gaffney, Georgia Earnest Garcia, Ernest R. House, Judith A. Langer, Pamela McCollum, Michael S. Meloth, Ofelia B. Miramontes, Sharon Nelson-Barber, Annemarie Sullivan Palincsar, P. David Pearson, Maria de la Luz Reyes, Robert Rueda, Lorrie A. Shepard, Nancy Lawrence, Elfrieda H. Hiebert, Richard C. Anderson.

585. Hill, Charles A., David L. Wallace, and Christina Haas. "Revising On-Line: Computer Technologies and the Revising Process." *C&C* 9 (November 1991): 83–109.

Shows how word processing technology affects writers' cognitive processes for revision.

586. Hiltz, Starr Roxanne, Donna Dufner, Michael Holmes, and Scott Poole. "Distributed Group Support Systems: Social Dynamics and Design Dilemmas." *JOC* 1 (Spring 1991): 135–159.

Reviews a series of pilot studies that identify problems of implementing group decision support systems.

587. Hlynka, Denis, and Chris Chinlen. "Technological Visions in Education." *JT* 25 (Spring/Summer 1991): 66–80.

Discusses social and cultural implications of educational technology for a positivist and hermeneutic/aesthetic perspective; poses a postmodern paradigm.

588. Hooper, Susan, and Michael J. Hannafin. "Psychological Perspectives on Emerging Instructional Technologies: A Critical Analysis." *EdPsy* 26 (Winter 1991): 69–95.

Suggests that technological tools may improve classroom instruction for a variety of reasons; proposes a matrix for determining when to use technology in the classroom.

589. Horgan, John. "Word Games." *ScAm* 265 (October 1991): 34.

Examines the current progress of MIT researchers to develop a computer program that will parse sentences in any language.

590. Houlette, Forrest. "Applying AI to the Writer's Learning Environment." *CollM* 9 (August 1991): 159–164.

Describes an organizing schema for applying artificial intelligence technology to the tasks that writers perform.

591. Houston, R. A. *Literacy in Early Modern Europe: Culture and Education 1500–1800*. White Plains, NY: Longman, 1988. 266 pages

Discusses higher education, ways of teaching, ways of learning, sources and measures of literacy, profiles of literacy, the world of the book, and language and culture.

592. Hult, Christine. "The Role of Computers in the English Department of the Future: One University's Approach." *WI* 10 (Winter 1991): 97–101.

Describes Utah State University's reconstruction of English department curricula for the English major and teacher training programs in relation to computer technology.

593. Hutchinson, Leonard Carter. "Toward an Aesthetic Paradigm Encompassing Computer Art: A Descriptive Analysis of Artwork and Attitudes in a University Setting." *DAI* 51 (February 1991): 2548A.

Analyzes the use of microcomputers in the visual composing process; finds that artists using computers will "edit" more when using a microcomputer.

594. Janangelo, Joseph. "Technopower and Technoppression: Some Abuses of Power and Control in Computer-Assisted Writing Environments." *C&C* 9 (November 1991): 47–64.

Shows how electronic networks encourage abuse; suggests more humanistic uses of technology.

595. Jennings, Edward M., and Alan C. Purves, eds. *Literate Systems and Individual Lives: Perspectives on Literacy and Schooling*. Literacy, Culture, and Learning. Albany, NY: State University of New York, 1991. 222 pages

Raises questions concerning the impact of literacy/illiteracy on individuals who operate within/without society's literate systems.

Essayists: Edward M. Jennings, Alan C. Purves, Daniel Wagner, Douglas M. Windham, Philip Foster, Nyi Akinnaso, Bernardo M. Ferdman, Donald A. Biggs, Sean A. Walmsley, Lil Brannon, Catherine E. Snow, David K. Dickinson.

596. Jobst, Jack, and Billie Wahlstrom. "User Responses to Varying Persona in Computer-Assisted Instruction." *CollM* 9 (August 1991): 153–158.

Finds that students using computer-assisted instruction respond differently to different on-line personae.

597. Johnson, Gerald R. "Agents, Traffic, Objects and Illusions: Paradigms of Computer Science." *JTWC* 21 (1991): 271–283.

Examines some essential paradigms of computer science that permeate computer discourse; describes paradigms as clusters of metaphors through which we think and talk about computers.

598. Kaestle, Carl F., Helen Damon-Moore, Lawrence C. Stedman, Katherine Tinsley, and William Vance Trollinger, Jr. *Literacy in the United States: Readers and Readings since 1880*. New Haven, CT: Yale University Press, 1991. 338 pages

Addresses the history of literacy and readers, reading ability and test-score decline, changes in the uses of literacy over time and social groups, and literacy and diversity. Argues that higher-level critical literacy skills must become available for the reading public and that diversity and accessibility of reading materials must be ensured.

599. Kaler, Ellen Redding. "Programming, Prewriting, and Pedagogy: A Plan, a Critique, and a Rationale." *CACJ* 5 (Winter 1991): 34–43.

Encourages using computer aids for student writers and promotes programming one's own software. Includes a four-page bibliography on prewriting programs, articles, and books.

600. Kamphoefner, Kathleen R. "Voices from the Botton: Women of Cairo Review Literacy." *DAI* 52 (November 1991): 1572A.

Questions women's views of education and examines the relationships between society and lived experiences.

601. Kantrov, Ilene. "Keeping Promises and Avoiding Pitfalls: Where Teaching Needs to Augment Word Processing." *C&C* 8 (April 1991): 63–77.

Describes research reports and product development; concludes that teachers must integrate word-processing technology into writing instruction.

602. Keller, Ronald Edward. "Auditory and Visual Processes among Tutorial Literacy Students." *DAI* 51 (April 1991): 3304A.

Indicates that illiterate adults are deficient in the auditory and visual process skills of visual sequencing, auditory sequencing, and auditory memory.

603. Knight, Lee Ellen. "Gender Issues and Computer Conferencing: A Survey of Emerging Scholarship." *CACJ* 5 (Spring 1991): 54–58.

Describes current scholarship relating to gender issues and computer conferencing. Offers 18-item bibliography.

604. Knussen, Christina, Gary R. Tanner, and Michael R. Kibby. "An Approach to the Evaluation of Hypermedia." *CompEd* 17 (1991): 13–24.

Presents six models with suggested methodology and criteria that can be applied to the evaluation of hypermedia: classical experimental, research and developmental, illuminative, briefing decision-makers, teacher as researcher, and case-study model.

605. Koch, Tom. *Journalism for the Twenty-First Century: Online Information, Electronic Databases, and the News*. Contributions to the Study of Mass Media and Communications, no. 28. New York: Greenwood Press, 1991. 374 pages

Examines the relation between the content of public information and the potential effects of new technologies on the degree and type of information available in the public forum.

606. Kolich, Eileen M. "Effects of Computer-Assisted Vocabulary Training on Word Knowledge." *JEdR* 84 (January/ February 1991): 177–182.

Argues that students provided with sentence context, definitional or synonym clues, and optional word choices learn more words than students who receive definitional information only.

607. Kozma, Robert B. "Computer-Based Writing Tools and the Cognitive Needs of Novice Writers." *C&C* 8 (April 1991): 31–45.

Examines computer writing tools currently available; concludes that without instructor support and guidance most are unsuitable for novice writers.

608. Kozma, Robert B. "The Impact of Computer-Based Tools and Embedded Prompts on Writing Processes and Products of Novice and Advanced College Writers." *C&I* 8 (1991): 1–27.

Argues that advanced writers do better with an "idea organizer" whereas novice writers do better with an "outliner."

609. LaFollette, Marcel C., and Jeffrey K. Stine, eds. *Technology and Choice: Readings from Technology and Culture*. Chicago, IL: University of Chicago Press, 1991. 380 pages

Fourteen essays provide historical perspectives on how, when, or why individuals, societies, governments, and industries made choices regarding the use of technology.

Essayists: Marcel C. LaFollette, Jeffrey K. Stine, Carlos Flick, John G. Burke, Patrick W. O'Bannon, Claude S. Fischer, Fred E. H. Schroeder, Suellen Hoy, Carroll W. Pursell, George T. Mazuzan, J. Samuel Walker, Sylvia D. Fries, Christine E. Bose, Philip L. Bereano, Mary Malloy, Ruth Schwartz Cowan, David P. Billington, Robert Mark, Eugene S. Ferguson.

610. Lazere, Donald. "Orality, Literacy, and Standard English." *JBW* 10 (Fall 1991): 87–98.

Reconsiders Thomas Farrell's "I. Q. and Standard English"; stresses "greater repertory of both syntax and reasoning that becomes possible through the resources of a grapholetic system."

611. Lytle, Susan L. "Living Literacy: Rethinking Development in Adulthood." *L&E* 3 (1991): 109–138.

Argues that adult literacy education must interrogate its current assumptions about adult learners, accounting more fully for the complexities of learners' beliefs, practices, language processes, and plans.

612. Mabrito, Mark. "Electronic Mail as a Vehicle for Peer Response: Conversations of High- and Low-Apprehensive Writers." *WC* 8 (October 1991): 509–532.

Studies contrasting responses of high- and low-apprehensive first-year college writers to peer response received during face-to-face interactions or as electronic mail.

613. Madden, Frank. "Correct Grammar." *CHum* 25 (February 1991): 58–61.

Questions the usefulness of this editing software for teaching students to revise.

614. Manly, Donna, James E. Muharkey, Cindy Bentley, Pablo Cardona, Lisa Flesch, and Barbara Suyama. "Workplace Educational Skills Analysis: Training Guide." Wisconsin State Board of Vocational, Technical, and Adult Education, 1991. ERIC ED 334 442. 77 pages

Describes a program used to analyze literacy requirements in the workplace.

615. Marcus, Stephen. "Word Processing: Transforming Students' Potential to Write." *M&M* 27 (May/June 1991): 8, 35.

Discusses computer telecommunication among students and the use of hypermedia.

616. Masys, Daniel. "The National Research and Education Network." *AM* 66 (June 1991): 397–398.

Describes the development of the computer network and parallel projects to improve dissemination of educational and scientific knowledge.

617. McCabe, Allyssa, and Carole Peterson, eds. *Developing Narrative Structure*. Hillsdale, NJ: Lawrence Erlbaum Associates, 1991. 367 pages

Authors present new empirical studies on genres of narrative, the role narrative structure plays in emergent literacy, the relationship between narrative language and autobiographical memory, and ways in which teachers and parents facilitate or hinder children's narrative development.

Essayists: Allyssa McCabe, Carole Peterson, Earl Capron, David K. Dickinson, James Paul Gee, Deborah Hicks, Judith A. Hudson, Sarah Michaels, Lauren R. Shapiro, Elizabeth Sulzby, Lilliano Barro Zecker.

618. McCarron, Bill. "Encounters with Word Processing." *ET* 22 (Summer 1991): 33–35.

Reflects on his own composing process from 1973 to 1992.

619. McLellan, Hilary. "Virtual Environments and Situated Learning." *Multimedia Review* 2 (Fall 1991): 30–37.

Explores the use of virtual reality to support sophisticated training applications, noting how such applications promote situated learning.

620. Miller, Kathryn Elizabeth. "The Fit between Training and Use in a Vernacular Literacy Training Program: An Ethnographic Study of Four Papua New Guineans." *DAI* 51 (February 1991): 2663A.

Results indicate a lack of application of vernacular literacy training to local community needs when students return home.

621. Miller, Randolph A., and Nunzia B. Giuse. "Medical Knowledge Bases." *AM* 66 (January 1991): 15–17.

Using medicine as a model, the study describes how faculty in any discipline can set up a computerized knowledge base; shows how they can best use and enlarge it.

622. Miller, Richard E. "Bringing the Classroom into the Literacy Debate." *WI* 11 (Fall 1991): 23–30.

Uses his own classroom experience to argue that new forms of pedagogy must accompany new definitions of literacy.

623. Moberg, Goran. "The Politics of Computers in Schools." *ACE Newsletter* 7 (Summer-Fall 1991): 2–3.

Argues that placing computers in writing classrooms is a complex undertaking.

624. Monaghan, E. Jennifer. "Family Literacy in Early Eighteenth-Century Boston: Cotton Mather and His Children." *RRQ* 26 (1991): 342–370.

Examines diaries and other writings to reveal issues facing modern reading researchers: comprehension and study skills, cohesiveness between reading and writing, and relationship between literacy and life.

625. Monty, Melissa Lee. "Issues for Supporting Notetaking and Note Using in the Computer Environment." *DAI* 51 (January 1991): 3597B.

Explores cues for recall in class notes, index cards, and the Xerox NoteCards hypertext system.

626. Moran, Charles. "Using What We Have." *C&C* 9 (November 1991): 39–46.

Describes a structured writing class period that uses networked computers.

627. Mosenthal, Peter B., and Irwin S. Kirsch. "Toward an Explanatory Model of Document Literacy." *DPr* 14 (April–June 1991): 147–180.

Presents a model of how documents such as bus schedules are interpreted. Argues that certain variables such as type of information influence document processing.

628. Moulthrop, Stuart, and Nancy Kaplan. "Something to Imagine: Literature, Composition, and Interactive Fiction." *C&C* 9 (November 1991): 7–23.

Describes experimental course teaching literature and writing through interactive fiction on networked computers.

629. Murray, Denise E. "The Composing Process for Computer Conversation." *WC* 8 (January 1991): 35–55.

Analyzes the ways in which contextual constraints on composing messages during computer-mediated conversation influence the composing process.

630. Naficy, Hamid. "Exile Discourse and Television, a Study of Syncretic Cultures: Iranian Television in Los Angeles." *DAI* 51 (January 1991): 2180A.

Studies television programming aimed at Iranian exiles; analyzes how immigrants incorporate themselves into a dominant culture.

631. Nellhaus, Tobin Benjamin. "Changing the Script: Orality and Literacy in the Performance Strategies of the York Cycle, Ben Jonson, and Richard Steele." *DAI* 52 (November 1991): 1576A.

Uses plays to examine how communication responds to changes in the literacy level of the intended audience.

632. Nelson, G. Lynn. "Bringing Language Back to Life: Responding to the New Illiteracy." *EJ* 80 (February 1991): 16–20.

Argues that the literacy problem arises from a "language-polluted and language-deadened environment"; proposes teaching strategies to revive the power and beauty of language.

633. Newman, Diane. "Practical Writing Resource Kit and Computer Writing Resource Kit." *CHum* 25 (December 1991): 513–515.

Suggests that teachers use the exercises on these interactive software packages to help students prewrite, write, and edit assignments in the humanities and business communication.

634. Nye, Emily F. "Computers and Gender: Noticing What Perpetrates Inequality." *EJ* 80 (March 1991): 94–95.

Reviews research showing why "positive benefits of computer technology fail to distribute evenly between male and female students"; advocates teacher training to redress disparity.

635. Olson, Gary M., and Judith S. Olson. "User-Centered Design of Collaboration Technology." *JOC* 1 (Winter 1991): 61–83.

Illustrates the various stages of a user-centered approach to developing groupware.

636. Olson, Gary R. "Eideteker: The Professional Communicator in the New Visual Culture." *IEEE* 34 (March 1991): 13–19.

Traces the post-Gutenberg devaluation of the visual in Western culture. Argues that accessible computer-graphics capability will reverse the trend.

637. Otte, George. "Computer-Adjusted Errors and Expectations." *JBW* 10 (Fall 1991): 71–86.

Details computer analysis of upper-level developmental students' writing; emphasizes students' inability to recognize their own errors and their need for individualized instruction.

638. Overmyer, Dwayne. "On Situating Documents: Notes toward a Descriptive and Analytical Framework." *IDJ* 6 (1991): 199–209.

Describes a framework for the understanding and evaluating of typographic documents both as objects of design and as instances of language in use.

639. Panetta, Clayann Gilliam. "Computer-Assisted Composition: A Classical Interpretation." *CACJ* 5 (Spring 1991): 59–64.

Places computer-assisted writing instruction into the framework of classical rhetoric; shows how modern methods are a natural extension of classical communication theories.

640. Parenteau, Jean M. "Literacy from Birth." *DAI* 51 (February 1991): 2622A.

Concludes that parental involvement with literacy development results in significantly higher student achievement in school.

641. Paul, Marianne. "When Words Are Bars: A Guide to Literacy Programming in Correctional Institutions." Ontario Department of Education. 1991. ERIC ED 334 371. 104 pages

Provides a guide for literacy groups working with prisoners.

642. Pearce, Glenn C., and Randolph T. Barker. "A Comparison of Business Communication Quality between Computer Written and Handwritten Samples." *JBC* 28 (Spring 1991): 141–152.

Points out that an analysis of Grammatik II and ANOVA for business student texts proves inconclusive.

643. Perry, Devern. "The Impact of the Computer on the English Language." *BABC* 54 (June 1991): 51–54.

Presents a study of computer-related words found in computer industry marketing publications.

644. Petkosh, David George. "The Revising Behaviors of Three Undergraduate Technical Writers Assisted by the Word Processor: A Qualitative Case Study." *DAI* 51 (April 1991): 3319A.

Concludes that revision for these writers consisted mostly in surface changes. Offers suggestions for teaching revision with the word processor.

645. Phinney, Marianne. "Word Processing and Writing Apprehension in First and Second Language Writers." *C&C* 9 (November 1991): 65–82.

Shows that second language students benefitted more from using computers for writing than did first language student.

646. Poteet, Howard. "Computers Make Mark on Teaching of Writing." EDRS. 1991. ERIC ED 329 968. 5 pages

Reports on benefits of teaching students to write using computers.

647. Power, Brenda Miller, and Ruth Hubbard, eds. *Literacy in Process: The Heinemann Reader*. Portsmouth, NH: Heinemann, 1991. 352 pages

Leading practitioners and theorists in literacy education argue for and demonstrate the advantages of holistic theory and practice.

Essayists: Donald M. Murray, Marge Piercy, Ruth Nathan, Paulo Freire, Tim Gillespie, Ruth Hubbard, Brenda Miller Power, Jerome Harste, Virginia Woodward, Carolyn Burke, Donald Graves, Shirley Brice Heath, Kenneth Goodman, Louise M. Rosenblatt, Patrick Shannon, Lucy Calkins, Susan Sowers, Lynn K. Rhodes, Curt Dudley-Marling, Kathy G. Short, Toby Fulwiler, Nancie Atwell, Linda Rief, Pat McLure, Cora Lee Five, Linda Henke, Rene Galindo, Susan Stires, Leslie Funkhouser, Susan Ohanian.

648. Purves, Alan C. "Clothing the Emperor: Towards a Framework Relating Function and Form in Literacy." *JBW* 10 (Fall 1991): 33–53.

Conceptualizes literacy as "a culturally mediated technology"; explains why students need explicit textual and functional models of the literacy that they are expected to demonstrate.

649. Purves, Alan C. *The Scribal Society: An Essay on Literacy and Schooling in the Information Age*. White Plains, NY: Longman, 1990. 128 pages

Discusses literacy from a social, epistemological, psychological, and pedagogical perspective. Emphasizes the distinction between scribal society (falling in popularity) and popular culture (rising). Explores the various segments of the scribal society and their specialized vocabulary as well as their shared characteristics.

650. Rhodes, Barbara K., and Nancy Ives. "Computers and Revisions—Wishful Thinking or Reality?" EDRS. 1991. ERIC ED 331 045. 14 pages

Shows that students using pens and typewriters make more revisions than those using computers, but there were no significant differences in the final quality of the papers.

651. Roberts, David H. "Using *Conference Writer* as an Inexpensive, Effective Means of Fostering Collaborative Writing on Computers." *CompC* 4 (December 1991):

Characterizes a pedagogy using a Hypercard stack.

652. Rosenthal, Beverly Margaret. "Computer-Mediated Discourse in a Writing Workshop: A Case Study in Higher Education." *DAI* 52 (December 1991): 2117A.

Examines the application of computer-mediated communication to writing instruction.

653. Saito, Mioko. "Effect of Background Music on Computer Anxiety." *DAI* 51 (May 1991): 3555A.

Finds positive effects of music on reducing anxiety of 44 students using a CAI program.

654. Schaafsma, David W. "Eating on the Street: Teaching Literacy in a Multicultural Society." *DAI* 52 (July 1991): 137A.

Illustrates the value of multiple perspectives in learning about teaching. Shows that telling stories about teaching is useful to develop learning theories and a curriculum.

655. Scheibal, William J., and Gary F. Kohut. "An Assessment of Computerized Text Editing Programs." *BABC* 54 (June 1991): 38–42.

Discusses a study comparing the results of two text editing programs with those of an experienced editor.

656. Schmitz, Joseph, and Janet Fulk. "Organizational Colleagues, Media Richness, and Electronic Mail." *ComR* 18 (August 1991): 487–523.

Uses electronic mail to document how social influences affect the ways in which individuals perceive and use new information technology.

657. Schneiderman, Ben, Catherine Plaisant, Rodrigo Botafogo, Don Hopkins, and William Weiland. "Designing to Facilitate Browsing: A Look Back at the Hyperties Workstation Browser." *Hypermedia* 3 (Summer 1991): 101–117.

Presents an overview of Hyperties and design features that facilitate browsing: pie menus, multiple window selection strategies, and pop-out graphical buttons.

658. Schwalm, David E. "High School/Dual Enrollment." *WPA* 15 (Fall/Winter 1991): 51–54.

Explains why dual enrollment is a threat to the development of college-level literacy and offers strategies for resisting the arrangement.

659. Selfe, Cynthia L., and Marilyn M. Cooper. "Cynthia L. Selfe and Marilyn M. Cooper Respond [to Bruffee and Blair, *CE* 53 (December 1991)]." *CE* 53 (December 1991): 953–955.

Selfe and Cooper respond to issues concerning technology in educational settings, teachers' authority in conferencing, and the multiple uses of literacy in society.

660. Selfe, Cynthia L., and Paul R. Meyer. "Testing Claims for On-Line Conferences." *WC* 8 (April 1991): 163–192.

Analyzes the influence of gender, status, and use of pseudonyms on participation in an on-line conference.

661. Shamonsky, Dorothy. "Rancho Deluxe." *Multimedia Review* 2 (Summer 1991): 3–8.

Chronicles the historical development of multimedia applications, noting the evolution of screen designs.

662. Simpson, Mark. "The Practice of Collaboration in Usability Test Design." *TC* 38 (November 1991): 527–531.

Points out that at Microsoft Corporation, document usability testers must collaborate with internal "clients," often switching roles, and organizing around tasks rather than traditional company roles.

663. Spaulding, Cheryl L., and Daniel Lake. *Interactive Effects of Computer Network and Student Characteristics on Students' Writing and Collaboration*. Chicago, IL: AERA, April 1991. ERIC ED 329 966. 26 pages

Reports on a study of fifteen remedial writers who used networked computers to assist in writing instruction.

664. Sproull, Lee, and Sara Kiesler. "Two-Level Perspective on Electronic Mail in Organizations." *JOC* 1 (Spring 1991): 125–134.

Summarizes a two-level perspective on computing and reviews research demonstrating strong organizational effects of electronic mail.

665. Stafford, Janice Yvonne. "Effects of Active Learning with Computer-Assisted or Interactive Video Instruction." *DAI* 52 (August 1991): 517A.

Uses meta-analysis procedures to examine the effects of active learning with computer-assisted and interactive video instruction.

666. Steelman, Jane Davis. "Facilitating Cognitive Development and Improving Writing Achievement of Middle Level Students through a Role-Taking Experience (Newspaper) Using Computers (Word Processors)." *DAI* 51 (January 1991): 2354A.

Compares composing strategies of students using word processors, pen-paper, and traditional writing methods.

667. Sticht, Thomas G. "Evaluating National Workplace Literacy Programs." Applied Behavioral and Cognitive Sciences, Inc. 1991. ERIC ED 334 431. 13 pages

Discusses government-mandated program evaluation requirements of the National Workplace Literacy Program.

668. Stuart, Rory, and John C. Thomas. "The Implications of Education in Cyberspace." *Multimedia Review* 2 (Summer 1991): 17–27.

Contrasts the impact cyberspace may have on education with the impact of earlier technologies; examines how cyberspace can engage students more powerfully.

669. Sudol, Ronald A. "The Accumulative Rhetoric of Word Processing." *CE* 53 (December 1991): 920–932.

Asserts that the efficiency of word processing has "potentially harmful effects" for inexperienced writers; identifies two ways to avoid those effects.

670. Sudol, Ronald A. "The Prospects and Consequences of Private Access to Computers." *WI* 10 (Winter 1991): 89–96.

Argues that choices universities make about computer hardware and software may be potentially limiting to students' freedom to write creatively.

671. Sugg, Deborah. "Word Processor Versus Braille Writing: A Comparative Study of Essays Written by Blind Students." *DAI* 51 (February 1991): 2709A.

Results show no clear differences in efficiency or quality, although more revisions were made by students using a word processor. Suggests ways in which writing pedagogy might be modified for visually impaired students.

672. Swearingen, C. Jan. *Rhetoric and Irony: Western Literacy and Western Lies*. New York: Oxford University Press, 1991. 344 pages

Integrates the histories of rhetoric, literacy, and literary aesthetics up to the time of Augustine, focusing on Western concepts of rhetoric as dissembling and of language as deceptive. Points out that these concepts have received prominent emphasis in Western aesthetics and language theory.

673. Taylor, Peter Leigh. "Rhetoric, Restructuring and Economic Democracy in Three Spanish Production Cooperatives." *DAI* 52 (December 1991): 2290A.

Argues that the emergence of an exclusive rhetoric reduces the space for competing perspectives and weakens democratic debate.

674. Thomas, Gordon P., and Dene Kay Thomas. "Judging and Adapting Style-Analysis Software." *C&C* 8 (April 1991): 17–30.

Describes study of student and teacher responses to computer-generated comments on students' compositions.

675. Trummel, Paul. "Shape Concept: Color Percept . . . Graphics, Geometry, and *Gestalt*." *IEEE* 34 (September 1991): 174–185.

Considers the relation of shape and color to the comprehension and meaning of a document through the lens of *gestalt* psychology.

676. Turoff, Murray. "Computer-Mediated Communication Requirements for Group Support." *JOC* 1 (Winter 1991): 85–113.

Presents an overview of the historical evolution of CMC systems for group support. Discusses advantages of asynchronous support and the integration of CMC with other resources.

677. Valeri-Gold, Maria, and Mary P. Deming. "Computers and Basic Writers: A Research Update." *JDEd* 14 (Spring 1991): 10–14.

Authors provide suggestions for effective computer use and warn readers concerning their limitations and misuse in the teaching of basic writers.

678. Vamos, T. "Cooperative Communication: Computerware and Humanware." *JOC* 1 (Winter 1991): 115–123.

Emphasizes the combined requirements of computer systems and humanistics.

679. Wallace, F. Layne, J. Michael Flanery, and Gerald A. Knezek. "The Effect of Subliminal Help Presentations on Learning a Text Editor." *IPM* 27 (1991): 211–218.

Points out that students learning PITA with a subliminal reinforcement of command needed less assistance. Suggests additional tests.

680. Walther, Joseph B. "Relational Communication in Computer-Mediated Interaction." *DAI* 51 (June 1991): 3958A.

Examines effects of time and communication channel on impression development, message personalization and relational communication; finds that computer-mediated groups experienced positive increases in relational dimensions.

681. Waterworth, John A., and Mark H. Chignell. "A Model for Information Exploration." *Hypermedia* 3 (Spring 1991): 35–58.

The authors clarify roles of humans and systems for browsing and information retrieval by using a three-dimensional model of information exploration.

682. Watters, Carolyn, and Michael A. Shepherd. "Hypertext Access and the New Oxford English Dictionary." *Hypermedia* 3 (Spring 1991): 59–79.

Presents a conversion of the dictionary to a hypertext document. Provides users with the ability to browse rather than query the program for information.

683. Wiley, Terrence. "Measuring the Nation's Literacy: Important Considerations (ERIC Digest)." National Clearinghouse for Literacy Education, 1991. ERIC ED 334 870. 4 pages

Reviews efforts to measure literacy levels in the United States, agreeing that illiteracy levels are alarmingly high; questions the ecological validity of available measures.

684. Williams, William F. "Teaching Literature, Canon Formation, and Multiculturalism." *ELQ* 13 (October 1991): 2–3.

Questions the practice of giving token recognition to multiculturalism while clinging to the belief that cultural literacy equals a knowledge of the traditional canon.

685. Willinsky, John. *The New Literacy: Redefining Reading and Writing in the Schools.* New York: Routledge, 1990. 256 pages

Brings together programs that have changed the way reading and writing have been taught over the last decade. Allows educators, parents, and other concerned readers to assess the promise of these programs that promote literacy as the means to greater public participation and the exploration of personal meaning.

686. Winn, William. "Color in Document Design." *IEEE* 34 (September 1991): 180–185.

Outlines a model of the process of perception which includes "preattentive" and "attentive" processing. Calls for a theoretical framework for research in graphics.

687. Wresch, William, ed. *The English Classroom in the Computer Age: Thirty Lesson Plans*. Urbana, IL: NCTE, 1991. 145 pages

Describes detailed, practically oriented lesson plans for teaching writing using computers. Presents three groups of lessons, for students with little, moderate, or advanced familiarity with computers. Lessons range from creative writing exercises to autobiographical journalism assignments to practices using critical thinking skills.

Essayists: Jean Bowen, John F. Beaver, Nancy Deal, Jeff Golub, Dan Gravely, Joseph Hackett, Joan Hamilton, Gail Hawisher, John Heyn, Mary Hoppe, Elizabeth A. Jones, Patricia LeRoy, Sandra Lucht, Stephen Marcus, Rick Monroe, Jessica Hohman, Catherine Morics, Thomas Neumann, Elray L. Pedersen, Stuart Rivard, James Ross, Vicki Sadowski, Mary Schenkenberg, Rae C. Shipke, Jeffrey Schwartz, Lee Sebastiani, Deborah Trimble, Michael D. Ubbelohde, Dwight Worman, William Wright.

688. Yohner, William A. "Effective Ideation in Written Texts: An Empirical Study of the Rhetorical Structures of First-Year College Writers' Essays Produced by Word Processing and by Handwriting." *DAI* 51 (April 1991): 3401A.

Concludes that students with computers produce longer and more varied, though not more contextually aware, writing.

689. Youmans, Gilbert. "A New Tool for Discourse Analysis: The Vocabulary Management Profile." *Language* 67 (December 1991): 763–789.

Presents a quantitative method for producing computer-generated graphics and for analyzing the distribution of vocabulary in a text.

See also 674, 713, 856, 1578, 1593, 1606, 1615, 1626, 1698, 1741, 1796, 1803, 1832

2.5 ADVERTISING, PUBLIC RELATIONS, AND BUSINESS

690. Ahlawat, Sucheta S. "The Relative Effects of Comparative and Noncomparative Advertising on Evaluation Processes." *DAI* 51 (February 1991): 2810A.

Supports the hypothesis that comparative messages are superior to noncomparative messages.

691. Albrecht, Terrance L., and Bradford 'J' Hall. "Facilitating Talk about New Ideas: The Role of Personal Relationship in Organizational Innovation." *ComM* 58 (September 1991): 273–288.

Focuses on relational and network conditions conducive to talk about new ideas.

692. Ambuske, Gail C. "A Narrative Analysis of the Subjective Experience of U. S. Expatriate Managers." *DAI* 51 (May 1991): 3814A.

Analyzes the narratives of fifteen returned expatriate managers to develop an understanding of the subjective experience of the individual while abroad.

693. Andrews, Victoria L. "Women in Advertising." *PC* 11 (Winter 1991): 27–28.

Presents the results of a survey of the readers of *Advertising Age* on depictions of women in advertising. Suggests possibilities for change.

694. Beason, Larry. "Strategies for Establishing an Effective Persona: An Analysis of Appeals to Ethos in Business Speeches." *JBC* 28 (Fall 1991): 326–346.

Analyzes the "signalled ethos" of the use of similitude, deference, self-criticism, expertise, and inclination to succeed in eight business speeches.

695. Brown, Mary Helen, and Jill J. McMillan. "Culture as Text: The Development of an Organizational Narrative." *SCJ* 57 (Fall 1991): 49–60.

Presents a method for integrating subtexts and diverse points of view to gain insight into the lower levels of the organizational hierarchy.

696. Bullis, Connie. "Communication Practices as Unobtrusive Control: An Observational Study." *ComS* 42 (Fall 1991): 254–271.

Explores the role of communication in inculcating decision premises; points out anomalies such as failures or contradictions in control.

697. Cheney, George. *Rhetoric in an Organizational Society: Managing Multiple Identities*. Columbia, SC: University of South Carolina Press, 1991. 208 pages

Explains how in an industrial society many messages are associated with large, powerful organizations that use advertising, annual reports, policy statements, and newsletters. Claims that citizens and scholars more tuned to the individual often have trouble interpreting messages from a collective body.

698. Crowley, Ayn Elizabeth. "The Golden Section: An Information Theoretic Approach to Understanding Two-Sided Persuasion." *DAI* 51 (April 1991): 3465A.

Examines the impact of various proportions of positive and negative information on the processing and effectiveness of persuasive communication.

699. Djeddah, Richard. "The Impact of Advertising on Security Returns." *DAI* 51 (May 1991): 3805A.

Proposes that advertising affects purchasing behavior of security investors in a similar way as it affects consumer behavior in product purchasing.

700. Dobos, Jean, Margaret Hilton Bahniuk, and Susan E. Kogler. "Power-Gaining Communication Strategies and Career Success." *SCJ* 57 (Fall 1991): 35–48.

Authors present a study of 258 managers that supports the relationship of connection and information adequacy variables to perceptual, attitudinal, and behavioral success indicators.

701. Dorrell, Jean T., and Nancy S. Darsey. "An Analysis of the Readability and Style of Letters to Stockholders." *JTWC* 21 (1991): 73–83.

Examines 30 shareholder letters in annual reports written by successful executives; finds that they conform to modern-day standards of style and readability.

702. DuBose, Philip B., and Peter A. Veglahn. "Labor-Management Mediation: The Mediator in a Complex Communication Situation." *JTWC* 21 (1991): 55–64.

Describes the complexities of the labor-management context in which the communicator plays numerous roles in the mediation process.

703. Farrell, Amy E. "Feminism in the Mass Media: '*Ms.*' Magazine, 1972–1989." *DAI* 52 (October 1991): 1401A.

Dramatizes how *Ms.* worked as a powerful yet contradictory channel for the women's movement.

704. Gengler, Charles Edward. "The Architecture of Advertising Strategy: A Structural Perspective on Persuasive Communications." *DAI* 51 (March 1991): 3141A.

Supports the cognitive structure approach to advertising strategy design and assessment.

705. Goodstein, Ronald C. "How Do Consumers Screen Advertisements? A Heuristic Model of Ad Processing." *DAI* 51 (June 1991): 4201A.

Predicts and tests when consumers will process ads in a detailed versus cursory manner.

706. Gordon, William I., and Dominic A. Infante. "Test of a Communication Model of Organizational Commitment." *ComQ* 39 (Spring 1991): 144–155.

Argues that employees are less committed to the organization and less satisfied with supervisors when their freedom of speech is restricted.

707. Gregory, James B. "Projecting a Global Image." *PC* 11 (Winter 1991): 18–19.

Argues that corporate communication programs must present a worldwide image; offers examples of Japanese and American companies that have achieved this objective.

708. Harcourt, Jules, Virginia Richerson, and Mark J. Wattier. "A National Study of Middle Managers' Assessment of Organization Communication Quality." *JBC* 28 (Fall 1991): 348–365.

A survey of 3600 middle managers reveals that most believe that the quality of organizational communication is poor. Authors point out that networks and grapevine are cited as better communication than official information.

709. Hobbs, Jeffrey D. "A Rhetorical Analysis of Corporate Advocacy Strategies during Public Relations Crises: Three Case Studies." *DAI* 51 (May 1991): 3558A.

Analyzes strategies used by the Chrysler, Toshiba, and Audi Corporations and finds that the rhetoric of image crises are influenced by apologia, identification, and narrative.

710. Horn, J. Kenneth. "Personnel Administrators' Reaction to Job Application Follow-Up Letters Regarding Extending Interviews and Offering Jobs." *BABC* 54 (September 1991): 24–27.

Reports on a study of the impact of follow-up letters on the offering of interviews and jobs.

711. Infante, Dominic A., and William I. Gorden. "How Employees See the Boss: Test of an Argumentative and Affirming Model of Supervisors' Communicative Behavior." *WJSC* 55 (Summer 1991): 294–304.

Investigates supervisory styles associated with subordinates' satisfaction and organizational commitment.

712. Jackson, Janice Jaquenetta. "The Communication Competence of Managers with Liberal Arts Versus Professional/Technical Undergraduate Backgrounds." *DAI* 51 (March 1991): 3135A.

Finds that better communicators have social science—not technical—education and that neither a liberal arts background nor institution had significant effects on communication skills.

713. Johansen, Robert. "Groupware: Future Directions and Wild Cards." *JOC* 1 (Spring 1991): 219–227.

Explores future directions for groupware in the marketplace and for business teams.

714. Kleimann, Susan D. "The Complexity of the Workplace." *TC* 38 (November 1991): 520–526.

Points out the complexity of document review which often involves multiple internal and external readers, many of whom demand major revisions.

715. LaDuc, Linda. "Infusing Practical Wisdom into Persuasive Performance: Hermeneutics and the Teaching of Sales Proposal Writing." *JTWC* 21 (1991): 155–164.

Uses hermeneutic theory to teach sales proposal writing by classifying the process by which ethical know-how intersects with persuasion.

716. Llewellyn, John T. "The Rhetoric of Corporate Citizenship." *DAI* 52 (July 1991): 22A.

Uses content analysis to examine the theological issues raised in annual reports and employee newsletters published by Ball Corporation and Eli Lilly Company.

717. March, James G. "How Decisions Happen in Organizations." *HCI* 6 (Spring 1991): 95–117.

Presents three visions of decision making in organizations: a social science view, a logic of appropriateness view, and an artifactual view.

718. Meyers, Douglas G. "Thinking Styles and the Writing Group." *BABC* 54 (March 1991): 17–20.

Discusses the importance of research on thinking styles and writing groups in the future of business communication.

719. Miller, Chip E. "Effects of Pictures and Words as Cognitive Cues on Information Processing and Print Ads." *DAI* 51 (January 1991): 2459A.

Postulates that print ads combining words and pictures of similar valence are more effective; finds that words are the more important medium.

720. Mumby, Dennis K., and Cynthia Stohl. "Power and Discourse in Organization Studies: Absence and the Dialectic of Control." *D&S* 2 (July 1991): 313–332.

Presents a deconstructive analysis of three texts to demonstrate that discourse is a major means of maintaining power in an organization.

721. Nixon, Judy C., and Marilyn M. Helms. "An Evaluation of Business Communication and Business Policy/Strategic Planning Textbooks: Readability Measures." *BABC* 54 (December 1991): 48–54.

Describes a study of methods of text selection and the readability level of business communication and business policy/strategic planning texts.

722. O'Malley, Sharon. "Women in a 'Man's World.' " *PC* 11 (Feb/March 1991): 19, 26.

Discusses the difficulties female professional communicators experience in nontraditional fields.

723. Powell, Melissa L. "The Language of Letters: A History of Persuasive and Psychological Strategies in American Business Letters from 1905 through 1920." *JBTC* 5 (January 1991): 33–47.

Analyzes persuasion, "you" viewpoint, and the five C's in American sales letters from 1905–1920.

724. Quinn, Robert, Herbert Hildebrandt, Priscilla Rogers, and Michael Thompson. "A Competing Values Framework for Analyzing Presentational Communication in Management Contexts." *JBC* 28 (Summer 1991): 213–232.

An empirical model contrasts characteristics of four general types of presentational communication.

725. Ramer, Mary Ann. "Globalization." *PC* 11 (Fall 1991): 10–13, 40.

Discusses the impact of globalization on the communications profession and offers "10 commandments for international success."

726. Rank, Hugh. *The Pitch*. Park Forest, IL: Counter-Propaganda Press, 1991. 160 pages

Presents a guide to analyzing advertisements. Discusses the purposes, strategies, and effects of messages that represent "examples of carefully crafted nonrational persuasion."

727. Reinsch, Lamar. "Editorial: What Is Business Communication?" *JBC* 28 (Fall 1991): 305–310.

Editor offers deliberately narrow definitions of business communication, management communication, and organizational communication to clarify the central nature of each.

728. Rossetti, Jane. "Deconstructing Economic Texts." *DAI* 51 (February 1991): 2819A.

Contrasts the post-structuralist deconstructive approach to economic texts with "internalist," "externalist," and rhetorical approaches to the history of economic thought.

729. Schramm, Robert M., and R. Neil Dortch. "An Analysis of Effective Résumé Content,

Format, and Appearance Based on College Recruiter Perceptions." *BABC* 54 (September 1991): 18–23.

Summarizes a study of college recruiters' résumé preferences.

730. Shelby, Annette N. "Applying the Strategic Choice Model to Motivational Appeals: A Theoretical Approach." *JBC* 28 (Summer 1991): 187–212.

Applies the strategic choice model to motivational options useful in constructing persuasive messages.

731. Sides, Charles H. "Collaboration in a Hardware Technical Writing Group: A Real-World Laboratory." *BABC* 54 (June 1991): 11–15.

Describes a group writing project in industry, as observed by the instructor of a corporate training program.

732. Smeltzer, Larry R., and James E. Suchan. "Guest Editorial: Theory Building and Relevance." *JBC* 28 (Summer 1991): 181–186.

Explains the theory behind the Summer 1991 issue of *JBC*. Discusses the theoretical relevance and the importance of the issue.

733. Smith, Peter Worthington. "Examining the Effects of Liked and Disliked Television Commercials on Consumer Brand Attitudes: An Application of Classical Conditioning Principles." *DAI* 51 (March 1991): 3142A.

Points out that experiments support using classical conditioning to explain the effects of advertising.

734. Wagner, Richard J. "The Media of the Message? An Empirical Study of the Importance of Selection System Attribute on Job Choice." *DAI* 51 (May 1991): 3842A.

Investigates the effect of the attributes of the selection system on perception of the selecting process, on the regard for the company, and on the probability of accepting a job.

735. Washington, Durthy A. "Developing a Corporate Style Guide: Pitfalls and Panaceas." *TC* 38 (November 1991): 553–555.

Discusses the gathering of information, designing the guide, and testing the document.

736. Wells, Barron, and Nelda Spinks. "Readability: Theory and Practice." *BABC* 54 (December 1991): 46–47.

Describes a study of the readability level of 100 pieces of business correspondence.

737. Werckmeister, O. K. *Citadel Structure.* Chicago, IL: University of Chicago Press, 1991. 232 pages

Uses cultural artifacts (novels, comic books, electronic music) to argue that despite media documentation of crises and our awareness of vulnerability we avoid rational discourse of calls for change.

738. Wernick, Andrew. *Promotional Culture: Advertising, Ideology, and Symbolic Expression.* Theory, Culture, and Society Series. Newbury Park, CA: Sage Publications, 1991. 208 pages

Assesses the cultural impact of advertising. Traces the impact from sale of consumer goods to electoral politics to the university.

739. Wert-Gray, Stacia, Candy Center, Dale E. Brashers, and Renee A. Meyers. "Research Topics and Methodological Orientations in Organizational Communication: A Decade in Review." *ComS* 42 (Summer 1991): 141–154.

Content analysis reveals that the research focused primarily on three topics, that the majority of studies was framed in modernistic-empirical methodology, and that it was conducted in actual settings.

740. Wright, Alice A. "Advertising Versus Direct Experience as Modes of Communicating Information about Products." *DAI* 52 (July 1991): 233A.

Examines the strengths and weaknesses of these two media in communicating product information.

741. Zorn, Theodore E. "Construct System Development, Transformational Leadership and Leadership Messages." *SCJ* 56 (Spring 1991): 178–193.

Studies leadership and communication in small businesses.

742. Zorn, Theodore E., and Gregory B. Leichty. "Leadership and Identity: A Reinterpretation of Situational Leadership Theory." *SCJ* 57 (Fall 1991): 11–24.

Applies a message analysis approach to studying leadership processes in management training.

2.6 LITERATURE, FILM, AND THEATER

743. Abarry, Abu Shardow. "The Significance of Names in Ghanian Drama." *JBS* 22 (December 1991): 157–167.

Analyzes names as a rhetorical device in modern plays.

744. Allan, Tuzyline J. "Feminist and Womanist Aesthetics: A Comparative Study." *DAI* 51 (April 1991): 3403A.

Tests Alice Walker's definition of "womanism" in *The Color Purple* by examining Woolf's *Mrs. Dalloway* and Drabble's *The Middleground.* Demonstrates the limits of "womanism" through an analysis of Emecheta's *The Joys of Motherhood.*

745. Baker, Barbara Louise. "Reaffirmation and Transformation of Gender in Popular Film: A Feminist Approach to Mythic Rhetoric." *DAI* 51 (January 1991): 2197A.

Examines *Indiana Jones* and *Star Wars* movies; concludes that the films reinforce rather than challenge patriarchy.

746. Baker, Houston A., Jr. *Workings of the Spirit: The Poetics of Afro-American Women's Writing*. Chicago, IL: University of Chicago Press, 1991. 256 pages

Compares current critical approaches to the theoretical character of African-American intellectual history. Argues for theoretical return to the vernacular of African-Americans and to autobiographical expressions.

747. Barrett, Lindon Warren. "In the Dark: Issues of Value, Evaluation, and Authority in Twentieth-Century Critical Discourse." *DAI* 51 (February 1991): 2742A.

Details a theoretical mode of value in order to investigate recent revolutions in literary critical authority.

748. Bernard-Donals, Michael Francis. "Discourse in Art, Discourse in Life: Mikhail Bakhtin and Contemporary Critical Theory." *DAI* 52 (October 1991): 1305A.

Traces connections between sociolinguistic theory and recent postformal critical work, including reader-response criticism and historical criticism.

749. Bove, Paul. *In the Wake of Theory*. Wesleyan, CT: Wesleyan University Press, 1991. 192 pages

Critiques the practice and politics of intellectuals and disciplines in postmodern society.

750. Bowers, Bradley R. *Toward Decentralizing the Study of Literature, or Who Do We Think We Are?* Boston, MA: CCCC, March 1991. ERIC ED 334 596. 5 pages

Explores three issues facing English departments: the canon debates, the teaching role of the department, and the role of theory.

751. Brown, Brenda Gabioud. "Battle Hymns: The Rhetorical Strategies of Twentieth-Century American War Novels." *DAI* 52 (October 1991): 1326A.

Analyzes rhetorical techniques and language in eight representative works.

752. Bundy, Rosalee. "Japan's First Woman Diarist and the Beginnings of Prose Writings by Women in Japan." *WS* 19 (1991): 79–97.

Discusses the tenth-century autobiographical journal of a woman whose records influenced the development of the modern Japanese romance.

753. Carey-Webb, Allen. "Auto/Biography of the Oppressed: The Power of Testimonial." *EJ* 80 (April 1991): 44–47.

Recommends testimonials as "ideal texts" for focusing on "the experience of the unlettered, marginalized, and oppressed"; encourages critical thinking about "generic, disciplinary, and institutional boundaries."

754. Cindoglu, Dilek. "Re-Viewing Women: Images of Patriarch and Power in Modern Turkish Film." *DAI* 52 (August 1991): 322A.

Examines representations of gender ideology in Turkish society by examining 1980s women's films.

755. Cole, Carole L. "The Search for Power: Drama by American Women, 1909–1929." *DAI* 52 (December 1991): 2185A.

Analyzes 24 plays by 16 American women as social documents; discovers that dramatic discourse does not reflect material improvement in conditions for women.

756. Connolly, Paula. "Giving Testimony: Social Reform and the Politics of Voice in Four Nineteenth-Century American Texts." *DAI* 52 (December 1991): 2142A.

Examines the ways in which four female authors contest the separation of spheres and the prevailing notions of domesticity.

757. Conquergood, Dwight. "Rethinking Ethnography: Towards a Critical Cultural Politics." *ComM* 58 (June 1991): 179–194.

Examines ethnographic research in light of critical theory.

758. Cooper, Brenda Kay. "Through the Eyes of Gender and Hollywood: Conflicting Rhetorical Visions of Isak Dinesen's Africa." *DAI* 52 (November 1991): 1551A.

Uses a rhetorical framework to compare Dinesen's writings with Pollack's film version of her work.

759. Decker, Jeffrey L. "The Interpretation of American Dreams: The Political Unconscious in American Literature and Culture." *DAI* 51 (June 1991): 4165A.

Attempts to produce a theory of the American Dream that facilitates interpretation and political awareness.

760. Denzin, Norman K. *Images of Postmodern Society: Social Theory and Contemporary Cinema*. Newbury Park, CA: Sage Publications, 1991.

Addresses the relations between Hollywood films of the 1980s, their constructions of self, and the structures of lived experience. Offers a postmodern sociology that addresses the increasingly conservative basis of postmodern ideologies of race, class, and gender.

761. Ekanger, Victoria Kill. "Teaching Stories: Enabling U.S. Literatures and Pedagogies." *DAI* 51 (March 1991): 3072A.

Explores how teaching U.S. literature can challenge rather than reinforce dominant strategies about "Americanness."

762. Esposito, Dawn G. "Speaking the Image: The Representation of Women in Culture." *DAI* 52 (November 1991): 1900A.

Develops a feminist, post-structural theoretical framework and applies it to Faulkner's *Sanctuary* and *Requiem for a Nun*.

763. Faust, Mark Andrew. "Reconsidering What We Talk about When We Talk about Literature: Social Constructionist Metaphors in Criticism and Teaching." *DAI* 51 (February 1991): 2664A.

Questions the claim that reader response theory and criticism represent a revolutionary departure from formalist theory and criticism.

764. Felch, Susan M. "Paradigms and Perspectives: The Application of Tagmemics and Dialogics to Religious Literary Criticism." *DAI* 52 (October 1991): 1314A.

Devises a model for religious literary criticism based upon theories from Kenneth Pike and Mikhail Bakhtin.

765. Fusfield, William D. "Walden's 'Conclusion': Henry David Thoreau's Transcendental Synthesis of the Classical Peroration and Early-Romantic Combinational Writing." *DAI* 52 (November 1991): 1570A.

Concludes that the literary and inspirational force of Thoreau's writing results from a selective appropriation, transformation, and synthesis of rhetorical forms.

766. Garvey, Johanna X. K. "Difference and Continuity: The Voices of Mrs. Dalloway." *CE* 53 (January 1991): 59–76.

Argues that Woolf's water imagery creates voices which both unify and fragment urban time and space, creating a "feminist revisioning of the cityscape."

767. Graham, Kenneth J. E. "The Performance of Conviction: Anti-Rhetorical Plainness from Wyatt to Shakespeare." *DAI* 51 (March 1991): 3082A.

Claims that aspiring to plainness creates a paradox between the desires for personal truth and public approval, resulting in anger and withdrawal.

768. Guss, Donald L. "Enlightenment as Process: Milton and Habermas." *PMLA* 106 (October 1991): 1156–1169.

Cites the rhetoric developed in Habermas as a method for a cooperative discourse that is grounded in a common capacity for reason.

769. Hagen, Patricia. "Revision Revisited: Reading (and) *The French Lieutenant's Woman*." *CE* 53 (April 1991): 439–451.

Shows how *The French Lieutenant's Woman* deconstructs the fact/fiction, writer/reader dichotomies, paralleling the shift in emphasis from product to process in composition theory.

770. Hayles, N. Katherine, ed. *Chaos and Order: Complex Dynamics in Literature and Science*. Chicago, IL: University of Chicago Press, 1991. 312 pages

Fourteen theorists use the relationship between chaos and order to develop its implications for understanding texts.

Essayists: William Paulson, David Porush, Peter Stoicheff, Kenneth J. Knoespel, Robert Markley, Sheila Emerson, Linda K. Hughes, Michael Lund, Adalaide Morris, Thomas P. Weissert, Istvan Csicsery-Ronay, Jr., Eric Charles White, Maria L. Assad.

771. Hesse, Douglas. "The Recent Rise of Literary Nonfiction: A Cautionary Essay." *JAC* 11 (Fall 1991): 323–333.

As scholar, Hesse identifies and refutes arguments for "the literary status of the essay," but as teacher he acknowledges the concept's "enabling fiction."

772. Hickey, James. "Cinemaesthetics: A College-Level Curriculum in Film and Communication Theory, Aesthetics, and Ethics, Critical Thinking and Articulation Skills." *DAI* 51 (June 1991): 3932A.

Describes a college-level course in film study and communication that reinforces a variety of communication and critical thinking skills.

773. Hoefel, Roseanne Louise. "Connecting the French Connection: Emily Dickinson and Virginia Woolf Writing the (Female) Body." *DAI* 51 (January 1991): 2372A.

Examines the authors' texts with the help of Irigaray, Cixous, and Kristeva; addresses the question of women's discourse across time, space, and genre.

774. Jones, Ann Rosalind. "Enabling Sites and Gender Difference: Reading City Women with Men." *WS* 19 (1991): 239–249.

Analyzes the impact of exclusive "teaching circuits, coteries, cities, social and linguistic environments" upon the work of three sixteenth-century women poets.

775. Joyrich, Lynne. "Re-Viewing Reception: Television, Gender, and American Culture." *DAI* 51 (February 1991): 2546A.

Examines how television has been figured in popular and critical discourse as a "feminized" or nonrational medium.

776. Judy, Ronald A. Trent. "The Rhetorics of Vernacular Corpora: The African-American Slave Narrative and the Challenge of Narrative Indeterminacy." *DAI* 51 (February 1991): 2735A.

Uses a nineteenth-century Arabic text to investigate the linguistic and historical problems of reading slave narratives.

777. Keller, Eve Miriam. "The Certain Sign: The Language of Geometry in Seventeenth-Century English Literature." *DAI* 51 (February 1991): 2753A.

Studies how three renaissance writers applied the language of geometry to effect a higher level of discourse.

778. Kintz, Linda. "On Performing Deconstruction: Postmodern Pedagogy." *CCrit* (Fall 1990): 87–107.

Analyzes the 1985 interview with Jacques Derrida in which he reveals his phallogocentric pedagogy that refuses to differentiate the "Other."

779. Lerer, Seth. *Literacy and Power in Anglo-Saxon Literature*. Lincoln, NE: University of Nebraska Press, 1991. 352 pages

Considers the construction of an early English cultural mythology of writing. Examines scenes of reading and writing in *Beowulf*, *Daniel*, Bede's *Ecclesiastical History* and the Exeter Book riddles, reassessing the social and historical nature of Old English literature.

780. Levenduski, Cristine. " 'Remarkable Experiences in the Life of Elizabeth Ashbridge': Portraying the Public Woman in Spiritual Autobiography." *WS* 19 (1991): 271–281.

Describes Ashbridge's process of "self-invention" through accounts of unconventional experiences within a traditional, normative form.

781. Lundman, John Peter. "Suppressed Discourse: William Blake's Use of the Language of Entropy." *DAI* 51 (January 1991): 2385A.

Examines the rhetoric and semiotics of Blake's poetry, makes suggestions for teaching it, and warns that students must work to retain their own discourse.

782. Marchalonis, Shirley. "Leaving the Jargons: Adeline D. T. Whitney and the Sphere of God and Women." *WS* 19 (1991): 309–325.

Presents the spiritual guest novels, poetry, and other religious writings of this late nineteenth-century woman "in the context of her life and time."

783. Marshall, Gary Thomas. "William Stafford: A Writer Writing." *DAI* 52 (November 1991): 1572A.

Describes the "everydayness" of Stafford's creative process and writing theory by constructing a "hermeneutic circle."

784. Mayer, Elsie F. "A Truce in the Battle of Books." *CEAF* 21 (Winter 1991): 1–3.

Advocates pairing compatible texts, one by a male, the other by a female, in teaching literature.

785. Meier, Cynthia M. "A Feminist Archetypal Analysis of Diane Di Prima's Loba Poems for Performance." *DAI* 51 (June 1991): 3956A.

Focuses on ancient images of the goddess as a metaphor for the feminine myth.

786. Melaver, Martin Edward. "The Resistance of Narrative." *DAI* 51 (January 1991): 2372A.

Uses texts from Carlyle, Melville, and James to show how narrative enables us to construct versions of our worlds despite theoretical limitations.

787. Millsapps, Jan Leah. "A Study of Moving Image Discourse." *DAI* 51 (June 1991): 3932A.

Examines moving image media within the interactive context of rhetoric and discourse.

788. Moffat, Wendy. "Identifying with *Emma*: Some Problems for the Feminist Reader." *CE* 53 (January 1991): 45–58.

Critiques new critical readings of the novel by arguing that Austen's *Emma* is neither autonomous nor representative.

789. Morey, Ann-Janine. "Lamentations for the Minister's Wife, by Herself." *WS* 19 (1991): 327–340.

Concerns the "documentary fictions" written by wives of Protestant ministers about the life of parsonage in the mid-nineteenth century.

790. Morton, Donald, and Mas'ud Zavarzadeh, eds. *Theory/Pedagogy/Politics: Texts for Change*. Baltimore, MD: University of Illinois Press, 1991. 264 pages

Seeks to effect change through attention to difference and its critique of verities, not only of the humanistic kind, but also of those of post-structuralism.

Essayists: Mas'ud Zavarzadeh, Donald Morton, Anthony Easthope, Chris Weedon, Juliet Flower MacCannell, Katherine Cummings, R. Radhakrishnan, Gregory L. Ulmer, Henry Giroux, Peter McLaren, Heather Murray, Evan Watkins, Adam Katz.

791. "Movies and History, Japanese Style." *QRD* 17 (July 1991): 11–12.

Cites Japanese editing of films as rewriting history; raises similar concerns over effect of Japanese ownership of Columbia Pictures and MCA.

792. Mwachofi, Ngure Wa. "Apprehending the Rhetorical Function of Politicizing Metaphors in Ngugi's *Petals of Blood*." *DAI* 51 (March 1991): 2925A.

Offers a critical analysis of Ngugi's political novel and establishes some of the groundwork for generic criticism of counter-discourse.

793. Otter, Samuel. "Melville's Anatomies: Rhetoric, Discourse, and Ideology in Antebellum America." *DAI* 51 (March 1991): 3075A.

Demonstrates Melville's interest in the rhetorical shaping of antebellum ideology about gender, race, and class through an analysis of four texts.

794. Payne, Paula H. "Tracing Aristotle's *Rhetoric* in Sir Philip Sidney's Poetry and Prose." *RSQ* 20 (Summer 1990): 241–250.

Argues that Sidney's acquaintance with and regard for Aristotle's *Rhetoric* are reflected in *Astrophil and Stella* and *The Defence of Poesy*.

795. Pearce, Frederick William. "An Analysis of Frank Capra's 'Why We Fight' Films (1942–1945) as Documentary Film Rhetoric." *DAI* 52 (August 1991): 323A–324A.

Examines Capra's work and concludes that documentary films are inherently rhetorical and persuasion-oriented.

796. Pearlman, Mickey, and Katherine Usher Henderson. *A Voice of One's Own*. Boston, MA: Houghton Mifflin, 1991. 224 pages

Presents conversational profiles of 28 writers who explain "what inspires, directs, infuriates, and sustains them."

797. Pennino, Dorothy E. "Engendering the Text: Self-Reliant Women in American Self-Help Literature (1848–1896)." *DAI* 52 (August 1991): 579A.

Attempts to restore women to the canon of nineteenth-century American self-help literature.

798. Pullman, George L. "Rhetoric and Literature." *FEN* 19 (Fall 1991): 19–21.

Argues that rhetoric belongs in the literature classroom because it can explain interpretation as systems of topoi.

799. Reid, Allan Patrick. "Literature as Communication and Cognition in Bakhtin and Lotman." *DAI* 51 (January 1991): 2401A.

Establishes a connection between the literary theories of the two authors; shows how their methodologies integrate literature with cultural reality.

800. Robinson, Douglas. "Henry James and Euphemism." *CE* 53 (April 1991): 403–427.

Argues that a euphemistic approach to ideology could allow people to choose a comfortable critical approach while remaining open to new approaches without defensiveness.

801. Saunders, David, and Ian Hunter. "Lessons from the 'Literatory': How to Historicize Authorship." *CritI* 17 (Spring 1991): 479–509.

Explores technological, economic, cultural, and legal forces that determined the concept of author. Focuses primarily on the eighteenth century.

802. Schindley, Wanda B. "A Rhetorical Analysis of Mark Twain's 'Letters from the Earth.'" *DAI* 52 (July 1991): 161A.

Presents a rhetorical analysis of Mark Twain's "Letters fom the Earth."

803. Scholes, Robert. "In the Brothel of Modernism: Picasso and Joyce." *The American Journal of Semiotics* 8 (1991): 5–25.

Discusses modernism as a literary and artistic movement that has a masculine structure embodied in "its images of the brothel."

804. Sewell, Marilyn J. "All That Is within Me, A Novel (Original Work), and, Contemporary Women's Spiritual Autobiography: A Search for Self, a Critical Essay." *DAI* 52 (October 1991): 1548A.

Presents a novel and accompanying essay that explore criteria for contemporary women's spiritual autobiography.

805. Shumway, David R., Walter Ulrich, Bryan C. Short, and Maureen Newlin. "Four Comments on 'Beyond Literary Darwinism' [*CE* 52 (September 1990)]." *CE* 53 (November 1991): 831–841.

Authors debate adversarial methods of criticism and advocate a system that best promotes intellectual goals; they argue that feminist voices should seek unifying approaches to literature.

806. Smith, Andrew Richard. "A Theory of Transcultural Rhetoric: 'Poiesis' and Mishima Yukio's Textuality." *DAI* 52 (September 1991): 739A.

Demonstrates how an understanding of poiesis "can help situate a critical analysis of transcultural rhetoric."

807. Spencer, Stacy Lee. "Women Writers and the Literary Journey, 1832–1844." *DAI* 52 (September 1991): 973A.

Explores how American and British women altered the generic expectations of travel literature.

808. Stadler, Harald Alfred. "Film as Experience: Phenomenology and the Study of Film Reception." *DAI* 52 (September 1991): 718A.

Argues that viewers of film and television "construct" meaning in much the same way as readers do.

809. Stewart, Veronica Jane. "Emily Dickinson and the Rhetoric of Conversion." *DAI* 51 (May 1991): 3747A.

Explores poetic applications of conversion rhetoric as it relates to the gender-differentiated development of the conversion narrative and the spiritual American autobiography.

810. Stone, John Fred. "A Burkean Analysis of Oliver Stone's *Salvador, Platoon, Wall Street*: Towards a Rhetoric of the Political Fiction Film." *DAI* 51 (March 1991): 2927A.

Demonstrates how these films "attempt to shape viewer perception of contemporary political issues" and concludes that the films are shaped by Stone's role as "cinematic rhetor."

811. Strine, Mary S. "Critical Theory and 'Organic' Intellectuals: Reframing the Work of Cultural Critique." *ComM* 58 (June 1991): 195–201.

Considers the relationship between critical theory and practice by using Antonio Gramsci's idea of the "organic intellectual."

812. Suleri, Sara. *The Rhetoric of English India*. Chicago, IL: University of Chicago Press, 1991. 232 pages

Challenges focus on otherness that marks current study of colonial discourse.

813. Travitsky, Betty S. "Reconstructing the Still, Small Voice: The Occasional Journal of Elizabeth Egerton." *WS* 19 (1991): 193–200.

Shows how the unpublished manuscripts of a seventeenth-century English countess raise the issue of multiple voices in autobiographical texts.

814. Troyan, Scott D. "Textual Decorum: A Rhetoric of Attitudes in Medieval Literature." *DAI* 52 (November 1991): 1742A.

Examines how a text's intratextual associations shape audience response.

815. Ward, Steven Craig. "Postmodernism as the Sociocultural Deconstruction of Modernity." *DAI* 52 (November 1991): 1918A.

Argues that postmodernism is a skeptical theoretical and cultural system that levels all ideational distinctions between belief and knowledge and truth and rhetoric.

816. Weinsheimer, Joel. *Philosophical Hermeneutics and Literary Theory*. New Haven, CT: Yale University Press, 1991. 192 pages

Discusses how the insights of Hans-Georg Gadamer alter our understanding of literary theory and interpretation.

817. Willinsky, John. *The Triumph of Literature/The Fate of Literacy: English in the Secondary School Curriculum*. Bloomington, IN: Indiana University Press, 1991. 240 pages

Examines the pedagogical influence of literary critics and theorists such as Arnold, Leavis, Rosenblatt, and Frye; finds the promise of democratic literacy unfulfilled in practice.

818. Wilson, Rob. "Producing American Selves: The Form of American Biography." *Boundary* 18 (Summer 1991): 104–129.

Illustrates and challenges the "rhetoric of consensus" in American biography and calls for the "reimagining of biography in inventive forms and pluralized modes."

819. Wischner, Claudia M. "The Storytelling Experience: How Selected Contemporary Storytellers Perceive Their Art." *DAI* 52 (September 1991): 743A.

Uses open-ended interviews and finds individual styles to result from the functions of verbal, visual, and kinesthetic images.

820. Yau, Ching-Mei Esther. "Filmic Discourse on Women in Chinese Cinema (1949–1965): Art, Ideology, and Social Relations." *DAI* 52 (July 1991): 4A.

Argues that women were used as rhetorical figures to support the socialist transformation of China.

See also 300

2.7 READING

821. Albrecht, Jason E., and Edward J. O'Brien. "Effects of Centrality on Retrieval of Text-Based Concepts." *JMemC* 17 (September 1991): 932–939.

Suggests that central concepts are recognized more quickly and responded to more accurately than peripheral concepts.

822. Beck, Isabel L., Margaret G. McKeown, Gale M. Sinatra, and Jane A. Loxterman. "Revising Social Studies Text from a Text-Processing Perspective: Evidence of Improved Comprehensibility." *RRQ* 26 (1991): 251–276.

Argues that the text-processing approach (encoding information and combining it with information in and outside the text) can create a more comprehensive text.

823. Carlson, Laura A., AnnJanette R. Alejano, and Thomas H. Carr. "The Level of Focal-Attention Hypothesis in Oral Reading: Influence of Strategies on the Context of Specificity of Lexical Repetition Effects." *JMemC* 17 (September 1991): 924–931.

Shows that the linguistic organization and the level of linguistic processing in the material read may be interdependent.

824. Daneman, Meredyth, and Murray Stainton. "Phonological Recoding in Silent Reading." *JMemC* 17 (July 1991): 618–632.

Discusses homophone confusion in proofreading tasks.

825. DeFord, Diane E., Carol Lyons, and Gay Su Pinnell, eds. *Bridges to Literacy: Learning from Reading Recovery*. Portsmouth, NH: Heinemann, 1991. 240 pages

Shows how one-on-one instruction techniques, developed by Marie Clay to help students with learning difficulties as part of the Reading Recovery program, can be used to help students in group settings. *Essayists:* M. D. Frieds, R. Estice, C. Dunkeld, M. M. Clay, K. G. Short, B. Peterson, K. E. Holland, D. P. Woolsey, C. S. Huck.

826. Firment, Michael Joseph. "Interpretation Components as a Measure of Learning for Proverb-Based Conceptual Categories." *DAI* 51 (May 1991): 5613B.

Finds a positive relationship between completeness of interpretation and later ability to recognize new instances.

827. Flynn, Elizabeth A. "Engendering the Teaching of Reading." *CollL* 18 (June 1991): 80–93.

Discusses feminist reader-response theory and "the implications of its position for the teaching of literature"; emphasizes the role of writing in this process.

828. Gambrell, Linda B., Patricia S. Koskinen, and Barbara A. Kapinus. "Retelling and the Reading Comprehension of Proficient and Less-Proficient Readers." *JEdR* 84 (July/August 1991): 356–362.

Argues that practice in retelling improves both the quantity and quality of propositions recalled by both groups.

829. Grossen, Bonnie. "The Fundamental Skills of Higher Order Thinking." *JLD* 24 (June/July 1991): 343–352.

Describes ways in which instruction in reasoning—analogical and logical—can be used as a strategy for learning critical reading and critical thinking.

830. Horning, Alice. "Readable Writing: The Role of Cohesion and Redundancy." *JAC* 11 (Winter 1991): 135–145.

Surveys relevant research on both reading and writing; defines key terms; concludes that increasing cohesive ties and redundancy make writing more readable.

831. Huckin, Thomas, and Linda Flower. "Reading for Points and Purpose." *JAC* 11 (Fall 1991): 347–362.

Explores the nature of the point-driven and purpose-driven understanding experienced by students who are reading de-contextualized material.

832. Hunter, Nancy, and Jacqueline Liederman. "Right Hemisphere Participation in Reading." *B&L* 41 (November 1991): 475–495.

Results suggest that skilled reading requires the controlled modulation of interhemispheric interaction.

833. Jou, Jerwen, and Richard Jackson Harris. "Processing Inflections: Dynamics in Sentence Comprehension." *JMemC* 17 (November 1991): 1082–1094.

Examines reading as a stimulus-driven process and suggests ways of altering inflection processing.

834. Karis, William, and Stephen Doheny-Farina. "Collaboration with Readers: Empower Them and Take the Consequences." *TC* 38 (November 1991): 513–519.

Studies the composition of two government pollution reports, each with different reader involvement, and each with unique problems.

835. Lee-Sammons, William H., and Paul Whitney. "Reading Perspectives and Memory for Text: An Individual Differences Analysis." *JMemC* 17 (November 1991): 1074–1081.

Examines encoding perspectives and their effects on memory for text.

836. Maloney, Wendy Hall. "Teaching a Question Schema to Improve College Students' Literal, Interpretive, and Evaluative Comprehension of Narrative Text." *DAI* 51 (January 1991): 2330A.

Finds that story-general questions and theme-centered texts can be taught to underprepared college students, thereby enhancing their reading comprehension and written responses.

837. McLain, K. Victoria Mayer, Betty E. Gridley, and David McIntosh. "Value of a Scale Used to Measure Metacognitive Reading Awareness." *JEdR* 85 (November/Decmeber 1991): 81–87.

Suggests that the Jacobs and Paris "Index of Reading Awareness" should be used cautiously as a measure of metacognitive reading.

838. Miholic, Vincent. "Metacognitive Abilities of College Developmental Reading, Freshman English Composition, and Eighth Grade Students: Effects of Passage Level and Error Type." *DAI* 52 (November 1991): 1699A.

Finds that metacognitive comments increase but comprehension declines when students read a more difficult passage.

839. Murray, Heather. "Close Reading, Closed Writing." *CE* 53 (February 1991): 195–207.

Argues that a close reading assignment is not achievable and is a contradiction in terms.

840. O'Brien, Edward J., and Jason E. Albrecht. "The Role of Contexts in Accessing Antecedents in Text." *JEPL* 17 (January 1991): 94–102.

Study illustrates that in antecedent search and retrieval readers either find the antecedent or generate a substitute if given the context.

841. Rauenbusch, Frances, and Carl Bereiter. "Making Reading More Difficult. A Degraded Text Microworld for Teaching Reading Comprehension Studies." *C&I* 8 (1991): 181–206.

Argues that meaning-based strategies improve the ability to decode degraded texts. Points out that such strategies can be transferred to normal texts as well.

842. Recchio, Thomas E. "A Bakhtinian Reading of Student Writing." *CCC* 42 (December 1991): 446–454.

Illustrates how student texts enact resistance to reading. Argues that resistances have to be recognized before they can be overcome.

843. Reutzel, D. Ray, and Paul M. Hollingsworth. "Investigating Topic-Related Attitude: Effect on Reading and Remembering Text." *JEdR* 84 (July/August 1991): 334–344.

Argues that experimentally created topic attitudes do not interfere with the immediate recall of text-based information.

844. Reutzel, D. Ray, and Paul M. Hollingsworth. "Reading Time in School: Effects on Fourth Graders' Performance on a Criterion-Referenced Comprehension Test." *JEdR* 84 (January/February 1991): 170–176.

Finds significant growth in reading comprehension for all three treatment groups: reading only, reading/skill instruction, and skill instruction only.

845. Rieben, Laurence, and Charles A. Perfetti, eds. *Learning to Read: Basic Research and Its Implications*. Hillsdale, NJ: Lawrence Erlbaum Associates, 1991. 240 pages

Essayists present conceptual and theoretical analyses of learning to read, research on the beginning processes of learning to read, and research on phonological abilities. Authors also discuss children who have problems in learning how to read.

Essayists: Isabelle Lieberman, Keith Stanovich, Philip Gough, Linnea Ehri, Brian Bryne, William Tnmer, Virginia Mann, Jesus Alegria, Rebecca Treiman.

846. Rogers, Theresa. "The Role of Personal Response in High School Students' Thematic Interpretations of Complex Short Stories." *EQ* 23 (1991): 51–61.

Examines the role of the reader's personal response in the formation of story themes. Results suggest that textual analysis and personal response are both involved in story interpretation.

847. Rogers, Trumbull. "Dyslexia: A Survivor's Story." *JLD* 24 (February 1991): 121–123.

The author recounts his personal and academic experience as a person with dyslexia.

848. Runyan, M. Kay. "The Effect of Extra Time on Reading Comprehension Scores for University Students with and without Learning Disabilities." *JLD* 24 (February 1991): 104–107.

Presents evidence that learning-disabled students cannot perform to their capacity under timed conditions but show significant improvement when given extra time.

849. Sadoski, Mark, Allan Paivio, and Ernest T. Goetz. "A Critique of Schema Theory in Reading and a Dual Coding Alternative." *RRQ* 26 (1991): 463–486.

Argues that dual coding explains cognition better than does schema theory.

850. Schwanenflugel, Paula J., and Calvin R. White. "The Influence of Paragraph Information on the Processing of Upcoming Words." *RRQ* 26 (1991): 160–177.

Results show that for college students both local and discourse-level context arise prior to word recognition.

851. Sessoms-Fennelly, Lois. "Effects of Composition Strategies upon the Response of College Students to a Short Story." *DAI* 51 (March 1991): 3029A.

Shows the effects of different types of composition strategies on the responses made by African-American college students. Analyzes the recall comprehension of the text and the use of primary traits in writing about the text.

852. Stanovich, Keith E. "Discrepancy Definitions of Reading Disability: Has Intelligence Led Us Astray." *RRQ* 26 (1991): 7–29.

Argues that basing defintions of dyslexia on IQ potential has been misleading. Instead, the field should use a relevant aptitude measure like listening comprehension.

853. Stoddard, Sally. *Text and Texture: Patterns of Cohesion.* Advances in Discourse Processes, edited by Roy Freedle, vol. 40. Norwood, CA: Ablex Publishing, 1991. 152 pages

Considers the relationship between cohesion and texture in written texts and investigates how they contribute to the derivation of meaning.

854. Stoker, Cheryl Lynn. "Toward Constraints for Beginning Reading Programs." *DAI* 51 (February 1991): 2626A.

Examines propositions of Paulo Freire and identifies implications for further research.

855. Topham, Ronald William. "Reading and Writing Relationships: Community College Readers' and Writers' Use of Working Systems." *DAI* 52 (November 1991): 1770A.

Finds that each of the six reasoning dimensions derived by Judith Langer (1986) are used in differing proportions in reading and in writing.

856. Vetcher, Johanna Hester. "The Utilization of *Writing to Read* and its Effects on the Reading and Writing Skills of Kindergarten and First-Grade Students." *DAI* 51 (February 1991): 2693A.

Finds significant difference in the scores of students participating in the *Writing to*

Read program over those receiving writing instruction in the regular classroom.

857. Webster, Cameron Dale. "Readability Formulas and Textuality: An Historical Perspective and Critique." *DAI* 51 (January 1991): 2369A.

Argues that readability formulas used in business and technical communications fail because they ignore intratextual factors of written discourse.

858. Withrow, Mark Houston. "Enhancing Students' Relationship with Language: Instructional Strategies for Teaching Reading and Writing." *DAI* 52 (October 1991): 1242A.

Finds that process-centered considerations of reading and writing interactions foster improvement in student attitudes toward reading and writing.

859. Wolf, Maryanne. "Naming Speed and Reading: The Contribution of the Cognitive Neurosciences." *RRQ* 26 (1991): 123–141.

Discusses findings from neuropyschological and reading research and analyzes differences between discrete-trial and continuous-naming formats as procedures for helping dyslexic readers.

860. Yoder, W. Barry. "The Effect of Mental Imagery as a Study Strategy on the Comprehension and Recall of College Readers." *DAI* 51 (February 1991): 2693A.

Studies high-risk and regular college students who were provided with instructional methology or teacher-modeled interaction. Finds that no significant improvement was achieved.

2.8 LINGUISTICS, GRAMMATICAL THEORY, AND SEMANTICS

861. Ahn, Hee-Don. "Light Verbs, VP-Movement and Clausal Architecture in Korean and English." *DAI* 52 (October 1991): 1236A.

Examines the principles underlying verbal projections in Korean and English.

862. Alder, Kenneth Ludwig. "Forging the New Order: French Mass Production and the Language of the Machine Age, 1763–1815." *DAI* 52 (December 1991): 2255A.

Argues that interchangeable parts manufacturing developed in intimate relation with the metric system.

863. Aldridge, Michelle. "How the Language Grows Up." *EnT* 7 (January 1991): 14–20.

Outlines the language development of preschool monolingual English-speaking children.

864. Allan, Keith, and Kate Burridge. *Euphemism and Dysphemism: Language Used as Shield and Weapon*. New York: Oxford University Press, 1991. 263 pages

Examines linguistic, social, and psychological aspects of the human tendency to use euphemistic and dysphemistic (offensive) language.

865. Andersen, Peter A. "When One Cannot Not Communicate: A Challenge to Motley's Traditional Communication Postulates." *ComS* 42 (Winter 1991): 309–325.

Contrasts sender and receiver perspectives.

866. Arias-Gonzalez, Pedro. "Linguistic and Cultural Crisis in Galicia, Spain." *DAI* 52 (December 1991): 2190A.

Describes the effects of Castilian dialect supremacy on the regional dialects of Spain.

867. Bahns, Jens. "What Did You Bought? Explaining a Typical Error in the Acquisition of English." *IRAL* 29 (August 1991): 213–228.

Studies second language acquisition of "do" support and its relevance for ESL/EFL teachers.

868. Bailey, Richard W. "Dialects of Canadian English." *EnT* 7 (July 1991): 20–25.

Reviews the many varieties of English in mainland Canada.

869. Bamberg, Michael, and Virginia Marchman. "Binding and Unfolding: Towards the

Linguistic Construction of Narrative Discourse." *DPr* 14 (July–September 1991): 277–305.

Argues that speakers structure narratives by differentiating events in a plot and by integrating events into an overall theme. Points out that English and German narrators show similar tendencies.

870. Banks, David. "Some Observations concerning Transitivity and Modality in Scientific Writing." *LangS* 13 (1991): 59–78.

Analyzes the frequency and linguistic effect of 252 modal verbs found in 11 academic articles published in *Oceonologica Acta*.

871. Bellwood, Peter. "The Austronesian Dispersal and the Origin of Languages." *ScAm* 265 (July 1991): 88–93.

Examines how migration of agrarian tribes in Southeast Asia spread a common-root language through the Pacific basin beginning approximately 4000 B.C.

872. Bernstein, Richard. "When Parentheses Are Transgressive." *QRD* 18 (October 1991): 10–11.

Applies Orwell's definition of jargon to literary critics' terminology. Concludes that not all words are jargon but that some are "seductive" and "cultish."

873. Black, William. "Briefingspeak." *QRD* 17 (July 1991): 8–9.

Satirizes military doublespeak by using imaginary dialogue between a general in the Persian Gulf War and George Orwell.

874. Borowsky, Ron, and Derek Besner. "Visual Word Reflection across Orthographies: On the Interaction between Context and Degradation." *JMemC* 17 (March 1991): 272–276.

Investigates the "orthographic-depth hypothesis" which focuses on the relationship between orthography and phonology.

875. Botan, Carl, and Geneva Smitherman. "Black English in the Integrated Workplace." *JBS* 22 (December 1991): 168–185.

Argues that "industrialized work settings" have created distinct speech communities for African-Americans and white Americans. Analyzes features of Black English that distinguish the two communities.

876. Bourdieu, Pierre. *Language and Symbolic Power*. Translated by Gino Raymond and Matthew Adamson. Cambridge, MA: Harvard University Press, 1991. 302 pages

Maintains that linguistic utterances or expressions can be understood as the product of the relation between a "linguistic market" and "linguistic habitus." Claims that every linguistic interaction bears the traces of the social structure that it expresses and helps to reproduce.

877. Bowden, Darsie Minor. "The Mythology of Voice." *DAI* 52 (December 1991): 2123A.

Provides a sociolinguistic reconceptualization of the metaphor of "voice" in writing. Argues that persona is a co-construction authored by the writer and the reader.

878. Capozuca, John Christopher. "Syntactic and Semantic Complexity, Emotional Adjustment, and the Thematic Apperception Test: Discourse Analysis of Adult Dyslexics." *DAI* 52 (September 1991): 1709B.

Argues that intervention with enriched language experiences facilitates semantic and emotional maturity.

879. Capps, Douglas. *Revisioning Vygotsky*. Boston, MA: CCCC, March 1991. ERIC ED 332 219. 17 pages

Recapitulates Vygotsky's views on the development of oral and written language.

880. Carrell, David. "Gender Scripts in Professional Writing Textbooks." *JBTC* 5 (October 1991): 463–468.

Provides an historical analysis of professional writing textbooks as they reflect and perpetuate sexual stereotypes.

881. Cavalli-Sforza, Luigi Luca. "Genes, Peoples, and Languages." *ScAm* 265 (November 1991): 104–110.

Describes theory tracing human evolution back to a single source, using both DNA patterns and worldwide linguistic similarities.

882. "CCTE Doublespeak and Plain English Awards." *QRD* 17 (July 1991): 5.

Announces *Revenue Canada* as winner of Doublespeak Award, cites runners-up, and announces winner of Canadian version of Orwell Award.

883. Chapman, Raymond. "A Versatile Suffix." *EnT* 7 (October 1991): 39–42.

Reviews the history and current uses of the suffix "ee."

884. Chen, Rong. "Verbal Irony as Conversational Implicature." *DAI* 51 (February 1991): 2728A.

Applies a revised version of Grice's theory to constructing a heuristic of irony production.

885. Cheshire, Jenny, ed. *English around the World: Sociolinguistic Perspectives.* New York: Cambridge University Press, 1991. 684 pages

Forty-four essays discuss the development of English as a world language and describe variations in the form and use of English in 11 geographical regions around the world. *Essayists:* Jenny Cheshire, Jeffrey L. Kallen, Sandra Clarke, Allan Bell, Richard A. Benton, David Bradley, Margaret S. Steffensen, Kamal K. Sridhar, Peter H. Lowenberg, Mohamed Abdulaziz, Maurice Chishimba, Eyamba G. Bokamba, John Victor Singler, Genevieve Escure, Peter Muhlhausler, John Harris, James Milroy, John H. Esling, Janet Holmes, Koenraad Kuiper, Edina Eisikovits, Farhat Khan, Mary W. J. Tay, John Platt, Musimbi Kanyoro, Rajend Mesthrie, Nicholas Faraclas, Donald Winford, John R. Rickford, Charlene J. Sato, Markku Filppula, J. K. Chambers, Howard B. Woods, Donn Bayard, Gregory R. Guy, Thiru Kandiah, Anju Sahgal, Andrew B. Gonzalez, Joseph J. Schmied, J. Keith Chick, Alice K. Siachitema, Munsali Jibril, Hubert Devonsih, Suzanne Romaine, Jeff Siegel.

886. Christophersen, Paul. "A Bilingual Denmark." *EnT* 7 (July 1991): 7–10.

Suggests that problems may occur when every citizen in a small country can speak English as well as the national language.

887. Chuk, Denise D. "The Semiotic Interaction of Image and Work in Theatre." *DAI* 51 (May 1991): 3562A.

Uses a semiotic framework to argue that sight and sound produce the written text as speech and action within a defined space.

888. Cintron, Ralph E. "The Use of Oral and Written Language in the Homes of Three Mexicano Families." *DAI* 51 (March 1991): 3055A.

Three families in Chicago provided the test subjects for documenting the link between oral and written comunication and various cultural traits.

889. Clevenger, Theodore, Jr. "Can One Not Communicate? A Conflict of Models." *ComS* 42 (Winter 1991): 340–353.

Suggests that a hybrid construct of communication behavior offers a possible bridge between the behavioral- and communication-process models.

890. Coupland, Nikolas, Justine Coupland, and Howard Giles. *Language, Society, and the Elderly: Discourse, Identity, and Aging.* Cambridge, MA: Basil Blackwell, 1991. 224 pages

Presents a sociolinguistic study of language and interaction in later life.

891. Crafton, Linda K. *Whole Language: Getting Started . . . Moving Forward.* Katonah, NY: Richard C. Owen Publishers, 1991. 270 pages

Describes the theory and philosophy of whole language, details whole language experiences with children, and demonstrates the basic strategies. Incorporates commentary and vignettes from six practicing whole language teachers.

892. Creekmur, Corey Knox. "The Discourse of Psychoanalytic Film Theory." *DAI* 52 (September 1991): 717A.

Dramatizes semiotic shifts in film theory through the practice of writing.

893. Datskovsky, Galina. "A Semantic Methodology for Building Natural Language Interfaces to Expert Systems." *DAI* 52 (August 1991): 928A.

Describes a new model for semantic interpretation, derived from linguistic treatments of verbs, which successfully interprets sentences within the discourse context.

894. de la Luz Reyes, Maria. "A Process Approach to Literacy Using Dialogue Journals and Literature Logs with Second Language Learners." *RTE* 25 (October 1991): 291–313.

Examines bilingual students' ability to construct meaning in writing; concludes that process approach to second language literacy is inneffective without appropriate cultural and linguistic adaptations.

895. Declerck, Renaat. *Tense in English: Its Structure and Use in Discourse*. New York: Routledge, 1991. 400 pages

Develops a descriptive theory of tense and applies it to the tenses of English.

896. Delahunty, Gerald P. "The Powerful Pleonasm: A Defense of Expletive 'It Is.' " *WC* 8 (April 1991): 213–239.

Rejecting handbook prescriptions, the study examines the actual uses of "it is" in discourse: extrapositives, clefts, and inferentials. Offers advice on the construction's appropriate use.

897. DeRidder, Mitchell Lee. "How the Comprehender Assigns a Meaning to an Ambiguous Word." *DAI* 52 (July 1991): 549B.

Supports a model in which the selector does not have to go through alternate meanings but determines a congruent meaning "subattentionally" before accessing it.

898. Deverson, Tony. "New Zealand English Lexis: The Maori Dimension." *EnT* 7 (April 1991): 18–25.

Discusses the increasing use of Maori loanwords in New Zealand English.

899. "Doublespeak Here and There" (April 1991):

Provides examples of doublespeak in business, education, foreign countries, government, and legal, medical, military, and miscellaneous categories.

"The Doublespeak of Arms Control," *see* 986

"The Doublespeak of Brown University," *see* 987

900. Doyle, Anne E. "Readers' and Writers' Genre Expectations in Letters of Recommendations: Two Case Studies." *DAI* 52 (July 1991): 209A.

Examines the relationship of genre to readers' and writers' interpretation of letters of recommendation.

901. Dunn, Michelle Arlene. "The Effects of Sentence Topic and Single Word Priming on Lexical Processing in Connected Speech." *DAI* 51 (May 1991): 5612B.

Supports the idea that both semantic (topic context) and single-word priming have an effect on lexical processing.

902. Dyson, Anne Haas. "Towards a Reconceptualization of Written Language Development." *L&E* 3 (1991): 139–161.

Critiques traditional views of children's written language development; argues that children's written development is linked with other communicative development in authentic dynamic social contexts.

903. Dyson, Anne Haas. "Viewpoints: The Word and the World—Reconceptualizing Written Language Development or Do Rainbows Mean a Lot to Little Girls?" *RTE* 25 (February 1991): 2.8.

Discusses written language development as a symbolic option, not just an extension of oral language; describes its characteristics and possible sociopolitical and pedagogical implications.

904. Ferrara, Kathleen, Hans Brunner, and Greg Whittemore. "Interactive Written Discourse as an Emergent Register." *WC* 8 (January 1991): 8–34.

Analyzes the syntactic and stylistic features of what the authors term "Interactive Written Discourse," which is a register used for computer-mediated communication.

905. Finlay, Linda Shaw, and Nathaniel Smith. "Literacy and Literature: Making or Consuming Culture?" *CollL* 18 (June 1991): 53–68.

Connects Paulo Freire's work to recent developments in epistemological and sociolinguistic pedagogical theory; argues for educational reform that uses Freire's concept of literacy; relates his work to the teaching of literature.

906. Fischer, Ute. "How Students Learn Words from a Dictionary and in Context." *DAI* 52 (August 1991): 1099B.

Argues that definitions are insufficient for understanding new words; shows that contexts are critical, and novel words are learned by analogy to familiar words.

907. Fishman, Joshua. *Reversing Language Shift: Theoretical and Empirical Foundations of Assistance to Threatened Languages*. Bristol, PA: Multilingual Matters, 1991. 431 pages

Discusses the theory and practice of assisting speech communities whose native languages are threatened because fewer and fewer people in each generation use the language. Explains why most efforts to reverse language shifts are unsuccessful; seeks a rational, systematic approach to the problem.

908. Folly, Dennis Wilson. "The Poetry of African-American Proverb Usage: A Speech Act Analysis." *DAI* 52 (December 1991): 2239A.

Analyzes the form, aesthetics, and functions of proverbs in the speech acts of African-Americans.

909. Forrester, Michael A. "A Conceptual Framework for Investigating Learning in Conversations." *CompEd* 17 (1991): 61–72.

Argues for an "eco-structural" model; considers implications for designing software.

910. Goldinger, Stephen D., David B. Pisoni, and John S. Logan. "On the Nature of Talker Variability Effects on Recall of Spoken Word Lists." *JEPL* 17 (January 1991): 152–162.

Study supports the proposal that a subject's ability to recall spoken word lists varies according to the number of speakers.

911. Goodlett, Norma Claire. "An Analysis of the Influence of Verbal and Nonverbal Communication on the Perceptions of African-American and English-Speaking African-Caribbean Students at Selected Universities." *DAI* 52 (December 1991): 1941A.

Concludes that the communication between African-American and African-Caribbean students needs improvement; suggests that it is the responsibility of universities to promote a better relationship between the two groups.

912. Greenberg, Seth N., and Asher Koriat. "The Missing-Letter Effect for Common Function Words Depends on Their Linguistic Function in the Phrase." *JMemC* 17 (November 1991): 1051–1061.

Explores how letter detection in function words varies according to the linguistic role in a context.

913. Grisham, Therese. "Linguistics as an Indiscipline: Deleuze and Guattari's Pragmatics." *SubStance* 20 (November 1991): 36–54.

Argues that Deleuze and Guattari de-territorialize the domain of twentieth-century linguistics by putting linguistic texts to work in the service of politics.

914. "Guidelines for Doublespeak and Orwell Awards." *QRD* 17 (July 1991): 2–3.

Encourages nominations and provides guidelines for both Doublespeak and Orwell Awards.

915. Gyasi, Ibrahim K. "Aspects of English in Ghana." *EnT* 7 (April 1991): 26–31.

Considers the question of whether there exists a distinctive Ghanian English; speculates on the future of English in Ghana.

916. Halliday, M. A. K. *Linguistic Perspectives on Literacy: A Systematic-Functional Approach*. Geelong, Australia: Inaugural Australian Systematics Network Conference on "Literacy in Social Processes," January 1991. ERIC ED 329 135. 36 pages

Examines literacy from a systematic-linguistic viewpoint and concludes that the term "articulacy"—making meaning by using texts in context—is more descriptive than "literacy."

917. Harbaugh, Frederick W. "Accentuate the Positive." *TC* 38 (February 1991): 73–74.

Points out that statements expressed in the positive are more easily understood than those expressed in the negative.

918. Harper, Mary Patricia. "The Representation of Noun Phrases in Logical Form." *DAI* 51 (February 1991): 3936B.

Argues that pronouns, singular definite noun phrases, and singular indefinite noun phrases can be represented in logical form; tests the model with a variety of examples.

919. Harris, Randy. "The Life and Death of Generative Semantics." *DAI* 52 (August 1991): 525A.

Examines the rhetoric of persuasion in articles that generated a schism between Chomsky and other linguists after the publication of *Aspects of the Theory of Syntax*.

920. Hasselriis, Peter. "From Pearl Harbor to Watergate to Kuwait: *Language in Thought and Action*." *EJ* 80 (February 1991): 28–35.

Commemorates the 50th anniversary of *Language in Thought and Action*; describes the continuing influence of S. I. Hayakawa and general semantics on English education.

921. Hausman, Carl R. "Language and Metaphysics: The Ontology of Metaphor." *P&R* 24 (1991): 25–42.

Proposes an ontological picture based on the premise that metaphorical language produces "something new" through the interactions of meaning.

922. Hoffman, Barbara G. "The Power of Speech: Language and Social Status among Monde Griots and Nobles." *DAI* 52 (August 1991): 587A.

Presents an ethnography of communication in a West African society that investigates how people speak in ways that mark their classes.

922. Hughes, Geoffrey. *Swearing: A Social History of Foul Language, Oaths, and Profanity in English*. The Language Library. Cambridge, MA: Basil Blackwell, 1991. 283 pages

Provides a historical study of swearing from Anglo-Saxon times to the present. Finds that attitudes toward swearing oscillate between acceptance and repression. Argues that the focus of swearing has shifted "from the domains of gods and heroes, and is now largely indiscriminate, with sacred, profane, sexual, political and racist modes coexisting."

924. "Hugh Rank 'Retires' as Critic of Doublespeak." *QRD* 17 (July 1991): 9.

Satiric announcement of Rank's change from critic of advertising to promoter of "Ubiquitous Commercialism"; outlines his plans for "Rent-a-Rhetorician" network.

925. Jakobson, Roman. *On Language*. Edited by Linda R. Waugh and Monique Monville-Burston. Cambridge, MA: Harvard University Press, 1990. 640 pages

Presents a broad profile of Jakobson who suggested radical innovations in every area of linguistic theory. Overview of his work in linguistics taken from partial and complete works, arranged, introduced, and cross-referenced by Waugh and Monville-Burston.

926. Kaye, Alan S. "Is English Diglossic?" *EnT* 7 (October 1991): 8–14.

Proposes that the use of "who" and "whom" and other variants point to two distinct registers in the language.

927. "Keeping Up with PC Language." *QRD* 18 (October 1991): 9.

Lists 23 sources as sample and starting point through the "linguistic thicket" of "nonsense" about PC.

928. Kess, Joseph F. "On the Developing History of Psycholinguistics" *LangS* 13 (1991): 1–20.

Traces the formative, linguistic, and cognitive periods in modern psycholinguistics. States that psycholinguistics is now subsumed by the field of cognitive science.

929. Klopf, Donald W. "Japanese Communication Practices: Recent Comparative Research." *ComQ* 39 (Spring 1991): 130–143.

Characterizes the typical Japanese communicator by collocating seven studies that cover such aspects as argumentativeness, immediacy, verbal predispositions, and verbal aggressiveness.

930. Konishi, Toshiko. "Language and Thought: A Cross-Cultural Study on the Connotations of Gender." *DAI* 52 (September 1991): 1756B.

Using German and Spanish, where nouns often have opposite genders, the study shows that for native speakers neutral nouns carry connotations of femininity and masculinity.

931. Koriat, Asher, and Seth N. Greenberg. "Syntactic Control of Letter Detection: Evidence from English and Hebrew Nonwords." *JMemC* 17 (November 1991): 1035–1050.

Points out the function of morphemes in the initial definition of the structural frame of a phrase until meaning is uncovered.

932. Kwachka, Patricia. "The Effect of Language Shift on the Acquisition of Orientational Systems, Choctaw and English." *L&E* 3 (1991): 169–185.

Examines locatives and possessives in an exploration of Choctaw children's bilingual abilities; raises various socioeconomic issues pertaining to the retention of Choctaw.

933. Leahey, Margaret J. " 'To Hear with My Eyes': The Native Language Acquisition Project in the 'Jesuit Relations.' " *DAI* 51 (June 1991): 4246A.

Suggests a way in which the native language acquisition experiences of the Jesuit missionary linguists may be of value in validating modern ESL acquisition theory and practice.

934. Lennon, Paul. "Error and the Very Advanced Learner." *IRAL* 29 (February 1991): 31–44.

Points out the main problems with lexis and prepositions. Argues that one error frequency sample is not a reliable determinant of proficiency.

935. Levin, Harry, and Margaretta Novak. "Frequencies of Latinate and Germanic Words in English as Determinates of Formality." *DPr* 14 (July–September 1991): 389–398.

Listeners judged Latinate words to be more formal than Germanic ones in an experiment that controlled word frequency.

936. Lu, Min-Zhan. "Redefining the Legacy of Mina Shaughnessy: A Critique of the Politics of Linguistic Innocence." *JBW* 10 (Spring 1991): 26–40.

Critiques dominant assumption "that the essence of meaning precedes and is independent of language"; argues for a "fuller recognition of the social dimensions of students' linguistic decisions."

937. Lucas, Michael A. "Systematic Grammatical Simplification." *IRAL* 29 (August 1991): 241–248.

Proposes simplification of literary texts for language learners based on the basic grammatical structures of the original text.

938. Lutz, William. "The First Casualty" *QRD* 17 (July 1991): 1–2.

Argues that language is first casualty of war and cites examples from the Gulf War to demonstrate how it distorts and blunts reality.

939. Lutz, William. "A Gulf War Reading List" *QRD* 17 (July 1991): 3–4.

Lists 26 sources that offer views which "go beyond the superficial, sometimes irrelevant, and often censored coverage" of mass media.

940. Mahler, Karen. "Masculine Versus Neutral Pronoun Usage: Effects on Self-Esteem in Adolescents." *DAI* 51 (February 1991): 4059B.

Finds no direct effect of this linguistic feature; suggests that a "more naturalistic examination of sexism in language would be useful."

941. McArthur, Tom. "The Pedigree of Plain English." *EnT* 7 (July 1991): 13–19.

Outlines the tradition of plain English usage.

942. McCutchen, Deborah, Laura C. Bell, Ilene M. France, and Charles A. Perfetti. "Phoneme-Specific Interference in Reading: The Tongue-Twister Effect Reversed." *RRQ* 26 (1991): 87–103.

Study of undergraduate college students shows that the tongue twister effect results from phoneme rather than visual confusion.

943. McTague, Mark J. "A Sociolinguistic Description of Attitudes to and Usage of English by Adult Korean Employees of Major Corporations in Seoul." *DAI* 52 (July 1991): 153A.

Discusses spread of English among 700 Korean white collar workers.

944. Merrell, Floyd. *Signs Becoming Signs: Our Perfusive, Pervasive Universe*. Bloomington, IN: Indiana University Press, 1991. 264 pages

Discusses implications of semiotic theory that signs are not "re-presentations" of pre-existing realities but "pre-sentations" of a constructed world.

945. Mohanan, Tara Warrier. "Arguments in Hindi." *DAI* 51 (February 1991): 2730A.

Analyzes the case of grammatical subjects. Argues that the information contained in the lexical entry of a predicate is distributed over four levels of structure.

946. Morenberg, Max. *Doing Grammar*. New York: Oxford University Press, 1991. 192 pages

Offers an approach to grammar that actively involves students in the process and builds on their knowledge of language. Provides a comprehensive overview of grammatical analysis; uses "real world" sentences from recent books, magazines, and newspapers.

947. Morris, Robin Kay. "The Effect of Prior Semantic Context on Lexical Access during Reading: An Analysis of Fixation Time." *DAI* 51 (May 1991): 5616B.

Points out that a congruent sentence context is more important than syntactical relations in making the target word easier to process.

948. Moxey, Linda Mae. "A Psychological Investigation of the Use and Interpretation of English Quantifiers." *DAI* 52 (August 1991): 1042B.

Examines problems of proportion and emphasis as quantifiers are used to describe simple situations; finds that quantifiers can affect the focus of succeeding discourse.

949. Murnane, Kevin, and Richard Shiffrin. "Word Repetitions in Sentence Recognition." *M&C* 19 (1991): 119–130.

Points out that a positive list-strength occurs when words are repeated in the context of different sentences (while holding constant the total number of words per list).

"The Newt Gingrich Guide to Politically Correct Language," *see* 988

950. Ney, James W. "Collaborative Learning in University Grammar Courses." *Innovative Higher Education* 15 (Spring/Summer 1991): 153–165.

Reports on student attitudes in classes where a collaborative learning model was used to teach modern English grammar using peer teaching and student-centered activities.

951. Nielson, H. Richard, Jr. "Articulating Protest: The Personal and Political Rhetorics of Clifford Odets and Mari Sandoz in the 1930s." *DAI* 52 (November 1991): 1735A.

Uses theories of social aspects of language acts by Burke and Freire to examine each author's rhetorical practices.

952. Noda, Mari. "The Extended Predicate and Confrontational Discourse in Japanese." *DAI* 51 (March 1991): 3060A.

Examines the role of the extended predicate construction in confrontation avoidance by sampling discourse from varied social interactions.

953. Noguchi, Rei R. *Grammar and the Teaching of Writing: Limits and Possibilities*. Urbana, IL: NCTE, 1991. 127 pages

Examines ways in which grammar instruction can either frustrate or support writing instruction; describes and advocates teaching a "writer's grammar" that would transfer students' learning of grammar to specific, common problems that occur in their own writing, rather than asking students to learn grammar as a separate system in itself.

954. Oaks, Dallin Dixon. "Enablers of Grammatic Ambiguity." *DAI* 52 (July 1991): 147A.

Identifies sets of enablers and discusses their relationships with grammatical ambiguity.

955. Olawsky, Duane Evan. "The Syntactic and Semantic Processing of English Comparatives." *DAI* 51 (February 1991): 3942B.

Examines the syntactic and semantic makeup of comparative expressions, noting their inherent ambiguity; offers a grammatical theory that describes these expressions.

956. Oliensis, Ellen S. "The Construction of Horatian Decorum." *DAI* 52 (November 1991): 1737A.

Argues that decorum always enforces subordination, even during disruptive moments that threaten to collapse its dominion.

957. Olsson, Gunnar. *Lines of Power, Limits of Language*. Minneapolis, MN: University of Minnesota Press, 1991. 229 pages

Proposes a new socio-theoretical language that transcends the disciplinary boundaries of sociology, geography, political sciences, philosophy, literature, and cultural theory.

958. "On Definitions; and Who Writes Them." *QRD* 18 (October 1991): 7.

Analyzes President Bush's redefinition of wetlands as example of doublespeak.

959. Pandharipande, Rajeshwari. "The Perfected Language." *EnT* 7 (April 1991): 7–10.

Discusses the history and nature of Sanskrit and its complex relationship with English in present-day India.

960. Parakrama, Arjujna. "De-Hegemonizing Language Standards: Learning from (Post) Colonial Englishes about 'English.'" *DAI* 52 (August 1991): 523A.

Argues that the written/spoken discourse of nonstandard English in Sri Lanka threatens to expand linguistic tolerance.

961. Patinkin, Mark. "Making a Bad Situation Look Good." *QRD* 17 (January 1991): 11–12.

Gives hypothetical humorous examples of doublespeak in business.

962. Pederson, Lee. *Linguistic Atlas of the Gulf States, Volume 5: Regional Pattern*. Linguistic Atlas of the Gulf States. Athens, GA: The University of Georgia Press, 1991. 456 pages

Studies speech variations in an eight-state region in the southern United States. Encompasses 5000 hours of taped interviews with 1100 individuals in urban and rural areas. Shows patterns of dialect by mapping the incidence of linguistic features such as word usage, grammatical forms, and pronunciation.

963. Pelligrini, A. D., Lee Galda, Janna Dresden, and Susan Cox. "A Longitudinal Study of the Predictive Relations among Symbolic Play, Linguistic Verbs, and Early Literacy." *RTE* 25 (May 1991): 219–235.

Finds that the ability of three-and-a-half-year olds to play symbolically correlates strongly to their awareness of print and its "rules" at age four-and-a-half.

964. Porter, Kent. "Usage of the Passive Voice." *TC* 38 (February 1991): 87–88.

Explores the deficiencies and various ways of expressing the passive voice.

965. *Proceedings of the Ninth West Coast Conference on Formal Linguistics*. Edited by Aaron Halpern. Center for the Study of Language and Information. Chicago, IL: University of Chicago Press, 1991. 520 pages

Presents papers from the 1990 conference on formal linguistics.

966. "Project Censored." *QRD* 17 (April 1991): 10–11.

States history and purpose of *Project Censored*; announces the top five "censored" stories of 1990.

967. Pullum, Geoffrey K. *The Great Eskimo Vocabulary Hoax and Other Irreverent Essays on the Study of Language*. Chicago, IL: University of Chicago Press, 1991. 200 pages

Examines odd questions about language and looks at people who study language. Draws information from columns by the author published in *Natural Language and Linguistic Theory*.

968. *QRD* 17 (January 1991): 1–6.

Announces 1989 Orwell and Doublespeak Awards together with nominations for each category; provides the text of William Lutz's speech announcing the awards.

969. Rahman, Tariz. "The Use of Words in Pakistani English." *EnT* 7 (April 1991): 32–38.

Discusses vocabulary in four subvarieties of Pakistani English.

970. Rank, Hugh. "Analyzing War Propaganda." *QRD* 17 (January 1991): 10.

Presents "intensifying" and "downplaying" as major concepts for identifying and analyzing predictable patterns of language.

971. Reinthaler, Bee. "Verbal Communications." *PC* 11 (Fall 1991): 15, 17.

Identifies gender-based stylistic differences in verbal and nonverbal communication.

972. "Resources." *QRD* 17 (July 1991): 3.

Lists 18 books for research on doublespeak.

973. Ross, Philip E. "Trends in Linguistics: Hard Words." *ScAm* 264 (April 1991): 138–147.

Examines current debate among linguists concerning the possible monogenesis of language from which all other languages evolve.

974. Roy, Alice M. "Four Studies of Linguistics and Composition." *CE* 53 (September 1991): 580–586.

Reviews books dealing with some intersections of these two fields and discusses their relative usefulness for teachers.

975. Rundquist, Suellen Mae. "Flouting Grice's Maxims: A Study of Gender-Differentiated Speech." *DAI* 52 (July 1991): 153A.

Empirical study suggests that, in family conversation, men speak more indirectly than women.

976. Sawadogo, Geremie. "A Policy Analysis of the Language of Reform in Burkina Faso from 1979 to 1984." *DAI* 51 (June 1991): 4244A.

Provides an analysis of the factors in the policy process, including policy environment, policy formulation and adoption, and policy implementation.

977. Schiffman, Byron C. "Early New High German Technical Writings of Albrecht Durer: Focus on Translation and Linear Syntax." *DAI* 51 (March 1991): 3059A.

A comparison of linear-syntax conventions in Durer with those of High German reveals that Durer's idioms adhere to the norm.

978. Sebeok, Thomas A. *Semiotics in the United States*. Bloomington, IN: Indiana University Press, 1991. 84 pages

Presents a brief history of the development and influence of semiotics in the United States; suggests applications of the theory in a variety of fields.

979. Sebeok, Thomas A. *A Sign Is Just a Sign*. Bloomington, IN: Indiana University Press, 1991. 190 pages

Presents a collection of previously published essays in semiotics.

980. Seitz, James. "Roland Barthes, Reading, and Roleplay: Composition's Misguided Rejection of Fragmentary Texts." *CE* 53 (November 1991): 815–825.

Argues that the possibilities of the fragment have to be explored in addition to the "complete" text in order to provide students with the full range of rhetorical effects.

981. Shapiro, Lewis, P., Bari Brookins, Betsy Gordon, and Nicholas Nagel. "Verb Effects during Sentence Processing." *JMemC* 17 (September 1991): 983–996.

Explores thematic representations of verbs and their contributions to sentence processing.

982. Siple, Patricia, and Susan D. Fischer, eds. *Theoretical Issues in Sign Language Research. Volume 2: Psychology*. Chicago, IL: University of Chicago Press, 1991. 376 pages

Studies acquisition and processing of sign language, bimodal input, and use of sign language with atypical groups. Addresses issues related to universality of language processes, language plasticity, contributions of biology, and input to language acquisition and use.

Essayists: James J. DeCaro, Patricia Siple, Susan D. Fischer, Judy Snitzer Reilly, Marina L. McIntire, Ursula Bellugi, C. Tane Akamatsu, Carolyn Mylander, Susan Goldin-Meadow, James Paul Gee, Judith L. Mounty, Samuel J. Supalla, M. Virginia Swisher, Dale Evan Metz, Paula M. Brown, Frank Caccamise, Rhonda Wodlinger-Cohen, Madeline Maxwell, Mark E. Bernstein, Kimberly Matthews Mear, Carol A. Padden, Rachel I. Mayberry, Gloria S. Waters, Adele Abrahamsen, Maureen Lamb, Jacqueline Brown-Williams, Susan McCarthy, John D. Bonvillian, Deborah Webb Blackburn.

983. Skoll, Geoffrey R. "Walk the Walk and Talk the Talk: An Ethnography of a Drug Abuse Treatment Facility." *DAI* 51 (January 1991): 2439A.

Semiotic analysis of discourse demonstrates that staff members retain hegemonic control of residents by repressing and interrupting oppositional discourse.

984. Smith, Brian D. "English in Indonesia." *EnT* 7 (April 1991): 39–43.

Discusses the history of English in Indonesia and explains why a knowledge of English will remain essential for national development.

985. Steele, Meili. "Lyotard's Politics of the Sentence." *CCrit* (Fall 1990): 193–214.

Discusses the philosophy of Jean-Francois Lyotard: explains how types of sentences can silence or oppress and how power operates within sentences.

986. "The Doublespeak of Arms Control." *QRD* 18 (October 1991): 8–9.

Cites government's position on arms control for the Middle East as example of doublespeak.

987. "The Doublespeak of Brown University." *QRD* 18 (October 1991): 8.

Argues that Brown's expulsion of a student on the basis of redefining speech as action constitutes doublespeak.

988. "The Newt Gingrich Guide to Politically Correct Language." *QRD* 18 (October 1991): 7–8.

Argues that booklet designed for Republican candidates lists words designed to "eliminate" thought and promote "orthodoxy," which is an example of Orwell's "duckspeak."

989. Tilevitz, Orrin. "The Three Bears." *QRD* 17 (April 1991): 11.

Parody of tale as retold according to Internal Revenue Code of 1986.

990. Trauth, Gregory P. "German and English Academic Genres: A Contrastive Study of Astronomical Sublanguage and Discourse." *DAI* 51 (March 1991): 3060A.

Presents a cross-linguistic, cross-textual analysis of six texts from three scientific academic genres that correlates syntactic features with sociolinguistic factors.

991. Tubbs, Gail Lewis. "A Case for Teaching Grammar to Writers." *WLN* 15 (March 1991): 1–3.

Argues that a knowledge of grammar enables writers to take apart and reassemble sentences into clear, more precise prose.

992. Tyhurst, James J. "Logical Forms for English Sentences." *DAI* 51 (January 1991): 2368A.

Maps the continuum from surface syntactic forms to logical forms to truth values with the help of the Government and Binding (GB) theory.

993. VanDe Kopple, William J. "Themes, Thematic Progressions, and Some Implications for Understanding Discourse." *WC* 8 (July 1991): 311–347.

Supports Halliday's analysis of three kinds of theme/rheme relationships. Enumerates uses of Halliday's system of analysis in teaching composition.

994. Walker, Jeffrey. "Jeffrey Walker Responds [to Stowell, *CE* 53 (February 1991)]." *CE* 53 (February 1991): 231–233.

Argues that Stowell's criticism only strengthens Walker's argument about neurolinguistics and rhetoric.

995. Watabe, Masakazu, Cheryl Brown, and Yamiko Ueta. "Transfer of Discourse Function: Passives in the Writings of ESL and JSL." *IRAL* 29 (May 1991): 113–134.

Contrastive analysis shows interplay and transfer between form and function of passives in the native language and the target language.

996. Watanabe, Suwako. "Framing in American and Japanese Group Discussions." *DAI* 52 (December 1991): 2130A.

Shows that interaction in group discussion may be based on individualism or collectivism and other sociocultural values.

997. Whitworth, Richard. "A Book for All Occasions: Activities for Teaching General Semantics." *EJ* 80 (February 1991): 50–54.

Details class activities based on S. I. Hayakawa's *Language in Thought and Action*; promotes "student involvement and student creation" by using language effectively.

998. Wilkins, Harriet. "Computer Talk: Long-Distance Conversations by Computer." *WC* 8 (January 1991): 56–78.

Analyzes the linguistics and discourse features of the computer discourse of 33 participants on Presbynet, an electronic conference system.

999. Winkelmann, Carol L. "Social Acts and Social Systems: Community as Metaphor." *L&E* 3 (1991): 1–29.

Using linguistic analysis to examine the metaphor of community as used in composition studies, this study proposes that the more dynamic metaphor "collectivity" replace "community."

1000. Young, Lynne. *Language as Behavior, Language as Code: A Study of Academic English*. Philadelphia, PA: John Benjamins, 1990. 304 pages

Explores situational factors that affect codal choices in academic English. Bases study on introductory texts and lectures in economics, engineering, and sociology.

1001. Young, Thomas E. "The Subjunctive and You: What College Professors Think." *EJ* 80 (December 1991): 38–42.

Concludes from a survey completed by 205 professors that "individual teachers have individual preferences" regarding the subjunctive.

1002. Zughoul, Muhammad Raji. "Lexical Choice: Towards Writing Problematic Word Lists." *IRAL* 29 (February 1991): 45–60.

A study of 691 lexically deviant sentences written by Jordanian English students shows greatest difficulty with assumed synonymity.

See also 1187

2.9 PSYCHOLOGY

1003. Applegate, James L., and Ed Woods. "Construct System Development and Attention to Face Wants in Persuasive Situations." *SCJ* 56 (Spring 1991): 194–204.

Authors assess the impact of individual differences on identity management.

1004. Asciutto, Cathy Lynne. "The Effects of Subliminal Stimulation on the Interpretation of Ambiguous Sentences and Figures." *DAI* 52 (July 1991): 548B.

Argues that suggestibility may affect susceptibility to subliminal cues; shows that by themselves, subliminal cues do not bias interpretation, but with preceding supraliminal cues, they do.

1005. Baesler, Erland James. "Message Processing of Evidence and Long-Term Retention and Judgment of Beliefs." *DAI* 52 (September 1991): 737A.

Studies the characteristics of evidence that influence beliefs about juvenile delinquency across several time periods; includes recommendations for further research.

1006. Barrett, Harold. *Rhetoric and Civility: Human Development, Narcissism, and the Good Audience*. Albany, NY: State University of New York Press, 1991. 202 pages

Draws connections between narcissistic behavior and forms of McCarthyism, cult leader Jim Jones, Roman orator Tiberius Gracchus, and Paul Morel in *Sons and Lovers*.

1007. Beatty, Michael J., and Ralph R. Behnke. "Effects of Public Speaking Trait Anxiety and Intensity of Speaking Task on Heart Rate during Performance." *HCR* 18 (December 1991): 147–176.

Argues that whereas heart rates of anxious speakers were significantly higher than those of nonanxious speakers in low-intensity conditions, heart rates were the same in high-intensity environments.

1008. Beeman, Mark. "Coherence Inferencing and Structure Building in the Cerebral Hemispheres." *DAI* 51 (May 1991): 5610B.

Finds the right hemisphere essential for drawing coherence inferences but suggests that both hemispheres are necessary to draw inferences and build appropriate mental structures for discourse.

1009. Benoit, William L. "Two Tests of the Mechanism of Inoculation Theory." *SCJ* 56 (Spring 1991): 219–229.

Tests the hypothesized mechanism of resistance to persuasion.

1010. Boxer, Susan Eve. "A Private Space: An Object Relations Analysis of Keeping a Diary." *DAI* 52 (July 1991): 503B.

Points out that adult diarists create "an observation platform, separated from both external and internal worlds"; argues that whether subjective or objective, the diary seems to have a unitary function.

1011. Braithwaite, Dawn O. " 'Just How Much Did That Wheelchair Cost?': Management of Privacy Boundaries by Persons with Disabilities." *WJSC* 55 (Summer 1991): 254–274.

Reveals communication strategies disabled persons use to manage disclosure.

1012. Brand, Alice. "Social Cognition, Emotions, and the Psychology of Writing." *JAC* 11 (Fall 1991): 395–407.

Argues that writing ability, training, and social imperatives do not present a complete psychology of writing. Points out that they have to be explored for their descriptive, explanatory, and predictive powers.

1013. Brand, Alice, and Dick Graves. "Notes from beyond the Cognitive Domain." ERIC/RCS. March 1991. ERIC ED 332 221. 43 pages

Summarizes ideas growing out of the think tank at the 1991 CCCC on noncognitive sources of writing.

1014. Brennan, Susan Elise. "Seeking and Providing Evidence for Mutual Understanding." *DAI* 51 (May 1991): 5611B.

Views conversation as collaborative hypothesis-testing, that is, an exchange of utterance with evidence that results in mutual understanding as well as autonomous interpretations.

1015. Brett, Daniel J, and James Price Dillard. "Persuasion and the Internality Dimension of Cognitive Responses." *ComS* 42 (Summer 1991): 103–113.

Findings indicate that externally originated thoughts are more potent determinants of attitude change than internally originated thoughts.

1016. Brown, Sam C., Jerry N. Conover, Luis M. Flores, and Karen M. Goodman. "Clustering and Recall: Do High Clusterers Recall More Than Low Clusterers Because of Clustering?" *JMemC* 17 (July 1991): 710–721.

Concludes that clustering is a variable that does not facilitate recall within the parameters of subject ability.

1017. Cantor, Judy, Randall W. Engle, and George Hamilton. "Short-Term Memory, Working Memory, and Verbal Abilities: How Do They Relate?" *Intelligence* 15 (April–June 1991): 229–246.

Argues that although some correlation between systems exists, STM and WM "measure different memory mechanisms" and that both are "important to individual differences."

1018. Carpenter, Marlene. *The Link between Language and Consciousness: A Practical Philosophy*. Lanham, MD: University Press of America, 1991. 120 pages

Analyzes cursing as a manifestation of negative thinking and examines the relationship between the use of language and states of mind.

1019. Christensen, Mark Robert. "Interpersonal Cognitive Complexity and Abstractness, Degree of Self-Disclosure, and Solidarity with Addressee as Factors in the Quality of College Students' Autobiographical Writing." *DAI* 51 (May 1991): 3653A.

Explores differences in individual sociocognitive complexity to differences in writing ability.

1020. Cleary, Linda Miller. "Affect and Cognition in the Writing Process of Eleventh Graders: A Study of Concentration and Motivation." *WC* 8 (October 1991): 473–508.

Using phenomenological interviews with 40 students, the study examines ways in which emotion can disrupt concentration on writing and lower motivation to complete writing tasks.

1021. Collis, Glyn M. "Classes of Dialogue Theory for the Learning Process: A Commentary." *CompEd* 17 (1991): 25–27.

Argues that while the study of the level of representation and problems is necessary, meta-knowlege (beliefs about knowledge) must be considered.

1022. Cosgrove, Cornelius. "Unmasking Psycho/Biological Labels for Language Acts." *ELQ* 13 (May 1991): 2–5.

Points out the dangers inherent in accepting neurological, biological, and behavioral explanations for how language is acquired and used.

1023. Curtin, Thomas Duane. "The Relationship of Self-Determination and Storytelling in Human Action." *DAI* 52 (November 1991): 2770B.

Looks at how people use narrative to discover meaning and direction; offers an empirical study to demonstrate the links with self-determination.

1024. Dienes, Zoltan, Donald Broadbent, and Dianne Berry. "Implicit and Explicit Knowledge Bases in Artificial Grammar Learning." *JMemC* 17 (September 1991): 875–887.

Explores the manipulators that influence the storage or retrieval of implicit and explicit knowledge.

1025. Dimant, Rose J., and David J. Bearison. "Development of Formal Reasoning during Successive Peer Interactions." *DP* 27 (March 1991): 277–284.

Studies the effects of different kinds of peer interaction; identifies specific features that produce cognitive growth.

1026. Draper, Stephen W., and Anthony Anderson. "The Significance of Dialogue in Learning and Observing Learning." *CompEd* 17 (1991): 93–107.

Concludes that while dialogue promotes learning, private beliefs must be studied through interviews rather than naturalistic studies.

1027. Eger, Henrick. "Writer Perception, Writer Projection: The Influence of Personality, Ideology, and Gender on Letters of Recommendation." *DAI* 52 (December 1991): 3334B.

Finds that professionals perceive and judge others based on concealed subtexts of which they are not aware; advocates active acceptance of differences.

1028. Evans, Fred. "Cognitive Psychology, Phenomenology, and 'The Creative Tension of Voices.'" *P&R* 24 (1991): 105–127.

Argues that our understanding of the world and the self must be viewed not only through cognitive psychology but also within the perspective of phenomenology.

1029. Everson, Barbara J. "Vygotsky and the Teaching of Writing." *QNWP/CSW* 13 (Summer 1991): 8–11.

Summarizes Vygotsky's theories of inner speech and zone of proximal development; discusses their relevance to writing instruction.

1030. Fletcher, Ronald. "Intelligence, Equality, Character, and Education." *Intelligence* 15 (April–June 1991): 139–149.

Presents a historical analysis of the hereditarian-environmentalist debate; argues that it should be ended because it rests on "completely false foundations."

1031. Haut, Jennifer Stempel. "Gender Differences in Prose Memory after Acute Intoxication with Ethanol." *DAI* 51 (May 1991): 5561B.

Points out that, when sober, men and women recall information equally. Argues that ethanol impairs speed and recall in both; suggests that intoxicated men are slower than intoxicated women but recall more information.

1032. Haviland, Jeannette M., and Deirdre A. Kramer. "Affect-Cognition Relationships in Adolescent Diaries: The Case of Anne Frank." *HD* 34 (May–June 1991): 143–159.

A psychobiographical study suggests that passion precedes and may facilitate the development of abstract thought.

1033. Hawkins, Katherine, and Robert A. Stewart. "Effects of Communication Apprehension on Perceptions of Leadership and Intragroup Attraction in Small Task-Oriented Groups." *SCJ* 57 (Fall 1991): 1–10.

Examines effects of communication apprehension on other-reports and self-reports as a function of time.

1034. Howard, George S. "Culture Tales: A Narrative Approach to Thinking, Cross-Cultural Psychology, and Psychotherapy." *AmP* 46 (1991): 187–197.

Proposes that ethnic, class, racial, and cultural "stories" influence cultural differences.

1035. Hull, Philip Veryan. "Bilingualism: Two Languages, Two Personalities?" *DAI* 51 (March 1991): 4623A.

Suggests language-specific memory in bilinguals; points out that normative personality data collected in only one of the languages may be inadequate.

1036. Kirton, Michael, Andrew Bailey, and Walter Glendinning. "Adaptors and Innovators: Preference for Educational Procedures." *JPsy* 125 (July 1991): 445–455.

Tests the hypothesis that differences in student attitudes toward conflicting educational procedures depend upon the context of the presentation of these procedures and the individual's cognitive preference for adaptation or innovation.

1037. LeSueur, Laura Lynn. "Of Metaphors and Associations." *DAI* 52 (July 1991): 504B.

Finds that metaphors do not rely on existing relations between their elements for comprehension but create a new association between them.

1038. Lodtman, David Allen. "Therapeutic Discourse: An Analysis of Therapists at Work on a Case." *DAI* 52 (July 1991): 535B.

Finds that therapy model has less influence on the therapy delivered by a family therapy team than their discourse arising from the social situation.

1039. Logan, Carole E. "Message Design Logics and Moral Reasoning: A Social Cognitive Approach to Understanding Messages." *DAI* 51 (May 1991): 3559A.

Examines the realtionship between O'Keefe's message design logics, Kohlberg's moral reasoning, and Gilligan's moral orientation.

1040. Mallory, Loren Eugene. "Hemispheric Asymmetries of Cognitive Processing: Effects of Literal and Metaphoric Language on Event-Related Potentials and Alpha Power." *DAI* 51 (February 1991): 4094B.

Results show only slight differences in how the brain handles these two types of language; argues that hemispheric laterality is not a factor.

1041. Mann, Dana J. "Writing from Prison: A Phenomenological Study." *DAI* 51 (June 1991): 6114B.

Points out that four imprisoned poets used writing to "confront the discordant," achieve perspective, and discover possibility.

1042. Manusov, Valerie. "Perceiving Nonverbal Messages: Effects of Immediacy and Encoded Intent on Receiver Judgments." *WJSC* 55 (Summer 1991): 235–253.

Investigates nonverbal messages sent with specific intent versus those representing spontaneous *gestalt*.

1043. Massaro, Dominic C., Mary Susan Weldon, and Stephen N. Kitzis. "Integration of

Orthographic and Semantic Information in Memory Retrieval." *JMemC* 17 (March 1991): 277–287.

Investigates the evaluation and integration of multiple sources of information during memory retrieval.

1044. McKain, Thomas Lee. "Cognitive Affective, and Behavioral Factors in Writing Anxiety." *DAI* 52 (September 1991): 1729B.

Shows that writing anxiety is more related to beliefs about one's efficacy than to one's actual skills; argues that its most important consequence is procrastination.

1045. McMath, William Thomas, III. "The Effects of the Therapist's Language Style on Patient Referential Activity: A Psychotherapy Process Study." *DAI* 52 (November 1991): 2779B.

Finds that the therapist's use of language was considered negative when frequent interpretations were made.

1046. McNamara, Timothy P., Robert J. Sternberg, and James K. Hardy. "Processing Verbal Problems." *Intelligence* 15 (April–June 1991): 193–221.

After four experiments on vocabulary problem solving, proposes an information-processing model of the mental representations and processes used in verbal comprehension.

1047. Merikle, Philip M., and Eyal M. Reingold. "Comparing Direct (Explicit) and Indirect (Implicit) Measures to Study Unconscious Memory." *JEPL* 17 (March 1991): 224–233.

Experiments using cued and uncued words indicate ways to reveal the unconscious processes in adults.

1048. Messer, Wayne Spencer. "Interpretational Ambiguities in Conjunction Problems." *DAI* 52 (July 1991): 551B.

Argues that common conversational conventions in language create ambiguities in conjunction problems, but a clarifying phrase can create the correct interpretation.

1049. Minot, Walter S., and Kenneth R. Gamble. "Self-Esteem and Writing Apprehension of Basic Writers: Conflicting Evidence." *JBW* 10 (Fall 1991): 116–129.

Challenges the idea that basic writers are a homogeneous group; emphasizes that some writers have high self-esteem and low writing apprehension.

1050. Musen, Gail. "Effects of Verbal Labeling and Exposure Duration on Implicit Memory for Visual Patterns." *JMemC* 17 (September 1991): 954–962.

Examines the importance of verbal labeling and the effect of study time versus number of repetitions on implicit and explicit memory.

1051. Niehoff, Brian P., and Debra J. Mesch. "Effects of Group Reward Structures on Academic Performance and Group Processes in a Classroom Setting." *JPsy* 125 (July 1991): 457–468.

Tests the thesis that cooperative, intergroup competitive, and individualistic reward structures produce different patterns of academic success. Concludes that cooperative reward systems produce higher levels of group processes.

1052. Osterhout, Lee Edward. "Event-Related Brain Potentials Elicited during Sentence Comprehension." *DAI* 51 (February 1991): 4082B.

Argues that syntactic anomalies produce different ERPs from semantic or interpretive anomalies. Points out that where syntactic ambiguity exists, readers seem to construct a single syntactic representation.

1053. Padilla, Amado M., Kathryn J. Lindholm, Andrew Chen, Richard Duran, Kenyi Hakuta, Wallace Lambert, and G. Richard Tucker. "The English-Only Movement: Myths, Reality, and Implications for Psychology." *AmP* 46 (1991): 120–130.

Argues that English-only will have negative effects on social-psychology education, testing, and health services.

1054. Parker, Nancy Eliot. "A Study on the Relationship between Hemispheric Preference and Writing Development." *DAI* 52 (December 1991): 2011A.

Links research in hemispheric specialization that supports the concept of left and right hemispheric modes in problem solving with techniques for teaching composition.

1055. Paulson, Lynn E. "The Identification of Differences in Patterns of Content and Functional Organization of Expressive, Conventional and Rhetorical Messages in Three Message Genres." *DAI* 51 (June 1991): 3957A.

Explores O'Keefe's model of message design logic by examining the performance of 235 college students and finds differences in content and structure between message genres.

1056. Rada, Muriel M. "The Relationship between Voice and Power: The Internal Acquisition and Development of Personal Expressive Voice." *DAI* 52 (December 1991): 2123A.

Analyzes the assumptions writers must make about themselves in order to develop a voice. Argues that the search for voice parallels defining the self.

1057. Riger, Stephanie. "Gender Differences in Sexual Harassment Policies and Procedures." *AmP* 46 (1991): 497–505.

Argues that policy and procedure statements are written in a way that discourages women from pursuing grievances.

1058. Rind, Bruce Laurence. "A Model for What Makes a Message Persuasive." *DAI* 51 (May 1991): 5642B.

Suggests that persuasive messages are resonant, relevant, attractive, plausible, and novel; points out that they require a recipient who is able to process the contents.

1059. Robertson, Lynn C., and Marvin R. Lamb. "Neuropsychological Contributions to Theories of Part/Whole Organization." *CPsy* 23 (April 1991): 299–330.

Suggests that a hierarchical organization of objects within objects includes the coordination of global properties, local properties, distributing attentional resources, and interconnecting global and local properties.

1060. Rosnow, Ralph L. "Inside Rumor: A Personal Journey." *AmP* 46 (1991): 484–496.

New findings suggest that minor transmission and generation result from combined effects of personal anxiety, general anxiety, credulity, and outcome-relevent involvement.

1061. Samson, Severine, and Robert J. Zatorre. "Recognition Memory for Text and Melody of Songs after Unilateral Temporal Lobe Lesion: Evidence for Dual Encoding." *JMemC* 17 (July 1991): 793–804.

Suggests that songs can be encoded in the left as well as the right temporal lobe.

1062. Schober, Michael F. "Spatial Perspective in Language Use." *DAI* 51 (May 1991): 5618B.

Points out that describing an object's location requires taking the vantage point of the addressee; argues that when that vantage point is similar to the describer's, the task is easier.

1063. Schumacher, Gary M., and Jane Gradwohl Nash. "Conceptualizing and Measuring Knowledge Change Due to Writing." *RTE* 25 (February 1991): 67–96.

Suggests that researchers studying "writing-to-learn" draw on theories of knowledge when choosing tasks/conditions and assess primarily structural knowledge changes. Discusses particular theories and methods.

1064. Shapiro, Lauren R., and Judith A. Hudson. "Tell Me a Make-Believe Story: Coherence and Cohesion in Young Children's Picture-Elicited Narratives." *DP* 27 (November 1991): 960–974.

Demonstrates that with proper stimuli, young children are cognitively equipped to construct complete and coherent stories.

1065. Stern, Leonard, Richard Dahlgren, and Linda Gaffney. "Spacing Judgments as an Index of Integration from Context-Induced Relational Processing: Implications for the Free Recall of Ambiguous Prose Passages." *M&C* 19 (1991): 579–592.

Results imply that improved comprehension of prose passages derived from context information provided at the time the passages were encoded.

1066. Stotsky, Sandra. "On Developing Independent Critical Thinking: What We Can Learn from Studies of the Research Process." *WC* 8 (April 1991): 193–212.

Surveys literature according to ways in which reading and writing involved in the research process foster critical thinking.

1067. Stowell, Hilton. "A Comment on 'Of Brains and Rhetoric' [*CE* 52 (March 1990)]." *CE* 53 (February 1991): 229–230.

Claims that Jeffrey Walker's article is outdated in its understanding of neuroscience.

1068. Thompson, Laura A., and Reinhold Kliegel. "Adult Age Effects of Plausibility on Memory: The Role of Time Constraints during Encoding." *JMemC* 17 (May 1991): 542–555.

Study illustrates that older adults have less recall of schema-discrepant words than younger adults; points out that both groups have better recall of schema-coherent words.

1069. Tomlinsen, Rebecca Joy. "An Application of the Personality Theories Developed by Gordon W. Allport to the Process of Character Analysis." *DAI* 52 (July 1991): 24A.

Explores the applicability of Allport's personality theories to textual and character analysis.

1070. Weiler, Marc, and Gery d'Ydewalle. "Continuity in Cognitive Skill: Comment on Kolers and Duchicky [JEPL 11 (1985)]." *JEPL* 17 (January 1991): 170–173.

Argues against the Kolers and Duchnicky report that "cognitive skills develop in a discontinuous way."

1071. Wercklc, Gerard Joseph, Jr. "Progoff's Intensive Journal Method: A Phenomenological Study." *DAI* 51 (May 1991): 5599B.

Argues that Progoff's method of journal-keeping enables access to inner experience; points out that this access releases creative direction for dealing with external experience.

1072. Willerman, Lee, Robert Schultz, J. Neal Rutledge, and Erin D. Bigler. " 'In Vivi' Brain Size and Intelligence." *Intelligence* 15 (April–June 1991): 223–228.

Researchers conclude that brain size can explain differences on intelligence tests.

1073. Wood, Sarah Bane. "The Therapeutic Element in Student-Centered Writing Instruction." *DAI* 51 (March 1991): 3005A.

Argues that student-centered writing shares much with psychotherapy. Points out that despite the praiseworthy goals, student-centered writing presents difficulties in practice. Makes recommendations to overcome difficulties.

1074. Young, Candace Anne. "An Investigation of Object Relations, Ego Development, and Reality Testing in Male and Female Creative Writers." *DAI* 52 (October 1991): 2321B.

Finds gender differences in all three areas.

1075. Zeitz, Colleen Mary. "Expert-Novice Differences in Memory and Analysis on Literary and Nonliterary Texts." *DAI* 51 (April 1991): 5061B.

Demonstrates that superior memory, abstract representation, and superior reasoning skills characterize expertise in literature.

1076. Zolliker, Susan. *Putting "Meta" Terms into Context: Constructing a Developmental*

Picture and Exploring Philosophical Implications. Boston, MA: CCCC, March 1991. ERIC ED 332 194. 18 pages

Claims that students need to use language to learn about language; points out that teachers need to become sensitive to this process that they, unlike their students, have internalized.

2.10 EDUCATION

1077. Barzun, Jacques. *Begin Here: The Forgotten Conditions of Teaching and Learning*. Edited by Morris Philipson. Chicago, IL: University of Chicago Press, 1991. 232 pages

Fifteen essays, articles, and other writings describe Barzun's thoughts on what teaching and learning are, what they can be, and what they must become if schools are to recover their purpose and effectiveness.

1078. Booth, Wayne C. *The Vocation of a Teacher: Rhetorical Occasions, 1967–1988*. Chicago, IL: University of Chicago Press, 1991. 372 pages

Argues for rhetoric as the center of a liberal education. Exposes political and economic situations that frustrate teachers. Includes a personal account of the pleasures of teaching.

1079. Brown, Gillian, and Stephanie Markman. "Discourse Processing and Preferred Information." *L&E* 3 (1991): 47–62.

This study suggests that some learners will pay less attention to and remember less information in stressful situations when verbal information is not fully consistent with visual information.

1080. Clifford, Margaret M. "Risk Taking: Theoretical, Empirical, and Educational Considerations." *EdPsy* 26 (Summer/Fall 1991): 263–298.

Presents findings on risk taking derived from theories of economics which are relevant to education; introduces a research program designed to isolate factors in academic risk taking.

1081. Counihan, Timothy John. "Gilbert Ryle and the Philosophy of Education." *DAI* 52 (August 1991): 461A.

Examines Ryle's philosophy of education, focusing on *The Concept of Mind*.

1082. D'Souza, Dinesh. "Illiberal Education." *The Atlantic Monthly* (March 1991): 51–79.

Discusses transformations in the intellectual and moral underpinnings of the American university. Focuses on Duke University, where radical academic theories and radical politics have proved complementary.

1083. DeVaney, Ann. "Rules of Evidence." *JT* 25 (Spring/Summer 1991): 6–18.

Argues that "knowledge" in the field of education can be based, as in law and science, on the specific, the inductive, and the analogy.

1084. Dzuback, Mary Ann. *Robert M. Hutchins: Portrait of an Educator*. Chicago, IL: University of Chicago Press, 1991. 336 pages

Compares Hutchins' programs with those at other institutions of the time and evaluates his contributions to intellectual and moral reform of higher education in the United States.

1085. Gless, Darryl J., and Barbara Herrnstein Smith, eds. *The Politics of Liberal Education*. Durham, NC: Duke University Press, 1991. 288 pages

Contributors discuss canon-formation in the ancient world, the idea of a "common culture," and the educational implications of the social movements of feminism, technological changes including computers and television, and intellectual development such as "theory."

Essayists: Stanley Fish, Phyllis Franklin, Henry Louis Gates, Jr., Henry A. Giroux, Darryl J. Gless, Gerald Graff, Barbara Herrnstein Smith, George A. Kennedy, Bruce Kuklick, Richard A. Lanham, Elizabeth Kamarck Minnich, Alexander Nehamas, Mary Louise Pratt, Richard Rorty, Eve Kosofsky Sedgwick.

1086. Graham, Robert J. *Reading and Writing the Self: Autobiography in Education and the Curriculum*. New York: Teachers College Press, 1991. 192 pages

Argues for the use of autobiography as a tool for learning across grade-levels and across the curriculum from the perspectives of literary theory, Deweyan philosophy, and curriculum studies.

1087. Jones, Beau Fly. "Thinking and Learning: New Curricula for the Twenty-First Century." *EdPsy* 26 (Spring 1991): 129–143.

Proposes that education must reform and that the third-wave reforms, employing a needs-based perspective, will have significant implications for curriculum, instruction, and assessment.

1088. Kerr, Stephen T. "Educational Technology Is Not about Technology." *JT* 25 (Spring/Summer 1991): 19–33.

Maintains that educational technology is about "the work done in schools," its definition, purpose, participants, and effects it has on learning and our democratic society.

1089. Macintyre, Peter D., and R. C. Gardner. "Investigating Language Class Anxiety Using the Focused Essay Technique." *MLJ* 75 (Autumn 1991): 296–304.

Finds that beginning language learners' essays reveal anxiety-arousing and confidence-building language experiences and change students' self-perceptions of proficiency.

1090. McLeod, Susan H. "Writing as a Mode of Learning." *CompC* 4 (March 1991): 7.

Argues that the definition of "learning" in WAC research must be expanded beyond "remembering."

1091. McNeill, William H. *Hutchins' University: A Memoir of the University of Chicago, 1929–1950*. Chicago, IL: University of Chicago Press, 1991. 208 pages

McNeill, a student and instructor during Hutchins' tenure, not only provides insight on Hutchins' influence on the university, but also on the way the university was affected by world events such as the red scare, the abolition of football, and the inauguration of the nuclear age.

1092. Meier, Kenneth J., and Joseph Stewart, Jr. *The Politics of Hispanic Education: Un Paso Pa'lante y Dos Pa'tras*. Albany, NY: State University of New York Press, 1991. 275 pages

Authors discuss problems of educational opportunity among Hispanic students in the United States with intra-group comparisons of Cubans, Mexicans, and Puerto Ricans. The study is based on data from 142 school districts with a minimum of 5000 students and a five percent Hispanic enrollment.

1093. Miller, Suzanne. "Room to Talk: Opening Possiblilities with the 'At-Risk.' " *ELQ* 13 (May 1991): 10–11.

Advocates the use of classroom conversation as a means of engaging at-risk students in reading and writing activities.

1094. Pignattelli, Frank Charles. "Toward a Practice of Freedom in Education: An Investigation and Analysis of the Work of Michel Foucault." *DAI* 51 (March 1991): 3010A.

Identifies an educational discourse-practice and develops a critical strategy for dealing with this discourse practice by examining the philosophy of Michel Foucault.

1095. Root, Robert L., Jr. "The Virgule Variations: Learning/Language/Literature." *EJ* 80 (October 1991): 18–27.

Details four variations of the "virgulian circle" showing an "infinite interrelationship of learning, language, and literature."

1096. Schiefele, Ulrich. "Interest, Learning, and Motivation." *EdPsy* 26 (Summer/Fall 1991): 299–324.

Argues that current theories of motivation do not include crucial aspects of the meaning of interest emphasized by classical American and German educational theorists.

1097. Snow, Catherine E., Wendy S. Barnes, Jean Chandler, Irene F. Goodman, and Lowry Hemphill. *Unfulfilled Expectations: Home and School Influences on Literacy*. Cambridge, MA: Harvard University Press, 1991. 251 pages

Examines home- and school-based factors that affected achievement in reading and writing among a group of ethically diverse low-income children who attended grades two, four, and six in a small-city school system in the industrial northeast.

2.11 JOURNALISM, PUBLISHING, TELEVISION, AND RADIO

1098. Almeida, Eugenie Photiadis. "Factuality and Nonfactuality in Newspaper Discourse." *DAI* 52 (October 1991): 1119A.

Analyzes how audiences interpret statements as factual or nonfactual and concludes that the interpretations are automatic and habitual.

1099. Atwater, Tony, and Anokwa Kwadwo. "Race Relations in Ebony: An Analysis of Interracial Statements in Selected Feature Stories." *JBS* 21 (March 1991): 268–286.

Analyzes selected stories to show the relation between media discourse and race relations. Focuses on four variables: sentence type, source, tone, and length.

1100. Bollinger, Lee C. *Images of a Free Press*. Chicago, IL: University of Chicago Press, 1991. 192 pages

Presents a guide to the evolution of a modern conception of freedom of the press and its strengths and weaknesses.

1101. Brandt, Richard. "Multimedia and Reality." *Multimedia Review* 2 (Spring 1991): 28–32.

Discusses mental models and what they mean to learning and multimedia.

1102. Butler, Susan Lowell. "The Media and the Military." *PC* 11 (Summer 1991): 32–33.

Reviews the Freedom Forum's "comprehensive report on how the press covered Operation Desert Storm and the events preceding it."

1103. Campbell, Karlyn Kohrs. "Hearing Women's Voices" *CEd* 40 (January 1991): 33–48.

Advocates the inclusion of more works by women in public address anthologies, *Vital Speeches of the Day*, and *Representative American Speeches*.

1104. Castrey, Margaret. "Student Editor Sets Precedent." *PC* 11 (Summer 1991): 20–21, 33.

Relates the case of a college journalist who challenged Southwest Missouri State University's refusal to release a security report involving a student athlete and won public access to university crime records.

1105. Dow, Bonnie Jean. " 'Woman's Place' on Television: A Feminist Critical Study of Situation Comedy." *DAI* 51 (March 1991): 2924A.

Discusses the portrayal of women in *The Mary Tyler Moore Show, Murphy Brown*, and *Designing Women*.

1106. Entman, Robert M. "Framing U.S. Coverage of International News: Contrasts in Narratives of the KAL and Iran Air Incidents." *JC* 41 (Autumn 1991): 6–27.

Investigates news frames (information-processing schemata) to see how events are constructed in narratives and how readers' interpretations are shaped by them.

1107. Evans, Martin G. "The Problem of Analyzing Multiplicative Composites: Interactions Revisited." *AmP* 46 (1991): 6–15.

Critiques nonexperimental researchers' continued use of multiplicative composites in bivariate correlational analysis. Suggests that journal editors and referees pay closer attention to methodology.

1108. Faxon, Linda, and Carolyne Allen. "Hiring and Programming." *PC* 11 (Summer 1991): 27, 29.

A panel at the Third Annual Conference of the National Association of College Broadcasters argues that persistent gender bias in media hirings influences programming decisions.

1109. Flander, Judy. "A Global Village." *PC* 11 (April/May 1991): 25–26.

Reports on "a major symposium on news gathering sponsored by the International Women's Media Foundation."

1110. Fowler, Roger. *Language in the News: Discourse and Ideology in the British Press.* New York: Routledge, 1991. 256 pages

Challenges the assumption that newspaper coverage of world events is an unbiased recording of facts. Examines the role of language in representations of gender, power, authority, and law and order, including stereotyping, terms of abuse and endearment, the editorial voice, and the formation of consensus.

1111. Friedheim, Jerry W. "The American People's First Amendment." *PC* 11 (April/May 1991): 22–23.

Argues that information technologies and rapidly changing world politics could endanger First Amendment freedoms in the twenty-first century.

1112. Garner, Thurmon, and Carolyn Calloway-Thomas. "Langston Hughes' Message for the Black Masses." *ComQ* 39 (Spring 1991): 164–177.

Describes how Hughes used the "Simple Columns" in the *Chicago Defender* to recommend how to resolve the problem of being Black in white America.

1113. Giddens, Elizabeth J. "John McPhee's Rhetoric of Balance and Perspective." *DAI* 52 (September 1991): 916A.

Studies McPhee's writings; shows that he employs a rhetorical strategy that balances journalistic fair-mindedness with persuasion.

1114. Gramsci, Antonio. *Selections from Cultural Writings.* Cambridge, MA: Harvard University Press, 1991. 464 pages

Edited from his journalism and his prison notebooks, Gramsci's first English translation of writings on culture are included here.

1115. Groswiler, Paul Ray. "The Shifting Sensorium: A Q-Methodology and Critical Theory Exploration of Marshall McLuhan's Visual and Acoustic Typologies in Media, Aesthetics, and Ideology." *DAI* 52 (August 1991): 329A.

Suggests that acoustic media and aesthetics factors are closely associated with visual ideology factors.

1116. Hacker, Kenneth L., Tara G. Coste, Daniel F. Kamm, and Carl R. Bybee. "Oppositional Readings of Network Television News: Viewer Deconstruction." *D&S* 2 (April 1991): 183–202.

Analyzes how people criticize and doubt what NBC news programs tell them and how they seek alternative sources of information.

1117. Hart, Roderick P., Deborah Smith-Howell, and John Llewellyn. "The Mindscape of the Presidency" *JC* 41 (Summer 1991): 6–25.

Analyzes how candidates have been portrayed to see how the media influences voters' expectations of a president.

1118. Henson, Kenneth T. *Writing for Successful Publication.* ERIC Clearinghouse on Reading and Communication Skills. 1991. ERIC ED 334 573. 289 pages

Offers suggestions for academics on book and article publication.

1119. Horn, John. "Dueling Buzzwords: Are Your 'Freedom Fighters' Their 'Terrorists'?" *QRD* 17 (January 1991): 7–8.

Analyzes media's use of labels and its difficulty in finding neutral terminology.

1120. Iyengar, Shanto. *Is Anyone Responsible? How Television Frames Political Issues*. Chicago, IL: University of Chicago Press, 1991. 195 pages

Argues that television affects the notion of political accountability by focusing on sensational dramas of individual perpetrators and victims rather than analysis and content.

1121. Julian, James Patrick. "The Self-Adjusting Propaganda System: Toward a Mid-range Theory of the Press." *DAI* 51 (March 1991): 3225A.

Explores the relationship between news content and social change within the context of the American media.

1122. Kaid, Linda Lee, and Anne Johnston. "Negative Versus Positive Television Advertising in U. S. Presidential Campaigns, 1969–1988." *JC* 41 (Summer 1991): 53–64.

Analyzes 830 commercials and concludes that recent campaigns have not been more negative than previous ones.

1123. Kaniss, Phyllis. *Making Local News*. Chicago, IL: University of Chicago Press, 1991. 248 pages

Presents interviews with journalists and city officials. Argues that agenda of local news is partly set by a need to capture more affluent audiences and boost circulation or ratings. Points out that the media focuses on stories that link a diverse, growing suburban audience with the central city.

1124. Lafky, Sue A. "The Women of American Journalism." *DAI* 51 (May 1991): 3926A.

Explores the general topic of gender-differentiated participation in the workplace.

1125. Leo, John. "Translations from the Journalese." *QRD* 17 (January 1991): 11.

Provides humorous examples of euphemisms designed to convey a writer's opinion without transgressing the confines of taste and libel law.

1126. Levine, Marilyn M. "Book Production: Patterns and Predictors." *IPM* 27 (1991): 559–573.

Argues that newspaper headline size, prime interest rate, mean rental price of videos, and purchase price of paperback books can predict yearly production of books per person.

1127. Lotz, Roy Edward. *Crime and the American Press*. New York: Praeger Publishers, 1991. 192 pages

Analyzes crime coverage in *The Chicago Tribune*, *The Los Angeles Times*, *The New Orleans Times-Picayune*, and *The Philadelphia Inquirer*.

1128. McDonald, Fred Lochland. "A Case Study of the Writing Process." *DAI* 51 (May 1991): 3543A.

Examines the protocol and recorded interview to reveal the composing process of a newspaper columnist.

1129. McGarry, Richard G. "Evaluating Interethnic Conflict in the Press: A Cross-Linguistic Discourse Analysis Model." *DAI* 52 (September 1991): 901A.

Analyzes contextual features of interethnic conflict in the Kenyan press.

1130. Michaelson, Herbert B. "Commentary: Unethical Blunders by Authors." *JTWC* 21 (1991): 425–428.

Discusses the question in ethics of omission, distortions of meaning, and improprieties of publication.

1131. Nicolescu, Nancy. "A Burkean Analysis of the Depiction of Women in Television Commercials." *DAI* 52 (November 1991): 1557A.

Analyzes 435 television advertisements based on the dramatistic theory of Kenneth Burke.

1132. Perkinson, Henry J. *Getting Better: Television and Moral Progress*. New Brunswick, NJ: Transaction Publishers, 1991. 306 pages

Argues that television has aided the critical scrutiny of existing culture, contributing to moral progress in society.

1133. Potter, Jonathan, Margaret Wetherell, and Andrew Chitty. "Quantification Rhetoric: Cancer on Television." *D&S* 2 (July 1991): 333–365.

Analyzes a television current affairs program that illustrates the manipulation of numbers to suit rhetorical purposes.

1134. "Public Television, as Approved by the CIA." *QRD* 17 (July 1991): 11.

Reports on Orwellian changes made in PBS program on Korean War after series was screened by General Stilwell.

1135. Redd, Teresa M. "The Voice of *Time*: The Style of Narration in a Newsmagazine." *WC* 8 (April 1991): 240–258.

Using Gibson's (1966) "Style Machine," the study analyzes the stylistic features of *Time*'s narrative voice in the news sections of the magazine.

1136. Ricchiardi, Sherry, Virginia Young, and Kay Mills. *Women on Deadline: A Collection of America's Best*. Ames, IA: Iowa State University Press, 1991. 201 pages

Presents biographical interviews and examples of writing from nine award-winning women journalists; includes assessments of women's progress in journalism.

1137. Rouse, Joy. "Positional Historiography and Margaret Fuller's *Public Discourse of Mutual Interpretation*." *RSQ* 20 (Summer 1990): 233–240.

Argues that Fuller's journalism expanded the idea of "public discourse" to include attention to everyday life.

1138. Russman, Linda deLauberfels. "Are Women Noteworthy?" *PC* 11 (Summer 1991): 25–26, 33.

Third annual study finds "little change since 1989 in news coverage of and by women on the front page of 10 major, general interest papers."

1139. Russman, Linda deLaubenfels. "Women TV Correspondents Lack Visibility." *PC* 11 (Summer 1991): 30–31.

Summarizes results of a "1990 Network Correspondent Visibility Study" that identifies the top 100 "most visible" network reporters.

1140. Sansom, Leslie. "Giving Up the Fight." *PC* 11 (Summer 1991): 34–35.

Discusses the aftereffects of sportswriter Lisa Olson's controversial exchange with players from the New England Patriots football team.

1141. Sansom, Leslie. "Women in the Newsroom: Making All the Difference." *PC* 11 (Summer 1991): 8–12.

Briefly profiles eight award-winning women journalists and explores why women journalists received a record number of awards this year.

1142. Speck, Bruce W. "Editiorial Authority in the Author-Editor Relationship." *TC* 38 (August 1991): 300–315.

Discusses techniques editors use in helping authors shape their work. Includes 138-item bibliography.

1143. Taylor, Welford Dunaway, ed. *The Newsprint Mask: The Tradition of the Fictional Journalist in America*. Ames, IA: Iowa State University Press, 1991. 268 pages

Examines fictional personalities used by American journalists from Addison and Steele in eighteenth-century England, Benjamin Franklin (writing as "Silence Dogood"), to the zenith of the genre in the mid-nineteenth century, and on to the present day.

Essayists: Benjamin Franklin, William Parks, Philip Freneau, Joseph Dennie, Seba Smith, James Russell Lowell, Frances M. Whitcher, George Washington Harris, William Tappan Thompson, Francis Bartow Lloyd, Charles Farrar Browne, David Ross Locke, Charles Henry Smith, Robert Henry Newell, Henry Wheeler Shaw, Samuel Langhorne Clemens, George Wilbur Peck, Samuel W. Small, Joel Chandler Harris, Charles Bertrand Lewis, Edward W. Townsend, Charles Follen Adams, Finley Peter Dunne, Donald Robert, Perry Marquis, Frank McKinney Hubbard, William Penn, Adair Rogers, Philander Chase Johnson, Sherwood Anderson, Edward Streeter, Richard E. Yates, Charles R. McDowell, Jr.

1144. Tebbel, John, and Mary Ellen Zuckerman. *The Magazine in America, 1740–1990.* New York: Oxford University Press, 1991. 448 pages

Traces the history of American periodical publishing since the era of Benjamin Franklin's *General Magazine.*

1145. Van Dijk, Teun A. *Racism and the Press.* New York: Routledge, 1991. 276 pages

Uses discourse analysis to examine the portrayal of ethnic minorities in the British and Dutch press.

1146. Vipond, Douglas, and Russell A. Hunt. "The Strange Case of the Queen-Post Truss: John McPhee on Writing and Reading." *CCC* 42 (May 1991): 200–210.

John McPhee comments on changes suggested for his original texts ("discourse-based interview") and on readers' observations about his work ("probes").

1147. Walton, Douglas N. *Begging the Question: Circular Reasoning as a Tactic of Argumentation.* New York: Greenwood Press, 1991. 340 pages

Analyzes begging the question as a systematic tactic used by the proponent of an argument to evade fulfilling a legitimate burden of proof. The technique uses a circular structure of argument to block the further progress of dialogue, particularly the respondent's ability to respond with legitimate critical questions.

1148. Witt, Nancy L. "The 'Hidden' Story." *PC* 11 (Winter 1991): 30–32.

Argues that the media ignore people with disabilities; offers tips on how to communicate appropriately about this segment of the population.

1149. Zelizer, Barbie. " 'Covering the Body': The Kennedy Assassination and the Establishment of Journalistic Authority." *DAI* 51 (February 1991): 2558A.

Explores journalists' narrative reconstruction of the JFK assassination—how they have turned their retelling of the assassination coverage into stories about themselves in an effort to establish authority.

2.12 PHILOSOPHY

1150. Burchell, Graham, Colin Gordon, and Peter Miller, eds. *The Foucault Effect: Studies in Governmentality.* Toronto: Harvester Wheatleaf, 1991. 320 pages

Includes lectures given at the College de France in 1978 and 1980 and an interview from 1977. Argues that the object and activity of government are not instinctive and natural, but invented and learned.

Essayists: Colin Gordon, Michel Foucault, Pasquale Pasquino, Graham Burchell, Giovanna Procacci, Jacques Donzelot, Ian Hacking, Francois Ewald, Daniel Defert, Robert Castel.

1151. Chang, Briankle G. "Deconstructing Communication." *DAI* 51 (June 1991): 3954A.

Analyzes Husserl's theory of intersubjectivity and Derrida's notion of the "postal principle" to critique the philosophical foundation underlying modern communication theories.

1152. Desan, Philippe. "The Platonization of the Gauls or French History According to Ramus." *Arg* 5 (November 1991): 375–386.

Argues that Ramus uses the *Traitte des meurs et facons des anciens gaulois* to advocate the reform of rhetoric, mathematics, and the teaching of philosphy.

1153. Findler, Richard. "The Problem of the Imagination for Subjectivity: Kant and Heidegger on the Issue of Displacement." *DAI* 52 (August 1991): 562A.

Develops the problem of displacement, explains the Kantian conception of subjectivity, examines the relationship between imagination and subjectivity, and explores Heideggers's understanding of the imagination.

1154. Golden, James L. "An Application of Michael Meyer's Theory of Problematology to David Hume's *Dialogues concerning Natural Religion*." *Arg* 5 (February 1991): 69–89.

Contends that Hume's *Dialogues concerning Natural Religion* fulfills four basic elements of Michael Meyer's theory of problematology.

1155. Griswold, Charles L., Jr. "Rhetoric and Ethics: Adam Smith on Theorizing about the Moral Sentiments." *P&R* 24 (1991): 213–237.

Examines the relationship between theory and praxis in Adam Smith's *Theory and Moral Sentiment*.

1156. Heckman, Peter. "Nietzsche's Clever Animal: Metaphor in 'Truth and Falsity.' " *P&R* 24 (Winter 1991): 301–321.

Argues that Nietzsche's use of metaphor in "Truth and Falsity" is less successful than in his later works. Points out that a "degree of confusion" in the text works in Nietzsche's favor.

1157. Hyde, Richard B. "Saying the Clearing: A Heideggerian Analysis of the Ontological Rhetoric of Werner Erhard." *DAI* 52 (July 1991): 21A.

Argues that Erhard's rhetoric is a variant of dialogic communication; proposes pedagogical implications of ontological rhetoric.

1158. Jamison, David L. "Michael Meyer's Philosophy of Problematology: Toward a New Theory of Argumentation." *Arg* 5 (February 1991): 57–68.

Argues that problematology focuses on questions rather than answers and thus contributes to our understanding of informal reasoning and the propositional model.

1159. Johnson, Ralph H. "In Response to Walton [*P&R* 24 (Winter 1991)]." *P&R* 24 (Winter 1991): 362–366.

Defends his articles on Hamblin's *Fallacies*. Points out that he did not critique the scope, nature, or purpose of the book but only discussed Hamblin's account of fallacies.

1160. Lyon, Arabella. "Rhetoric and Disciplinary Change: A Study of Wittgenstein's 'Tractatus' and 'Investigations.' " *DAI* 52 (August 1991): 344A.

Uses models of disciplinary change from the philosophy of science to develop a rhetorical model accounting for evolutionary and revolutionary discourses as well as interdisciplinarity.

1161. Martens, David Bryan. "Some Descriptional Theories of First-Person Thoughts." *DAI* 51 (February 1991): 2772A.

Reviews classical and contemporary theories from Russell through the present. Notes data, arguments, and putative counter-examples that a theory must accommodate.

1162. Meerhoff, Kees. "Logic and Eloquence: A Ramusian Revolution." *Arg* 5 (November 1991): 357–374.

Examines the European intellectual trends of the humanist movement and their influence on the work of Peter Ramus.

1163. Riddell, Terence Joseph. "Reference and Structure: Literary Modernism and the Philosophy of Language." *DAI* 51 (February 1991): 2757A.

Argues that literary modernism is an essential step in the progress from Edenic or medieval models of language to contemporary ones such as Derrida and McCanles.

1164. Riley-Nuss, Kerry K., trans. " 'Friedrich Nietzsche and the Greek Sophistic': A Comparative Lecture Given by Dr. Max Wiesenthal in 1903." *Arg* 5 (May 1991): 201–220.

Argues that Nietzsche's greatest insights are "the revived thoughts of his unacknowledged cultural, philosophical, and stylistic model—the Sophists."

1165. Sharratt, Peter. "Introduction: Ramus, Perelman and Argumentation, a Way through the Wood." *Arg* 5 (November 1991): 335–345.

Argues that the work of sixteenth-century French philosopher Peter Ramus is relevant to argumentation. Presents bibliography of works by and about Ramus.

1166. Steele, Meili. "Lyotard's Politics of the Sentence." *CCrit* (Fall 1990): 193–214.

Discusses the philosophy of Jean-Francois Lyotard: explains how types of sentences can silence or oppress and how power operates within sentences.

1167. Stokes, Karina Nancilee. "A Dialogic Method for Natural Language Cognition." *DAI* 51 (April 1991): 3401A.

Stokes rejects the application of formal logic in producing natural language machines, offering instead a method that allows dialogic merging of a plurality of approaches.

1168. Whitson, Steve. "On the Misadventures of the Sophists: Hegel's Tropological Appropriation of Rhetoric." *Arg* 5 (May 1991): 187–200.

Argues that "Hegel's history of the Sophists operates along tropological lines, the exact same lines that the truth claims of his philosophy oppose."

1169. Wildeson, Daniel L. "The Speech Perspective of Hannah Arendt and Its Implications for Rhetorical Theory." *DAI* 52 (November 1991): 1574A.

Focuses on the relationship between individual and community experience by examining speech, the activity through which humans reveal their unique identities.

1170. Ziarek, Krzysztof Marek. "Being and the Ethical: Language in the Writings of Heidegger, Stevens, Levinas, and Celan." *DAI* 51 (February 1991): 2738A.

Emphasizes the linguistic "resistance" to difference; suggests that otherness and difference may be disengaged. Implies the necessity of novel modes of philosophical thinking and critical analysis.

2.13 SCIENCE AND MEDICINE

1171. Ambron, Joanna. "Conceptual Learning and Writing in the Sciences." *TETYC* 18 (May 1991): 114–120.

Argues that clustering is effective as prewriting for learning biological concepts.

1172. Barnard, David. "Review of *Stories of Sickness* by Howard Brody (Yale, 1987)." *AM* 66 (June 1991): 324–325.

Commends Brody's attention to and explication of "narratives of human life" in his study of patients' "narratives of illness."

1173. Bowen, Elizabeth C., and Beverly E. Schneller, eds. *Writing about Science*. 2d ed. New York: Oxford University Press, 1991. 400 pages

Twenty-seven essays show that scientific writing can be imaginative and concise, efficient and entertaining. Introductions outline each author's life and contribution to science and place each selection in chronological and thematic context.
Essayists: Michael Faraday, Charles Darwin, James Watson, Francis Crick, Lynn Margulis, Stephen J. Gould, J. B. S. Haldane, Isaac Asimov, Bertrand Russell, George Gamow, Stephen Toulmin, June Goodfield, Keith Tinkler, Howard Ensign Evans, Lewis Thomas, Rachel Carson, Norbert Wiener, Thomas Jefferson, Al-

mira Phelps, Richard P. Feynman, Marian C. Diamond, Julian Huxley, Gregory Bateson, Garrett Hardin, Dorion Sagan, George Beadle, Muriel Beadle, Gerald Holton, Jens Feder.

1174. Buller, David B., and Richard L. Street, Jr. "The Role of the Perceived Affect and Information in Patients' Evaluations of Health Care and Compliance Decisions." *SCJ* 56 (Spring 1991): 230–237.

Addresses the question whether communicator style alters compliance with treatment directives.

1175. Ciolli, Russ T. "A Rhetorical Analysis of Two Public Addresses by C. P. Snow: 'The Two Cultures and the Scientific Revolution' and 'The Moral Un-Neutrality of Science.' " *DAI* 52 (November 1991): 1570A.

Uses the rhetorical guidelines of Richard Weaver to examine themes of cultural polarity between scientists and nonscientists, overspecialization in education, and world hunger.

1176. Dear, Peter, ed. *The Literary Structure of Scientific Argument*. Philadelphia, PA: University of Pennsylvania Press, 1991. 208 pages

Seven historians of science examine the historical creation and meaning of a range of scientific textual forms from the seventeenth to the late nineteenth centuries. They consider examples from chemistry, medicine, physics, zoology, physiology, and mathematics.
Essayists: Thomas H. Broman, Frederic L. Holmes, Bruce J. Hunt, Lynn K. Nyhart, Lissa Roberts, Lisa Rosner.

1177. Dombrowski, Paul M. "The Lessons of the Challenger Investigations." *IEEE* 34 (December 1991): 211–216.

Argues that the reports of the two major investigations of the events preceding the Challenger disaster were shaped by "powerful though unacknowledged social contingencies."

1178. Ellis, P. M., G. Blackshaw, G. L. Purdie, and G. W. Mellsop. "Clinical Information in Psychiatric Practice: What Do Doctors Know, What Do They Think Is Known, and What Do They Record?" *MEd* 25 (September 1991): 438–443.

Discusses doctors' audience and subject assumptions, and the effects of these on what is recorded; considers the effect of omissions on subsequent readers and reviewers.

1179. Gopen, George, and Judith A. Swan. "The Science of Scientific Writing." *American Scientist* 78 (January 1991): 550–558.

Presents several rhetorical principles, based on a reader's expectations, that can produce clarity in scientific communication without oversimplifying scientific issues.

1180. Gross, Alan G. "Does Rhetoric of Science Matter? The Case of the Floppy-Eared Rabbits." *CE* 53 (December 1991): 933–943.

Argues that scientific communication is "deeply rhetorical" and that it conveys a world view through its style and organization.

1181. Gross, Alan G. *The Rhetoric of Science*. Cambridge, MA: Harvard University Press, 1990. 272 pages

Applies the principles of rhetoric to the interpretation of classical and contemporary scientific texts to show how they persuade author and audience.

1182. Harris, R. Allen. "Rhetoric of Science." *CE* 53 (March 1991): 282–305.

Suggests that rhetoric of science is occupied with argumentation and with the dialectic that unearths truths, grafting them to form knowledge.

1183. Lee, Donald Paul. "A Rhetorical Analysis of the Scientific-Romantic Synthesis in the Popular Scientific Writings of Lewis Thomas." *DAI* 51 (March 1991): 2925A.

Demonstrates how Thomas successfully synthesized two apparently contradictory perspectives: the scientific and the romantic.

1184. Levine, George. "Scientific Realism and Literary Representation." *Raritan* 10 (Spring 1991): 18–39.

Reviews and critiques contemporary theories of "ways of knowing" and "realistic description."

1185. Lewontin, R. C. "Facts and the Factitious in Natural Sciences." *CritI* 18 (Autumn 1991): 140–153.

Drawing on the work of Thomas Kuhn, explores how facts are constructed by scientific theories.

1186. Moss, John Dietz. "Dialectic and Rhetoric: Questions and Answers in the Copernican Revolution." *Arg* 5 (February 1991): 17–37.

Examines the prevalence of dialectic in scientific discourse during the Copernican revolution. Compares the use of dialectic and rhetoric in writings by Copernicus, Kepler, and Galileo.

1187. Myers, Greg. "Lexical Cohesion and Specialized Knowledge in Science and Popular Science Texts." *DPr* 14 (January–March 1991): 1–26.

Argues that readers of scientific articles need to detect implicit lexical cohesion, while readers of polarizations require cohesive devices such as repetition and conjunctions.

1188. Nwogu, Kevin N. "Structure of Science Popularizations: A Genre-Analysis Approach to the Schema of Popularized Medical Texts." *ESP* 10 (1991): 111–123.

Examines 15 medical research articles as popularized journalistic reported versions and analyzes them as to schema and "moves" within the specific genre.

1189. Riley, Kathryn. "Passive Voice and Rhetorical Role in Scientific Writing." *JTWC* 21 (1991): 239–257.

Analyzes passive voice in 12 experimental studies; suggests passive structures are more appropriate for expository purposes and active structures more appropriate for argumentative purposes.

1190. Selzer, Richard. "An Expostulation." *L&M* 10 (1991): 34–41.

Reflecting on volume three of *Literature and Medicine*, Selzer argues that both scholars and physicians must "shift emphasis from the writings of living doctors to the whole of world literature written by men and women, be they doctors or not."

1191. Sullivan, Dale L. "The Epideictic Rhetoric of Science." *JBTC* 5 (July 1991): 229–245.

Illustrates how epideictic rhetoric—a "rhetoric of orthodoxies"—with its five rhetorical functions can be applied to internal scientific discourse.

1192. Tanno, Dolores Valencia. "Toward Savage Peace: A Conflict of Narratives in J. Robert Oppenheimer's Public Discourse, 1945–1967." *DAI* 51 (February 1991): 2566A.

Discusses the struggles of Oppenheimer to maintain faith in science after the near destruction of Hiroshima and Nagasaki.

1193. Taylor, Charles A. "The Rhetorical Construction of Science: Demarcation as Rhetorical Practice." *DAI* 51 (June 1991): 3957A.

Explores science as a discipline created by scientists constructing operative definitions and advancing proprietary interests over research domains.

1194. Weimer, Donna Schimeneck. "A Rhetorical Analysis of a Scientific Controversy: Margaret Mead Versus Derek Freeman in Cultural Anthropology." *DAI* 51 (March 1991): 2928A.

Concludes that Freeman's refutation of Mead's work is unsatisfying in that his arguments attack Mead personally instead of focusing on her scientific work.

1195. Yanos, Susan B. "A Rhetorical Analysis of the Current Challenges to the Evolutionary Paradigm." *DAI* 51 (June 1991): 4256A.

Asserts that Darwin's theories were not scientifically revolutionary because he established rather than overthrew the existing paradigm in biology.

See also 870

2.14 CROSS-DISCIPLINARY STUDIES

1196. Adegbija, Efurosibina. "A Survey of Students' Prewriting Activities and Their Implications for Teaching." *ESP* 10 (1991): 227–235.

Presents results of a survey among college students in Nigeria; encourages the teaching of more prewriting strategies that can be applied to different disciplines.

1197. Audiger, Jean Y. *Connections*. Lanham, MD: University Press of America, 1991. 172 pages

Argues for presentational symbolism as a complement to discursive language in the classroom. Stresses the limits of discursive language to communicate aesthetic appreciation. Studies the relationships among discursive language, images, and music.

1198. Berkenkotter, Carol. "Paradigm Debates, Turf Wars, and the Conduct of Sociocognitive Inquiry in Composition." *CCC* 42 (May 1991): 151–169.

Urges the importance of both cognitive (empirical) and social (hermeneutic) approaches to issues in composition studies.

1199. Burdette, Martha Bruner. "Narrative Response: A Developmental Perspective." *DAI* 52 (October 1991): 1314A.

Offers strategies for developing narrative skills by using anthropology, psychology, and literary theory as heuristic devices.

1200. Clark, Suzanne. "Writing and Revolutionaries." *JTW* 10 (Spring/Summer 1991): 87–94.

Argues that art replaces "dogma with experience." Conects modernist art, politics, and pedagogy. Reviews Paul Avarich's *The Modern School Movement*, Emma Goldman's *Anarchism and Other Essays*, and Robert Henri's *The Art Spirit*.

1201. Collins, Deanne Margaret. "Releasing Potential: An Investigation of the Use of Theatre Sports for Developing Selected Creativity Skills in Human Resource Development Professionals." *DAI* 52 (September 1991): 740A.

Argues that performing arts creativity training is applicable to other disciplines.

1202. Comprone, Joseph J. *Writing across the Disciplines: Where Do We Go from Here?* Boston, MA: CCCC, March 1991. ERIC ED 331v053. 27 pages

Seeks connections between literary theory and WAC practices; looks to current theory and functional contexts for both questions and answers.

1203. Dethier, Brock. "Using Music as a Second Language." *EJ* 80 (December 1991): 72–76.

Explains how music can be used "as a chief source of examples and analogies" in teaching key concepts of composition and/or literature courses.

1204. Ebisutani, Kay, Dan Donlan, and Elizabeth Siebers. "The Effects of Music on Reading, Oral Language, and Writing Abilities: A Review of Literature." ERIC/RCS, 1991. ERIC ED 333 356. 33 pages

Identifies and describes relevant literature to indicate how music should be used to facilitate language skill development of at-risk students.

1205. Farnsworth, Rodney. "How the Other Half Sounds: An Historical Survey of Musical Rhetoric during the Baroque and after." *RSQ* 20 (Summer 1990): 207–224.

Discusses topics, figures, and composing methods of composers and theorists who employed a now-neglected musical rhetoric that reflected the principles of verbal rhetoric.

1206. Fontelar, Pilar Franche. "Composition-Based Problem Solving as a Function of Expertise." *DAI* 51 (April 1991): 3303A.

Using writing as the problem-solving activity, compares differences in the problem-solving ability of individuals with primarily social-science versus technical-science educational backgrounds.

1207. Gallagher, Victoria J. "Repositioning the University: Organizational Symbolism and the Rhetoric of Permanence and Change." *DAI* 51 (June 1991): 3955A.

Examines rhetoric as a means by which institutions can reconcile and transcend the conflict and contradictions of competing contexts to achieve consensus or stability.

1208. Haber, Samuel. *The Quest for Authority and Honor in the American Professions, 1750–1900*. Chicago, IL: University of Chicago Press, 1991. 448 pages

Traces the cultural evolution of the professions and argues that values embedded in the American professions have their origins in the class position and occupational prescriptions of eighteenth-century English gentlemen.

1209. Harris, Lois Ann. "Bridges and Barriers to Learning: An Interdisciplinary Exploration of Issues of Authority, Knowledge, Power, and Discipline in Higher Education." *DAI* 52 (August 1991): 462A.

Examines the incongruency between ideas about what constitutes humane teaching and what appears normative in practice.

1210. JanMohamed, Abdul R., and David Lloyd, eds. *The Nature and Context of Minority Discourse*. New York: Oxford University Press, 1991. 488 pages

Emphasizes works that are theoretically centered in the political experiences of minority cultures. Creates a paradigm for critical cultural studies that accounts for the similarities and differences of minority and Third World cultures.

Essayists: Abdul R. JanMohamed, David Lloyd, Nancy Hartstock, Barbara Christian, R. Radhakrishnan, Henry Louis Gates, Jr., Renato Resaldo, Elaine H. Kim, Allogan Slagle, Jose Rabasa, Kumkum Sangari, Josaphat B. Kubayanda, Hannan Hever, Arlene A. Teraoka, Lata Mani, Caren Kaplan, Arif Dirlek, Sylvia Wynter.

1211. Kalamaras, George. *Effecting Institutional Change through Writing across the Curriculum: Ideology and Inner Dialogue*. Boston, MA: CCCC, March 1991. ERIC ED 332 220. 15 pages

Describes the emergent perceptions of curricular change by a writing consultant to a biology department.

1212. McCarthy, Lucille Parkinson, and Stephen M. Fishman. "Boundary Conversations: Conflicting Ways of Knowing in Philosophy and Interdisciplinary Research." *RTE* 25 (December 1991): 419–468.

Argues that learning occurs when authority for knowledge is redistributed. Points out that redistribution leads to closer listening, which promotes the ability to juxtapose conflicting ways of knowing.

1213. Purnell, Kenneth N., and Robert T. Solman. "The Influence of Technical Illustrations on Students' Comprehension of Geography." *RRQ* 26 (1991): 277–299.

Studied 25 Australian high school students' response to texts and illustrations. Found that comprehension was higher when both texts and illustrations were included.

1214. Seabury, Marcia Seabury. "Critical Thinking Via the Abstraction Ladder." *EJ* 80 (February 1991): 44–49.

Recommends the use of S. I. Hayakawa's image to promote "effective thinking, writing, and evaluation" in courses across the curriculum; describes its use in cross-disciplinary teachers' workshops.

1215. Stanley, Linda C., and Joanna Ambron, eds. *Writing across the Curriculum in Community Colleges*. New Directions for Community Colleges, no. 73. Los Angeles, CA: ERIC Clearinghouse for Junior Colleges and Office of Educational Research and Improvement, 1991. ERIC ED 330 420. 113 pages

Provides 15 articles on various aspects of WAC theory and practice to assist program planners and administrators at community colleges in initiating WAC programs. *Essayists:* Barbara R. Stout, Joyce N. Magnotto, Lee Odell, Martin B. Spear, Dennis McGrath, Evan Seymor, Marsha Z. Cummins, Jacqueline Stuckin-Paprin, Judith R. Lambert, Julie Bertch, Debryn R. Fleming, Hannah Karp Laipson, Patricia Durfee, Ann Sova, Libby Bay, Nancy Leech, Robert Fearrien, Ruth Lucas, Gail Hughes-Wiener, Susan K. Jensen-Cekalla, Linda Hirsch, Joanne Nadal, Linda Shohet, JoAnn Romeo Anderson, Nora Eisenberg, Harvey S. Wiener, Christine M. Godwin, Stanley P. Witt, Dana Nicole Williams.

1216. Tavakolian, Abdolhosain. "Spaces for Human Communication: The Inner Life of Two Urban Plazas in Philadelphia: Rittenhouse and Washington Squares." *DAI* 52 (February 1991): 2546A.

Argues that the spatial design of a location affects communication.

1217. Tremblath, Paul. "The Limits of Critical Culture and the Possibility of Local Aesthetics: A Study of Postmodern Rhetoric, Contemporary Theory, and Conceptual Art." *DAI* 51 (May 1991): 3735A.

Indicates that the postmodern theories of Lyotard, Rorty, Foucault, and Derrida demonstrate how theory can promote a local aesthetics of daily life.

1218. Tudjman, Miroslav. "Culture and Information Society: The Japanese." *IPM* 27 (1991): 229–243.

Contrasts Japanese corporate knowledge (cognition and communication emphasis) with western public knowledge (documentation and information emphasis); points out that these are two different "paths toward information society."

1219. Ward, Jay A. *WAC Reconsidered: Issues for the 90s*. Boston, MA: CCCC, March 1991. ERIC ED 333 456. 14 pages

Advocates approaching discourse in ways that include the diversity of academic discourse communities and their epistemological assumptions and pedagogical practices.

1220. Weissmann, Katherine E. " 'Rust-Out' Protection for College Science Teachers." *JCST* 20 (December 1990/January 1991): 140–143.

Describes the phenomenon of "rust-out"; tells how successful teachers in many disciplines avoid it and how teachers and two-year colleges can help prevent it.

See also 677, 957, 1463

2.15 OTHER

The Almanac of Higher Education, see 1230

1221. Altman, Karen E., and Thomas K. Nakayama. "Making a Critical Difference: A Different Dialogue" *JC* 41 (Autumn 1991): 116–128.

Identifies theoretical and empirical research on gender and race that needs to be conducted in cultural communication studies.

1222. Hardymon, Betsy L. "A Mother Reenvisions Her Daughter's Writing." *JTW* 10 (Fall/Winter 1991): 137–150.

Analyzes motivations that prompt personal and academic writing. Emphasizes the importance of real audiences and investment in writing. Debunks the myth that children do not like to write.

1223. Klapp, Orrin Edgar. *Inflation of Symbols: Loss of Values in American Culture*. New Brunswick, NJ: Transaction Publishers, 1991. 199 pages

Describes a process of cultural inflation involving, for example, the rhetorical expansion of a conflict into a war between good and evil or self-expansion through identifying with the deeds of heroes or celebrities.

1224. Koenigsberg, Lisa M. "Professionalizing Domesticity: A Tradition of American Women Writers on Architecture: 1848–1913." *DAI* 52 (July 1991): 197A.

Identifies previously unrecognized American women who wrote about extant architecture for several generations.

1225. Levi-Strauss, Claude, and Didier Eribon. *Conversations with Claude Levi-Strauss*. Translated by Paula Wissing. Chicago, IL: University of Chicago Press, 1991. 192 pages

Levi-Strauss responds to interview questions about his career and to questions that clarify his intellectual motives and the development of his research.

1226. Litke, Rebecca A. "The Development of Ethnographic Research in Communication." *DAI* 51 (February 1991): 2564A.

Demonstrates the need for a framework to classify ethnographic research and clarify various approaches to that research.

1227. Mann, Lian Hurst. "Architecture as Social Strategy: Structures for Knowledge for Change." *DAI* 51 (March 1991): 2901A.

Analyzes how the social construction of knowledge effects architectural design pedagogy.

1228. Pylkko, Pauli. "Game-Theoretical Aesthetics." *AJS* 8 (1991): 101–111.

Discusses writing and reading from the perspective of game theory.

1229. Reynolds, Mark. "Writing for Professional Publication." *TETYC* 18 (December 1991): 290–296.

Provides tips for busy teachers on how to find ideas and time for research and writing.

1230. *The Almanac of Higher Education*. Edited by The Chronicle of Higher Education. Chicago, IL: University of Chicago Press, 1991. 362 pages

Provides an overview of national indicators of health and financing of U. S. higher education. Gives state-by-state reports on demographics, political leadership, and statistics about faculty, students, costs, and spending.

1231. Urban, Greg. *A Discourse-Centered Approach to Culture*. Austin, TX: University of Texas Press, 1991. 224 pages

Argues against the view that culture is a single entity transmitted over time and equally accessible to all members of a community.

3

Teacher Education, Administration, and Social Roles

3.1 TEACHER EDUCATION

1232. Beere, Carole A., Lynda A. King, and Daniel W. King. "Gender-Related Instruments as Instructional Devices in the Communication Classroom" *CEd* 40 (January 1991): 73–93.

Focuses on 19 psychometric instruments. Cautions teachers to use them carefully in classes.

1233. Belanger, Kelly. *Gender and Teaching Academic Discourse: How Teachers Talk about "Facts, Counterfacts, and Artifacts."* Boston, MA: CCCC, March 1991. ERIC ED 334 577. 34 pages

Interviews 10 composition teachers about their use of a textbook; notes that responses were gender-specific.

1234. Bird, John. "What We Want to Learn: A Tone-Setting, Focus-Shifting First-Day Exercise." *ET* 22 (Winter 1990): 6–8.

Describes his method of making the first day of class useful throughout the semester.

1235. Bishop, Wendy. "Teachers as Learners: Negotiated Roles in Writing Teachers' Learning Logs." *JTW* 10 (Fall/Winter 1991): 217–240.

A coded pattern analysis, identified in nine writers' learning logs, yields three models of learning: scholar, practitioner, and analyst. Draws four conclusions about log use.

1236. Carson, Gatti. "Predictors of Future Teacher Effectiveness for Nontraditional Teacher Certification Candidates." *DAI* 52 (July 1991): 134A.

Evaluates potential measures for predicting future teacher effectiveness of participants in nontraditional teacher certification programs.

1237. Cayton, Mary Kupiec. "Writing as Outsiders: Academic Discourse and Marginalized Faculty." *CE* 53 (October 1991): 647–660.

Analyzes circumstances that prevent marginalized faculty from attaining fluency in academic discourse and asks for examination of values that structure such discourse.

1238. Chastonay, P., J. J. Guilbert, and A. Rougemont. "The Construction of a 'Topic Tree': A Way of Familiarizing a Teaching Staff to Problem-Oriented Learning in a Master's Programme in Public Health." *MEd* 25 (September 1991): 405–413.

Demonstrates the usefulness and relevance of this prewriting technique for problem-oriented learning. Gives examples.

1239. Cochran-Smith, Marilyn. "Learning to Teach against the Grain." *HER* 61 (August 1991): 279–310.

Analyzes conversations among student teachers and experienced teachers in four urban schools; argues that student teachers can learn to see themselves as agents for change.

1240. Cooper, Allene, and D. G. Kehl. "Development of Composition Instruction through Peer Coaching." *WPA* 14 (Spring 1991): 27–39.

Discusses the benefits of a nonjudgmental system of peer coaching to improve teaching by graduate assistants; uses Arizona State University's program as an example.

1241. Dragga, Sam. "Responding to Technical Writing." *TWT* 18 (Fall 1991): 202–221.

Suggests that technical writing teachers adopt practices of technical editors' explicit, systematic use of directives, questions, and suggestions to improve the usefulness of their response commentary.

1242. Etheridge, Chuck. "Memo to Myself." *ET* 22 (Summer 1991): 15–16.

Looks back in time to his college graduation (1985) and gives himself advice on how to become a good teacher.

1243. Fox, Dana Leigh. "From English Major to English Teacher: Case Studies of Student Teachers and Their First Year Teaching." *DAI* 52 (December 1991): 2003A.

Describes the participants' adaptation to the role of teacher of English and the factors that influence this transformational process.

1244. Griffith, Kevin. *Readers, Writers, Teachers: The Process of Pedagogy*. Boston, MA: CCCC, March 1991. ERIC ED 332 206. 13 pages

Surveys indicate that teaching assistants need to be acclimated to the discourse of composition before teaching.

1245. Grossman, Pamela L. *The Making of a Teacher: Teacher Knowledge and Teacher Education*. New York: Teachers College Press, 1991. 200 pages

Studies the effectiveness of a trained and untrained group of secondary school teachers. Argues that professionally trained teachers are more flexible and understand students' perspectives, while those not trained imitate their previous teachers.

1246. Harris, Jeane. "Confessions of a Backslider: Or, How I Lost My *Ethos* Because I Couldn't Read the Map of the Terrain of the Mind of Rhetoric." *FEN* 19 (Spring 1991): 26–28.

Personal account by a composition director of shifts in goals and purpose during her first three years out of graduate school.

1247. Hogan, Mark Alan. "The Effects of an Inservice Education Program on Teaching Basic Writing in Secondary Classrooms." *DAI* 51 (February 1991): 2665A.

Samples and scores student writing using two holistic measures. Finds no significant differences.

1248. Jarvis, Donald K. *Junior Faculty Development: A Handbook*. New York: MLA Publications, 1991. 128 pages

Designed to encourage mentoring and developmental programs for junior professors. Serves as a self-help manual for faculty members at a variety of institutions, from junior colleges to research universities, and as a guide for job seekers who want to evaluate an academic institution's developmental programs.

1249. Kennedy, Mary M., ed. *Teaching Academic Subjects to Diverse Learners. What Teachers Need to Know*. New York: Teachers College Press, 1991. 312 pages

Examines questions of teacher preparation relating both to knowledge of subject matter and to knowledge of diverse students. *Essayists:* Alonzo B. Anderson, Charles W. Anderson, Deborah Loewenberg Ball, James A. Banks, Herbert Clemens, Siegfried Engelmann, Robert Floden, John T. Gage, Carl A. Grant, George Hillocks, Jr., Mary M. Kennedy, Anton E. Lawson, G. Williamson McDiarmid, Tony Romano, Suzanne M. Wilson.

1250. Leland, Bruce H. *Partners in the Process: Professionalism for Writing Instructors*. Boston, MA: CCCC, March 1991. ERIC ED 331 076. 12 pages

Presents a model for involving temporary writing instructors in curriculum development, boosting morale and professional interest.

1251. Lombardo, Sally. "On Being a Teacher." *ET* 22 (Summer 1991): 32–33.

Discusses the various roles of a teacher.

1252. Magnotto, Joyce. "Faculty Writing Groups a Useful Addition to WAC Programs." *CompC* 4 (May 1991): 7–8.

Describes formal faculty groups that included "non-fiction serious," "non-fiction fun," and "fiction and fun."

1253. Mahala, Daniel. *Empowering/Being All That You Can Be: An Experiment toward a Multi-Cultural Practice*. Boston, MA: CCCC, March 1991. ERIC ED 332 182. 15 pages

Presents a course to train new teachers of composition that emphasizes desocializing students from sexist, racist, and classist ideologies.

1254. McCarron, Bill. "Encounters with Writing Assignments." *ET* 21 (Summer 1990): 30–32.

Uses writing assignments he has received and developed from 1950–1990 to chronicle changes in his career and in the English teaching profession.

1255. Montgomery, Nancy Kathleen. "The College Composition Teacher's Role in Facilitating Writing Workshops Which Emphasize Collaborative Talk about Student Texts." *DAI* 51 (February 1991): 2667A.

Finds a consistent relationship between the experience and training of the teacher with collaborative learning in writing workshops and the degree of congruence in the enactment of these concepts.

1256. Morton, Johnnye L. *Modelling Effective Writing Strategies for Preservice and Inservice Content Area Teachers*. Las Vegas, NV: The International Reading Association, March 1991. ERIC ED 333 450. 6 pages

Reports on a study that concludes that modelling desired teaching strategies can produce teachers who can use those techniques and set up writing programs.

1257. Patterson, Leslie, John C. Stansell, and Sharon Lee. *Teacher Research: From Promise to Power*. Katonah, NY: Richard C. Owen, 1991. 150 pages

Invites classroom teachers to become researchers using a naturalistic approach to data collection. Its eight chapters focus on the process of teacher research, theory building, and publication of research, illustrated with examples of teacher research by R. Kay Moss and Terresa Payne Katt.

1258. Phelan, Anne Mary. "An Examination of Teaching as Practical Political Activity." *DAI* 51 (March 1991): 2974A.

Examines the teacher as an agent of democratic citizenship and social justice. Critiques the university institution and the rationalistic definitions of the transformative intellectual.

1259. Protherough, Robert, and Judith Atkinson. *The Making of English Teachers*. Bristol, PA: Open University Press, 1991. 148 pages

Studies the approaches used in Britain for preparing English teachers.

1260. Robbins, Bruce Wayne. "Teachers as Writers: Relationships between English Teachers' Own Writing and Instruction." *DAI* 51 (May 1991): 3565A.

Explicates the concept of composition teachers as writers and discusses potential difficulties with implementing theory into practice.

1261. Sandler, Bernice Resnick. "Women Faculty at Work in the Classroom, or, Why It Still Hurts to Be a Woman in Labor" *CEd* 40 (January 1991): 6–15.

Offers nine strategies women can use to promote equity in their classes.

1262. Shrofel, Salina. "Developing Writing Teachers." *EEd* 23 (October 1991): 160–177.

Describes a faculty member's successful and unsuccessful activities to help preservice teachers use writing process approaches effectively.

1263. Sperling, Melanie. *Metaphors We Live by*. Boston, MA: CCCC, March 1991. ERIC ED 332 191. 13 pages

Finds controlling metaphors in the autobiographical narratives of preservice teachers describing their experiences in student teaching.

1264. Stratton, Charles R. "Qualifications for Teaching Technical Writing." *TETYC* 18 (February 1991): 59–64.

Suggests criteria concerning education, experience, and professional writing ability for teachers at various levels of technical writing.

1265. Swilky, Jody. *Cross-Curricular Writing Instruction: Can Writing Instructors Resist Institutional Resistance?* Boston, MA: CCCC, March 1991. ERIC ED 331 066. 14 pages

A study of two faculty members in a WAC seminar shows the need for collaboration between WAC seminar leaders and faculty who will need to change pedagogic strategies.

1266. Tindall, Mary Ellen. "Process-Oriented Writing Instruction: The Effect of Training on Instructional Practice." *DAI* 52 (August 1991): 511A.

Examines the effects of training on instructional practice related to the teaching of writing and teacher perception of what constitutes quality in student writing.

1267. Tryneski, John. *Requirements of Certification of Teachers, Counselors, Librarians, Administrators for Elementary and Secondary Schools*. 56th ed. Chicago, IL: University of Chicago Press, 1991. 250 pages

Provides an annually updated state-by-state listing of certification requirements.

1268. Van Nortwick, Thomas. "Collaborative Learning, Cultural Literacy, and the State Humanities Councils." *CEAF* 21 (Winter 1991): 6–9.

Claims that college teachers have much to learn from the success of collaborative programs for adults.

1269. Yearwood, Stephanie. "Is this Nirvana? Meditations on Our Future." *ET* 22 (Fall 1990): 34–36.

Meditates through vignettes on the future of writing teachers, including cooperation between colleges and high schools, better teacher training, and less adherence to prescriptive forms.

3.2 ADMINISTRATION

1270. Burgan, Mary, George Butte, Karen Houck, and David Laurence. "Two Careers, One Relationship: An Interim Report of "Spousal" Hiring and Retention in English Departments." *ADEB* 98 (Spring 1991): 40–45.

Reviews a sample of 80 responses regarding hiring in and outside academe, discusses problems, and presents six suggestions for department chairs.

1271. Fishbein, Estelle A. "Ownership of Research Data." *AM* 66 (March 1991): 129–133.

Johns Hopkins' General Counsel reviews current ethical and legal standards for ownership of and access to research data; makes recommendations for university policy statements on the subject.

1272. Flora, Joseph M., and Erika Lindemann. "English Chairs and Writing Program Administrators: An Antiphonal Reading." *ADEB* 100 (Winter 1991): 35–40.

Explores the relationship between the director of composition and department chair at a research institution; describes present and future pressures and how to overcome them.

1273. Glick, Nancy Lea Parsons. "Job Satisfaction among Academic Administrators at Selected American Colleges and Universities." *DAI* 52 (August 1991): 436A.

Examines job satisfaction among academic administrators in higher education. Finds that chief academic officers and deans are dissatisfied with the content of the job they do.

1274. Halstead, Kent. *State Profiles: Financing Public Higher Education, 1978 to 1991.* Washington, DC: Research Associates of Washington, 1991. 221 pages

Presents 15 measures of how states rank in providing support for public higher education.

1275. Hammond, P. Brett, and Harriet P. Morgan. *Ending Mandatory Retirement for Tenured Faculty: The Consequences for Higher Education.* Washington, DC: National Academy Press, 1991. 149 pages

Speculates on the consequences of retirement rule changes that will come into effect in 1994. Draws on data from studies of 17 colleges and universities, selected to represent a variety of institutional types.

1276. Harris, Muriel. "Solutions and Trade-Offs in Writing Center Administration." *WCJ* 12 (Fall 1991): 63–79.

Presents a series of problems that encourage collaborative, flexible, individualized solutions to administrative concerns inside writing centers.

1277. Huber, Bettina J., Denise Pinney, and David Laurence. "Patterns of Faculty Hiring in Four-Year English Programs: Findings from a 1987–1988 Survey of *Job Information List* Advertisers." *ADEB* (Fall 1991): 38–48.

Analyzes positions that have been filled in English according to such factors as specialization, rank, tenure status, and institutional characteristics.

1278. Janangelo, Joseph. "Somewhere between Disparity and Despair: Writing Program Administrators, Image Problems, and *The MLA Job Information List.*" *WPA* 15 (Fall/Winter 1991): 60–66.

Examines sample advertisements to support a claim that the job information list "militates against writing program administrators' professional advancement."

1279. Laurence, David. "Writing and Literature in the University." *CompC* 4 (March 1991): 5–6.

Argues that an institutional bias against education—not literature faculty attitudes—best explains the poor working conditions of writing faculty.

1280. Livingston-Weber, Joan. "Limits on the Power of Naming." *WPA* 14 (Spring 1991): 7–20.

Discusses the consequences of word choice, especially regarding predicates, when writing job description for writing programs by using the Western Writing Program proposal for illustration.

1281. Machann, Ginny Brown. "Andrews Hall—1963" *ET* 22 (Spring 1991): 17–20.

Examines ways in which modern students are "short-changed" by the educational system by reviewing her college education career and her love of literature.

1282. Miller, Susan. *Textual Carnivals: The Politics of Composition.* Carbondale, IL: Southern Illinois University Press, 1991. ERIC ED 326 889. 283 pages

Miller argues that historical myths, institutional structures, lack of academic rewards, and personal "self-abnegation" frequently combine to relegate teachers of composition to marginal positions.

1283. Mitoraj, Suzanne Ogorzalek. "The Impact of Technology on the Secondary School English Curriculum: A National Survey of the Views of English Department Chairs." *DAI* 52 (September 1991): 794A.

A panel of 22 English chairs identified 10 technological developments that will affect the teaching of English by shifting the emphasis and broadening curriculum content.

1284. Moss, Malcom William. "Student Affairs Administrators' University Relationships: A Study of Language Usage in Departmental Meetings." *DAI* 52 (September 1991): 765A.

A study of figurative language used by student affairs professionals reveals several perceptions of dominant relationships.

1285. Perdue, Virginia. "Writing Center Faculty in Academia: Another Look at Our Institutional Status." *WPA* 15 (Fall/Winter 1991): 13–23.

Uses Foucault's statements about power relations to encourage Writing Center faculty to reexamine how they present their work to their colleagues and administrators.

1286. *Profession 91.* Edited by Phyllis Franklin. New York: MLA Publications, 1991. 64 pages

Deals with questions college and university teachers and departments are regularly called on to answer. Subject matter ranges from electronic media to multiculturalism.

1287. Sledd, James. "Why the Wyoming Resolution Had to Be Emasculated: A History and a Quixotism." *JAC* 11 (Fall 1991): 269–281.

Argues that administrators, literati, and emininent compositionists have perpetuated an old injustice. Points out that "emancipation proclamations" unsupported by determined power are obstructive.

1288. Thomas, Trudelle. "The Graduate Student as Apprentice WPA: Experiencing the Future." *WPA* 14 (Spring 1991): 41–51.

Suggests ways in which writing progam administrators can help graduate students gain knowledge and hands-on experience in writing program administration.

1289. Wenzler, Ivo. "Project Assessment Game: (PAG): A New Approach to Development Planning." *DAI* 51 (January 1991): 2180A.

Develops an assessment procedure using multiple-perspective, small-group problem-solving, and decision-making approaches to planning situations.

1290. White, Edward M. "Use It or Lose It: Power and the WPA." *WPA* 15 (Fall/Winter 1991): 3–12.

Discusses the potential power struggles facing WPAs, gives examples of sources of WPA power, and urges all to use them.

1291. White, Ron. *Management in English Language Teaching.* New York: Cambridge University Press, 1991. 348 pages

Presents a guide to management for English language instructors making the transition to administrative responsibilities.

1292. Wilson, Allison. "The New Composition-and-Literature Textbooks: Innovative Writing Stimuli or Recycled Anthologies?" *Focuses* 4 (Summer 1991): 19–23.

Evaluates five textbooks for suitability in writing instruction.

1293. Wood, Julia T., and Lisa Firing Lenze. "Strategies to Enhance Gender Sensitivity in Communication Education." *CEd* 40 (January 1991): 16–21.

Encourages institutional leaders to create a conducive environment for men and women. Outlines specific actions to be taken by administrators, academic support services, and instructors.

See also 247

3.3 SUPPORT SERVICES

1294. Bennett, David, and Paul Hightower. "Computerizing Visual Journalism: Lessons from the Writing Labs." *JourEd* 46 (Spring 1991): 46–49.

The authors present an exploratory survey of journalism professors responsible for writing labs to determine what their aims, purposes, and costs are.

1295. Bergman, Jill. "Tutor Selection: Assessing Applicants through Group Interviews." *WLN* 15 (January 1991): 1–6.

Argues that by observing applicants discuss sample writings, the director can assess an applicant's communication skills—diplomacy, sensitivity, and ability to listen. Points out the limitations of this method.

1296. Besser, Pam. "Bridging the Gap: The Theoretically and Pedagogically Efficient Writing Center." *WLN* 16 (November 1991): 6–8.

Cites six ways in which a director can create an interdisciplinary writing center: hiring full-time tutors, engaging faculty assistance, providing orientations, selecting materials, and advertising.

1297. Bosley, Deborah S., and Linda Droll. "Creating Collaborative Writing Centers." *WLN* 15 (April 1991): 12–14.

Argues that writing centers should offer assistance in "small group dynamics and collaborative writing instructions" to assist students who take collaborative writing/learning theory and business professional courses.

1298. Brooks, Jeff. "Minimalist Tutoring: Making the Student Do All the Work." *WLN* 15 (February 1991): 1–4.

Argues that tutors can avoid becoming editors by practicing minimalist tutoring strategies.

1299. Campbell, Kermit E. *"Bad English" and "Slang": Students' Perceptions of Dialect in Writing*. Boston, MA: CCCC, March 1991. ERIC ED 332 218. 16 pages

Finds different concepts of the appropriateness of Black English in the writing of two Afro-American university students attending tutoring sessions.

1300. Carino, Peter, Lori Floyd, and Marcia Lightle. "Empowering a Writing Center: The Faculty Meets the Tutors." *WLN* 16 (October 1991): 1–5.

To increase rapport between tutors and faculty, Carino arranged for a panel presentation in which tutors described their function in tutorials and answered faculty questions.

1301. Castellucci, Karen. "Tutor's Column: Getting to Know You . . . Building Relationships as a Tutor." *WLN* 16 (September 1991): 9–11.

Describes gaining the trust of a shy student who eventually appreciates the tutor as a person with whom to explore, develop ideas, and improve writing skills.

1302. Crisp, Sally. "Our Bill of Writes." *WLN* 15 (January 1991): 8.

Lists 56 phrases containing plays on the word "write." Examples include "We have the 'write' stuff," and "All the 'write' people come here."

1303. Davis, Candice. "Tutor's Column: Qualities of a Good Writing Assistant." *WLN* 15 (January 1991): 9–10.

Argues that a good writing assistant should engage in active listening, offer meaningful feedback, gear the session to the individual, and guide by asking questions.

1304. Davis, Kevin. "Notes from the Inside." *TETYC* 18 (February 1991): 18–21.

Argues that peer tutors can help teachers to develop clear and specific writing assignments.

1305. Devet, Bonnie. "Laundry Day at the Writing Lab." *WLN* 15 (January 1991): 16.

Relates an incident in which a client asked his tutor how to remove stains from his jeans.

1306. Dixon, Mimi Still, and Maureen S. Fry. "Raising Consciousness across the Curriculum: How Faculty Can Own Responsibility for Student Writing." *WLN* 16 (October 1991): 12–15.

Cites efforts to engage university faculty in student writing. Describes writing center's involvement with outreach program, the junior exam, writing fellows, and writing-intensive programs.

1307. Dossin, Mary M. "Conference Teaching: How Writing Instructors Can Become Better 'Tutors.'" *CompC* 4 (November 1991): 5–6.

Points out that effective conferencing techniques are more than exhaustive annotations of sentence errors and tutor monologues.

1308. Dyer, Patricia M. "Business Communication Meets in the Writing Center: A Successful Four-Week Course." *WLN* 15 (March 1991): 4–6.

Describes how the center "served as an environment" for collaborative learning. Points out tht students improved their brainstorming, organizing, writing, and revising skills and learned how to incorporate the computer in the writing process.

1309. Gajewski, Geoff. "The Tutor/Facility Partnership: It's Required." *WLN* 15 (June 1991): 13–16.

Points out that peer tutors have achieved increased respect from all faculty through working closely with faculty members teaching first-year college courses to develop and evaluate writing assignments.

1310. Gamboa, Sylvia H., and Angela W. Williams. "Writing Centers on the Ropes: Using a Wilderness Lab for Discovery." *WCJ* 11 (Spring/Summer 1991): 29–40.

Describes a staff training course where tutor-trainees faced physical challenges geared toward group cooperation and communication applicable to their work at the writing center.

1311. Gillam, Alice M. "Writing Center Ecology: A Bakhtinian Perspective." *WCJ* 11 (Spring/Summer 1991): 3–12.

Explains dynamics of tutorials as interplay between centripetal and centrifugal language forces. Suggests reconceptualizing current practice according to Bakhtinian notions of dialogism, addressivity, and answerability.

1312. Healy, Dave. "Specialists Versus Generalists: Managing the Writing Center-Learning Center Connection." *WLN* 15 (May 1991): 11–16.

Argues for the propriety of involving staff in "tutorial-based learning strategies instruction." Cites his program's strengths and weaknesses.

1313. Healy, David. "Tutorial Role Conflict in the Writing Center." *WCJ* 11 (Spring/Summer 1991): 41–50.

Describes several roles tutors play and proposes ways for supervisors to help tutors clarify ambiguity and manage conflict.

1314. Hoye, Marj, and Greg Lyons. "Teachers and Tutors Talk." *WLN* 16 (November 1991): 1–5, 10.

Authors describe ways to improve tutorials. They point out that teachers can provide detailed assignments, use standard marking symbols, and make comments explanatory.

1315. Hubbuch, Susan. "Some Thoughts on Collaboration from a Veteran Tutor." *WLN* 16 (September 1991): 1–3, 8.

Discusses limitations of current collaborative learning ideology for writing center practice. Cites the center as a place where students can test and explore their individual ideas.

1316. Hughes, Bradley T. "Review of *When Tutor Meets Student: Experiences in Collaborative Learning*." *WCJ* 12 (Fall 1991): 101–104.

Reviews Martha Maxwell's collection of nineteen vignettes by undergraduate writing tutors at Berkeley between 1987 and 1989.

1317. Impson, Beth, Burl Self, Susan Dorsey, Lucinda Hudson, and Laura Johnson. "Integrating WAC and Tutoring Services: Advantages to Faculty, Students, and Writing Center Staff." *WLN* 16 (October 1991): 6–8, 11.

Describes the specific benefits of WAC and tutoring services from the perspectives of the teacher, the WAC/writing center director, and the peer tutors.

1318. Italia, Paul G. "The Curriculum Loop: The Role of the Writing Task Force in Curriculum Development at CUNY." *TETYC* 18 (October 1991): 186–190.

Describes the role of the task force in curricular development, details specific writing-curriculum recommendations, and outlines the political dynamics of its university-wide curricular endeavors.

1319. Jessop, Ann. "Tutor's Column." *WLN* 15 (May 1991): 9–10.

Argues that students' racist/sexist statements show ignorance or are mistakes. Suggests that tutors should not preach but demonstrate the effect of such statements.

1320. Johanek, Cindy. "Learning Styles: Issues, Questions, and the Roles of the Writing Center Tutor." *WLN* 16 (December 1991/January 1992): 10–14.

Recommends four styles—diverter, assimilator, converger, and accommodator—so that tutors can better understand their own learning style and appreciate the different styles in their clients.

1321. Johnstone, Sally M. "Research on Telecommunicated Learning: Past, Present, and Future." *Annals* 514 (March 1991): 49–57.

Suggests that well-designed courses offered through distance learning programs are effective, though the research is limited. Points out that researchers have begun investigating interactive systems.

1322. Jordan, Gillian. "Humor in Tutorials." *WLN* 15 (May 1991): 8, 10.

Advocates using gentle, friendly humor to dispel fears, to illustrate grammar and punctuation points, and to introduce serious but controversial ideas.

1323. Kuriloff, Peshe C. "Reaffirming the Writing Conference: A Tool for Writing Teachers across the Curriculum." *JTW* 10 (Spring/Summer 1991): 45–57.

Argues that writing conferences help teachers discover what students know and what they intend in their writing. Describes positive experience of WAC conferences at the University of Pennsylvania.

1324. Kussrow, Paul G. "Faculty Writers and the Writing Center." *CompC* 4 (February 1991): 4–5.

Describes operations and benefits of a program for faculty at a writing center.

1325. Leahy, Richard. "On Being There: Reflections on Visits to Other Writing Centers." *WLN* 15 (April 1991): 1–6.

Leahy points out that he changed the name and design of his center, the term for his tutors, and the recruiting process after seeing other centers. Recognizes the importance of a writing center for the community.

1326. Leslie, Charles J. "Learning a Lesson in the Writing Lab." *WLN* 16 (September 1991): 12–13.

Warns against encouraging students to try sophisticated writing strategies beyond their ability and experience. Cites an incident in which his suggestions were harmful rather than helpful.

1327. Litow, Ann B. "Negotiating Teaching/Learning Interactions: A Study in Reciprocity in Tutorial Discourse." *DAI* 52 (October 1991): 1313A.

This case study concludes that increased speaker confidence leads to control in writing.

1328. Lunsford, Andrea. "Collaboration, Control, and the Idea of a Writing Center." *WCJ* 12 (Fall 1991): 3–10.

Argues that collaborative projects in writing centers are most effective when power and control are negotiated and shared among staff and students.

1329. Lyons, Greg. "Writing Activities for Tutors." *WLN* 15 (March 1991): 14–16.

Requires tutors to write detailed (140 words) annotations of 10 articles and a 10–15 page report. Compiles and "publishes" research for in-house library.

1330. MacDonald, James C. "The State of Louisiana Writing Programs." *CompC* 4 (October 1991): 4–6.

Presents the results of a 1989 survey of 16 writing programs' staffing, salaries, training, and work loads.

1331. MacDonald, Ross B. "An Analysis of Verbal Interaction in College Tutorials." *JDEd* 15 (Fall 1991): 2–12.

Results of study contradicts tutor trainers' commonly held belief that tutors lead the tutees to answers by asking skillful questions.

1332. Malikowski, Steve. "Tutors' Column: Have You Heard What Your Students Have Been Saying?" *WLN* 15 (February 1991): 9–10.

Points out that tutors can demonstrate effective listening skills by repeating key parts of the student's statement, by paraphrasing the comments, and by occasionally remaining silent.

1333. Marx, Michael Steven. "Bringing Tutorials to a Close: Counseling's Termination Process and the Writing Tutorial." *WCJ* 11 (Spring/Summer 1991): 51–60.

Discusses parallels between psychological counseling and tutorials. Proposes that students and tutors benefit from "full termination process" used in counseling relationships.

1334. Masiello, Lea, and Malcolm Hayward. "The Faculty Survey: Identifying Bridges between the Classroom and the Writing Center." *WCJ* 11 (Spring/Summer 1991): 73–79.

Indicates that although tutorials suggested by faculty members match those identified by the writing center, some faculty resist supporting the services.

1335. Maxwell, Martha. "The Effects of Expectations, Sex, and Ethnicity on Peer Tutoring." *JDEd* 15 (Fall 1991): 14–18.

Concludes that tutor training programs need to address cultural sex stereotypes as well as ethnic differences and tutee expectations.

1336. McCleary, Bill. "Writing Research Center Begins Second Five Years." *CompC* 4 (November 1991): 1–4.

Summarizes the activities and main findings of the Center for the Study of Writing.

1337. Medway, Frederic J. "A Social Psychological Analysis of Peer Tutoring." *JDEd* 15 (Fall 1991): 20–26, 32.

Reviews research and recommendations for structuring tutoring programs.

1338. Mohr, Ellen. "Model of Collaboration: The Peer Tutor." *WLN* 16 (September 1991): 14–16.

Describes general effectiveness of peer tutors. Lists eight writing concerns tutors address in tutorials. Cites three strategies for teaching tutors to be good leaders.

1339. Murphy, James P. "Tutors and Fruitflies." *WLN* 15 (May 1991): 5–6.

Assigns a research topic but leaves the research and writing up to students and nonmajor tutors to make students assume responsibility for their learning.

1340. O'Flaherty, Carol. "Tutor's Column." *WLN* 16 (December 1991/January 1992): 9.

Describes tutoring a student whose teacher appropriated her text, disregarding her opinions. Encourages student to write what her teacher wants, but feels unethical.

1341. Parry, Robin. "Techniques for Assisting Adult Students Returning to Formal Education." *WLN* 15 (February 1991): 13–16.

Points out that tutors can create a supportive environment for anxious, unsure, hostile adults and, using specified strategies, encourage them to become self-confident and self-sufficient.

1342. Pobo, Kenneth G. "Creative Writing and the Writing Center." *WLN* 15 (February 1991): 5–7.

Argues that tutors can assist creative writers by encouraging them to select precise language, giving honest but tactful responses, interpreting assignments, and providing a sympathetic audience.

1343. Pomerance, Anita Humphreys. "Volunteers Tutoring Adults: The Construction of Literacy by Tutor-Student Pairs." *DAI* 51 (February 1991): 2693A.

Explores tutors' and adult learners' beliefs about literacy and learning and the relationship between their stated beliefs and actual practices.

1344. Powers, Suzanne. "What Composition Teachers Need to Know about Writing Centers." *FEN* 19 (Spring 1991): 15–21.

Discusses five writing centers in terms of concept, staffing, structure, services, and future development; also draws on scholarly studies of writing centers.

1345. Renaud, Judith. "Tutor's Column: The Writing Center Story." *WLN* 15 (March 1991): 11–12.

Compares interactions in the writing center to the plot and subplot in a story.

1346. Robins, Adrienne. "Teaching the Conferencing Strategies that Improve Student Writing." *WLN* 15 (June 1991): 1–4.

Focuses on writing and advising as a process. Writing advisors analyze videotapes of tutorials (including their own) to distinguish effective from noneffective strategies.

1347. Sams, Ed. "The Weekly Tutor Meeting." *WLN* 15 (May 1991): 104.

Divides 18-week training sessions into four categories, alternating discussions of thinking, writing, reading, and tutoring. Gives examples and sequences of several issues discussed.

1348. Schramm, Mary Jane. "Tutor's Column: Just Like Joe." *WLN* 15 (June 1991): 9–10.

Describes her misconceptions about and subsequent strategies for working with a student with a learning disability. Includes a 14-point "Checklist of Possible Learning Disabled Characteristics."

1349. Sherwood, Steve. "White Lies in the Writing Center: The Fragile Balance between Praise and Criticism." *ET* 22 (Spring 1991): 29–32.

Discusses the lies told by students in order to protect their egos and by writing center personnel in order to spare students undue trauma.

1350. Strickland, Judy. "Tutor's Column: Working with International Students." *WLN* 16 (November 1991): 9–10.

Points out that tutors should not equate language skills with mental ability. Suggests that tutors can assist ESL students by clarifying assignments and helping them develop confidence in using English.

1351. Vavra, Ed. "A Tip for Tutors." *WLN* 15 (May 1991): 6.

Suggests that tutors can help students correct subject/verb agreement problems by asking them to underline subjects and verbs in sentences rather than by referring to rules.

1352. Walker, Carolyn. "Communication with the Faculty: Vital Links for the Success of Writing Centers." *WLN* 16 (November 1991): 11–16.

Cites eight ways to "bridge the communications gap" and three ways to involve faculty. Describes presentations at faculty orientations. Urges "constant, repeated contact."

1353. Wallace, Ray, and Jeanne Simpson, eds. *The Writing Center: New Directions.* Source Books on Education, vol. 27. New York: Garland Publishing, 1991. 304 pages

Eighteen essays investigate how writing centers identify new roles, new constituencies, and new methodologies across college curricula.

Essayists: Katherine H. Adams, James Addison, Henry Wilson, Don Bushman, Robert D. Child, Irene Lurkis Clark, Sallyanne H. Fitzgerald, Peggy Mulvihill, Ruth Dobson, Karyn L. Hollis, Bradley T. Hughes, Jay Jacoby, Stan Pattan, Nadene A. Keene, Richard Leahy, Christina Murphy, Curtis E. Ricker, Donald Samson, Maurice Scharton, Janice W. Neuleib, Jeanne Simpson, Ray Wallace, William C. Wolff.

1354. White, Linda. "Spelling Instruction in the Writing Center." *WCJ* 12 (Fall 1991): 34–47.

Offers specific instructions for spelling workshops inside writing centers.

1355. Williams, Sharon. "Body Language: The Nonverbal Path to Success in the Writing Conference." *WLN* 16 (December 1991/January 1992): 6–7.

Describes positive and negative nonverbal cues such as the use of space, listener feedback, eye behavior, facial expressions, body position, and physical appearance.

1356. Wolterbeck, Marc. "Writing Center Directors Speak." *WLN* 15 (April 1991): 14–16.

Presents a survey in which 20 colleges defined the strengths and weaknesses of the writing centers. Common weaknesses pointed out are inadequate staffing, location, space, and lack of computers.

1357. Yahner, William, and William Murdick. "The Evolution of a Writing Center: 1972–1990." *WCJ* 11 (Spring/Summer 1991): 13–28.

Documents shifts in the role of writing centers based on California University of Pennsylvania's Jensen Papers and traces the history of the university's writing center.

1358. Yardas, Mark. "Tutor's Column: Achieving Rapport with Quiet Students." *WLN* 16 (October 1991): 9–10.

Shows that Yardas learned to distinguish the causes of silence, to ask open-ended questions, and to wait patiently for a response.

3.4 ROLE IN SOCIETY

1359. Bourne, Jill. "Languages in the School Systems of England and Wales." *L&E* 3 (1991): 81–102.

Describes educational provisions for minority language groups in England and Wales; argues that future provisions must challenge territoriality as a basis for language policy.

1360. CCCC Committee on Professional Standards. "A Progress Report from the CCCC Committee on Professional Standards." *CCC* 42 (October 1991): 330–344.

Clarifies Committee's "positions on certain controversial aspects" of the Statement of Professional Standards. Proposes recommendations for implementing and enforcing the statement.

1361. Clarke, Ben. "Writing in Community." *QNWP/CSW* 13 (Winter 1991): 15–18.

Describes a unique community-based learning and resource center for homeless people and residents of a low-income neighborhood in San Francisco.

1362. Clotfelter, Charles T., Ronald G. Ehrenberg, Malcolm Getz, and John J. Siegfried. *Economic Challenges in Higher Education.* Chicago, IL: University of Chicago Press, 1991. 424 pages

Analyzes the growth and composition of undergraduate enrollment, the supply of faculty in the academic labor market, and the cost of operating colleges and universities.

1363. Cole, Suzanne C. *Write Where You Are: The Off-Campus Composition Course.* Boston, MA: CCCC, March 1991. ERIC ED 332 183. 12 pages

Describes a community college's efforts to offer first-year college composition off-campus in business, industrial, and professional workplaces.

1364. Etheridge, Chuck. "Now It's *My* Turn." *ET* 22 (Spring 1991): 11–13.

Contradicts a *Newsweek* article that said college English teachers have little to do and are more interested in research than in teaching.

1365. Fagen, Laurie. "Keys to Career Independence." *PC* 11 (February/March 1991): 6–9.

Advises actual and potential entrepreneurs on securing a loan, planning for growth, selecting a partner, and hiring employees.

1366. Guthrie, James W. "The World's New Political Economy Is Politicizing Educational Evaluation." *EdEPA* 13 (Fall 1991): 309–321.

Outlines the evaluation dynamics which develop when state governments reshape higher educational systems to enhance natural economic growth; offers alternative assessment model.

1367. Haiman, Franklyn S. "Sexist Speech and the First Amendment" *CEd* 40 (January 1991): 1–5.

Identifies and describes sexist communication that occurs in classrooms, campuses, and dormitories.

1368. Lobdell, James. "Interview with James Britton: 'It Needs to Be from Within.' " *QNWP/CSW* 13 (Winter 1991): 3–6.

Reflects on composing, research, and classroom teaching in the U.S. and the U.K.; provides national curricula and social processes of education, writing, and literature.

1369. McCleary, Bill. " 'Tyrannical Machines' Hold Sway over Education, Says Cheney." *CompC* 4 (February 1991): 1–2.

Summarizes a report by Lynn Cheney and cites its aptness for the state of composition pedagogy.

1370. Peshkin, Alan. *The Color of Strangers, the Color of Friends: The Play of Ethnicity in School and Community.* Chicago, IL: University of Chicago Press, 1991. 320 pages

Presents an ethnographic study of "Riverview," an ethnically diverse town. Finds that ethnic students learned how to frame their demands in such a way that other groups could understand them, and friends gradually came to be defined by actions rather than color.

1371. Peterson, Jane E. "Valuing Teaching: Assumptions, Problems, and Possibilities." *CCC* 42 (February 1991): 25–35.

The Chair of CCCC invites its members to "approach teaching as active, committed learners" and to explore teaching as a valid "mode of inquiry."

1372. Raign, Kathrin Rossner. *Philosopher to Moderator: The Shifting Paradigm of "Ethos" in Education.* Boston, MA: CCCC, March 1991. ERIC ED 333 457. 18 pages

Traces the dichotomy between teacher as philosopher and as moderator; argues that writing teachers must determine what ethical stance is best for them.

1373. Smith, Louise Z. "Family Systems Theory and the Form of Conference Dialogue." *WCJ* 11 (Spring/Summer 1991): 61–72.

Describes conferencing in terms of family systems theory as a way of looking at the shifting roles of tutor and student.

1374. Stotsky, Sandra, ed. *Connecting Civic Education and Language Education: The Contemporary Challenge*. New York: Teachers College Press, 1991. 256 pages

Essays suggest the teaching of reading, writing, speech, and literature to strengthen the development of civic identity in students at the secondary and college level.

Essayists: John W. Cameron, Richard Catula, Jeanne S. Chall, Barbara Hardy Deierl, Lisa Ede, Dorothy Henry, Richard L. Larson, Sandra Stotsky.

1375. Tuman, Myron C. "Unfinished Business: Coming to Terms with the Wyoming Resolution." *CCC* 42 (October 1991): 356–364.

Poses "unfinished" questions about supporting "positions" rather than people, defining professional life, and staffing writing courses in research universities.

3.5 OTHER

1376. Calderonello, Alice. *Professionalism of Rhetoric/Composition: Consequences and Commitment*. Boston, MA: CCCC, March 1991. ERIC ED 333 464. 12 pages

Calls attention to the consequences and trends resulting from professionalization.

1377. Dent, Thomas, and Thomas J. Liebrandt. "Interest in Medical Editors as Staff Members of Residency Programs." *AM* 66 (July 1991): 426.

Argues that trained writing professionals help departments not only with publications but also in other writing-related fields.

1378. Phelan, James. *Beyond the Tenure Track: Fifteen Months in the Life of an English Professor*. Columbus, OH: Ohio State University Press, 1991. 235 pages

Presents a journal of an Ohio State faculty member who records his observations on teaching, advising, research, and the values of the academic reward system.

1379. Reagan, Sally Barr. *Women in Composition: Where Are We Going and How Do We Get There*. Boston, MA: CCCC, March 1991. ERIC ED 333 466. 12 pages

Reports on a survey study of 20 women considered leaders in the field of composition.

1380. Robinson, William S. "The CCCC Statement of Principles and Standards: A (Partly) Dissenting View." *CCC* 42 (October 1991): 345–349.

Argues that the CCCC Statement "needs to argue as forcefully for professionalism in the field as it does for improved status and working conditions."

4

Curriculum

4.1 GENERAL DISCUSSIONS

1381. Aber, John. *Political Commitment in the Writing Class: A Look at the Practice of Five Teachers*. Boston, MA: CCCC, March 1991. ERIC ED 331 059. 11 pages

Studies five politically progressive writing teachers; finds that they were often political in the classroom, for example, in writing assignments.

1382. AFR320/LIN325. "Language as Social Fabric: Ties That Bind and Separate." *WI* 10 (Spring 1991): 149–158.

Describes an undergraduate course at the University of Texas at Austin in the Fall of 1990 where Black English was examined through videotape, research, and discussion.

1383. Agatucci, Cora. "The Lessons of Student Autobiography." *TETYC* 18 (May 1991): 138–145.

Describes a creative writing course in autobiography.

1384. Ahlstrom, Amber Dahlin. "Reflects Actions: Theory and Practice in Teaching Writing." *DAI* 52 (November 1991): 1712A.

Argues that private as well as public theory is essential to understanding the practice of teaching writing.

1385. Alexander, Valerie. "Allusion as Heuristic." *TETYC* 18 (February 1991): 22–28.

Argues that students need to expand their understanding of classical mythology to become competent readers. Provides sample assignments.

1386. Andrews, James R. *The Practice of Theoretical Criticism*. White Plains, NY: Longman, 1990. 386 pages

Acquaints students with elements in the rhetorical situation that warrant serious attention. Teaches them a strategy with which to begin their practice of criticism. Explains that students can refine their judgments through the study of discourse, theory, and critical works written by others.

1387. Atwell, Nancie. *Side by Side: Essays on Teaching to Learn*. Portsmouth, NH: Heinemann, 1991. 184 pages

Presents eight essays that continue the ideas for expanding reading and writing instruction set forth in her previous book *In the Middle*.

1388. Atwell, Nancie, ed. *Workshop 3 by and for Teachers: The Politics of Process*. Portsmouth, NH: Heinemann, 1991. 152 pages

Presents annually written articles by and for elementary teachers ("teacher-researchers") concerned with ways of improving the language arts curriculum.

Essayists: Linda Hazard Hughs, Mary Ellen Giacobbe, Mem Fox, Mark Milliken, Lynn Parsons, Thomas Newkirk, Mimi DeRose, Yetta Goodman, Ken Goodman, Sigmund A. Boloz, Patrick Shannon, Ed Kenny, Marguerite Graham, Ralph Fletcher, Margaret Lally Queenan.

1389. Baker, Tracey. "Collaborating the Course and Organized Flexibility in Professional Writing." *JBTC* 5 (July 1991): 275–284.

Develops an entire course using shared-document writing.

1390. Berrill, Deborah P. "The Development of Written Argument at Eleven, Sixteen, and Twenty-Two Years of Age." *DAI* 51 (January 1991): 2294A.

Looks at cognitive and social/affective development; suggests that teachers concentrate on their students' strengths rather than on teaching formal argument.

1391. Biggs, Margaret M. "The Effect of Journal Writing on the Reading Comprehension and the Metacognitive Awareness of College Students." *DAI* 51 (February 1991): 2690A.

Finds that teacher interaction, and not journal writing with or without dialogue, affects reading comprehension scores.

1392. Bizzell, Patricia. "Power, Authority, and Critical Pedagogy." *JBW* 10 (Fall 1991): 54–70.

Rejects the concept of power as "unitary force with uniform effects"; explains how power and authority are interrelated in composition courses promoting "alternative critical literacy."

1393. Blohm, Paul J., and Stephen L. Benton. "Effect of Prewriting Interventions on Production of Elaboration in Informative Writing." *JRDEd* 24 (Winter 1991): 28–31.

Extends the utility of student-generated metacognitive prewriting activities to promote and embellish top-level ideas.

1394. Bloom, Lynn Z. "Be It Ever So Humble, They Can Go Home Again." *ExEx* 37 (Fall 1991): 31–32.

Argues that students become comfortable in the composition classroom and develop their writing and analysis skills by writing about their homes and other buildings familiar to them.

1395. Bodino, Angela Adamides. "An Analysis of the Construing Processes of Twelve Student Writers as They Read, Write, Revise, and Interpret Personal Narrative: A Constructivist View of Language." *DAI* 51 (January 1991): 2295A.

Uses a case study to compare skilled and unskilled writers; traces levels of writers' metaphorical uses of language.

1396. Boswell, Grant. "Using Kenneth Burke's 'Linguistic Skepticism' in a Composition Class." *CompC* 4 (September 1991): 9–11.

Explains strategies implicit and explicit in Burke's work for teaching students to recognize persuasive techniques.

1397. Brooke, Robert E. *Writing and Sense of Self: Identity Negotiations in Writing Workshops*. Urbana, IL: NCTE, 1991. 166 pages

Argues that learning is influenced by identity negotiations that necessitate a change in the structure of writing classes. Shows that workshop teaching helps students develop writers' roles because it focuses on identity negotiations, helps students understand themselves as writers, and teaches writing more effectively.

1398. Brown, Hazel, and Vonne Mathie. *Inside Whole Language: A Classroom View*. Portsmouth, NH: Heinemann, 1991. 96 pages

Looks at translating a basic belief in whole language teaching into classroom practice.

1399. Brunner, Diane D. "Who Owns This Work? The Question of Authorship in Professional/Academic Writing." *JBTC* 5 (October 1991): 393–411.

Explores social, cultural, and political assumptions implicit in the concept of authorship.

1400. Buckelew, Mary. *Group Discussion Strategies for a Diverse Student Population*. Boston, MA: CCCC, March 1991. ERIC ED 334 576. 12 pages

Reports writing student responses to a questionnaire on classroom discussion.

1401. Bularzik, Eileen M. *Reading Processes: Responding to Discourse Community Constraints*. Boston, MA: CCCC, March 1991. ERIC ED 333 359. 13 pages

Describes a course where students learn to read the texts of and write for particular discourse communities.

1402. Cadet, Lorraine Page. "A Description of the Evolution of Computer-Supported Composition Curricula in Kansas Public Community/Junior Colleges." *DAI* 52 (October 1991): 1185A.

Examines variables governing institutional implementation of microcomputer curricula; offers suggestions for further research.

1403. Cain, Mary Ann. "The Role of the Writer in the Academy: Narrative, Gender, and Cultural Inscription." *DAI* 51 (January 1991): 2295A.

Concludes that the cultural "text" of the classroom is created through personal narrative.

1404. Carroll, Michael. "A Comment on 'Pedagogy of the Distressed' [*CE* 52 (October 1990)].' " *CE* 53 (September 1991): 599–601.

Contends that Tompkins' student-centered approach is unrealistic for junior faculty and writing instructors.

1405. Chappell, Virginia A., Mary Louise Buley-Meissner, and Chris Anderson, eds. *Balancing Acts: Essays on the Teaching of Writing in Honor of William F. Irmscher*. Carbondale, IL: Southern Illinois University Press, 1991. 216 pages

First section presents six essays offering a personal and immediate look at the paradoxes and compromises of student-teacher interaction. Second section includes five essays focusing on the dynamics of teachers' decision-making about theory and pedagogy within their own institutional communities.

Essayists: Kurt Spellmeyer, Chris Anderson, Mary Louise Buley-Meissner, Virginia A. Chappell, Kathleen Doty, Edward P. J. Corbett, Christine R. Farris, Anne Ruggles Gere, Richard Lloyd-Jones, Richard Young, Charles I. Schuster, Richard Tracey.

1406. Chesin, Martin F. "Teaching and Using Computers, Literature, and Writing in the Electronic Classroom." *CACJ* 5 (Winter 1991): 29–33.

Argues that students experiment with literature texts, manipulate sentence order and develop an appreciation for reading and writing skills by using computers.

1407. Clark, John, and Anna Lydia Motto. "Masking—In Style." *ExEx* 37 (Fall 1991): 15–16.

Argues for revising peer writing in the style of authors such as Hemingway, Dickens, Faulkner, or Tom Wolfe.

1408. Collazo Bhakuni, Rosa. "The Revision Spiral: A Questioning Strategy for Effective Composing." *DAI* 51 (May 1991): 3653A.

Discusses effective revision by students in relation to an awareness of the individual writing process, a self-questioning strategy, and a check of surface matters throughout the process.

1409. Corder, Jim. "Collaboration and Autonomy, Owning and Sharecropping." *FEN* 19 (Spring 1991): 11–12.

Suggests that although the social constructionist/intertextual pedagogy appears powerful currently, pedagogy needs to accept lone author theory as well.

1410. Cortes, Carlos, Elizabeth Minnich, and Martin Bernal. "Rethinking the Curriculum: Three Scholars on Their Work." *AAHE* 43 (June 1991): 3–8.

Presents three ways of implementing multicultural perspectives ("curriculum of inclusion") in the classroom.

1411. Danis, M. Francine. *Soup Sandwiches and Box Cars: Using Images to Teach Organization*. Boston, MA: CCCC, March 1991. ERIC ED 333 429. 14 pages

Advocates using images and metaphors to help students heighten their perception of themselves as organizers.

1412. Dinan, John, and Robert Root, eds. *Book Bindings and Boundaries*. Language Arts Journal of Michigan. Rochester, MI: Michigan Council of Teachers of English, 1990. 83 pages

Essays suggest ways in which teachers can move beyond the confines of traditional curricula or facilities, opening the classroom to a wide variety of learning experiences; suggestions include using oral traditions and encouraging interaction between students at different ages, students and the elderly, and students of different cultural backgrounds.

Essayists: Terry Blackhawk, Mary M. Dekker, Saly J. Dorenbusch, Marguerite H. Helmers, Sarah Henderson, William Palmer, Carol Bender, Elizabeth Spatz, Stephen Tchudi, Margaret Tebo-Messina, Doris Blough, Marybeth Tessmer, Eleanor L. Wollett.

1413. "Disputed Composition Syllabus at University of Texas Still on Hold." *CompC* 4 (February 1991): 7.

Summarizes events leading to the suppression of a syllabus developed by Linda Brodkey and others.

1414. Dittmer, Allan F. "Letters: The Personal Touch in Writing." *EJ* 80 (January 1991): 18–24.

Recommends letter writing to activate interest and improve students' appreciation of the power of written communication.

1415. Dossin, Mary M. "Getting beyond the Typo: Effective Peer Critiquing." *CompC* 4 (May 1991): 4–5.

Argues that teachers should use modeling, examples, and specific directions to teach peer evaluation.

1416. Dryden, Phyllis. *Alexander Bain's CUE in the Post-Modern World: Unity Revisited.* Boston, MA: CCCC, March 1991. ERIC ED 332 213. 14 pages

Argues that values of coherence, unity, and emphasis (Bain, 1866) remain embedded in current composition textbooks. Recommends creative writing as an antidote.

1417. Egghe, L. "Theory of Collaboration and Collaborative Measures." *IPM* 27 (1991): 177–202.

Suggests principles for good collaborative measures and presents a new method for measuring collaborative efforts in various situations (e.g., consulting papers).

1418. Ehrhart, Margaret J. " 'Dear Journal.' " *CollT* 39 (Spring 1991): 55–56.

Suggests that a teacher's personal responses to students' authentic journal writing builds a class relationship of understanding.

1419. Elliot, David. "Sharing Language: A Conversation with William Stafford." *TETYC* 18 (December 1991): 255–260.

Provides advice from a poet/teacher on writing as process, with a warning about the hazards of praising students.

1420. Englert, Carol Sue, and Troy V. Mariage. "Shared Understandings: Structuring the Writing Experience through Dialogue." *JLD* 24 (June/July 1991): 330–342.

Describes classroom dynamics that provide the basis for establishing a literacy context where students learn common text structures and metacognitive processes to guide their writing.

1421. Erwin, T. Dary. *Assessing Student Learning and Development: A Guide to Principles, Goals and Methods of Determining College Outcomes*. San Francisco, CA: Jossey-Bass Publishers, 1991. 250 pages

Describes key issues, strategies, terminology, and challenges in developing an assessment program within an academic department. Shows how to select reliable and valid existing assessment methods that fit institutional needs. Details how to design new assessment methods.

1422. Eubanks, Ilona M. "Nonstandard Dialect Speakers and Collaborative Learning." *WI* 10 (Spring 1991): 143–148.

Argues that the needs of students with nonstandard dialect are not being met by traditional instruction methods; offers bidialecticality as an alternative.

1423. Flower, Linda, Rebecca Burnett, Thomas Hajduk, David Wallace, Linda Norris, Wayne Peck, and Nancy Spivey. "Making Thinking Visible: An Introduction to Collaborative Planning (Revised)." Carnegie-Mellon University, Center for the Study of Writing, 1991. ERIC ED 334 593. 72 pages

Reports on materials for teaching collaborative planning gathered by elementary, high school, and college teachers.

1424. Fulkerson, Tahita. "The Jump-Start: A Collection of Energizing Strategies for Stalled Writers and Teachers." *ET* 22 (Summer 1991): 17–21.

Collects ideas from a variety of teachers to help students begin writing when they are having trouble thinking of anything to say.

1425. Gabriel, Susan L., and Isaiah Smithson, eds. *Gender in the Classroom: Power and Pedagogy*. Baltimore, MD: University of Illinois Press, 1990. 208 pages

Essays range from theoretical contributions to discussions of classroom dynamics. Contributors discuss issues of gender and gender equity in education.
Essayists: Isaiah Smithson, Carolyn G. Heilbrun, Cheris Kramarae, Paula Treichler, Nina Baym, Patrocinio P. Schweickart, Robert Con Davis, Elizabeth A. Flynn, Susan L. Gabriel, Linda Laube Barnes, Penny L. Burge, Steven M. Culver, Myra Sadker, David Sadker.

1426. Gardner, Phillip. "Introductory Paragraphs and Revision." *TETYC* 18 (February 1991): 55–58.

Argues that student "truths," a method for creating introductions, can provide both means and measure for essay revision.

1427. Gatherwall, Frances Mary. "Bridging the Gap from Oral to Written Discourse through Dialogue Journals." *DAI* 52 (September 1991): 790A.

Presents six case studies and concludes that writing in dialogue journals enables authors to build on their oral language resources in learning to write.

1428. Gilbert, Pamela K. "Letter to the Readers: Black English in the University." *WI* 10 (Spring 1991): 113–115.

Introduces theme of journal issue: how do writing instructors validate the voice of black students while simultaneously telling them their language is substandard.

1429. Gillis, Candida. *The Community as Classroom: Integrating School and Community through Language Arts*. Portsmouth, NH: Boynton/Cook, 1991. 224 pages

Discusses how students can explore their own communities through language-centered activities.

1430. Good, Howard. "Teaching Writing as a Beautiful and Bleak Passion." *CHE* 37 (17 July 1991): B3.

Discusses the exhaustion and rewards of writing. Contends that obsession with writing must be learned, not taught.

1431. Gourdine, Angeletta K. M. "Exploring the Rhetoric of Science." *WI* 10 (Spring 1991): 136–142.

Asks students to examine their own linguistic histories through a sociolinguistic autobiography; ends with discussion of the formal ritual of the writing classroom.

1432. Graves, Donald H. *Build a Literate Classroom*. Portsmouth, NH: Heinemann, 1991. 208 pages

Presents a practical guide of various classroom activities to help make students into life-long readers and writers.

1433. Greenberg, Steven R. "Approval-Guided Learning: Its Impact on Self-Esteem and Written Expression Skills." *DAI* 51 (May 1991): 3617A.

Investigates the effects of approval-guided (praise for correct response) learning to teach written expression.

1434. Harris, Joseph. "After Dartmouth: Growth and Conflict in English." *CE* 53 (October 1991): 631–646.

Reviews conflicts uncovered by Dartmouth Seminar of 1966 to help assess how English can best be taught today.

1435. Hawkes, Peter. "Fire, Flag, Feud, and Frost: Teaching the Interpretation of Symbols." *ExEx* 36 (Spring 1991): 6–11.

Provides examples of three activities—flag burning, *Family Feud* game show, and Frost poem discussion—that strengthen students' abilities to connect symbol with meaning.

1436. Hayward, Nancy M. "The Reluctant Writer: A Descriptive Study of Student Behavior and Motivation in the Composition Class." *DAI* 52 (December 1991): 2054A.

Examines the motivations and attitudes of university students in writing classes and addresses the lack of research concerning the affective aspects of writing.

1437. Hobson, Eric. "Where Do College Students Come From?: School/University Articulation on Writing Theory." *FEN* 19 (Fall 1991): 26–28.

An explanation of whole language theory for post-secondary language instructors with a plea that they listen to "other agents within literacy education."

1438. Holman, Elizabeth Vanderventer. "Intuition and College Student Writers: A Phenomenological Study." *DAI* 52 (July 1991): 98A.

Identifies points in the writing process where intuition is most likely to occur.

1439. Jackson, Alan. "A Lesson in Transitions." *ExEx* 36 (Spring 1991): 23–24.

Points out that students collaborate and learn the importance of transition in a pass-around story.

1440. Joyner, Michael. "The Writing Center Conference and the Textuality of Power." *WCJ* 12 (Fall 1991): 80–89.

Points out that students need to be made aware by writing tutors that their texts are expressions of ideology, explicit or not, empowering them to enter into academic discourse.

1441. Kecht, Maria-Regina, ed. *Pedagogy Is Politics: Literary Theory and Critical Teaching*. Champaign, IL: University of Illinois Press, 1991. 240 pages

Points out that education's primary purpose is to develop students' ability to think critically. Argues that all teachers of literature, composition, and culture are active critical theorists.

1442. Kelly, Priscilla. *Metaphor, Narrative, and Point of View: Shifting Our Perspectives about "Literary Techniques" in Composition.* Boston, MA: CCCC, March 1991. ERIC ED 332 196. 13 pages

Three concepts from creative writing offer advantages in the teaching of exposition.

1443. Kiedaisch, Jean, and Sue Dinitz. "Learning More from the Students." *WCJ* 12 (Fall 1991): 90–100.

Evaluates a tutoring program that is organized around student self-reporting; examines gender issues, non-English majors, nonverbal communication, ESL, and learning disabilities.

1444. Kiewra, Kenneth. "Aids to Lecture Learning." *EdPsy* 26 (Winter 1991): 37–53.

Describes instructional aids that improve students' abilities to learn through lectures and presents an integrated learning system as an alternative to the lecture method.

1445. Kirby, Dan, and Carol Kuykendall. *Mind Matters: Teaching for Thinking.* Portsmouth, NH: Boynton/Cook, 1991. 248 pages

Argues and demonstrates that mental growth comes from having students grapple with real issues.

1446. Kirschner, Paul A., Henk van den Brink, and Marthie Meester. "Audiotape Feedback for Essays in Distance Education." *Innovative Higher Education* 15 (Spring/Summer 1991): 185–195.

Authors point out that students who received audio-feedback considered their experience as personal, complete, and clear, whereas students who received written feedback considered their experience only as adequate.

1447. Knoblauch, C. H. "The Albany Graduate English Curriculum." *ADEB* (Spring 1991): 19–21.

Explains DA program titled *Writing, Teaching, and Criticism* that emphasizes coherence within English studies, outlining eight aims reached by five areas of study.

1448. Knodt, Ellen Andrews. "'I Can Do That!' Building Basic Writers' Confidence and Skill." *TETYC* 18 (February 1991): 29–33.

Sequences writing assignments on the Moffett model: observation, narration, generalization, and theory. Provides sample assignments.

1449. Kort, Melissa Sue. "Classroom Research and Composition Classes." *TETYC* 18 (May 1991): 98–102.

Points out that classroom research conducted by the individual teacher provides valuable information; describes one model.

1450. Kumar, Amitava. "Brecht and His Friends: Writing as Critique." *JAC* 11 (Fall 1991): 301–314.

Kumar's semester daybook provides insight into Brecht's critical thinking pedagogy.

1451. Kuriloff, Peshe C. "Writing across the Curriculum and the Future of Freshman English: A Dialogue between Literature and Composition." *ADEB* 98 (Spring 1991): 34–39.

Argues that first-year college composition taught as textual studies can facilitate integration of composition and literature.

1452. Kutz, Eleanor, and Hephzibah Roskelly. *An Unquiet Pedagogy: Transforming Practice in the English Classroom.* Portsmouth, NH: Boynton/Cook, 1991. 376 pages

Presents a new approach to teaching English; draws on the work of Freire; helps students resist existing practices.

1453. Laditka, James N. "Language, Power, and Play: The Dance of Deconstruction and Practical Wisdom." *RR* 9 (Spring 1991): 298–311.

Links deconstruction, cultural criticism, and Covino's *The Art of Wondering* for a composition practice; argues that it fosters students' ethical judgment and results in their empowerment.

1454. Lamb, Catherine E. "Beyond Argument in Feminist Composition." *CCC* 42 (February 1991): 11–24.

Suggests moving beyond "monologic argument" to "collaborative, cooperative, and structured" forms of negotiation and mediation so that "power is experienced as mutually enabling."

1455. Latona, John. "What Do We Mean by 'Writing-Intensive.'" *CompC* 4 (October 1991): 8–9.

A survey of WAC programs reveals that "writing intensive" is defined by the program's aims and principles or by the quantity of writing (average: 4800 words).

1456. Leeds, Bruce, and Sharon Sieber. "Classroom Writing Strategies." *CEAF* 21 (Winter 1991): 12–16.

Gives reminders and advice for student writers to encourage creativity and communication.

1457. Liggett, Sarah. "Creativity and Nonliterary Writing: The Importance of Problem Finding." *JTW* 10 (Fall/Winter 1991): 165–179.

Correlates three characteristics of creativity with three different characteristics of problem solving. Applies findings to a student example.

1458. Lisowski, Marylin. "Other Voices, Other Times—Ideas with Lasting Meaning." *JCST* 20 (February 1991): 220–221.

Presents a collection of quotations about knowledge and discovery as thinking, writing, and discussion prompts for students.

1459. Ludeman, Sandra Guth. "Encouraging Reflection in Teachers of Writing: Two Case Studies." *DAI* 52 (September 1991): 763A.

A year-long study documents the teaching methods used by two teachers and the justification for their use.

1460. Martin, Judy L. "Removing the Stumbling Blocks: Twenty-Five Ways to Help Our Learning-Disabled College Writers." *TETYC* 18 (December 1991): 283–289.

Provides a guide for improving the learning environment for students in general and for learning-disabled students in particular.

1461. McCleary, Bill. "Topics Are Always an Issue." *CompC* 4 (September 1991): 7–8.

Summarizes five approaches for assigning topics in writing classes.

1462. McClish, Glen. "Controversy as a Mode of Invention: The Example of James and Freud." *CE* 53 (April 1991): 391–402.

Suggests using ideological readings as the framework for a confrontation-based approach to invention and looks briefly at a student paper produced by this practice.

1463. Means, Barbara, Carol Chelemer, and Michael S. Knapp, eds. *Teaching Advanced Skills to At-Risk Students: Views from Research and Practice*. Jossey-Bass Education Series. San Francisco, CA: Jossey-Bass, 1991. 280 pages

Eight essays present six instructional models that have proven successful in teaching reading comprehension, written composition, and mathematical reasoning to students at risk in typical school programs. *Essayists:* Michael S. Knapp, Lauren B. Resnick, Sharon B. Lesgold, Penelope L. Peterson, Thomas Carpenter, Annemarie Sullivan Palincsar, Marlene Scardamalia, Allan Collins, Sharon M. Carver, Barbara Means, Victoria L. Bill, Mary N. Leer, Elizabeth Fennema, Laura J. Klenk, Mary Bryson, Robert Calfee, Jan Hawkins, Carol Chelemer.

1464. Moffett, James, and Betty Jane Wagner. *Student-Centered Language Arts, K–12*. 4th ed. Portsmouth, NH: Boynton/Cook, 1991. 460 pages

Provides a new edition of the landmark 1968 textbook that attempted to provide the basis for a comprehensive, K–12, language arts curriculum.

1465. Murray, Bertha Flowers. "Improvement in Reading Comprehension and Writing Performance as a Function of Text-Interactive

Instruction." *DAI* 52 (September 1991): 794A.

Indicates that students receiving text-interactive instruction improved their writing performance.

1466. Murray, Donald M. "One Writer's Curriculum." *EJ* 80 (April 1991): 16–20.

Illustrates 10 basic elements of a self-directed composition curriculum which "begins in solitude and ends in community"; recommends being attentive to anything that improves writing.

1467. Nash, Cornelia Lynne. "Teaching Undergraduates Writing Skills: A Cognitive Approach Based on Modelling." *DAI* 52 (October 1991): 1225A.

Finds that process-oriented instruction leads to some gains in the abilities of students in newswriting classes.

1468. Neuman, Michael. "Rightwriter 3.1." *CHum* 25 (February 1991): 55–58.

Suggests using this editing software to help students revise their papers—after teachers adapt it to their specific classes.

1469. Nunnally, Thomas E. "Breaking the Five-Paragraph-Theme Barrier." *EJ* 80 (January 1991): 67–71.

Encourages teachers and students to recognize "the FPT" as "helpful but contrived exercise useful in developing solid principles of composition."

1470. Ochsner, Robert. *Physical Eloquence and the Biology of Writing*. Albany, NY: State University of New York Press, 1990. 230 pages

Recommends an approach to teaching writing that stresses the neurological foundations of written English. Emphasizes the neurological processes of hand, eye, and ear that every writer must control to generate and simultaneously interpret a text and the innate abilities that all people have for acquiring prose.

1471. Odom, Keith C. "If I Write It, They Will Come: Thoughts on the Process of Personal Writing." *ET* 22 (Spring 1991): 22–25.

Discusses his rationale for writing autobiography.

1472. Pack, Robert, and Jay Parini, eds. *Writers on Writing*. Middlebury, VT: Middlebury College Press, 1991. 307 pages

Presents the act and art of writing for practitioners, teachers, and readers by established poets and fiction writers.

Essayists: Marvin Bell, Rosellen Brown, Nicholas Delbanco, Stanley Elkin, Richard Ford, Gail Godwin, David Huddle, T. R. Hummer, John Irving, Erica Jong, Donald Justice, Sydney Lea, Philip Levine, William Matthews, Paul Mariani, Joyce Carol Oates, Tim O'Brien, Robert Pack, Jay Parini, Linda Pastan, Francine Prose, Lynne Sharon Schwartz, Ellen Bryant Voigt, Nancy Willard, Hilma Wolitzer.

1473. Parry, Sally E. "The Doctor Is a Woman: Using Sexual Stereotypes to Explore Gender Roles." *ExEx* 37 (Fall 1991): 10–11.

Presents a device to encourage students to consider gender issues in a nonthreatening atmosphere.

1474. Perrin, Robert. "When Junk Mail Isn't Junk." *EJ* 80 (January 1991): 30–32.

Explains how mail can be used in class activities such as analyzing advertisers' concepts of audience and techniques of persuasion.

1475. Prentice, Penelope. "Some Applications of Brief Therapy to Teaching Creative Writing and Literature and to Teaching in General." *ET* 21 (Summer 1990): 35–37.

Describes how a psychological counseling method can be used to develop writing abilities.

1476. Proctor, Margaret B. "The Writer's Voice: An Overview, and an Analysis of Voice in Student Writing." *DAI* 51 (January 1991): 2299A.

Defines voice as a presence of the implied author, measures it against qualitative and linguistic features, and suggests classroom applications.

1477. Raban, Birdie, and Maggie Sanders Bolton. "Writing What They Mean." *EQ* 23 (1991): 40–50.

Authors point out that students make changes which enhance meaning when reading their writing aloud.

1478. Reagan, Sally Barr. "Warning! Basic Writers at Risk: The Case of Javier." *JBW* 10 (Fall 1991): 99–115.

Demonstrates that teachers should "take a researcher's view" in determining changes that they themselves must undergo to encourage students' academic success.

1479. Reaves, Rita Reavis. "The Effects of Writing-to-Learn Activities on the Content Knowledge, Retention of Information, and Attitudes toward Writing of Selected Vocational Agricultural Education Students." *DAI* 52 (November 1991): 1614A.

Finds that writing-to-learn activities enable students to retain more of the information learned and to gain confidence in their ability to write.

1480. Rico, Gabriele Lusser. *Writing the Natural Way*. New York: Teachers & Writers Collaborative, 1991. 286 pages

Presents Rico's "clustering" technique, which is a way to break through writer's block, explore sensibilities more fully, and shape one's work.

1481. Roberts, Patricia Jenkins. "Enabling Factors in the Development of Writing Competence: What Writers and Teachers Say." *DAI* 52 (October 1991): 1241A.

Identifies and compares items that contribute to competence; offers suggestions on incorporating these items.

1482. Rule, Rebecca. *Writers Welcome Here: Evolution through Diversity: The University of New Hampshire's Workshop Model for Teaching Writing*. Boston, MA: CCCC, March 1991. ERIC ED 333 424. 7 pages

Describes the writing workshop as observed by an English faculty member, both as a teacher and as a student in the writing program.

1483. Scheurer, Erika. *Voice and the Collaborative Essay*. Boston, MA: CCCC, March 1991. ERIC ED 332 222. 14 pages

Relates teaching experience in which co-writing proved problematic for students; points out that they ultimately incorporated their own voices in the essay.

1484. Schiff, Peter. "Developing Student Writing Essays." *ExEx* 36 (Spring 1991): 21–22.

Students imitate in writing the voices of three school figures based on Walker Gibson's tough, sweet, and stuffy categories in a casebook assignment.

1485. Schine, Rena. "The Role of Language Communication Acquisition Experience in Developing Abstract Thought in Deaf Students." *DAI* 51 (February 1991): 2682A.

Concludes that deaf children should receive a curriculum that teaches thinking strategies directly in order to compensate for their lack of natural access to life and language experience.

1486. Schmudde, Carol. "Teaching Accommodation in Argument through Negotiations Roleplay." *ExEx* 36 (Spring 1991): 17–20.

As "Student Activities Council" or "Alumni Association Members," students roleplay to establish a balance of power, determine a budget, and resolve an issue of principle.

1487. Scholes, Robert. "A Flock of Cultures—A Trivial Proposal." *CE* 53 (November 1991): 759–772.

Refutes "Great Books" curricula for lacking intellectual, disciplinary, and historical basis; proposes modernized trivium to link cultures past and present.

1488. Secor, Marie, and Davida Charney, eds. *Constructing Rhetorical Education*. Carbondale, IL: Southern Illinois University Press, 1991. 480 pages

Authors assume that a rhetorical education is not limited to teaching first-year composition, and that the classroom is not the only place in which such education occurs. Volume stresses that the larger goal of a rhetorical education is to foster critical thinking.

Essayists: Anuradha Dingwaney, Lawrence Needham, JoAnn Campbell, Katherine Borland, Valerie M. Balester, Anne J. Herrington, Louise Wetherbee Phelps, Carmen B. Schmersahl, Byron L. Stay, Cynthia L. Selfe, Evangeline Marlos Varonis, Janice N. Hays, Kathleen S. Brandt, Jeanne Fahnestock, V. Melissa Holland, Barbara M. Sitko, Elizabeth A. McCord, Mary Rosner, Diane Dowdey, Jeffrey Walker, Steven B. Katz, Aletha Hendrickson.

1489. Sheridan, Daniel. "Changing Business as Usual: Reader Response in the Classroom." *CE* 53 (November 1991): 804–814.

Discusses classroom practices of reader-response theory and the recognition of a teacher's authority amid diverse functions as reader, lecturer, and discussion leader.

1490. Steckfuss, Richard. "Good Writing Can Be Taught with Critiques and Rewrites." *JourEd* 46 (Autumn 1991): 64–68.

Identifies six writing characteristics that differentiate between professional and amateur writers; describes how students are guided to improve their writing.

1491. Stephens, Diane. *Research on Whole Language: Support for a New Curriculum.* Katonah, NY: Richard C. Owen Publishers, 1991.

Reviews research on whole language classrooms and helps educators sift through competing ideas about literacy. The first section explores the roots of whole language and discusses the philosophical basis for whole language. The bulk of the book is an annotated list of research since 1985.

1492. Stires, Susan, ed. *With Promise: Redefining Reading and Writing Needs for Special Students.* Portsmouth, NH: Heinemann, 1991. 200 pages

Teachers and researchers share their experience with teaching reading and writing to "at-risk" students.

Essayists: T. Romano, A. Furnas, E. S. Fine, I. Johnson, K. Robinson, P. T. Cousin, M. J. Throne, W. L. Wansart, D. Graves, K. S. Goodman, B. S. Sunstein, L. Hoyt, J. Bailey, L. Prentice, E. Aragin, C. Leonard, L. A. Rose, T. Weekley, C. Chee, C. Etsetty, D. Kiyaani, L. Kiyaani, L. Lockhard, L. Tsosie.

1493. Strickland, Kathleen. "Toward a New Philosophy of Language Learning." *ELQ* 13 (February 1991): 2–4.

Provides a brief overview of the beliefs of a whole language philosophy and the common elements that such classrooms share.

1494. Suhor, Charles. "Surprised by Bird, Bard, and Bach: Language, Silence, and Transcendence." *EJ* 80 (February 1991): 21–26.

Encourages classroom activities allowing teachers and students to experience "the silence of transcendence towards which literature and all other arts ultimately point us."

1495. Sullivan, Mary Margaret. "Revision from a Reader's Perspective: Conferences and Peer Editing." *ET* 22 (Fall 1990): 22–25.

Suggests that students need guidance that is provided better by conversation than by written comments; dicusses methods she uses for conferencing and peer editing.

1496. Taylor, Hanni. "Ambivalence toward Black English: Some Tentative Solutions." *WI* 10 (Spring 1991): 121–135.

Describes instruction that uses a bidialectical language pedagogy by teaching basic linguistic components and comprehension within an affective and conative domain of social context.

1497. Tingle, Nick. "Returning to the Self Psychoanalytically." *FEN* 19 (Fall 1991): 17–19.

Suggests a post-Freudian pedagogy for composition and literature that would help students transform narcissistic injuries.

1498. Tobin, Lad. "Reading Students, Reading Ourselves: Revising the Teacher's Role in the

Writing Class." *CE* 53 (March 1991): 333–348.

Suggests that instructor's role needs redefining by examining writing in the context of the student-teacher relationship.

1499. Tompkins, Jane. "Jane Tompkin Responds [to Carroll, *CE* 53 (September 1991)]." *CE* 53 (September 1991): 601–604.

Sympathizes with Carroll but also defends her student-centered pedagogy by asserting that teachers have "more freedom than we think."

1500. Torgovnick, Marianna. "Writing Cultural Criticism." *The South Atlantic Quarterly* 91 (Special Issue, Winter 1991): 295 pages.

Takes up the debate over how to teach "culture" and the establishment of national "cultural" policies. Discusses the effects of texts, specific movements, and works of art on the individual writer's understanding of "culture."

1501. Tremmel, Robert. "Taking a Backward Step: Reflecting on the Writing Process, Critical Thinking, and Other Pitfalls." *FEN* 19 (Fall 1991): 21–25.

Suggests that teachers avoid a reductionist approach to composition by reflecting on practice and by teaching students to reflect "in a self-conscious way."

1502. Vivion, Michael J. "High School/Dual Enrollment and the Composition Program." *WPA* 15 (Fall/Winter 1991): 55–60.

Supports dual enrollment plans when carefully considered and implemented; describes how the author's department developed an effective plan.

1503. Wallace, Robert K. "Creating a Class Magazine Based on the Fine Arts and *The New Yorker*." *ExEx* 37 (Fall 1991): 12–14.

Incorporates a variety of fine arts experiences plus a study of *The New Yorker* in a writing class.

1504. Ward, Dean A. "The 'Reader's Outline': A Toll for Global Revision." *JTW* 10 (Fall/Winter 1991): 201–215.

Emphasizes "visual accessibility to the elements of a text to which readers respond." Defines and describes examples of the reader's outline.

1505. Webster, Janice Gohm. "Using Popular Culture Materials in the Composition Classroom." *DAI* 51 (January 1991): 2300A.

Supports the use of advertisements, television, film, and popular music in composition courses; suggests specific assignments.

1506. Weiler, Kathleen. "Freire and a Feminist Pedagogy of Difference." *HER* 61 (November 1991): 449–479.

Questions Freirean assumption of a single experience of oppression; identifies three ways on which a feminist pedagogy builds; enriches Freire's pedagogy.

1507. Wheeler, Phyllis. "At the Top: 'This Stuff Really Works!' " *ET* 22 (Fall 1990): 28–32.

Illustrates the use of Nancie Atwell's *In the Middle* for college composition. Emphasizes reading and places more importance on the quality of graded essays than on quantity.

1508. Woodward, Branson L., Jr. "A Comment on 'Relativism, Radical Pedagogy, and Ideology of Paralysis' [*CE* 51 (October 1989)]." *CE* 53 (February 1991): 226–227.

Argues that a theistically based curriculum would provide an emancipatory pedagogy.

1509. Wright, William W. "Students as Ethnographers: Encouraging Authority." *TETYC* 18 (May 1991): 103–108.

Argues that teaching students to see themselves as ethnographers encourages them to become authorities in their writing and moves them towards the center of the composition course.

See also 103, 120, 329, 1086, 1215

4.2 HIGHER EDUCATION

4.2.1 DEVELOPMENTAL WRITING

1510. Bowser, June. "Talking about It: Identifying a Sociability Factor in the Writing Process." *Leaflet* 90 (Fall 1991): 2–7.

Argues that beginning writers function best when they experience social interaction within the writing process.

1511. Bushey, Barbara Carol. "What Helps Weak Writers Learn to Write Better? A Pilot Study in the Harvard Expository Writing Program." *DAI* 52 (December 1991): 2034A.

Focuses on activities that help students improve their writing; points to the importance of effective communication between students and teachers.

1512. Cohen, Roberta Parish. "The Use of Newspapers with Underprepared Community College Students as a Means of Improving Reading and Writing." *DAI* 52 (August 1991): 406A.

Investigates the effectiveness of newspapers in developing reading and writing skills in underprepared community college students.

1513. Condravy, Jace. "Sentence Combining: A Spoonful of Sugar." *ELQ* 13 (December 1991): 10–12.

Reports on success with sentence combining exercises for underprepared first-year college students in a developmental writing course.

1514. Courage, Richard Arthur. "Nontraditional Students and the Basic Writing Course: A Case Study of Classroom Interactions." *DAI* 52 (September 1991): 826A.

Studies 24 nontraditional students; explores their interactions with their teacher, themselves, and their text.

1515. De Beaugrande, Robert, and Jean Olson Mar. "Using a 'Write-Speak-Write' Approach for Basic Writers." *JBW* 10 (Fall 1991): 4–32.

Examines linguistic, psychological, and social concepts of basic writing; proposes "participant orientation" to error analysis; describes pilot project emphasizing the development of students' "fluency and involvement."

1516. Grow, Shanna. "Revision with Basic Writers: A Case Study." *UEJ* 19 (1991): 4–10.

Reports on classroom practice that uses four phases in a revision process: conceptual revision, substantive revision, stylistic revision, and editing.

1517. Harris, Joseph. *Criticism and the Other Reader*. Boston, MA: CCCC, March 1991. ERIC ED 331 070. 11 pages

Describes assignments for a basic writing class to make students more aware of the actuality of messages that popular texts may bear.

1518. Heilker, Paul. "The Bi-Polar Mind and the Inadequacy of Oppositional Pedagogies (Or the Dead Poets Society Revisited)." *FEN* 19 (Fall 1991): 5–8.

Argues for a composition pedagogy that will teach students to both accommodate and resist "isms"; suggests a way to have students collaborate and work alone.

1519. Henning, Barbara. "The World Was Stone Cold: Basic Writing in an Urban University." *CE* 53 (October 1991): 674–685.

Discusses how current-traditional as well as method-oriented process textbooks and pedagogies exclude the nontraditional student.

1520. Hull, Glynda, Mike Rose, Kay Losey Fraser, and Marisa Castellano. "Remediation as Social Construct: Perspectives from an Analysis of Classroom Discourse." *CCC* 42 (October 1991): 299–329.

Analysis suggests that general cognitive failure is often presumed when a student exhibits particular classroom difficulties.

Includes four suggestions for teachers and researchers.

1521. Hull, Glynda, Mike Rose, Cynthia Greenleaf, and Brian Reilley. "Seeing the Promise of the Underprepared." *QNWP/CSW* 13 (Winter 1991): 6–13, 25.

Studies at a community college, state college, and university reveal the richness and complexity of the strategies, rules, and assumptions of underprepared students.

1522. Kinder, Rose Marie. "A Piece of the Streets." *JBW* 10 (Spring 1991): 67–72.

Shows how students can improve interpretive and analytical skills by using newspaper, journal, and magazine articles as texts in composition classrooms.

1523. Korth, Philip A. *The Developmental Level Writing Program at Michigan State University*. Boston, MA: CCCC, March 1991. ERIC ED 332 214. 10 pages

Describes the aims and premises of one university's developmental writing program.

1524. Lounsberry, Barbara. " 'Accuse Not Nature, She Hath Done Her Part': Ten Writing Assignments Involving Nature." *CEA* 54 (Fall 1991): 75–77.

Assignments involve all the language arts skills and offer students a clear subject, audience, and purpose.

1525. Mangelsdorf, Katherine Ward. "Claiming Authority: A Case Study of Two Female Basic Writers." *DAI* 51 (March 1991): 3005A.

Examines gender issues in marginalized students by looking at four Mexican-American Basic Writers, an area previously given little attention in Basic Writing scholarship.

1526. McCleary, Bill. "Study Finds 16 Percent of College Freshman Taking Basic Writing." *CompC* 4 (December 1991): 1–2.

Summarizes statistics survey from the National Center for Education.

1527. Pollard, Rita H. "Another Look: The Process Approach to Composition Instruction." *JDEd* 14 (Spring 1991): 30–32, 37.

Defends and clarifies process approaches in composition for developmental students.

1528. Posey, Evelyn, and Dorothy Ward. "Ideas in Practice: Computer-Supported Writing Instruction: The Student-Centered Classroom." *JDEd* 15 (Winter 1991): 26–30.

Describes the University of Texas at El Paso's use of software to develop students' writing skills through interaction with other students and instructors.

1529. Rondinone, Peter. "Teacher Background and Student Needs." *JBW* 10 (Spring 1991): 41–53.

Argues that students and teachers alike need to analyze conflicting demands of academic and home communities; explains strategies for helping students develop "alternate world views."

1530. Schor, Sandra. "The Short, Happy Life of Ms. Mystery." *JBW* 10 (Spring 1991): 16–25.

Describes experimental summer intensive course in basic writing; shows how writing and reading letters can "sustain and educate the imagination."

1531. Smith, Maggy. "Paragraph Scavenger Hunt: Looking for Paragraph Partners." *ExEx* 37 (Fall 1991): 17–18.

Students learn paragraph construction, collaboration with peers to build paragraphs, and to report orally on their analysis of these paragraphs.

1532. Smith, Susan Belasco. "Basic Writers and the Control of Our Environment." *CEA* 54 (Fall 1991): 52–54.

Describes a course based on ecology theme.

1533. Troiano, Edna M., and Julia Draus. *Integrating Academic Information into Developmental Writing Courses*. Boston, MA: National Association for Developmental Education, March 1991. ERIC ED 333 919. 31 pages

Describes assignments used in a community college's basic writing course to promote cultural literacy.

1534. Valeri-Gold, Maria, James R. Olson, and Mary P. Deming. "Portfolios: Collaborative Authentic Assessment Opportunities for College Developmental Learners." *JR* 35 (December 1991): 298–305.

Describes five factors that portfolios need to address in order to be used in college level classrooms; suggests components that should be included.

See also 508, 527, 583, 637, 677, 1545, 1570

4.2.2 FIRST-YEAR COLLEGE COMPOSITION

1535. Christensen, Norman. "Avoidance Pedagogy in Freshman English." *TETYC* 18 (May 1991): 133–136.

Suggests that in order for teachers to maximize classroom interaction, they need to bring their own writing to the students and make writing enjoyable.

1536. Clark, Carol Lea, and Bill Bolin. "Index to Freshman English News 1972–1991." *FEN* 19 (Fall 1991): 29–35.

Index to 19 years of publication; categories include theory and research; teacher education, administration, and social roles; curriculum; testing, measurement, and evaluation; and bibliography.

1537. Coldiron, A. E. B. "*Refutatio* as a Prewriting Exercise." *TETYC* 18 (February 1991): 40–42.

Provides an exercise that helps first-year college students to support their argument and to address audience objections.

1538. Coxwell, Deborah Loretta. "The Effects of CLAST Instruction on the Development of Freshman Writers." *DAI* 52 (September 1991): 827A.

Demonstrates that instruction in CLAST essay skills does not ensure higher CLAST essay scores.

1539. Erickson, Bette LaSere, and Diane Weltner Strommer. *Teaching College Freshmen.* San Francisco, CA: Jossey-Bass Publishers, 1991. 255 pages

Identifies common first-year student anxieties, assumptions, and habits that can impede the learning progress; illustrates what faculty can do to overcome and dispel these obstacles. Presents strategies for developing and maintaining more personalized academic support through advising, mentoring, and using office hours effectively.

1540. Frazier, Hood. "Exploring Art and the Artistic Process in the Composition Classroom." *TETYC* 18 (December 1991): 266–271.

Describes an integrated first-year college student art and composition course; points out that students see similarities in the creative processes of both fields.

1541. Gale, Fredric G. "A Probability Theory of Communication and the Freshman Writer." *FEN* 19 (Spring 1991): 12–15.

Applies Claude Shannon's 1949 communication theory to the teaching of first-year college student composition, suggesting use of more extensive freewriting.

1542. Gillam, Alice M. "Returning Students' Ways of Writing: Implications for First-Year College Composition." *JTW* 10 (Spring/Summer 1991): 1–20.

Suggests that an analysis of out-of-school writing and of initial academic attitudes and performance reveals gender differences. Argues that "experience" portfolios emphasize students' strengths.

1543. Glossner, Alan Joseph. "College Students' Personal Constructs for Writing and for Learning to Write: A Descriptive Study during English 101." *DAI* 51 (January 1991): 2297A.

Finds that community college students bring complex personal constructs to 101.

Argues they rely on the influence of their instructors, but support peer collaboration.

1544. Gold, R. Michael. "How the Freshman Essay Anthology Subverts the Aims of the Traditional Composition Course." *TETYC* 18 (December 1991): 261–265.

Argues that anthologized essays are too specialized or sophisticated for use as models; points out that conversational topics emphasize subject matter rather than rhetoric. Author recommends literary works as readings.

1545. Golden, Louise. "What's Not Right with Writing: The Effects of Grammar Instruction and Writing Apprehension on the Composing Processes of Basic Writers at the American State College." *DAI* 52 (July 1991): 98A.

Shows that the effects of grammar instruction on writing apprehension, overall improvement in writing essays, and grammar mechanics were not significant.

1546. Hairston, Maxine C. "Required Writing Courses Should Not Focus on Politically Charged Social Issues." *CHE* 37 (23 January 1991): B1, B3.

Rejects proposed revisions of a first-year course at the University of Texas at Austin. Argues that a high-risk context will encourage dishonesty among students and subjects best understood by sociologists.

1547. Haskell, Dale. "Show Off & Tell: Another Look at Teachers Writing with Their Students." *EJ* 80 (April 1991): 65.

Lists "eight rules for minimizing the danger of showing off" when writing with students.

1548. Hicks, Kim. *Negotiation, Authority, and Confidence: Freshmen Writers Collaborate*. Boston, MA: CCCC, March 1991. ERIC ED 333 361. 12 pages

Examines two first-year writing sections; finds that difficulties in collaboration reveal much about the ways students struggle to write alone as well as with others.

1549. Hill, Charles A. *The Impact of Persona on the Success of Written Arguments*. Boston, MA: CCCC, March 1991. ERIC ED 332 227. 11 pages

A study of first-year college students suggests that attitude is a strong factor in the complex reaction to persona.

1550. Kinder, Rose Marie. "Grading Students' Writing in College Writing: A History." *DAI* 51 (March 1991): 2971A.

Argues that the merge between the ranking of students' work and first-year college composition has contributed to an emphasis on surface details and obscured the larger issues in writing.

1551. Landis-Groom, Eileen. "College Writers Composing for Correspondence." *ArEB* 33 (Spring 1991): 15–17.

Describes a peer-response approach in which students in composition classes—one in Florida and one in Arizona—offered long distance critiques.

1552. Luckett, Sharon. *Informal Freshman Writing of Orally-Based Literature and Its Relationship to Formal Writing*. Boston, MA: CCCC, March 1991. ERIC ED 333 430. 24 pages

Suggests that the informal journal be used to introduce disciplined composition pedagogy through creative assigment with an emphasis on oral literary traditions.

1553. Mangan, Katherine S. "Entire Writing-Course Panel Quits at U. of Texas." *CHE* 37 (13 February 1991): A16.

Reports on the resignation of the members of the panel whose course proposal, which emphasized court cases on affirmative action and civil rights, was rejected.

1554. Mangan, Katherine S. "U. of Texas's Postponement of Controversial Writing Course Kindles Debate over Role of Outsiders in Academic Policy." *CHE* 37 (20 February 1991): A15, A18.

Points out that MLA and AAUP voiced concerns about the university's postponement of the proposed first-year course "Writing about Difference." Cites professors who consider outside interference as inappropriate.

1555. Marx, Michael Steven. *Writing Abilities, Writing Attitudes, and the Teaching of Writing*. Boston, MA: CCCC, March 1991. ERIC ED 332 215. 15 pages

Studies attitudes of first-year college writers at three ability levels. Finds unexpected results for lower and middle groups.

1556. McCleary, Bill. "Reworked Writing Course Adopted Quietly at Texas." *CompC* 4 (September 1991): 1–2.

Summarizes the first-year college student writing syllabus adopted in May 1991 at the University of Texas at Austin.

1557. Meyers, Douglas G. "The Natural World and the World of Discourse: Nature Writing in Freshman Composition." *CEA* 54 (Fall 1991): 43–46.

Offers assignments that engage students in Kinneavy's discourse aims.

1558. Murdick, William, and Rosalie Segan. "Placing Whole Language in a Workshop Setting." *ELQ* 13 (December 1991): 4–6.

Authors apply whole language philosophy to a writing workshop; includes a chart to contrast it with the skills-based pedagogy of a traditional classroom.

1559. Newton, Evangeline V. "Developing Metacognitive Awareness: The Response Journal in College Composition." *JR* 34 (March 1991): 476–478.

Describes how journal entries influenced the development of the metacognitive abilities of a first-year college student class.

1560. Otte, George. *The Diversity within: From Finding One's Voice to Orchestrating One's Voices*. Boston, MA: CCCC, March 1991. ERIC ED 331 084. 13 pages

Suggests that teachers should aim to encourage a multiplicity of student voices in composition with a focus on discovery.

1561. Peterson, Linda H. "Gender and the Autobiographical Essay: Research Perspectives, Pedagogical Practices." *CCC* 42 (May 1991): 170–183.

Studies the autobiographical writing of 44 first-year college students. Findings show gender differences in topic choices and aspects of writing success, leading to suggestions for pedagogy.

1562. Randic, Jasna. *Employing Freire's Notion of Dialogue as the "Sealing Power" in the Writing Classroom: Theoretical Base and a Call for Change*. Boston, MA: CCCC, March 1991. ERIC ED 331 069. 14 pages

Advocates the use of dialogic strategies to enhance collaborative learning.

1563. Ruszkiewicz, John. *"Reason Is but Choosing": Ideology in First Year English*. Boston, MA: CCCC, March 1991. ERIC ED 331 058. 10 pages

Argues that courses which incorporate "critical literacy" intimidate students. Advocates a multicultural syllabus that can be incorporated into the existing syllabus.

1564. Shaw, Margaret L. "What Students' Don't Say: An Approach to the Student Text." *CCC* 42 (February 1991): 45–54.

Analyzes several students' texts for gaps between the said and the unsaid, thereby encouraging the writers to "establish new configurations or to change their minds."

1565. Siebert, Bradley Gene. "Freshman Rhetorics: Composition Studies Research and Theory into Practice." *DAI* 51 (February 1991): 2669A.

Examines first-year college writing textbooks in terms of how they are adapting current influences and trends within the field of composition studies.

1566. Sirc, Geoffrey. *One of the Things at Stake in the Peer-Group Conferences: The Feminine*. Boston, MA: CCCC, March 1991. ERIC ED 332 187. 13 pages

Describes the feminine style of peer response to student writing; argues that it is difficult for students to make a "transition" between gender styles.

1567. Slattery, Patrick J. "The Argumentative, Multiple-Source Paper: College Students Reading, Thinking, and Writing about Divergent Points of View." *JTW* 10 (Fall/Winter 1991): 181–199.

Points out that a study of 12 first-year composition students revealed dogmatic, noncommittal, and analytical approaches to sources.

1568. Wallace, David L., and John R. Hayes. "Redefining Revision for Freshmen." *RTE* 25 (February 1991): 54–66.

Describes research indicating that students instructed to revise globally do more global revision and produce better revisions than students simply asked to revise.

1569. Wenner, Barbara. *Hearing or Ignoring Audience: The Dilemma of the Freshman Writer*. Boston, MA: CCCC, March 1991. ERIC ED 332 197. 16 pages

Reminds us that students should sometimes ignore the idea of audience in the process of writing.

1570. Wenzel, Gary Edwin. "Basic Writers: Qualitative Case Studies Identifying Patterns of Success." *DAI* 52 (September 1991): 831A.

Studies the progress of first-year college students who develop behavior patterns and acquired skills as writers.

1571. White, Fred D. *Freshman Composition and Creative Writing: Another Gap to Bridge*. Boston, MA: CCCC, March 1991. ERIC ED 331 061. 12 pages

Advocates the use of creative writing in first-year composition classes since many of the processes are valid in both kinds of writing classes.

1572. Winkelmann, Carol. *Obscured by Metaphor: "Community" Versus the Reality of a Writing Class*. Boston, MA: CCCC, March 1991. ERIC ED 334 579. 15 pages

Offers a case study of one student in a college composition class; notes that her use of metaphor reveals ambiguities in the notion of writing.

1573. Yeilding, Donnie Deverne Cook. "Freshman Composition Instruction in Texas: The State of the Art." *DAI* 51 (June 1991): 4049A.

Outlines composition requirements of 92 institutions, including details about syllabi, goals, texts, and pedagogy.

See also 563

4.2.3 ADVANCED COMPOSITION

1574. Chapman, David W. "Forming and Meaning: Writing the Counterpoint Essay." *JAC* 11 (Winter 1991): 73–81.

Argues for the heuristic value of some modern nonfiction forms. Uses John McPhee as a source and model; discusses student essays.

1575. Ewald, Helen Rothschild. "What We Could Tell Advanced Student Writers about Audience." *JAC* 11 (Winter 1991): 147–158.

Argues that telling students everything from reading research about readers as active constructors of meaning may create new complex problems.

1576. Kaufer, David S., and Cheryl Geisler. "A Scheme for Representing Written Argument." *JAC* 11 (Winter 1991): 107–122.

Offers a visual method for schematizing arguments involving complex responses to prior sources; uses a passage from Gould as illustration.

1577. Woolever, Kristin R. *Reassessing the Role of Collaborative Writing in Advanced Composition*. Boston, MA: CCCC, March 1991. ERIC ED 333 455. 11 pages

Explains the benefits of collaborative writing in advanced composition.

4.2.4 BUSINESS COMMUNICATION

1578. Applegate, Lynda M. "Technology Support for Cooperative Work: A Framework for

Studying Introduction and Assimilation in Organizations." *JOC* 1 (Winter 1991): 11–39.

Focuses on the transfer and assimilation of new technology innovations from research and development units to larger units.

1579. Barker, Randolph T., and Marilyn Finnemore-Bello. "Use of Overhead Transparencies in Collaborative Business Writing." *BABC* 54 (December 1991): 67–70.

Discusses the use of transparencies created by collaborative student groups in a business communication class.

1580. Blake, Bonnie L. "Student Research in the Classroom: Solving the Teacher/Researcher Dilemma." *BABC* 54 (December 1991): 73–75.

Describes the use of student research projects for formal business communication reports; discusses one project in detail.

1581. Blaszczynski, Carol. "Writing the Letter of Resignation." *BABC* 54 (September 1991): 66–67.

Describes a management communication assignment to write a letter of resignation.

1582. Blyler, Nancy Roundy. "Reading Theory and Persuasive Business Communications: Guidelines for Writers." *JTWC* 21 (1991): 383–396.

Provides background on reading theory to illustrate the role of inferring, reasoning analogically, and learning in building consensual meaning; proposes four supplementary guidelines.

1583. Boris, Edna Zwick. "Résumés: A Student Handout." *BABC* 54 (December 1991): 76–79.

Addresses the business communication student in a discussion of techniques for résumé writing.

1584. Butler, Marilyn S. "The Persuasive Use of Numerical Data in Influential Business Periodicals." *BABC* 54 (March 1991): 13–16.

Describes a study of persuasion and the presentation of data in three types of business periodicals.

1585. Campbell, Patty Glover. "Business Communication of Technical Writing?" *BABC* 54 (June 1991): 6–10.

Analyzes how well business writing texts and technical writing texts meet the communication needs of engineering and business students.

1586. Carroll, E. Ruth. "Improved Interpersonal Relationships: A Result of Group Learning." *JBTC* 5 (July 1991): 285–299.

Describes procedures for structuring and implementing cooperative learning groups.

1587. Carson, John Stanton. "Writing across the Business Disciplines at Robert Morris College: A Case Study." *DAI* 52 (October 1991): 1236A.

Catalogues successes and failures of the WAC program at this particular institution.

1588. Casady, Mona J. "Using an nglish and Spelling Pretest to Maximize Performance in Business Communication Classes." *BABC* 54 (December 1991): 11–18.

Describes a study examining the effectiveness of a grammar and spelling pretest on business communication performance; discusses results.

1589. Ceccio, Joseph F. "Job-Related Stress among Business and Professional Writing Faculty Members." *JBTC* 5 (January 1991): 3–32.

Examines job-related stress among collegiate business and professional writing faculty members in the United States.

1590. Cross, Mary. "Aristotle and Business Writing: Why We Need to Teach Persuasion." *BABC* 54 (March 1991): 3–6.

Discusses why Aristotle's principles of persuasion are relevant to business writing; presents four persuasive strategies.

1591. Cullinan, Mary, and Ce Ce Iandoli. "What Activities Help to Improve Your Writing? Some Unsettling Student Responses." *BABC* 54 (December 1991): 8–10.

Compares business communication students' responses on a precourse questionnaire to responses on a postcourse questionnaire.

1592. Curry, Jerome. "Teaching Definition to Technical Students: Beyond the Course Textbook." *BABC* 54 (June 1991): 16–18.

Describes a 10-stage approach to teaching definition; presents an assignment.

1593. DeBauche, Susan Clark. "The Effects of Word Processing in Teaching Writing in Business Comunication Courses at Southwest Baptist University." *DAI* 52 (August 1991): 401A.

Compares students' writing quality on assignments completed by word processing and by typewriter in a business communication course.

1594. Faulkenburg, Marilyn. "Casing a Method for News." *BABC* 54 (December 1991): 71–72.

Describes the use of *Wall Street Journal* articles for cases in a managerial communications class.

1595. Flatley, Marie E. "The Newsletter: An Excellent Alternative to the Long Report." *BABC* 54 (June 1991): 20–21.

Describes a business communication assignment requiring students to develop a business newsletter.

1596. Forman, Janis. "Collaborative Business Writing: A Burkean Perspective for Future Reseach." *JBC* 28 (Summer 1991): 233–257.

Offers a Burkean framework for the study of collaborative business writing; argues for a research agenda that emphasizes qualitative studies followed by quantitative research.

1597. Fox, Jean. "Profiles in Confidence." *TETYC* 18 (May 1991): 146–151.

Argues that early practice in writing résumés and business letters helps students gain confidence, build self-esteem, and improve writing skills.

1598. Frank, Jane. "A Discourse Analysis of the Language Used in Direct Mail Communications (Volume I and II)." *DAI* 51 (April 1991): 3399A.

Finds that "speech-like" writing aids persuasion in sales letters.

1599. Frisch, Adam. "Escaping the Authoritative Reader: Writing to Small Groups." *BABC* 54 (December 1991): 36–38.

Describes a proposal assignment in a "Research and Argument" class that introduces the concept of peer readership.

1600. Gasarch, Pearl. "Rhetoric and Technical Writing: A Working Relationship." *BABC* 54 (June 1991): 3–5.

Reviews literature on the importance of rhetorical principles in effective technical writing.

1601. Gilsdorf, Jeanette W. "Write Me Your Best Case for . . ." *BABC* 54 (March 1991): 7–12.

Discusses aspects of persuasion in business messages and explains how persuasive writing differs from informative writing.

1602. Haight, Robert. *Infusing a Global Perspective into Business Communication Courses: From Rhetorical Strategies to Cultural Awareness*. Boston, MA: CCCC, March 1991. ERIC ED 333 454. 10 pages

Introduces a model that allows traditional course objectives to be met while presenting international materials and perspectives.

1603. Hall, Mary Ann. "A Cognitive Language Model for Business Writing." *DAI* 51 (May 1991): 3719A.

Suggests that studying the "analytic language" inherent in interviews with business writers can help students become independent, critical thinkers.

1604. Hashim, Safaa H. "WHAT: An Argumentative Groupware Approach for Organizing and Documenting Research Activities." *JOC* 1 (Fall 1991): 275–302. Describes a hypertext-based tool for argumentative writing and its impact on organizational computing applications in business education and training.

1605. Hebert, Margaret. "Searching for the Right Job." *BABC* 54 (September 1991): 62–63.

Describes a business communication unit on the job search, including the writing of résumés and letters.

1606. Javed, M. Latif. "Integrating Computers in a Business Report Writing Class." *BABC* 54 (June 1991): 22–23.

Describes a method of incorporating computer use in a report writing class.

1607. Joy, Robert O. "Providing a Flexible Course in Writing Reports with the Use of the Computer within a Traditional University College of Business." *BABC* 54 (June 1991): 24–28.

Explains how computers are used in a report-writing course; presents the course evaluation and course outline.

1608. Karis, Bill. "Climbing the Corporate Ladder: Becoming Aware of the Rungs." *JBTC* 5 (January 1991): 76–87.

Describes audience-analysis exercises to help business-writing students understand how discourse communities affect communication.

1609. Kryder, LeeAnne Giannone. "Project Administration Techniques for Succesful Classroom Collaborative Writing." *BABC* 54 (December 1991): 65–66.

Describes writing and nonwriting techniques to help students manage collaborative projects in a business writing class.

1610. Larsen, Elizabeth. "Producing Effective Writing in the Managerial Communication Course." *BABC* 54 (March 1991): 38–42.

Describes a series of assignments designed to strengthen specific aspects of students' writing in a managerial communication course.

1611. Limaye, Mohan, and Richard Pompian. "Brevity Versus Clarity: The Comprehensibility of Nominal Compounds in Business and Technical Prose." *JBC* 28 (Winter 1991): 7–21.

Shows that brevity achieved by using noun chains results in reduced comprehension. Includes teaching suggestions.

1612. Limback, E. Rebecca. "Language Skills: Can a Value-Added Approach Make a Difference." *JBTC* 5 (July 1991): 300–306.

Presents the results of a pretest/posttest assessment to determine if instruction in business writing improves students' language skills.

1613. Loughman, Tom. "Activating Students to Generate Report Topics." *BABC* 54 (March 1991): 29.

Describes an "agenda memo and meeting" assignment to help business communication students develop report and project topics.

1614. Lund, Donna. *Extra-Rhetorical Restraints on Writing in Acounting*. Boston, MA: CCCC, March 1991. ERIC ED 332 193. 9 pages

Argues that subjectivism undergirds the ideology of objectivism in the field of accounting. Finds significant barriers to intervention in this discourse community.

1615. Mayer, Kenneth R. "The Role of Style Analyzers in Business Communication." *BABC* 54 (June 1991): 35–37.

Discusses eight points concerning the use of style analyzers by business communication students.

1616. McCord, Elizabeth A. "The Business Writer, the Law, and Routine Business Communication: A Legal and Rhetorical Analysis." *JBTC* 5 (April 1991): 173–199.

Uses social rhetorical theory to show how awareness of the rhetorical situation can help writers avoid liability-prone prose.

1617. McCord, Elizabeth A. "Meeting the Reader's Needs: Audience Response through Reader-Focused Testing." *BABC* 54 (December 1991): 39–45.

Discusses current methods of assessing audience needs and describes a "reader-focused" business writing assignment that teaches students to test a document's effectiveness.

1618. Merrier, Patricia A. "The Extent to Which Students' Reactions to Usage Errors Change as a Result of Having Completed a Business Communication Course." *BABC* 54 (December 1991): 27–30.

Describes a study of students' responses to usage errors in a business communication course without basic skills instruction.

1619. Michael, Catherine. "The Persuasive Letter: From Start to Finish." *BABC* 54 (March 1991): 28–29.

Describes how persuasive letter assignments can be used throughout a business communication course.

1620. Nichols, Patsy. "Desktop Packaging." *BABC* 54 (June 1991): 43–45.

Presents seven principles of page design for business communication students; describes a classroom exercise.

1621. Pollard, Canstance. "Streamlining the Writing Process in Business Communication." *BABC* 54 (June 1991): 29–31.

Discusses the use of word processing in all stages of the writing process, including composing.

1622. Rosenberg, Roberta. "The Community-Based Report: A Strategy for College-Community Collaboration." *BABC* 54 (March 1991): 43–51.

Describes a business communication report assignment that requires students to work in groups and collaborate with a community organization.

1623. Scheiber, H. J. "Open-Ended Cases and Collaborative Learning in the Business Communication Course." *BABC* 54 (December 1991): 60–64.

Describes the development of analytical report cases for business communication; presents a sample case.

1624. Schierhorn, Ann. "The Role of the Writing Coach in the Magazine Curriculum." *JourEd* 46 (Summer 1991): 46–53.

Explores how the use of writing coaches and a writing process concept can be applied to the teaching of magazine writing.

1625. Schneider, Carolyn. "Supplementary Graphics Exercises." *BABC* 54 (June 1991): 19–20.

Describes a business communication assignment requiring students to develop graphics to illustrate data found in newspaper articles.

1626. Smith, Carolena L., and Richard A. Hatch. "Selection of an Integrated Software Package for the Business Communication Course." *BABC* 54 (June 1991): 32–34.

Discusses the use of integrated software, as opposed to word processing software, and compares features of three integrated software packages.

1627. Spencer, Barbara, and Carol M. Lehman. "Creative Thinking: An Integral Part of Effective Business Communication." *BABC* 54 (March 1991): 21–27.

Discusses the creative thinking process and presents a business communication project that encourages creative thinking.

1628. Stanley-Weigand, Pam. "Organizing the Writing of Your Résumé." *BABC* 54 (September 1991): 11–12.

Describes the process of writing a résumé in terms of a flowchart.

1629. Vassallo, Philip. "The Roles of Literature in Business and Expressiveness in Technical Writing." *TETYC* 18 (December 1991): 278–282.

Argues that literature and expressiveness are important and often unrecognized in business and technical writing.

1630. Warlaumont, Hazel G. "Problem-Solving Strategies in the Classroom: A Business Writing Paradox." *BABC* 54 (December 1991): 55–59.

Describes a study of contradictions between business writing students' beliefs and problem-solving behavior exhibited in assignments. Discusses how cognitive theory applies to the study.

1631. Wayne, F. Stanford, and Jolene D. Scriven. "Problem and Purpose Statements: Are They Synonymous Terms in Writing Reports for Business?" *BABC* 54 (March 1991): 30–37.

Analyzes the discussion of business report problem and purpose statements in selected business communication textbooks.

1632. Wedell, Allen J., and Robert Allerheiligen. "Computer-Assisted Writing Instruction: Is It Effective?" *JBC* 28 (Spring 1991): 131–140.

Points out that business students who use Writer's Workbench perceived significant improvement in oral but not in written communication.

1633. Wells, Barron, and Nelda Spinks. "What Do You Mean People Communicate with Audiences?" *BABC* 54 (September 1991): 100–102.

Describes the various audiences involved in organizational communication.

1634. Wiegand, Richard. "The Job Application Letter." *BABC* 54 (September 1991): 63–65.

Describes a job application letter assignment that is less threatening for management communication skills.

1635. Williams, Paula, Jolene D. Scriven, and Stan Wayne. "A Ranking of the Top 75 Misused Similar Words that Business Communication Students Confuse Most Often." *BABC* 54 (December 1991): 19–25.

Describes a study to determine any relationship between business communication student characteristics and correct word usage.

See also 131

4.2.5 SCIENTIFIC AND TECHNICAL COMMUNICATION

1636. Allen, Jo. "Gender Issues in Technical Communication Studies: An Overview of the Implications for Profession, Research, and Pedagogy." *JBTC* 5 (October 1991): 371–392.

Presents major gender issues related to technical communication.

1637. Allen, Jo. "Thematic Repetition as Rhetorical Technique." *JTWC* 21 (1991): 29–40.

Examines William Harvey's rhetorical strategies in *On the Motion of the Heart and Blood in Animals* to find out how he reduced resistance to his ideas.

1638. Allen, Nancy J. "Collaboration Squared: Writing Groups Working Together." *TWT* 18 (Winter 1991): 69–74.

Describes a classroom exercise in which students prepared a complex collaborative document assembled from collaboratively produced subparts.

1639. *Among the Professions*. Edited by T.R. Girill. Arlington, VA: Society for Technical Communication, 1991. 64 pages

Twenty-six essays reprinted from *Technical Communication* compare other disciplines such as architecture and library science to technical communication.

1640. Baker, Margaret Ann, and Patricia Goubil-Gambrell. "Scholarly Writing: The Myth of Gender and Performance." *JBTC* 5 (October 1991): 412–443.

Presents an empirical study to determine if gender influences academic performance and scholarly writing.

1641. Barclay, Rebecca O., Michael L. Keene, Thomas E. Pinelli, John M. Kennedy, and Myron Glassman. "Technical Communication in the International Workplace: Some Implications for Curriculum Development." *TC* 38 (August 1991): 324–335.

Offers suggestions for technical communication curriculum based on results of 188 questionnaires from U.S. and European engineers and scientists.

1642. Beck, Charles E. "Implications of Metaphors in Defining Technical Communication." *JTWC* 21 (1991): 3–15.

Examines the limitations of some common metaphors for technical communication and explores new alternatives that lead to a new definition of technical communication.

1643. Belcher, Diane D. "Nonnative Writing in a Corporate Setting." *TWT* 18 (Spring 1991): 104–115.

Describes an on-site technical writing course for advanced ESL students. Addresses the need for a corporate environment acculturation; shows linguistic and rhetorical disadvantages.

1644. Bocchi, Joseph S. "Forming Constructs of Audience: Convention, Conflict, and Conversation." *JBTC* 5 (April 1991): 151–172.

Compares two groups of professional writers and their problems in conceptualizing audiences.

1645. Boiarsky, Carolyn. "Relating Purpose and Genre through James Britton's Functional Categories." *TWT* 18 (Spring 1991): 95–102.

Expresses need for a technical document model that recognizes the relationship between technical genre and the rhetorical context of a document.

1646. Bosley, Deborah S. "Designing Effective Technical Communication Teams." *TC* 38 (November 1991): 504–512.

Discusses corporate and personnel factors to consider when selecting collaborative team members.

1647. Brasseur, Lee Ellen. "An Examination of the Visual Composing Process of Graph, Chart and Table Designers." *DAI* 51 (February 1991): 2731A.

Suggests that graphics instruction could be improved by emphasizing process skills.

1648. Brockmann, R. John. "The Unbearable Distraction of Color." *IEEE* 34 (September 1991): 153–159.

Surveys research comparing the effectiveness of color and black-and-white graphics. Advises caution in the use of color graphics.

1649. Burnett, Rebecca E. "Substantive Conflict in a Cooperative Context: A Way to Improve the Collaborative Planning of Workplace Documents." *TC* 38 (November 1991): 532–539.

Argues that successful collaboration often occurs when document writers (1) elaborate key ideas, (2) consider alternatives, and (3) voice disagreements.

1650. Bush, Don. "Comparing the Two Cultures in Technical Writing." *IEEE* 34 (June 1991): 67–69.

Drawing on his own experience, the author compares the approaches taken by industry and the academy to such topics as grammar and editing.

1651. Campbell, Kim Sydow. "Structural Cohesion in Technical Texts." *JTWC* 21 (1991): 221–237.

Supplements Halliday and Hasan's semantic cohesive devices with structural cohesion types such as the repetition found in thematic progression, parallelism, and graphic devices.

1652. Connor, Jennifer J. "History and the Study of Technical Communication in Canada and the United States." *IEEE* 34 (March 1991): 3–6.

Argues that historical studies play a role in the teaching of technical writing and in helping the discipline define itself.

1653. Curtis, Donnelyn, and Stephen A. Bernhardt. "Keywords, Titles, Abstracts, and Online Searchers: Implications for Technical Writing." *TWT* 18 (Spring 1991): 142–161.

Describes current indexing systems; argues for a shift to automated methods; discusses the importance of clear, precise diction in documents to facilitate access to technical and scientific prose.

1654. Debs, Mary Beth. "Recent Research on Collaborative Writing in Industry." *TC* 38 (November 1991): 476–484.

Defines collaboration and argues that workers may not be aware that they write collaboratively. Offers guidelines for improving efficiency and dealing with problems in collaboration.

1655. Dragga, Sam. "Classifications of Correspondence: Complexity Versus Simplicity." *TWT* 18 (Winter 1991): 1–13.

Rejects the traditional, complex classifications of correspondence (forms) in favor of a simpler system (direct and indirect communication) requiring writers to address the demands of specific rhetorical moments.

1656. Dulek, Ronald E. "The Challenge to Effective Writing: The Public Policymaker's Multiple Audiences." *IEEE* 34 (December 1991): 224–227.

Describes the multiple audiences addressed by writers in the Occupational Safety and Health Administration (OSHA).

1657. Elliot, Norbert, and Margaret Kilduff. "Technical Writing in a Technological University: Attitudes of Department Chairs." *JTWC* 21 (1991): 411–424.

Recommends a course and programs in technical writing within specific institutional contexts to meet a growing agenda of competitiveness in engineering.

1658. Flynn, Elizabeth A., Gerald Savage, Marsha Penti, Carol Brown, and Sarah Watke. "Gender and Modes of Collaboration in a Chemical Engineering Design Course." *JBTC* 5 (October 1991): 444–462.

Defines three collaborative modes that show different power relationships among collaborative groups.

1659. Forman, Janis. "Novices Work on Group Reports: Problems in Group Writing and in Computer-Supported Group Writing." *JBTC* 5 (January 1991): 48–75.

Analyzes problems of novice writers and users of technology and draws conclusions related to pedagogy.

1660. Goodwin, David. "Emplotting the Reader: Motivation and Technical Documentation." *JTWC* 21 (1991): 99–115.

Argues that good technical manuals motivate by giving the reader an action-oriented role in a narrative of progress and improvement throughout the document.

1661. Halterman, Carroll, Jody Dutkiewicz, and Eve Halterman. "Men and Women on the Job: Gender Bias in Work Teams." *JBTC* 5 (October 1991): 469–481.

Assesses characteristics of effective work teams and the degree to which these characteristics are gender marked.

1662. Hartley, Peter. "Writing for Industry: The Presentational Mode Versus the Reflective Mode." *TWT* 18 (Spring 1991): 162–169.

Points out that industrial communication is action oriented and requires a focus on the reader's needs in the social context of an organizational role.

1663. Hashimoto, Takehiko. "Theory, Experiment and Design Practice: The Formation of Aeronautical Research, 1909–1930." *DAI* 52 (December 1991): 2256A.

Emphasizes the function of intermediaries, translators, and graphs as knowledge passed from scientific theorists to engineering practitioners.

1664. Haugen, Diane. "Editors, Rules, and Revision Research." *TC* 38 (February 1991): 57–64.

Argues that the academic community is superior to industry in recognizing that the best writing involves editing as process.

1665. Haynes, Kathleen J. M., and Linda K. Robertson. "An Application of Usability Criteria in the Classroom." *TWT* 18 (Spring 1991): 236–242.

Describes a classroom application of contextual factors, ease-of-use factors, and document design criteria.

1666. Horton, William. "Overcoming Chromophobia: A Guide to the Confident and Appropriate Use of Color." *IEEE* 34 (September 1991): 160–171.

Argues that technical communicators and teachers should not avoid the use of chromatic color. Offers suggestions for the effective use of color in documents.

1667. Horton, William. *Secrets of User-Seductive Documents*. Arlington, VA: Society for Technical Communication, 1991. 64 pages

Presents techniques that draw on readers' natural curiosity and intelligence in order to ensure that documents are read, understood, and acted upon.

1668. Howell, Carles. *Composition and Professional Education: A Case Study of an Engineering Student*. Botson, MA: CCCC, March 1991. ERIC ED 333 460. 12 pages

Tests the hypothesis that rhetorical theory can help students make sense of specialized discourse.

1669. *Internships in Technical Communication*. Edited by Bege K. Bowers and Chuck Nelson. Arlington, VA: Society for Technical Communication, 1991. 96 pages

Presents a self-help guide for students, faculty supervisors, and internship sponsors. Includes several generic forms and letters that may be adapted for individual use.

1670. Jewett, John W., Jr. "Learning Introductory Physics through Required Writing Assignments." *JCST* 20 (September 1991): 20–25.

Describes both advantages and drawbacks of writing assignments in courses at Cal Poly. Gives case samples.

1671. Johnson, Pamela R. "Employee Handbooks: An Integration of Technical Writing Concepts—Part II." *TWT* 18 (Winter 1991): 60–68.

Describes employment at-will doctrine; discusses legal cases surrounding employee handbooks. Provides samples from manuals and classroom exercises.

1672. Karis, Bill, and Susan Ross. "Communicating in Public Policy Matters: Addressing the Problem of Noncongruent Sites of Discourse." *IEEE* 34 (December 1991): 247–254.

Describes a course in technical communication that draws heavily on the theoretical work of such rhetoricians as Toulmin and Burke.

1673. Lay, Mary M. "Feminist Theory and the Redefinition of Technical Communication." *JBTC* 5 (October 1991): 348–370.

Discusses six common characteristics of feminist theory and traces their impact on a new conception of technical communication pedagogy and research.

1674. Lay, Mary M., and William M. Karis, eds. *Collaborative Writing in Industry: Investigations in Theory and Practice*. Technical Communication Series. Amityville, NY: Baywood Publishing, 1991. 286 pages

Presents 12 essays from academic and industrial experts on the theories of collaboration, industrial case studies of collaborative writing, classroom techniques for collaborative assignments, and gathering, verifying, and editing strategies that enhance collaboration. Includes annotated bibliography.
Essayists: David K. Farkas, Timothy

Weiss, James R. Weber, Meg Morgan, Mary Murray, Barbara Couture, Jone Rymer, Elizabeth L. Malone, Elizabeth Tebeaux, Ann Hill Duin, Linda A. Jorn, Mark S. DeBower, William Van Pelt, Alice Gillam, Dixie Elise Hickman, Roger A. Grice, Henrietta Nickels Shirk, Margaret Batschelet, Thomas Trzyna, Mary M. Lay, William M. Karis.

1675. Levine, Linda, Linda H. Pesante, and Susan B. Dunkle. "Implementing the Writing Plan: Heuristics from Software Development." *TWT* 18 (Spring 1991): 116–125.

Draws on software engineering experience to provide insight into the planning and revision of technical prose.

1676. Markel, Mike. "Criteria Development and the Myth of Objectivity." *TWT* 18 (Winter 1991): 37–47.

Provides a method for creating standards for technical reports and studies that accommodates the subjective nature of the task.

1677. Marshall, Stewart. "A Genre-Based Approach to the Teaching of Report-Writing." *ESP* 10 (1991): 3–13.

Investigates the teaching of genre analysis for scientific report writing and proposes a "genre for feedback" from the instructor, using a computer expert system.

1678. McDowell, Earl E. *Interviewing Practices for Technical Writers*. Amityville, NY: Baywood, 1991. 274 pages

Discusses the fundamentals of interviewing, informational interviews, employment cycle interviews, and internal and external interviews. Provides the necessary foundation of building the effective interviewing skills that are essential in today's workplace.

1679. McDowell, Earl E. "Surveys of Undergraduate and Graduate Technical Communication Programs and Courses in the United States." *TWT* 18 (Winter 1991): 29–35.

Argues that professionals and educators perceive that practical coursework such as publication management, and document testing is most important at both graduate and undergraduate levels for technical communication students.

1680. McNair, John R. "Ancient Memory Arts and Modern Graphics." *JTWC* 21 (1991): 259–269.

Discusses theoretical and practical applications of ancient memory arts for modern graphics.

1681. Mirel, Barbara. "Critical Reviews of Experimental Research on the Usability of Hard Copy Documentation." *IEEE* 34 (June 1991): 109–117.

Examines 22 experimental usability studies. Discovers limitations caused by such factors as sample selection, composition, and size. Recommends alternate research designs.

1682. Mirel, Barbara, Susan Feinberg, and Leif Allmendinger. "Designing Manuals for Active Learning Styles." *TC* 38 (February 1991): 75–87.

Argues that effective manuals avoid "hand holding" and instead encourage users to perform "active, exploratory learning." Researchers offer four methods for accomplishing this.

1683. Montgomery, Tracy T. "Negotiating Corporate Culture: An Exercise in Documentation." *TWT* 18 (Winter 1991): 75–80.

Presents an exercise in which students confront operational, political, and ethical demands of the workplace; assignment refines notions of appropriate documentation.

1684. Morgan, Meg. "Patterns of Composing: Connections between Classroom and Workplace Collaborations." *TC* 38 (November 1991): 540–545.

Identifies successful techniques of collaborative methods and argues for their use in industry.

1685. Morgan, Meg. "Using Modules to Teach Advanced Technical Writing." *TC* 38 (April 1991): 240–244.

Discusses use of *modules*—"packets of materials on specialized topics," such as *Manual Design, Writing for Clients*, or *Using Writer Aids*, for teaching writing.

1686. Nern, Michael G. "How I Avoided Becoming a Victim of the Process Approach." *TWT* 18 (Winter 1991): 81–84.

Defends a product-oriented approach to technical writing instruction. Argues that technical writing is formulaic and accommodates product approach.

1687. Olds, Barbara M., and Karen B. Wiley. "Public Policy and Technical Communication across the Curriculum at the Colorado School of Mines." *IEEE* 34 (December 1991): 240–246.

Describes a four-semester course sequence in which students work in groups on "real world" projects.

1688. Painter, Teresa. "Collaboration between Business and Academy." *TC* 38 (November 1991): 498–503.

An IBM facility offers "training linkages" with academics as teachers, technical writers, and researchers, thereby generating a symbiotic relationship.

1689. Pena-Paez, Alberto, and John R. Surber. "Effect of Study Strategy Skill Level on Test Performance." *EQ* 23 (1991): 31–39.

Argues that technical college students who were skilled in summarizing performed better than unskilled students.

1690. Pieper, Gail W. "Effective Roadmaps or Signs of Construction Ahead?" *TWT* 18 (Spring 1991): 127–131.

Argues that the traditional approach to report writing fails to motivate readers. Suggests an alternate "roadmap" that is precise, excites curiosity, and offers navigational assistance.

1691. Popken, Randall. "A Study of Topic Sentence Use in Technical Writing." *TWT* 18 (Winter 1991): 49–58.

Compares topic sentence use in technical writing to other discourse communities. Shows that rhetorical genre and paragraph length are influencing textual factors of topic sentences.

1692. *Proceedings of the 38th International Technical Communication Conference*. San Diego, CA: UNIVELT, 1991. 763 pages

Subjects in this collection of papers presented in New York, May 1991, include education, training, and professional development, management, research and technology, and visual communications.

1693. Rivers, William E., and Diane Rose Carr. "The NCR-USC Document Validation Laboratory: A Special Collaboration between Industry and Academia." *JBTC* 5 (January 1991): 88–103.

Describes problems in laboratory manuals; points out reasons for these problems.

1694. Rodman, Lilita. "Anticipatory 'It' in Scientific Discourse." *JTWC* 21 (1991): 17–27.

Examines the communicative value of 205 anticipatory "it" clauses in scientific and technical texts, categorizing them by discourse function and recommending their effective use.

1695. Rowan, Katherine E. "When Simple Language Fails: Presenting Difficult Science to the Public." *JTWC* 21 (1991): 369–382.

Discusses ineffective and effective strategies for helping lay readers understand difficult science news and concepts and their implications for health and safety.

1696. Rutter, Russell. "History, Rhetoric, and Humanism: Toward a More Comprehensive Definition of Technical Communication." *JTWC* 21 (1991): 133–153.

Argues for increased attention to questions of what a person needs to be and know in order to become an effective practicing technical communicator.

1697. Shapiro, Ann. *WAC and Engineering or Why Engineers Can't Write*. Boston, MA: CCCC, March 1991. ERIC ED 332 199. 9 pages

Reports that a faculty debate over the inadequacy of student writing led to the articulation of discipline-specific requirements and interdisciplinary responsibilities at one university.

1698. Shirk, Henrietta Nickels. " 'Hyper' Rhetoric: Reflections on Teaching Hypertext." *TWT* 18 (Fall 1991): 189–200.

Identifies some of the issues and questions for creating a set of rhetorical concepts to evaluate the effectiveness of hypertextual communication.

1699. Smith, Robert E., III. "Functional Teaching: Using Obsolescence to Teach Definition." *JTWC* 21 (1991): 175–180.

Presents a method for teaching an extended technical definition through exercises centered around a term that is lapsing into obsolescence.

1700. Spyridakis, Jan H., Michael J. Wenger, and Sarah H. Andrew. "The Technical Communicator's Guide to Understanding Statistics and Research Design." *JTWC* 21 (1991): 207–219.

Presents simple definitions of selected research designs and statistical concepts; accompanies these definitions with concrete examples related to the field of technical communication research.

1701. Stephens, Irving E. "Citation Indexes Improve Bibliography in Technical Communication." *JTWC* 21 (1991): 117–125.

Offers systematic methods for researchers to improve their efforts at comprehensive bibliographic coverage by using citation indexes and a few other databases.

1702. Stock, Juanita K. "Tinkering with Rhetorical Forms." *TETYC* 18 (October 1991): 200–203.

Argues that students who have to write technical reports can have creative fun in following a teaching strategy using Tinker Toys.

1703. Sullivan, Patricia. "Collaboration between Organizations: Contributions Outsiders Can Make to Negotiation and Cooperation during Composition." *TC* 38 (November 1991): 485–492.

Suggests methods useful to writers responsible for collaboration between different organizations in industry.

1704. Tebeaux, Elizabeth. "Technical Communication, Literary Theory, and English Studies: Stasis, Change, and the Problem of Meaning." *TWT* 18 (Winter 1991): 15–27.

Suggests that technical communication curricula must emphasize connections between reading and writing, historical-cultural contexts of communication, and the technological, global complexity of multicultural audiences to maintain effectiveness.

1705. Tebeaux, Elizabeth. "Visual Language: The Development of Format and Page Design in English Renaissance Technical Writing." *JBTC* 5 (July 1991): 246–274.

Uses Pollard's and Redgrave's *Short Title Catalogue* to show early concern with design techniques such as partition and visual aids.

1706. Thompson, Isabelle. "The Speech Community in Technical Communication." *JTWC* 21 (1991): 41–54.

Explores context through the idea of the speech community by examining language, culture, and thought and by expanding notions of grammatical competence and cognitive structures.

1707. Thralls, Charlotte. "Bridging Visual and Verbal Communication: Training Videos and Written Instructional Texts." *JTWC* 1991 (1991): 285–306.

Describes the use of training videos for teaching the writing of effective instructions; includes information-processing strategies, cultural themes, and learning objectives important to written instructions.

1708. Treweek, David John. "Designing the Technical Communication Résumé." *TC* 38 (April 1991): 257–260.

The author, a manager of professional technical writers, offers tips to the job-seeker and the teacher of résumé writing.

1709. Van Buren, Robert, and Mary Fran Buehler. *Levels of Edit*. Pasadena, CA: Jet Propulsion Laboratory, California Institue of Technology, 1976. Reprint. Arlington, VA: Society for Technical Communication, 1991. 36 pages

Defines stages of editing by the amount of work involved.

1710. VanDeWeghe, Richard. "What Is Technical Communication? A Rhetorical Analysis." *TC* 38 (August 1991): 295–299.

Responding to criticism that technical communicators "rank low" in prestige, the author analyzes the phrase "technical communication" and discovers a complex profession requiring many skills.

1711. Vaughan, David K. "Abstracts and Summaries: Some Clarifying Distinctions." *TWT* 18 (Spring 1991): 132–141.

Discusses the subtle distinctions between two forms of technical prose.

1712. Von Koenigseck, Edward V., James Irvin, and Sharon Irvin. *Technical Writing for Private Industry*. Malabar, FL: Krieger, 1991. 164 pages

Includes subjects on the technical writer's functions, where the technical document fits in, how military specifications and standards affect technical documents, the procurement process, reevaluating sources and planning the job, and preparing, validating, verifying, and writing the manual.

1713. White, Jan V. "Color: The Newest Tool for Technical Communicators." *TC* 38 (August 1991): 346–351.

Discusses advantages and disadvantages of using color in a technical document.

See also 142, 637, 645, 664, 688, 1180, 1191, 1665

4.2.6 WRITING IN LITERATURE COURSES

1714. Broughton, Esther, and Janine Rider. "Writing about Literature with Large-Group Collaboration: The We-Search Paper." *ELQ* 13 (October 1991): 7–9.

Suggests a collaboration assignment requiring students to write as a large group responsible for one research paper.

1715. Carey-Webb, Allen. "Homelessness and Language Arts: Contexts and Connections." *EJ* 80 (November 1991): 22–28.

Explains how students benefit from reading and writing about literature related to homelessness; advocates critical awareness of the "social, historical, and thematic content" of literature.

1716. Cross, Alice. "Reading Unlimited." *ExEx* 37 (Fall 1991): 29–30.

Argues that in courses where individual students choose from a variety of works, teachers can use both traditional critical and connective responses.

1717. Demastes, William W. "Using 'Public' Dramas to Debate 'Private' Assumptions: Susan Glaspell's *Trifles* and Marsh Norman's *'Night, Mother*." *ExEx* 36 (Spring 1991): 12–16.

Provides plot-summary, analysis and points for discussion, in-class activities, and writing assignments that draw upon issues of gender, dominance, and oppression.

1718. Elder, John. "Hiking off the Trail: One Teacher's Approach to Nature Writing." *CEA* 54 (Fall 1991): 19–21.

Supports canon revision by focusing on a form outside conventional categories of poetry, fiction, and drama.

1719. Freedman, Diane P. "Case Studies and Trade Secrets: Allaying Student Fears in the 'Litcomp' Classroom." *CollL* 18 (February 1991): 77–83.

Provides examples of ways in which she orients students to "disciplinary discourse" by helping them to see their role as constructors of text through reading.

1720. Frye, Barbara J. "Motivating Intermediate Grade Students to Read: An Ethnographic Study of Four Successful Teachers and Their Classrooms." *DAI* 51 (February 1991): 2665A.

Presents an ethnographic study of teachers' methods of promoting literature, their personal perceptions, and students' resulting actions and attitudes.

1721. Golbort, Robert C. "Science in Literature: Materials for a Thematic Teaching Approach." *EJ* 80 (March 1991): 69–73.

Outlines three reading and writing units that "draw students into the ongoing dialectic between the humanistic and scientific world-views."

1722. Goldstein, Norma W. "Using Exit Notes as Teaching Tool." *ExEx* 36 (Spring 1991): 25–27.

Explains the approach for exit and entrance notes; provides examples for a writing and an American literature course.

1723. Maitino, John R. "Gender: Classroom Models for Thinking and Writing about Literature and Film." *QNWP/CSW* 13 (Spring 1991): 13–20.

Describes a course that integrates reading and writing around gender issues and helps students reflect on their own experience.

1724. Mullin, Anne Johnson. "See What We're Saying: An Interpretive Approach to Teaching Writing." *DAI* 52 (August 1991): 451A.

Documents a pedagogical approach using psychoanalytic interpretation, literary critical theory, and reader response theory.

1725. Nystrand, Martin, and Adam Gamoran. "Instructional Discourse, Student Engagement, and Literature Achievement." *RTE* 25 (October 1991): 261–290.

Examines the kinds of instruction that foster student engagement with literature and the effects of such instruction on achievement.

1726. Price, Jody. "Feminism and the Reconstruction of Family." *ELQ* 13 (October 1991): 3–5.

Explores ways that critical theory, especially feminist theory, can create a dialogic, liberating classroom for reading and writing about literature.

1727. Rocklin, Edward. "Converging Transformations in Teaching Composition, Literature, and Drama." *CE* 53 (February 1991): 177–192.

Argues that a unified theory of composition includes analogues to drama; points out that pedagogy is itself a type of script.

1728. Thompson, Edgar H. "Tying Reader Response to Group Interaction in Literature Classrooms." *ELQ* 13 (October 1991): 9–10.

Extends reader response pedagogy to include written responses to exchanges that develop in large and small group classroom considerations of written responses to text.

1729. Tritt, Michael. "Straddling Two Worlds: Teaching Composition and Literature in Colleges." *CEAF* 21 (Summer 1991): 4–7.

Argues that composition will not integrate well into literature courses and vice versa.

1730. Wetzel, Gloria Hipps. "The Effect of 'Writing to Learn' on Literature Comprehension in English Literature." *DAI* 51 (February 1991): 2700A.

Determines significant improvement over traditional instructional methods; recommends further research in reading-thinking contexts.

4.2.7 COMMUNICATION IN OTHER DISCIPLINES

1731. Ames, Ina R. *The Student Journal: Integration through Creative and Critical Analy-*

sis. Pittsburgh, PA: Annual Meeting of the Eastern Communication Association, April 1991. ERIC ED 333 503. 11 pages

Discusses the use of three-component journals—classroom journals, reading journals, and listening journals—in an interpersonal communication theory class.

1732. Amyotte, Paul. "A Communication Course for Engineers." *EnEd* 81 (May/June 1991): 436–438.

Offers techniques for teaching undergraduates practical communication skills; includes a brief section on teaching writing with emphasis on organization.

1733. Bailey, Ronald A., and Cheryl Geisler. "An Approach to Improving Communication Skills in a Laboratory Setting: The Use of Writing Consultants." *JCE* 68 (February 1991): 150–152.

Graduate students from the language department at Rensselaer Polytechnic Institute serve as "writing consultants" to undergraduate science majors who have to write lab reports.

1734. Beall, H. "In-Class Writing in General Chemistry: A Tool for Increasing Comprehension and Communication." *JCE* 68 (February 1991): 148–149.

Argues that brief, ungraded responses to "thought questions" and to questions about students' science writing help the instructor judge comprehension and help students express themselves.

1735. Blank, Gary B. "Foresters, Public Policy, and Communication." *IEEE* 34 (December 1991): 233–239.

Argues that forestry curricula should include work that creates understanding of the rhetorical contexts in which foresters will write and speak.

1736. Cain, Mary Ann. *Researching Language Practices in Other Disciplines: Seeing Ourselves as "Other."* Boston, MA: CCCC, March 1991. ERIC ED 332 181. 13 pages

An ethnographic investigation of an economics class suggests that student papers are influenced by the demands of content course rather than by individualism in expression.

1737. Caplan, Richard, and Alan Widiss. "Medicine, Law, and Humanities." *AM* 66 (September 1991): 531.

Describes the advantages of offering an elective course in medicine, law, and the humanities. Argues that it will improve students' understanding of narrative and of patient cognitive processes.

1738. Cutts, Martin. "Clear Writing for Lawyers." *EnT* 7 (January 1991): 40–43.

Suggests a four-stage approach to avoid writing "legalese."

1739. Dennis, Sarah. "Discovery by Design: A Writing Course for Visual Arts." *DAI* 51 (May 1991): 3616A.

Reviews literature of symbolic expression in visual-verbal tradition; develops rationale linking visual and verbal instruction; presents a writing course to stimulate fine arts students.

1740. Evans, John C., John Mark Dean, and Scott Chapal. "Expert Witness or Advocate: Developing Oral Argument Skills in the Marine Science Student." *JCST* 21 (December 1991/January 1992): 149–153.

Includes rhetorical training for science professionals as a way of preparing them to write and speak publicly.

1741. Grantham, Charles E. "Social Science as a Basis for Design of Human-Computer Interactions." *Multimedia Review* 2 (Spring 1991): 21–27.

Discusses the paradigm shift occurring in human-computer research and software engineering.

1742. Hedley, Jane, and Jo Ellen Parker. "Writing across the Curriculum: The Vantage of the Liberal Arts." *ADEB* 98 (Spring 1991): 22–28.

Argues that a rhetorical approach based on disciplinary differences is better for research institutions and that an inquiry model based on commonalities is better for liberal arts colleges.

1743. Herrington, Anne J., and Deborah Cadman. "Peer Review and Revising in an Anthropology Course: Lessons for Learning." *CCC* 42 (May 1991): 184–199.

Describes the work of two students and an instructor in an anthropology course that incorporates peer review and revising.

1744. Jones, Marjorie A., and Michael Smith. "Letter to the Editor: Illinois State University Study Examines College Student Attitudes toward Writing." *JCST* 20 (March/April 1991): 262.

Points out that science students value good writing and instructor efforts to help them write better, but few take elective writing courses.

1745. Kahaney, Phyllis S. "Determining the Qualities of a Well-Written Brief: A Descriptive Study of Persuasive Writing in Law School." *DAI* 52 (December 1991): 2256A.

Studies reactions of three groups of readers' response to student appellate briefs and derives descriptions of successfully written briefs.

1746. LeGere, Adele. "Collaborative and Writing in the Mathematics Classroom." *MT* 84 (March 1991): 166–172.

A college algebra teacher reports on the effectiveness of using cooperative learning and writing activities in the classroom to elicit student participation and promote critical thinking.

1747. Mahala, Daniel. "Writing Utopias: Writing across the Curriculum and the Promise of Reform." *CE* 53 (November 1991): 773–789.

Compares British and American WAC programs; argues that American WAC has circumvented institutional conflict at the cost of weakening itself as agency of change.

1748. Maimon, Elaine. *Errors and Expectations in Writing across the Curriculum. Diversity, Equity, and the Ideology of Writing across the Curriculum.* Boston, MA: CCCC, March 1991. ERIC ED 331 092. 5 pages

Describes features of a WAC program that encourage writing to learn.

1749. Marteau, T. M., C. Humphrey, G. Mattoon, J. Kidd, M. Lloyd, and J. Horder. "Factors Influencing the Communication Skills of First-Year Clinical Medical Students." *MEd* 25 (March 1991): 127–134.

Argues that gender rather than communication training affects communication success. Manifests that confidence had no relation to students' abilities. Suggests strategies for improvement.

1750. McCarthy, Lucille. *Multiple Realities and Multiple Voices in Ethnographic Texts.* Boston, MA: CCCC, March 1991. ERIC ED 331 210. 15 pages

Reports efforts to collaborate in understanding how students are initiated into the discourse community in philosophy.

1751. McGrath, Dennis, and Martin B. Spear. *The Academic Crisis of the Community College*. Literacy, Culture, and Learning: Theory and Practice. Albany, NY: State University of New York, 1991. 185 pages

Examines the role of writing and writing across the curriculum program in the context of the general role/mission of the community college.

1752. McLeod, Susan H., and Margot Soven. "What Do You Need to Start—and Sustain—a Writing across the Curriculum Program?" *WPA* 15 (Fall/Winter 1991): 25–33.

Advises WPAs to inform their administrators before taking on the task of implementing a WAC program.

1753. Miller, L. Dianne. "Writing to Learn Mathematics." *MT* 84 (October 1991): 516–521.

Through a question-and-answer organization strategy, this college-level math teacher offers suggestions for using writing to teach mathematics.

1754. Moore, Benetta, and Gilbert L. Wergowske. "Participation of Nurses in the Evaluation of Residents' Interpersonal Skills." *AM* 66 (August 1991): 494–495.

Indicates that residents were more likely to take nurses' written evaluations of doctors' performances seriously when those written evaluations included positive as well as negative comments.

1755. Nekvasil, Nancy P. "Adding Writing Proficiency to Undergraduate Biology Research—A Formula for Success at St. Mary's (Indiana)." *JCST* 20 (March 1991): 292–293.

Describes a two-year research project required of junior/senior biology majors and the writing components now successfully integrated.

1756. Pagana, Michael P. "Communication Effectiveness of Medical Records." *AM* 66 (April 1991): 244.

Study of case records indicates that physicians do not write effectively; points out that writing courses in medical schools are needed to help physicians avoid legal and economic consequences of poor documents.

1757. Rau, Anita D. "Developing Analytical Reasoning and Judgment Skills in Nonscience Majors." *JCST* 21 (November 1991): 97–99.

Argues that writing, critical reading, and questioning strategies help nonscience majors grasp course content more easily and accurately.

1758. Recchio, Thomas E. "On Composing Ethnographically: Strategies for Enacting Authority in Writing." *RR* 10 (Fall 1991): 131–142.

Illustrates the multivoiced nature of authoritative discourse using James Clifford's anthropological essay "On Ethnographic Authority."

1759. Richlin-Klonsky, Judith, and Ellen Strenski, eds. *A Guide to Writing Sociology Papers*. 2d ed. New York: St. Martin's Press, 1991. 184 pages

Presents preliminary information about writing a paper—such as formulating a question, managing time, and the logic and structure of an essay. Describes typical writing assignments based on four data sources—textual analysis, library research, ethnographic field research, and quantitative research, including an annotated sample student paper for three of the categories.

Essayists: Roseann Giarusso, Judith Richlin-Klonsky, William G. Roy, Ellen Strenski, Constance Coiner, Arlene Dallalfar, Lisa Frohmann, Nancy A. Matthews.

1760. Shea, George Bernard, Jr. "Writing, Drawing, Photographing: Composing Texts to Learn in a Biology Class." *DAI* 52 (November 1991): 1705A.

Concludes that maintaining a balance between the three techniques, emphasizing depth of understanding, and focusing on the process enhances student learning and enjoyment.

1761. Sills, Caryl K. "Paired Composition Courses: 'Everything Relates.'" *CollT* 39 (Spring 1991): 61–64.

Proposes to reconceptualize the interdisciplinary model of first-year college composition courses paired with courses in other disciplines; uses "Introduction to Sociology" course as an example.

1762. Soven, Margot. "Writing Fellows Program: Peer Tutors in the WAC Class." *CompC* 4 (December 1991): 9–10.

Characterizes peer writing fellows program at La Salle University.

1763. Stanley, Linda C. "A Two-Tiered Writing Program for the Technology Curriculum." *TETYC* 18 (May 1991): 109–113.

Describes a WAC project that helps the engineering faculty with assignments such as journals, lab reports, and microthemes. Points out that in Tier II, the technical faculty redesign assignments independently of the WAC staff.

1764. Thaiss, Chris. "WAC at 35,000 Feet." *CompC* 3 (January 1991): 7–8.

Philosophy and art history professors discuss writing assignments in their courses.

1765. Wadsworth, John S., and Dennis C. Harper. "Training Health Care Professionals to Communicate with Patients with Mental Retardation." *AM* 66 (August 1991): 495–496.

Describes the University of Iowa's program to improve written and oral communication skills of professionals working with mentally disabled patients.

1766. Walvoord, Barbara E., and Lucille P. McCarthy. *Thinking and Writing in College: A Naturalistic Study of Students in Four Disciplines*. Urbana, IL: NCTE, 1990. 269 pages

Discusses writing as a means of teaching students to think critically in biology, business, history, and psychology courses.

1767. White, Edward M. "Shallow Roots or Taproots for Writing across the Curriculum." *ADEB* (Spring 1991): 29–33.

Analyzes seven common structures that lead to strong WAC programs; points out four pressure points that can endanger them.

1768. Whitehouse, C. R. "The Teaching of Communication Skills in U.K. Medical Schools." *MEd* 25 (July 1991): 311–318.

Points out that most U.K. medical schools provide communication training; offers suggestions how to improve the quality and affordability of such training.

1769. Woods, Donald R. "Handling the Large Class—Ways to Deal with a Potentially Big Problem." *JCST* 20 (March 1991): 312–315.

Describes a number of strategies, including Osterman's "Feedback Lecture," for obtaining written feedback and evaluations from a large class.

See also 1778

4.3 ADULT AND GRADUATE EDUCATION

1770. Ackerman, John M. "Reading, Writing, and Knowing: The Role of Disciplinary Knowledge in Comprehension and Composing." *RTE* 25 (May 1991): 133–178.

Discusses the differing rhetorical strategies employed by graduate students based on whether they had high or low knowledge of their subject.

1771. "Adult Literacy (Special Collection No. 2)." ERIC/RCS, 1991. ERIC ED 334 569. 58 pages

Collects two ERIC Digests and nine annotated bibliographies for teachers concerned with adult literacy training.

1772. Browning, M. Curt. *Opening Minds through the Liberal Arts, in a Program for Working Adults*. Boston, MA: CCCC, March 1991. ERIC ED 333 453. 6 pages

Describes a writing-intensive program for working adults that uses thematic assignments related to their own experiences.

1773. Courage, Richard Arthur. *The Interaction of Public and Private Literacies in Basic Writing Courses*. Boston, MA: CCCC, March 1991. ERIC ED 333 463. 11 pages

Two case studies indicate that public literacy is adaptable to academic literacy tasks, but private literacy is in conflict with the norms of academic literacy.

1774. Daly, Ann Marie. "The Writing of Poor and Working Class Women: Issues of Personal Power." *DAI* 51 (January 1991): 2296A.

A qualitative study of 10 women shows that their personal voices are powerful, but that they need support to develop public ones.

1775. Duppenthaler, Peter. "What about Pronunciation?" *EnT* 7 (July 1991): 32–35.

Examines recent research on the effect of the aging process on the acquisition of a second language and offers suggestions for teaching pronunciation.

1776. Fantine, Stephen Gary. "Forming and Reforming the Writing Curriculum of a Class of Nine Nontraditional Adult College-Level Composition Students at an Urban Open-Access Community College: A Study of Change in Teacher Attitude and Student Learning Behaviors as Students Become Socialized into the Expectations of Academia." *DAI* 52 (November 1991): 1668A.

Investigates the changes in teacher attitudes and student learning in a composition class at an urban open-access community college.

1777. Fox, Helen. "'It's More Than Just a Technique': International Graduate Students' Difficulties with Analytical Writing." *DAI* 52 (December 1991): 2050A.

Analyzes whether graduate students from non-Western backgrounds have difficulties with analytical writing, or if Western universities have difficulty interpreting them.

1778. Goodman, Michael B., James W. Hill, and Kenneth R. Greene. "Communication in Graduate Management Programs: Results of a Survey." *IEEE* 34 (March 1991): 24–35.

Describes a study of communication courses in graduate management programs. Finds a need for increased emphasis on oral and written communication in these programs.

1779. Henry, James. "What Are These Authors? A Narratological Analysis of Writing and Response in a Graduate Landscape Architecture Course." *DAI* 51 (February 1991): 2665A.

Analyzes authority as a function of articulation of various discursive traditions and practices by graduate students in a writing across the curriculum course.

1780. Kidder, Rushworth M. "Academic Writing Is Convoluted, Jargon-Ridden, and Isolated from the Messy Realities of the World." *CHE* 37 (January 30, 1991): B1–B3.

Urges tenure committees to quit rewarding esoteric, jargon-riddled publications; believes that scholars and media specialists should pool resources to make meaningful statements about contemporary problems.

1781. Mertesforf, Jane C. "Learning Styles and Barriers to Learning Perceived in Adult Students on Campus." *DAI* 51 (April 1991): 3304A.

Argues that a study of learning barriers (dispositional and institutional) does not reveal a relationship between the adaptive learning modes and perceived barriers to learning.

1782. Miller, Carlton Wayne. "Cognitive Styles of Functionally Illiterate Adults." *DAI* 51 (February 1991): 2604A.

Argues that while no significant relationship exists between cognitive styles and sex, age, race, or years in school, cognitive styles should nonetheless determine student/tutor matchings.

1783. O'Connor, Michael E., Jr. "An Exploratory Study of Adult Learners' Perceptions of the Professors' Communication of Power in the College Classroom." *DAI* 52 (November 1991): 1573A.

Examines 205 students and finds gender most closely associated with perceptions of power communication and affective learning.

1784. Peterson-Gonzales, Meg Joanna. "Vivencias: Writing as a Way into a New Language and Culture." *DAI* 52 (November 1991): 1666A.

A case study of four Peace Corps volunteers finds that the "life learning experience" approach to writing is a useful tool for language learning.

1785. Prior, Paul. "Contextualizing Writing and Response in a Graduate Seminar." *WC* 8 (July 1991): 267–310.

Studies how writing assignments in a graduate seminar were made by the professor and responded to by native and nonnative speakers.

1786. Resnick, Judith. "An Investigation of the Categorization Processes of Adult Developmental Reading Students Using a Think Aloud Protocol." *DAI* 52 (August 1991): 488A.

Studies the cognitive processes used by adult developmental reading students while categorizing.

1787. Rosenn, Barbara Hemley. "The Role of Perceptions of Audience in Writing Difficulty: An Exploratory Study of Ten Graduate Students Working on the Doctoral Dissertation." *DAI* 51 (February 1991): 2655A.

Determines issues that create writing difficulties; develops a way in which the academic community can assist graduate students with these issues.

1788. Santopietro, Kathleen, Joy Kreeft Peyton, Gary Pharness, Karen J. Bartlett, Flavio O. Vargas, and Janet Isserlis. "ERIC Digests on Adult Literacy Programs." National Clearinghouse for Literacy Education, 1991. ERIC ED 334 871–874. 16 pages

Four ERIC digests report on issues in adult education: assessing needs of ESL learners; a worker education program; needs of migrant workers; and workplace programs for ESL learners.

1789. Schildgen, Brenda Deen. "Master of Arts in Writing." *WPA* 15 (Fall/Winter 1991): 35–50.

Describes the Master of Arts in Writing as an attempt at reforming the master's degree in English in light of current criticisms of English studies.

1790. Stasz, Bird B., Roger Schwartz, and Jared Weeden. "Writing Our Lives: An Adult Basic Skills Program." *JR* 35 (September 1991): 30.

Describes how the writing process and oral history are combined in a whole language approach to develop literacy skills in adult learners.

1791. Stover, Lois. "Living with a Writer: Lessons for the Classroom." *JTW* 10 (Spring/Summer 1991): 59–71.

Presents 11 analyses of spouse/author's writing process with pedagogical implications for each.

4.4 ENGLISH AS A SECOND LANGUAGE

1792. Bobo, Sheilah Ann, and Pearl Monica Thompson. *Teaching English to Speakers of ESD, ESL, and EFL*. Lanham, MD: University Press of America, 1990. 216 pages

Describes the grammatical systems of Haitian Creole, Jamaican Creole, and the "Afro-American community dialect." Indicates problems these speakers may have learning Standard English and provides techniques for teaching Standard English grammar and the sound system.

1793. Brookes, Arthur, and Peter Grundy. *Writing for Study Purposes: A Teacher's Guide to Developing Individual Writing Skills*. New York: Cambridge University Press, 1990. 162 pages

Draws on the authors' experiences while teaching writing to native and nonnative speakers of English at the University of Durham.

1794. Brown, James Dean. "Do English and ESL Faculties Rate Writing Samples Differently?" *TESOLQ* 25 (Winter 1991): 587–603.

Points out that two faculties' holistic ratings of compositions by native and nonnative speakers did not show significant differences. Shows that the only difference lies in how each faculty "arrived at their scores."

1795. Browne, Sammy R. "Social Cognition as a Predictor of the Writing Quality of Students Using English as a Second Language in Freshman Composition." *DAI* 51 (April 1991): 3348A.

Argues that ESL students' expository and persuasive writing correlated positively with their social cognitive abilites. Points out that impression organization was the most significant predictor of writing quality.

1796. Butler-Pascoe, Mary Ellen. "Effective Uses of Computer Technology in the Development of Writing Skills of Students Enrolled in a College-Level English as a Second Language Program." *DAI* 51 (January 1991): 2295A.

Shows that computer writing has significant positive results on students' writing.

1797. Canilao, Paz N. D. A. "Audience Awareness: An Inquiry into Its Impact in ESL Composition." *DAI* 52 (July 1991): 147A.

Investigates ESL students' use of audience cues and the effect of audience awareness on overall writing quality.

1798. Carrell, Patricia L., and Ulla Connor. "Reading and Writing Descriptive and Persuasive Texts." *MLJ* 75 (Autumn 1991): 314–324.

Studies ESL reading-writing relationships with attention to the effects of genre, educational level, and language proficiency.

1799. Celce-Murcia, Marianne. "Grammar Pedagogy in Second and Foreign Language Teaching." *TESOLQ* 25 (Autumn 1991): 459–480.

Summarizes ESL/EFL grammar pedagogy (1966–1991), presenting theoretical foundations and resulting practices. Discusses the amount of grammar to teach, which methods to use, and error correction.

1800. Chiang, Johnson Chung Shing. "Effects of Speech Modification, Prior Knowledge, and Listening Proficiency on the Lecture Listening Comprehension of Chinese EFL (English as a Foreign Language) Students." *DAI* 51 (March 1991): 2922A.

Concludes that students are able to comprehend better when listening to a familiar-topic lecture; suggests curricula changes to accommodate these findings.

1801. Cummings, Victor. "Speech and Writing: An Analysis of Expository Texts Composed by Native and Nonnative Speakers of English at the City University of New York." *DAI* 51 (January 1991): 2296A.

Compares successful and unsuccessful written and oral texts, looking at global patterns as well as local features.

1802. Cunningham, Mary Elizabeth. "Prototype of a Content-Based ESL Textbook." *DAI* 51 (February 1991): 2664A.

Includes the design and structure for BASE (*Basic Academic Studies in English*), with teachers' guides and formative evaluations.

1803. Dalgish, Gerard M. "An ESL Writer's Query System: Theory and Practice." *CollM* 9 (November 1991): 205–209.

Describes a computer-based query system designed to assist ESL writers.

1804. Duncan, Edwin. "Vietnamese Problems with English Grammar." *ET* 21 (Spring 1990): 8–11.

Explains why Vietnamese students have difficulty learning English; decribes methods that can be used to improve their grammar.

1805. Dziombak, Constance E. "Searching for Collaboration in the ESL Computer Lab and the ESL Classroom." *DAI* 51 (January 1991): 2296A.

Notes that teachers consider collaborative activities an inappropriate preparation for writing assessment tests, but research suggests the contrary.

1806. El-daly, Hosney Mostafa. "A Contrastive Analysis of the Writing Proficiency of Arabic and Spanish Speakers: Linguistic, Cognitive, and Cultural Perspectives." *DAI* 52 (November 1991): 1624A.

Investigates the written performance of ten foreign students in order to understand the role of grammar knowledge in written production.

1807. Fotos, Sandra, and Rod Ellis. "Communicating about Grammar: A Task-Based Approach." *TESOLQ* 25 (Winter 1991): 605–628.

Explores the use of a "communicative grammar-based task" for studying EFL in Japan. Tests the level of student interaction and rule acquisition concerning dative verbs.

1808. Garcia Duran, Sara Soledad. "A Test of a Mastery Learning Approach for Teaching Basic Paragraph Writing Skills to Spanish Language Background Students." *DAI* 52 (November 1991): 1624A.

Investigates whether learning could be improved for students of Spanish language background through a mastery learning approach.

1809. Gillette, Barbara K. "Beyond Learning Strategies: A Whole-Person Approach to Second Language Acquisition." *DAI* 52 (August 1991): 524A.

Concludes that success in foreign language study depends on the students' goals in learning the language.

1810. Hall, Ernest. "Variations in the Composing Behaviors of Academic ESL Writers in Test and Nontest Situations." ERIC/FLL. January 1991. ERIC ED 328 062. 37 pages

Contrasts texts and behaviors of six graduate students, reinforcing concern about the validity of single writing samples.

1811. Hill, Elizabeth Frances. "A Comparative Study of the Cultural, Narrative, and Language Content of Selected Folk Tales Told in Burma, Canada, and Yorubaland." *DAI* 51 (January 1991): 2482A.

Presents a method of reading folk tales that assesses their usefulness in ESL instruction in developing language skills and cross-cultural understanding.

1812. Hobson, Eric H. "Working on the Olympic Goldmine." *ExEx* 37 (Fall 1991): 6–9.

Uses the 1996 Olympics as a context for making U.S. employment customs (letters of inquiry and application, résumé, and follow-up) relevant to ESL students.

1813. Johns, Ann M. "Interpreting an English Competency Examination: The Frustrations of an ESL Science Student." *WC* 8 (July 1991): 379–401.

Uses case-study and interview data to critique examinations of competency in written English often administered to ESL students.

1814. Kim, Hyun Sook. "Teaching English Definite Article Usage to Koreans: A Comparative Approach Based on Language Universals Using Written Discourse." *DAI* 52 (November 1991): 1732A.

Examines the commonalities between noun phrases preceded by "the" in English and those marked by Korean topic markers.

1815. Kim, Jong-Dae. "A Comparison of Learning Strategies of College Students Enrolled in Beginning and Advanced English as a Second Language." *DAI* 51 (February 1991): 2666A.

Concludes that second language learning is different in beginning and advanced stages.

1816. Kirkland, Margaret R., and Anne P. Saunders. "Maximizing Student Performance in Summary Writing: Managing the Cognitive Load." *TESOLQ* 25 (Spring 1991): 105–121.

Discusses internal and external constraints contributing to a high cognitive load in writing summaries. Explains approach to teaching summary writing; includes handouts.

1817. Kitchin, Deborah Anne. "Case Study of ESL Community College Stuents Using Computer-Based Writing Tools in a Composition Course." *DAI* 52 (October 1991): 1240A.

Holistic scores reveal gains that students attribute to the use of prewriting software, word processing, and grammar analysis software.

1818. Kotecha, Piyushi. "Problem Solving and Report Writing for Second Language Engineering Students." *JTWC* 21 (1991): 165–173.

Describes a report writing unit for second language engineering students in South Africa that challenges students linguistically and cognitively within their technical disciplines.

1819. Larsen-Freeman, Diane. *An Introduction to Second Language Acquisition Research.* White Plains, NY: Longman, 1990. 398 pages

Discusses methodology for gathering and analyzing data, history and development of second language research and substantive findings on interlanguage development, role of theory in social science and effects of formal instruction on language learning.

1820. Leki, Ilona. "A New Approach to Advanced ESL Placement Testing." *WPA* 14 (Spring 1991): 53–68.

Questions and challenges existing ESL placement tests and offers an innovative alternative exam with acknowledged limitations.

1821. Leki, Ilona. "The Preferences of ESL Students for Error Correction in College-Level Writing Classes." *FLA* 24 (May 1991): 203–218.

A survey of 100 ESL first-year students suggests that they equate good writing with error-free writing; suggests that their expectations may need adjustment to facilitate profit from teacher feedback.

1822. Leung, Constant H. "Bilingualism and English Language Teaching: An Underdeveloped Alliance." *DAI* 51 (February 1991): 2666A.

Examines the relationship between bilingualism and the ELT enterprise.

1823. Lucas, Tamara. "Individual Variation in Students' Engagement with a Genre." *The CATESOL Journal* 4 (November 1991): 7–39.

Explores adult ESL students' individual differences and ability to adapt to in-class journal writing requiring description and examination of writers' past experiences.

1824. MacGowan-Gilhooly, Adele. "Fluency First: Revising the Traditional ESL Sequence." *JBW* 10 (Spring 1991): 73–87.

Describes rationale, design, and results of whole-language approach to reading and writing instruction at CUNY; explains how ESL students gain essential academic skills.

1825. Martin, Aida Ramsical. "Teaching Writing as a Tool for Learning with Adult ESL Students: A Case Study." *DAI* 51 (April 1991): 3304A.

Studies the use of writing as a learning tool for ESL students, focusing on freewriting, learning logs, and summary logs. Finds evidence of literacy growth.

1826. Miriami, Djoudi. "Linguistic Competence and Strategic Competence of Second Language Learners in the Area of the English Verb System: A Cross-Sectional Study of Interlanguage." *DAI* 51 (February 1991): 2664A.

Suggests new pedagogical methods and ways of designing syllabi for ESL learners.

1827. Narain, Mona. *Nonnative Speakers: Some Problems of Language Usage*. Boston, MA: CCCC, March 1991. ERIC ED 334 588. 12 pages

Identifies three problems specific to Asian ESL students: concern about usage questions, confusions regarding self-identity, and choice of active or passive voice.

1828. Pery-Woodley, Marie-Paule. "Textual Designs: Signalling Coherence in First and Second Language Academic Writing." *DAI* 51 (February 1991): 2668A.

Shows that specific syntactic features of second language texts are likely to hamper identification of major topics and goals, and thus make processing difficult.

1829. Prineas, Julienne Swynny. "The Indigenous Writer: A Study of Nonfluent Writers among Academically Capable Upper Division College Students." *DAI* 52 (December 1991): 2041A.

Explores interacting sociocultural, affective, and cognitive factors in the educational background of academically successful students who experienced difficulty in writing.

1830. Rahman, Muhammed Asfah. "Some Effects of Computers on ESL Student Writing." *DAI* 51 (February 1991): 2719A.

Finds that computers do not make a significant difference over writing with a typewriter or pen in the quality of drafts or revisions. Argues that computers do not significantly reduce writing anxiety.

1831. Raimes, Ann. "Out of the Woods: Emerging Traditions in the Teaching of Writing." *TESOLQ* 25 (Autumn 1991): 407–430.

Summarizes ESL composition pedagogy (1966–1991); presents four focuses (form, writer, content, reader), explaining theory and practice. Discusses five controversial issues and five "emerging traditions."

1832. Rhodes, Frances Gates. "An Examination of Four Manners of Presentation of Computer Assisted Instruction in Teaching English Irregular Verbs to Fifth-Grade Spanish/English Bilinguals." *DAI* 52 (October 1991): 1241A.

Examines the effectiveness of four CAI manners of presentation and response for teaching irregular verbs.

1833. Rodriguez, Elizabeth. "Articulation: The Community College Task in Teaching ESL Writing." *The CATESOL Journal* 4 (November 1991): 97–101.

Discusses the issue of equivalency of ESL and regular freshman writing courses with suggestions for improving articulation and ESL programs.

1834. Salyer, Monte Gale. "The Significance of Difficult Vocabulary to Reading in a Second Language." *DAI* 51 (March 1991): 3058A.

Demonstrates that vocabulary development is important to ESL reading improvement.

1835. Sanchez-Villamil, Olga Irene. "The Effects of Two Metacognitive Strategies on Intermediate ESL College Students' Writing." *DAI* 52 (November 1991): 1670.

Investigates the effects of text-structure awareness and awareness of strategic behavior for self-monitoring on students' writing products.

1836. Shakir, Abdullah. "Coherence in EFL Student-Written Texts: Two Perspectives." *FLA* 24 (October 1991): 399–411.

Argues that EFL teachers in Jordan focus more on sentence structure and grammar in analyzing the coherence of 45 EFL texts than on interaction between contextual variables.

1837. Shaw, Philip. "Science Research Students' Composing Processes." *ESP* 10 (1991): 186–206.

Presents results of a study of 22 ESL/EFL dissertation writers' composing processes. Gives suggestions of intervention strategies for ESL/EFL teachers.

1838. Silva, Tony. "A Comparative Study of the Composing of Selected ESL and Native English-Speaking Freshman Writers." *DAI* 51 (April 1991): 3397A.

Reveals significant composing differences in personal, process, and product variables.

1839. Smoke, Trudy. "Becoming an Academic Insider: One Student's Experience of Attaining Academic Success in College." *DAI* 52 (December 1991): 2055A.

Describes using a long-term case study to explore academic success of a female developmental ESL student.

1840. Soh, Bee-Lay, and Yee-Ping Soon. "English by E-Mail: Creating a Global Classroom via the Medium of Computer Technology." *ELTJ* 45 (October 1991): 287–292.

Describes a project where EFL/ESL classes in Singapore and Quebec communicate via e-mail telecommunications to improve their written English and increase their cross-cultural awareness.

1841. Spanos, George, Teresa Castaldi, and Shelley Quezada. "ERIC Digests on Adult ESL Learning." National Clearinghouse on Literacy Education, 1991. ERIC ED 334866–868. 12 pages

Three ERIC digests report on issues in adult ESL instruction: cultural considerations, ethnography of workplace programs, and library services.

1842. *The Teacher as Integrator*. [videotape]. Roles of the ESL Teacher. Ames, IA: Iowa State University, n.d.

A class of advanced-proficiency ESL graduate students visits an art museum to complete tasks requiring real-world use of language skills.

1843. Teng, Chunghong. "Grammar, Imitation, and Process: How Teaching Methods Affect What Chinese ESL Students Learn about Written English." *DAI* 52 (August 1991): 452A.

Investigates the possible cause for the problems Chinese students have in writing well-developed, cohesive English prose; suggests how problems can be solved.

1844. Wongkhan, Siriporn. "The Influence of ESL Students' Cultural Schemata on the Quality of Their Writing." *DAI* 52 (November 1991): 1700A.

Finds that cultural schemata have an effect on the quality of both Thai and Japanese ESL students' writing.

1845. Yao, Lucy Chun-Kun. "Writing in English for Academic Purposes." *DAI* 52 (July 1991): 101A.

Employs think-aloud protocols to examine second language activity at the university.

1846. Yule, George. "Developing Communicative Effectiveness thorugh the Negotiated Resolution of Referential Conflicts." *L&E* 3 (1991): 31–45.

Demonstrates that adult second language learners' performance as speakers will improve more effectively if interactive listening experiences replace additional speaking practice.

See also 158, 240, 245, 1643

4.5 RESEARCH AND STUDY SKILLS

1847. Almeida, David A. "Do Underprepared Students and Those with Lower Academic Skills Belong in the Community College? A Question of Policy in Light of the 'Mission.' " *CCR* 18 (Spring 1991): 28–32.

Discusses strategies which two-year-college instructors can use to help students who are underprepared in writing and reading.

1848. Carr, Janet H. "Storytelling or Natural Narrative: A Way into the Academic Research Paper." *Leaflet* 90 (Winter 1991): 30–36.

Describes a pilot class in which physical therapy students wrote narrative-based, experientially-grounded research papers.

1849. Jacobs, Barbara Vogel. "Changing Locus-of-Control through Programmed Writing Assignments and Feedback." *DAI* 52 (September 1991): 849A.

A study of 249 students concludes that subjects became no more internally enhanced as a result of completing the written assignments with or without feedback.

1850. Licklider, Patricia. "A Comment on 'Anorexia: The Cheating Disorder' [*CE* 52 (December 1990)]." *CE* 53 (December 1991): 949–950.

Argues that teachers can help students avoid plagiarism by guiding students' writing choices and strategies.

1851. McCormick, Frank. "Quizzing the Suspected Plagiarist." *CompC* 4 (April 1991): 4–5.

Argues that written quizzes are helpful in proving plagiarism; provides examples.

1852. McIntyre, Susan Ruth. "The Relationship between Information Processing and Notetaking Effectiveness as Demonstrated by University Undergraduates." *DAI* 51 (May 1991): 3621A.

Explores the relationship between information processing and effective notetaking to distinguish between able and less able performers.

1853. Stahl, Norman A., James Riking, and William Henk. "Enhancing Students' Notetaking through Training and Evaluation." *JR* 34 (May 1991): 614–622.

Describes a four-stage instructional sequence of modeling, practicing, evaluating and reinforcing activities to develop student-directed notetaking strategies.

1854. Wilson, John T., and Mark S. Stensvold. "Improving Laboratory Instruction: An Interpretation of Research." *JCST* 20 (May 1991): 350–353.

Shows how various writing, reading, and critical thinking activities can help students understand lab work. Provides extensive bibliography.

See also 1538

4.6 OTHER

1855. Augustin, Harriet M. "The Written Job Search: A Comparison of the Traditional and a Nontraditional Approach." *BABC* 54 (September 1991): 13–14.

Describes nontraditional strategies for writing résumés and job application letters that appeal to employers.

1856. Branham, Robert James. *Debate and Critical Analysis: The Harmony of Conflict.* Hillsdale, NJ: Lawrence Erlbaum Associates, 1991.

Discusses debate as an integral part of academic inquiry in all disciplines which prepares students for critical analysis.

1857. Christensen, Kimberly. "Teaching Undergraduates about AIDS: An Action-Oriented Approach." *HER* 61 (August 1991): 337–356.

Describes content and pedagogy of a course on AIDS designed to help students combat feelings of powerlessness. Shows how journal-keeping can be integrated with action-oriented pedagogy.

1858. Erickson, Marianne. *Hear Together Eyes; Write Together Heart; American Sign Language in the (Verbocentric) Composition Classroom.* Boston, MA: CCCC, March 1991. ERIC ED 331 075. 16 pages

Discusses a number of problems unique to ASL students; suggests appropriate strategies necessary for the composition class.

1859. Greenway, William. "The House on the Second Floor." *CEAF* 21 (Summer 1991): 7–9.

Presents a collection of student bloopers.

1860. Murray, Donald M. "All Writing is Autobiography." *CCC* 42 (February 1991): 66–74.

Shares his own writings to suggest that "we become what we write."

1861. Pascarella, Ernest T., and Patrick T. Terenzini. *How College Affects Students: Findings and Insights from Twenty Years of Research.* San Francisco, CA: Jossey-Bass Publishers, 1991. 795 pages

Authors recognize and interpret a compilation of data that show how students grow and change as a consequence of attending college, including learning, critical thinking and decision making, values and attitudes, and education and career attainment. Shows how administrators and faculty can shape the educational and interpersonal settings of their campus.

1862. Romano, Thomas S. "One Writing Process: A Self-Reflective Analysis of the Creation of a Young Adult Novel." *DAI* 52 (December 1991): 2055A.

Describes the process of creation by analyzing a journal kept in conjunction with writing a young adult novel.

1863. "Vygotsky and the Bad Speller's Nightmare." *EJ* 80 (December 1991): 65–70.

Presents a first-person "confession" of a "terrible speller" completing a Ph.D. in English Education; asks teachers to reconsider how they respond to students' spelling problems.

5 Testing, Measurement, and Evaluation

5.1 EVALUATION OF STUDENTS

1864. Anbar, Michael. "Comparing Assessments of Students' Knowledge by Computerized Open-Ended and Multiple-Choice Tests." *AM* 66 (July 1991): 420–422.

Argues that computerized open-ended tests are feasible, can emulate oral exams, may allow better assessment of student performance than multiple-choice questions, and can identify "blatant ignorance" in distinct domains of knowledge.

1865. Anthony, Robert, Terry Johnson, Norma Mickelson, and Alison Preece. *Evaluating Literacy: A Perspective for Change*. Portsmouth, NH: Heinemann, 1991. 200 pages

Presents a practical guide for collecting, measuring, and reporting for teachers at all levels who use whole language teaching.

1866. Aubrecht, Gordon J. "Is There a Connection between Teaching and Testing?" *JCST* 20 (December 1990/January 1991): 152–157.

Demonstrates how teachers communicate the limitations in a course's scope and philosophy with tests. Provides an extended bibliography.

1867. Auten, Janet Gebhart. "A Rhetoric of Teacher Commentary: The Complexity of Response to Student Writing." *Focuses* 4 (Summer 1991): 3–18.

Argues that teachers' marginal comments should express the same rhetorical concerns about audience and purpose as they teach students to have about their readers.

1868. Belanoff, Pat. "The Myth of Assessment." *JBW* 10 (Spring 1991): 54–66.

Presents the keynote address at CUNY's ESL Conference in 1990; critiques misconceptions related to purpose, form, criteria, and validity of large-scale writing tests; proposes alternative evaluation process.

1869. Bentley, Robert H. *And Gladly Count: Examining the Error-Reduction Component of a Writing Program*. Boston, MA: CCCC, March 1991. ERIC ED 331 078. 15 pages

Finds that grading papers by counting errors results in a substantial—50%—decrease in errors.

1870. Brown, James Dean, Thomas Hilgers, and Joy Marsella. "Essay Prompts and Topics: Minimizing the Effect of Mean Differences." *WC* 8 (October 1991): 533–556.

Argues for pairings of a large number of stable placement exam prompts to correct the influence of a particular prompt on student responses or reader evaluation.

1871. Byrnes, Marie E., Garlie A. Forehand, Myrtle W. Rice, Douglas R. Garrison, Elizabeth Griffin, Margaret McFadden, and Eric R. Stepp-Bolling. "Putting Assessment to Work: Computer-Based Assessment for Developmental Education." *JDEd* 14 (Spring 1991): 2–8.

Authors claim that assessment which provides on-screen feedback and printed reports to student and instructor maximizes the opportunity for students to learn from the assessment itself.

1872. Cavallaro, Joanne. "The Effects of Selected Text Features on Teachers' Judgments of Student Writing." *DAI* 52 (September 1991): 826A.

Studies the relative effects of content, organization, vocabulary, and mechanics on the judgment of student essays.

1873. Cloutier, Richard Louis. "The Effect of Adding a Writing Skills Component to the General Education Development Test and the Impact of Preparation." *DAI* 52 (October 1991): 1175A.

Finds that adding an essay increases the number of passes; points out that the method of preparation affects performance.

1874. Cummings, Selden William. "The English Placement Practices of Fifteen Selected Southern California Community Colleges." *DAI* 52 (December 1991): 1958A.

Compares the English assessment practices of 15 selected Southern California community colleges in English departments for their sensitivity to cultural and/or linguistic differences.

1875. Daiker, Donald, and Nedra Grogan. "Selecting and Using Sample Papers in Holistic Evaluation." *JAC* 11 (Winter 1991): 159–171.

Explains and defends appropriate steps for selecting and using sample papers; stresses complexity of process as issues of authority and consensus are negotiated.

1876. DeFina, Allan A., and Linda L. Anstendig. "Alternative Integrated Reading/Writing Assessment and Curriculum Design." *JR* 34 (February 1991): 354–359.

Describes a test of reading and writing for incoming college students, as well as holistic scoring procedures used to assess students' performances.

1877. Dohrer, Gary. "Do Teachers' Comments on Students' Papers Help?" *CollT* 39 (Spring 1991): 48–54.

Examines the effect of teachers' actual comments on students' writing, students' reactions, and subsequent revisions.

1878. Elbow, Peter. "Writing Assessment: Do It Less, Do It Better." *AAF* (Winter 1991): 3–5.

Argues that fair assessment requires reliability based on judging rather than ranking, and validity based on multiple rather than single samples; endorses portfolios.

1879. Farr, Roger. "Portfolios: Assessment in Language Arts." ERIC/RCS, 1991. ERIC ED 334 603. 3 pages

Reviews the theory and practice of portfolio assessment.

1880. Frick, Jane, and Karen Fulton. *Promises Kept and Broken: Holistically Scored Impromptu Writing Exams*. Boston, MA: CCCC, March 1991. ERIC ED 333 449. 11 pages

Concludes that holistically scored timed writing tests should be viewed with caution as a curriculum evaluation tool, but they show promise as a placement instrument.

1881. Greenberg, Karen L. "The Vote against an Essay on the Scholastic Aptitude Test." *CHE* 37 (16 January 1991): B1, B3.

Argues that multiple-choice items—not essays—are unfair to minorities. Worries that the decision will encourage a return to grammar drills in high school.

1882. Harrison, Suzan. *Valuing Writing: Students and Their Portfolios*. Boston, MA: CCCC, March 1991. ERIC ED 334 574. 13 pages

Describes the writing portfolio assessment project at Eckerd College in Florida; notes positive student responses.

1883. Hourigan, Maureen M. "Poststructural Theory and Writing Assessment: 'Heady, Esoteric Theory' Revisited." *TETYC* 18 (October 1991): 191–195.

Argues that current theories of reading raise serious questions about large-scale holistic writing assessments.

1884. Hughes, Ronald Elliott, and Carlene H. Nelson. "Placement Scores and Placement Practices: An Empirical Analysis." *CCR* 19 (Summer 1991): 42–46.

Shows that the use of ASSET scores for placement is not a strong predictor of success in first-year college student composition.

1885. Jeffrey, Alan John, Henry Ruminski, and William Hanks. "Trends in Writing Skills Tests for Admission to Programs." *JourEd* 46 (Autumn 1991): 44.

Surveys 236 journalism programs to determine how many used commerical, standardized tests; also examines the scores required to pass and the differences between accredited and nonaccredited programs.

1886. Johanyak, Michael. "Comparing Student and Teacher Numerical Essay Evaluations." *TETYC* 18 (December 1991): 274–277.

Argues that numerical evaluations supplement marginal and end comments to enhance communication and reflective thinking.

1887. Jones, Joan, and Ronald Jackson. "The Impact of Writing Placement Testing and Remedial Writing Programs on Student Ethnic Populations at Oxnard College." Oxnard College, 1991. ERIC ED 335 081. 18 pages

Examines writing placement tests and remedial course enrollment by ethnic group.

1888. Kepner, Christine Goring. "An Experiment in the Relationship of Types of Written Feedback to the Development of Second-Language Writing Skills." *MLJ* 75 (Autumn 1991): 305–313.

Finds that teachers' message-related comments on student journal entries are more effective in promoting accuracy and higher-level thinking than error-correcting comments.

1889. Lavelle, Ellen. "Preliminary Development and Validation of an Inventory to Assess Processes in College Composition Writing." *DAI* 52 (November 1991): 1656A.

Develops and validates five scales for measuring individual differences in college writing processes: elaborationist, low self-efficacy, reflective-revisionist, spontaneous-impulsive, and methodological.

1890. Lehman, Carol M., and G. Stephen Taylor. "Participative Appraisal of Student Performance and Effective Communication Skills—Long-Run Success." *JBTC* 5 (July 1991): 307–320.

Describes a system for giving students feedback about writing performance.

1891. Linacre, John Michael. *Constructing Measurement with a Many Facet Rasch Model*. Boston, MA: CCCC, March 1991. ERIC ED 333 047. 16 pages

Argues that a many-faceted Rasch model (i.e., partial scoring technique) can be applied to the testing of composition.

1892. McCleary, Bill. "Placement Essays, Portfolios Widely Used in Missouri Colleges and Universities." *CompC* 4 (April 1991): 3.

Presents results of a survey of institutions of higher learning.

1893. Merwin, Debra Davis. "A Comparative Analysis of Two Tutoring Methods Assessing Student Achievement and Retention." *DAI* 52 (August 1991): 438A.

Compares the effectiveness of group tutoring and individual tutoring; examines levels of achievement and retention in high risk undergraduates.

1894. Miller, Emily P., and R. Stephen Richarde. *The Relationship between the Portfolio Method of Teaching Writing and Measures of Personality and Motivation.* Boston, MA: CCCC, March 1991. ERIC ED 332 184. 21 pages

Argues that the effectiveness depends equally on the grade received as well as using the portfolio approach.

1895. Peplow, P. V. "Performance of Medical Students in Case-Based and Essay Components of Written Anatomy Examinations." *MEd* 25 (July 1991): 287–292.

Points out that students in case-based courses that required a written report to be submitted for grading gained more in-depth knowledge than those in courses requiring ungraded writing.

1896. Petiprin, Gary L., and Mark E. Johnson. "Effects of Gender, Attributional Style, and Item Difficulty on Academic Performance." *JPsy* 125 (January 1991): 45–50.

Studies instances of learned helplessness in the reactions of male and female students to test items of varying difficulty.

1897. Riggenbach, Heidi. "Toward an Understanding of Fluency: A Microanalysis of Nonnative Speaker Conversations." *DPr* 14 (October–December 1991): 423–441.

Argues that instructors' evaluations of the fluency of nonnative speakers are based on three factors: hesitations, speech rate, and conversational repairs.

1898. Roemer, Marjorie Godlin. "What We Talk about When We Talk about School Reform." *HER* 61 (November 1991): 434–448.

Reflects on the complexities of school reform, telling the story of a high school-university collaboration that used writing portfolios in the assessment of high school English classes.

1899. Roemer, Marjorie, Lucille M. Schultz, and Russel K. Durst. "Portfolios and the Process of Change." *CCC* 42 (December 1991): 455–469.

Recounts and evaluates the implementation of portfolio assessment in a large Midwestern university.

1900. Rogers, Glenn E., and Carl R. Steinhoff. "Florida Community Colleges Meet the Challenge: Preparing Students for Minimum Competency Testing." *CCR* 18 (Spring 1991): 33–38.

Argues that performance on Florida CLAST has become a powerful motivator for administrators and faculties, perhaps more so than for students.

1901. Simmons, Jay. "Large-Scale Portfolio Evaluation of Writing." *DAI* 52 (November 1991): 1724A.

Demonstrates that timed writing samples poorly predict actual classroom writing, underestimating the weakest and overrating the highest.

1902. Starr, Douglas P. "Using Word Processor to Evaluate Student Papers Benefits Student and Instructor." *CollM* 9 (February 1991): 55–58.

Describes a procedure of on-line submission and evaluation of student writing in a journalism course.

1903. Sternberg, Robert J. "Death, Taxes, and Bad Intelligence Tests." *Intelligence* 15 (July–September 1991): 257–269.

Reviews six approaches to testing intelligence—classical psychometric, developmental, culture-sensitive, cognitive, biological, and systems approach. Concludes that a better assessment is possible.

1904. Stiver, Margaret Farrell. "Student Internalization of Written Teacher Response on English Compositions." *DAI* 52 (September 1991): 797A.

A study of 196 male college-bound seniors shows a desire and appreciation of written comments on English papers.

1905. Taylor, Victoria Hyrka. "Student Assessment of Writing Quality as a Predictor of Writing Proficiency." *DAI* 51 (March 1991): 3049A.

Describes and evaluates a holistic writing placement measure, the Projective English Placement Instrument. PEPI is assessed to be reliable, valid, and cost-effective.

1906. Thompson, Edgar H. "Assessment in a Whole Language Environment: Teaching Students to Document Their Own Writing Progress." *ELQ* 13 (February 1991): 11–12.

Advocates asking students to identify what they learned about writing from each piece of writing completed, guiding them in their assessment with collaboratively developed checklists.

1907. Tiffany, Gerald E., Edward Chenevat, and Nancy D. Howard. "Student Learning Outcomes Assessment for English 101 at the Wenatchee Campus of Wenatchee Valley College: The Relationship of Student Outcomes and Rater Consistency in English 101, Winter 1990 and Spring 1990." Wenatchee Valley College, 5 March 1991. ERIC ED 330 409. 70 pages

Finds that course grades in English 101 are not predictive of exam performance nor is the rater's evaluation influenced by knowing another rater's score.

1908. Tittle, Carol Kehr. "Changing Models of Student and Teacher Assessment." *EdPsy* 26 (Spring 1991): 157–165.

Proposes that cognitive, constructivist, and interpretist theories will dominate new directions for assessment of students and teachers in the twenty-first century.

1909. Van der Vleuten, C. P. M., G. R. Norman, and E. De Graaff. "Pitfalls in the Pursuit of Objectivity: Issues of Reliability." *MEd* 25 (March 1991): 110–118.

Authors claim that objectified methods in measurement do not inherently provide more reliable scores and may even provide unwanted outcomes.

1910. Wieland, Sharon. "Student Writers Set Their Own Goals." *ELQ* 13 (February 1991): 8–11.

After advocating this approach, the author finds that students' goals often involve lengthening their writing, finishing pieces, spending time on the task, and trying new techniques.

See also 1534

5.2 EVALUATION OF TEACHERS

1911. Coxwell, Deborah L. *The Clash between Teachers' Personal Views of Student Writing and Views Imposed by the State*. Boston, MA: CCCC, March 1991. ERIC ED 332 209. 16 pages

An informal study of Florida writing teachers suggests that teachers continue to focus on limited, product-based criteria for evaluation.

1912. Damisch, Jean Larson. "Teaching Techniques of Outstanding Teachers." *DAI* 52 (August 1991): 358A.

Examines "outstanding" and "other" teachers. Points out that "outstanding" teachers wait for student responses, use probing, elaboration, and "why" questions, move around the room, and give clear assignments.

1913. Edgerton, Russell, Patricia Hutchings, and Kathleen Quinlan. *The Teaching Portfo-*

lio: Capturing the Scholarship in Teaching. Washington, DC: American Association for Higher Education, 1991. 65 pages

Outlines "four core tasks" of teaching—course preparation, teaching, student assessment, and professional development—that can be displayed in a portfolio for formative (developmental) and summative (promotion and tenure) purposes; includes sample entries and suggestions for beginning teaching a portfolio program.

1914. Fandt, Patricia M., and George E. Stevens. "Evaluation Bias in the Business Classroom: Evidence Relating to the Effects of Previous Experiences." *JPsy* 125 (July 1991): 469–477.

Examines instances of gender bias in how students evaluate management professors. Concludes that previous experiences with a female faculty member reduce gender bias.

1915. Hampton, Sally B. "Changing Instructional Practice: Principles of Andragogy and the Ongoing Education of Writing Teachers." *DAI* 52 (August 1991): 393A.

Investigates to what extent the National Writing Project is andragogical if writing instruction changes after teacher training, and if students' writing improves after teacher training.

1916. Stacks, Don W., and Mark Hickson, III. "The Communication Investigator: Teaching Research Methods to Undergraduates." *ComQ* 39 (Fall 1991): 351–357.

Discusses how instructor attitude, student attitude, course requirements, and evaluation techniques contribute to the value of communication research courses.

5.3 EVALUATION OF PROGRAMS

1917. Beidler, Peter. "The WPA Evaluation: A Recent Case History." *WPA* 14 (Spring 1991): 69–73.

Describes the WPA consultation-evaluation team's visit to Lehigh University, discusses the recommendations and results, and advises other administrators to consider the benefits of an evaluation.

1918. Elliot, Norbert, Maximino Plata, and Paul Zelhart. *A Program Development Handbook for the Holistic Assessment of Writing*. Lanham, MD: University Press of America, 1990. 154 pages

Provides information on the history, underlying concepts, and process of conducting large-scale writing assessments at institutions of higher education.

1919. Fontaine, Sheryl I. *M. A. Programs in Composition: Existing Courses of Study*. Boston, MA: CCCC, March 1991. ERIC ED 333 465. 16 pages

Reports on a survey study of 111 programs.

1920. Friedman, Charles P., Dale S. Krams, and William D. Mattern. "Improving the Curriculum through Continuous Evaluation." *AM* 66 (May 1991): 257–258.

Describes an ongoing system of curriculum evaluation using portfolios, student input, interviews with faculty, and standard evaluation instruments.

1921. Larson, Richard. "Using Portfolios to Assess the Impact of a Curriculum." *Assessment Update* (March–April 1991): 9–11.

Argues that in their display of cognitive and rhetorical strategies, portfolios can point toward specific curricular and/or instructional changes.

1922. McLeod, Susan H. "Requesting a Consultant-Evaluation Visit." *WPA* 14 (Spring 1991): 73–77.

Discusses the reasons for requesting evaluation of one's own writing program and presents the benefits of such a request.

1923. Nelson, Sally Furber. "Influences on Composition at the Community Colleges: A

Descriptive Study of Writing Programs in the Community Colleges in Kentucky." *DAI* 52 (December 1991): 1996A–1997A.

Examines the writing programs of 14 community colleges in Kentucky.

1924. Perrin, Robert. "Teaching to TASP: Should We? Can We?" *ET* 21 (Spring 1990): 24–29.

Questions whether teaching methods currently used are an adequate preparation for standardized achievement and proficiency tests.

5.4 OTHER

1925. Emerling, Fred. "Identifying Ethnicity and Gender from Anonymous Essays." *CCR* 19 (Winter 1991): 29–33.

Examines whether readers of essays can correctly identify a subject's sex or ethnicity by studying an anonymous essay.

Subject Index
Name Index

Subject Index

Numbers in the right-hand column refer to sections and subsections (see Contents). For example, entries containing information on achievement tests appear in Section 5, Subsection 5.1 (Evaluation of Students). When the righthand column contains only a section number, information on the subject appears in several subsections. Entries addressing assignments in the classroom, for example, appear in several subsections of Section 4, depending on the kind of course for which the assignments are appropriate.

Academic Aptitude, 2.10
Academic Aptitude Tests, 5.1
Academic Freedom, 3.0
Academic Records, 3.2
Accountability, 3.4
Accountability Measures, 5.0
Accreditation, Institutional, 5.3
Accreditation of Teachers, 3.1
Achievement Tests, 5.1
Activities, Classroom, 4.0
Administration, 3.2
Admissions Tests, 5.1
Adolescent Development, 2.10
Adult Education Courses, 4.3
Adult Learning, 2.10
Advanced Composition Instruction, 4.2.3
Advanced Placement Tests, 5.1
Advertising in Instruction, 4.0
Advertising Research, 2.5
Affirmative Action, 3.2
Age/Grade Placement Policies, 3.2
Age/Grade Placement Tests, 5.1
Alphabets, 2.8
Ambiguity, 2.0
Anthropological Linguistics, 2.8
Anxiety Research, 2.9
Applied Linguistics, 2.8
Apprenticeships for Students, 4.3
Apprenticeships for Teachers, 3.1
Aptitude Tests, 5.1
Argumentive Discourse, 2.1
Argumentive Writing Instruction, 4.0
Arrangement in Discourse, Rhetorical, 2.1
Arrangement Instruction, Rhetorical, 4.0
Assignments, Classroom, 4.0
Assignments, Testing, 5.0
Attendance Policies, 3.2
Audience in Discourse, 2.0
Audience Instruction, 4.0
Autobiographical Writing Instruction, 4.0

Basic Skills Instruction, 4.0
Basic Writers, 2.0
Basic Writing Courses, 4.21
Behavior Theories, 2.9
Benefits, Employee, 3.2
Bibliographies, 1.0
Bilingual Instruction, 4.4
Bilingualism, 2.8
Boards, Governing, 3.2
Body Language, 2.15
Brain Research, 2.9
Budgets, 3.2

Business Communication Instruction, 4.2.4
Business Communication Theories, 2.5

Censorship, 3.4
Certification of Teachers, 3.1
Cheating, 4.5
Checklists, 1.0
Child Development, 2.10
Child Language, 2.8
Citizen Participation, 3.4
Classroom Communication, 4.0
Classroom Observation Techniques, 5.2
Class Size, 3.2
Cloze Procedure Measures, 5.0
Cloze Procedure Research, 2.7
Code Switching Instruction, Language, 4.0
Code Switching Research, Language, 2.8
Cognition, 2.9
Cognitive Development, 2.9
Cognitive Measurement, 5.1
Coherence, Teaching Techniques, 4.0
Coherence in Discourse, 2.1
Collaboration, Schools/Colleges, 3.4
Collaborative Learning, Teaching Techniques, 4.0
Collaborative Learning Research, 2.0
Collective Bargaining, 3.2
College Curriculum, 4.2
Community Relations, 3.4
Competency-Based Education, 4.0
Competency Tests, 5.1
Composing Processes, 2.1
Composition Instruction, 4.0
Composition Research, 2.1
Comprehension, 2.7
Comprehension Instruction, 4.0
Computer-Assisted Instruction, 4.0
Computer Literacy, 2.4
Computer-Managed Instruction, 4.0
Concept Formation, 2.9
Conferences, Professional, 3.3
Conferences, Student/Teacher, 4.0
Consulting as Professionals, 3.4
Consulting with Professionals, 3.4
Continuing Education Courses, 4.3
Continuing Education for Teachers, 3.1
Contract Grading, 5.1
Contracts, Teacher, 3.2
Contrastive Linguistics, 2.8
Core Curriculum, 4.0
Correctional Education, Prisons, 4.3
Correspondence Courses, 4.0
Course Descriptions, 4.0
Course Evaluation, 5.3
Courses, 4.0
Creative Writing Courses, 4.2.7
Creativity Research, 2.9
Creativity Tests, 5.1
Credentials, Teacher, 3.1
Critical Theory, 2.6
Critical Thinking, 2.9
Critical Thinking Instruction, 4.0
Cross-Curricular Writing Courses, 4.2.7
Cross-Disciplinary Research, 2.14
Cultural Literacy, 2.4
Cumulative Sentence Writing, 4.0
Curriculum, 4.0
Curriculum Evaluation, 5.3
Curriculum Research, 2.10

Day Care, Employee Benefits, 3.2
Deconstruction, 2.6
Degree Programs for Teachers, 3.1
Degree Programs in Writing, 4.0
Descriptive Discourse, 2.0
Descriptive Writing Discourse, 4.0
Development, Individual, 2.9
Developmental Studies Programs, 4.2.1
Diachronic Linguistics, 2.8
Diagnostic Tests, 5.1
Dialect Instruction, 4.0
Dialect Studies, 2.8
Dictionary Skills Instruction, 4.5
Discourse Theories, 2.1
Discussion, Teaching Techniques, 4.0
Doublespeak, 2.8
Doublespeak Instruction, 4.0
Drama, Teaching Techniques, 4.0
Drama as Literature, 2.6

Editing, Teaching Techniques, 4.0
Editing in Publishing, 2.11
Educational Administration, 3.2
Educational Assessment, 5.0
Educational Programs for Teachers, 3.1
Educational Research, 2.10
Educational Strategies, 4.0
Educational Television, 3.3
Educational Testing, 5.0
Emotional Development, 2.9
Employer/Employee Relationships, 3.2
Engineering Education, 4.2.7
English, Instruction, Second Language, 4.4
English, Research, Second Language, 2.8
English Coalition Conference, 3.4
English Language Instruction, 4.0
English Language Theories, 2.8

English Literary Criticism, 2.6
English Literature Instruction, 4.0
English-Only Legislation, 2.4
English Teacher Education, 3.1
Error, Theories of, 2.1
Error Evaluation, 5.1
Essay Test Instruction, 4.0
Essay Tests, 5.1
Essay Writing, 4.0
Ethnic Studies, 4.0
Ethnography, 2.0
Evaluation, 5.0
Experimental Curriculum, 4.0
Expository Discourse, 2.1
Expository Writing Instruction, 4.0

Faculty Development, 3.1
Faculty Evaluation, 5.2
Federal Legislation, 3.4
Figurative Language, 2.0
Figurative Language Instruction, 4.0
Film Courses, 4.0
Film Criticism, 2.6
Folk Culture Instruction, 4.0
Folklore Research, 2.14
Forced Choice Tests, 5.1
First-Year Composition Courses, 4.2.2

General Semantics, 2.8
Generative Rhetoric, 2.1
Generative Rhetoric Instruction, 4.0
Governing Boards, Institutional, 3.2
Grading, 5.1
Graduate Study for Teachers, 3.1
Graduate Teaching Assistants, 3.0
Graduate Writing Courses, 4.3
Grammar Instruction, 4.0
Grammatical Theories, 2.8
Grants, 3.3
Grievance Procedures, 3.2
Group Activities, 4.0
Group Discussion, 4.0
Grouping through Assessment, 5.1
Group Instruction, 4.0
Guidance Centers, 3.3

Handwriting, 2.15
Higher Education Curriculum, 4.2
History of Rhetoric, 2.2
Homework, 4.0
Honors Curriculum, 4.0
Humanities Instruction, 4.0

Illiteracy Studies, 2.4
Imagination, 2.9
Imitation, Teaching Techniques, 4.0
Individual Development, 2.9
Individualized Instruction, 4.0
Industrial Education, 4.0
In-Service Teacher Education, 3.1
Instructional Techniques, 4.0
Intellectual Development, 2.9
Intelligence Tests, 5.1
Interdisciplinary Course, 4.2.7
Interdisciplinary Research, 2.14
Interpretive Skills, 2.7
Interpretive Skills Instruction, 4.0
Invention Instruction, Rhetorical, 4.0
Invention Research, Rhetorical, 2.1

Journalism Education, 4.2.7
Journalism Research, 2.11
Journals, Teaching Techniques, 4.0
Judicial Rhetoric, 2.3

Laboratories, 3.3
Language Acquisition, 2.8
Language Disorders, 2.13
Language Instruction, Native, 4.0
Language Instruction, Second, 4.4
Language Planning, 2.4
Language Research, 2.8
Language Tests, 5.1
Language Theories, 2.8
Laws, 3.4
Learning Disabilities, 2.10
Learning Disabled, Programs for, 4.6
Learning Resources Centers, 3.3
Learning Theories, 2.10
Legal Rhetoric, 2.3
Legal Writing Instruction, 4.2.7
Levels of Abstraction in Discourse, 2.1
Levels of Abstraction Instruction, 4.0
Libraries, 3.3
Library Skills Instruction, 4.5
Linguistic Theories, 2.8
Listening Instruction, 4.0
Listening Research, 2.4
Literacy, 2.4
Literacy Instruction, 4.0
Literary Criticism, 2.6
Literature Courses, 4.2.6
Logic, 2.12

Mass Media Instruction, 4.0
Measurement, 5.0

Media Centers, 3.3
Medical Writing, 2.13
Medical Writing Instruction, 4.2.7
Memory Research, 2.9
Methods of Teaching, 4.0
Minimum Competency Testing, 5.1
Minority Cultures in Instruction, 4.2.7
Minority Teachers, 3.2
Miscue Analysis in Instruction, 4.0
Miscue Analysis Research, 2.7
Moral Development, 2.9
Morphology, Language, 2.8
Motivational Techniques, 4.0
Multicultural Instruction, 4.0
Multicultural Research, 2.14
Multimedia Instruction, 4.0
Multiple Choice Tests, 5.0

Narrative Discourse, 2.1
Narrative Writing Instruction, 4.0
Native Language Instruction, 4.0
Neurolinguistics, 2.8
Neurological Research, 2.9
Nonstandard Dialects in Instruction, 4.0
Nonstandard Dialect Studies, 2.8
Nonverbal Communication, 2.15
Note Taking Instruction, 4.5

Objectives, Educational, 4.0
Objective Tests, 5.1
Oral Language Instruction, 4.0
Oral Language Research, 2.4
Organization, Teaching Techniques, 4.0
Organization in Discourse, 2.1
Organizations, Professional, 3.3
Orientation Programs, 3.3

Paragraphs, Teaching Techniques, 4.0
Paragraphs in Discourse, 2.1
Parent/Teacher Conferences, 3.4
Parts of Speech, 2.8
Parts of Speech Instruction, 4.0
Part-Time Employment, 3.2
Peer Evaluation, 5.0
Peer Teaching, 4.0
Perception, 2.9
Personality Theories, 2.9
Personnel Evaluations, 5.2
Personnel Policies, 3.2
Persuasive Discourse, 2.0
Persuasive Writing Instruction, 4.0
Philosophy of Language, 2.12
Phonemics, 2.8
Phonology, 2.8
Placement Procedures, 5.1
Placement Tests, 5.1
Plagiarism, 4.5
Play Writing, 4.0
Poetry Instruction, 4.0
Police Education, 4.3
Political Rhetoric, 2.3
Popular Culture Instruction, 4.0
Position Statements, Instructional, 4.1
Position Statements, Professional, 3.2
Position Statements, Public Policies, 3.4
Practicums for Teachers, 3.1
Preaching (Religious Rhetoric), 2.3
Pre-Service Teacher Education, 3.1
Pretests/Posttests, 5.1
Prewriting Instruction, 4.0
Prewriting Research, 2.1
Priming Effects, 2.7, 2.9
Prison Programs, 4.3
Problem-Solving Instruction, 4.0
Problem-Solving Research, 2.1
Professional Development, 3.1
Professional Organizations, 3.3
Program Administration, 3.2
Program Descriptions, 4.0
Program Evaluation, 5.3
Promotion, Occupational, 3.2
Propaganda, Political, 2.3
Propaganda in Advertising, 2.5
Propaganda Instruction, 4.0
Proposal Writing Instruction, 4.0
Prose Instruction, 4.0
Prose Theories, 2.0
Psycholinguistics, 2.8
Psychological Services, 3.3
Psychology, 2.9
Public Relations, School/Community, 3.4
Public Relations Research, 2.5
Public Television, 3.3
Publishing Industry, 2.11
Punctuation, 2.8
Punctuation, Teaching Techniques, 4.0
Purpose, Teaching Techniques, 4.0
Purpose in Discourse, 2.1

Questioning Techniques, 4.0
Questionnaires, 5.0

Radio, 3.3
Rating Scales, 5.0

Readability Research, 2.7
Reader-Response Criticism, 2.6
Reading Centers, 3.3
Reading Instruction, 4.0
Reading Research, 2.7
Reading Tests, 5.1
Religious Rhetoric, 2.3
Remedial Instruction, 4.0
Report Writing Instruction, 4.0
Research Methodology, 2.0
Research Needs, 2.0
Research Skills Instruction, 4.5
Resource Centers, 3.3
Revision Instruction, 4.0
Revision Research, 2.1
Rhetorical History, 2.2
Rhetorical Instruction, 4.0
Rhetorical Theories, 2.1
Roleplaying, 4.0

Salaries, 3.2
School/Community Relationships, 3.4
Schools/Colleges, Collaboration, 3.4
Scientific Communication Theories, 2.13
Scientific Writing Instruction, 4.2.5
Second Language Instruction, 4.4
Self-Evaluation, 5.0
Semantics, 2.8
Semiotics, 2.8
Sentence-Combining Instruction, 4.0
Sentence-Combining Research, 2.8
Sentences, Teaching Techniques, 4.0
Sentences in Discourse, 2.1
Sociolinguistics, 2.8
Speech Act Theories, 2.1
Speech Communication Research, 2.0
Speech Instruction, 4.0
Spelling Instruction, 4.0
Staff Development, 3.1
Standardized Tests, 5.0
State Departments of Education, 3.2
State Legislation, 3.4
Storytelling, 4.0
Structural Linguistics, 2.8
Student Evaluation by Teacher, 5.1
Student Evaluation of Courses, 5.3
Student Evaluation of Teachers, 5.2
Student Placement, 5.1
Student/Teacher Conferences, 4.0
Study Skills Instruction, 4.5
Stylistic Instruction, 4.0
Stylistics, 2.1
Substitute Teachers, 3.2
Summer Programs for Students, 4.0
Summer Teachers' Institutes, 3.1
Syntax, 2.8
Syntax Instruction, 4.0
Systemic Linguistics, 2.8

Tagmemics, Teaching Techniques, 4.0
Tagmemic Theory, 2.8
Teacher Centers, 3.3
Teacher Education, 3.1
Teacher Evaluation, 5.2
Teacher/Parent Conferences, 3.4
Teacher Researchers, Training, 3.1
Teacher/Student Conferences, 4.0
Teacher Welfare, 3.2
Teaching Assistants, Training, 3.1
Teaching Load, 3.2
Technical Communication Theories, 2.13
Technical Writing Instruction, 4.2.5
Television, 3.3
Television Viewing Instruction, 4.0
Temporary Employment, 3.2
Tenure, 3.2
Testing Programs, 5.0
Test Taking Instruction, 4.5
Textbook Selection, 3.2
Thinking Instruction, Critical, 4.0
Thinking Research, 2.9
Traditional Grammar, 2.8
Traditional Grammar Instruction, 4.0
Transformational Grammar, 2.8
Translation in Publishing, 2.11
Tutoring, Peer, 4.0
Tutoring Programs, 3.3
Two-Year College Curriculum, 4.2

Unemployment, 3.2
Usage Instruction, 4.0
Usage Studies, 2.8

Verbal Development, 2.8
Verbally Gifted Students, 2.10
Verbally Gifted Students, Programs for, 4.0
Visual Literacy Instruction, 4.0
Visual Literacy Research, 2.4
Vocabulary Instruction, 4.5
Vocational Education, 4.0

Women's Studies, 4.0
Word Study Skills Instruction, 4.0

Work Load, Faculty, 3.2
Writing about Literature Instruction, 4.0
Writing across the Curriculum Courses, 4.2.7
Writing across the Curriculum Research, 2.0
Writing Centers, 3.3
Writing Exercises, Classroom, 4.0
Writing Exercises, Testing, 5.0
Writing Program Administrators, 3.2
Writing Program Evaluation, 5.3
Wyoming Conference Resolution, 3.2

Name Index

This index lists authors for anthologized essays as well as authors and editors for main entries.

Abarry, Abu Shardow, 743
Abdulaziz, Mohamed, 885
Aber, John, 26, 1381
Abrahamsen, Adele, 982
Ackerman, John M., 38, 114, 1770
Adams, Charles Follen, 1143
Adams, Katherine H., 1353
Adamson, David McLaren, 270
Adamson, Matthew, 876
Addison, James, 1353
Adegbija, Efurosibina, 1196
Afokpa, Kodjo, 27
Agar, Michael, 348
Agatucci, Cora, 1383
Ahlawat, Sucheta S., 690
Ahlstrom, Amber Dahlin, 1384
Ahn, Hee-Don, 861
Akamatsu, C. Tane, 982
Akinnaso, S. Nyi, 595
Al-Osaimi, Mohammed ‘Abd Al-Moshen, 349
Albrecht, Jason E., 821, 840
Albrecht, Terrance L., 691
Alder, Kenneth Ludwig, 862
Aldridge, Michelle, 863
Alegria, Jesus, 845
Alejano, AnnJanette R., 823
Alexander, Valerie, 1385
Allan, Keith, 864
Allan, Tuzyline J., 744
Allen, Carolyne, 1108
Allen, Jo, 1636, 1637
Allen, Julia M., 28
Allen, Nancy J., 1638
Allerheiligen, Robert, 1632
Allington, Richard L., 584
Allison, Alida Louise, 271
Allmendinger, Leif, 1682
Almeida, David A., 1847
Almeida, Eugenie Photiadis, 1098
Altman, Karen E., 1221
Alves, Julio, 29
Ambron, Joanna, 1171, 1215
Ambuske, Gail C., 692
Ames, Ina R., 1731
Amyotte, Paul, 1732
Anbar, Michael, 1864
Andersen, Kenneth E., 111
Andersen, Peter A., 865
Andersen, Wallis May, 504
Anderson, Alonzo B., 1249
Anderson, Anthony, 1026
Anderson, Charles W., 1249
Anderson, Chris, 40, 1405
Anderson, JoAnn Romeo, 1215

Anderson, Richard C., 566, 584
Anderson, Sherwood, 1143
Andrew, Sarah H., 1700
Andrews, James R., 1386
Andrews, Victoria L., 693
Angert, Marlene Rubin, 30
Ansani, Antonella, 272
Anstendig, Linda L., 1876
Antczak, Frederick J., 111
Anthony, Robert, 1865
Applebee, Arthur N., 103, 584
Applegate, James L., 1003
Applegate, Lynda M., 1578
Aragin, E., 1492
Arias-Gonzalez, Pedro, 866
Aristotle, 273
Armbruster, Bonnie B., 566
Arnett, Ronald C., 111
Arntson, Paul H., 474
Arrington, Phillip, 31
Asciutto, Cathy Lynne, 1004
Ashcroft, Joseph Gerard, 274
Ashton-Jones, Evelyn, 187
Asimov, Isaac, 1173
Assad, Maria L., 770
Atkinson, Judith, 1259
Atwater, Tony, 1099
Atwell, Nancie, 647, 1387, 1388
Atwill, Janet, 187
Au, Kathryn H., 104
Aubrecht, Gordon J., 1866
Audiger, Jean Y., 1197
Augustin, Harriet M., 1855
Aune, James Arnt, 350
Auten, Janet Gebhart, 1867
Autrey, Ken, 32
Ayers, Cathy Fallon, 351
Ayim, Maryann, 33

Bacig, Thomas D., 505
Baer, E. Kristina, 1
Baesler, Erland James, 1005
Bahniuk, Margaret Hilton, 700
Bahns, Jens, 867
Bailey, Andrew, 1036
Bailey, J., 1492
Bailey, Richard W., 868
Bailey, Ronald A., 1733
Baker, Barbara Louise, 745
Baker, Houston A., Jr., 746
Baker, Margaret Ann, 1640
Baker, Tracey, 1389
Balester, Valerie M., 1488
Ball, Carolyn C., 34
Ball, Deborah Loewenberg, 1249
Bamberg, Michael, 869
Banks, David, 870
Banks, James A., 1249
Bannister, Linda, 35
Barber, Liz, 179
Barclay, Rebecca O., 1641
Barker, K. Georgene, 570
Barker, Randolph T., 642, 1579
Barker, Thomas T., 506
Barnard, David, 1172
Barnes, Linda Laube, 1425
Barnes, Wendy S., 1097
Barr, Mary A., 103
Barrett, Harold, 1006
Barrett, Lindon Warren, 747
Bart, John A., 352
Bartlet, Andrew Hugh., 353
Bartlett, Karen J., 1788
Barton, David, 507
Barton, Elen, 582
Barzun, Jacques, 1077
Bateson, Gregory, 1173
Batschelet, Margaret, 508, 1674
Battenfeld, Mary, 36
Baumann, James F., 103
Bavelas, J.B., 248
Bay, Libby, 1215
Bayard, Donn, 885
Baym, Nina, 275, 1425
Bazerman, Charles, 37, 38
Beadle, George, 1173
Beadle, Muriel, 1173
Beall, H., 1734
Bearison, David J., 1025
Beason, Larry, 694
Beatty, Michael J., 1007
Beaver, John F., 687
Beck, Charles E., 1642
Beck, Isabel L., 822
Beckelman, Dana, 39
Beder, Hal, 509
Beeman, Mark, 1008
Beere, Carole A., 1232
Behnke, Ralph R., 1007
Beidler, Peter, 1917
Belanger, Kelly, 2, 1233
Belanoff, Pat, 40, 1868
Belcher, Diane D., 1643
Bell, Allan, 885
Bell, Laura C., 942
Bell, Martha Clark, 510

Bell, Marvin, 1472
Bell, Paula, 506
Bellugi, Ursula, 982
Bellwood, Peter, 871
Benardete, Seth, 276
Bender, Carol, 1412
Benelli, Beatrice, 268
Bennett, Beth S., 277
Bennett, David, 1291
Benoit, William L., 278, 279, 354, 355, 1009
Bentley, Cindy, 614
Bentley, Robert H., 1869
Bentley, Roy, 523
Benton, Richard A., 885
Benton, Stephen L., 1393
Bereano, Philip L., 609
Bereiter, Carl, 841
Bergman, Jill, 1295
Berkenkotter, Carol, 38, 1198
Berlin, James A., 133, 187, 284
Bernabo, Lawrance Mark, 356
Bernal, Martin, 1410
Bernard-Donals, Michael Francis, 748
Bernhardt, Stephen A., 1653
Bernstein, Mark E., 982
Bernstein, Richard., 872
Berrill, Deborah P., 1390
Berry, Dianne, 1024
Bertch, Julie, 1215
Berthoff, Ann E., 41, 42
Besner, Derek, 874
Besser, Pam, 1296
Bialostosky, Don H., 121
Biesecker, Susan L., 280
Biester, James Paul, 281
Biggs, Donald A., 595
Biggs, Margaret M., 1391
Bigler, Erin D., 1072
Bikai-Nyunai, Victor-Janvier, 511
Bill, Victoria L., 1463
Billington, David P., 609
Bird, John, 1234
Bishop, Walton Burrell, 43
Bishop, Wendy, 44, 1235
Bizzell, Patricia, 121, 512, 1392
Black, Kathleen, 513
Black, William, 873
Blackburn, Deborah Webb, 982
Blackhawk, Terry, 1412
Blackshaw, G., 1178
Blair, Kathleen M., 521
Blake, Bonnie L., 1580
Blank, Gary B., 1735
Blaszczynski, Carol, 1581
Blau, Sheridan, 40
Bleich, David, 187
Blitz, Michael, 133
Blohm, Paul J., 1393
Bloom, Lynn Z., 1394
Blough, Doris, 1412
Blyler, Nancy Roundy, 1582
Bobo, Sheilah Ann, 1792
Bocchi, Joseph S., 1644
Bodino, Angela Adamides, 1395
Boggs, William, 42
Boiarsky, Carolyn, 514, 1645
Bokamba, Eyamba G., 885
Bolin, Bill, 1536
Bollinger, Lee C., 1100
Boloz, Sigmund A., 1388
Bolter, Jay David, 515
Bolton, Maggie Sanders, 1477
Bonvillian, John D., 983
Booth, Wayne C., 1078
Boren Gilkenson, Francine Rose, 516
Boris, Edna Zwick, 1583
Borland, Katherine, 1488
Borowsky, Ron, 874
Bose, Christine E., 609
Bosley, Deborah S., 1297, 1646
Bosmajian, Haig, 357
Bostdorff, Denise M., 358
Boswell, Grant, 1396
Botafogo, Rodrigo, 657
Botan, Carl, 875
Botstein, Leon, 566
Bourdieu, Pierre, 876
Bourne, Jill, 1359
Bove, Paul, 749
Bowden, Darsie Minor, 877
Bowen, Elizabeth C., 1173
Bowen, Jean, 687
Bowers, Bege K., 1669
Bowers, Bradley R., 750
Bowers, Roger, 46
Bowser, June, 1510
Boxer, Susan Eve, 1010
Boyd, Melanie, 2
Boyd, Richard, 47
Bradley, David, 885
Braithwaite, Dawn O., 1011
Branciforte, Suzanne, 282
Brand, Alice G., 517, 1012, 1013
Brandt, Kathleen S., 1488
Brandt, Richard, 1101
Branham, Robert James, 1856

Brannon, Lil, 595
Brashers, Dale E. 739
Brasington, Bruce Clark, 283
Brasseur, Lee Ellen, 1647
Bratcher, Robert G., 447
Brause, Rita S., 103
Brennan, Susan Elise, 1014
Brent, Doug, 48, 518
Brett, Daniel J, 1015
Bridwell-Bowles, Lillian, 159
Briggs, John C., 49
Britten, Tracy, 570
Broadbent, Donald, 1024
Brockmann, R. John, 1648
Brodbeck, Felix, 557
Broderick, Bill, 527
Brodkey, Linda, 187
Broman, Thomas H., 1176
Brooke, Robert E., 1397
Brookes, Arthur, 1793
Brookins, Bari, 981
Brooks, Jeff, 1298
Broughton, Esther, 1714
Brown, Brenda Gabioud, 751
Brown, Carol, 1658
Brown, Cheryl, 995
Brown, David Donald, 50
Brown, Gillian, 1079
Brown, Hazel, 1398
Brown, James Dean, 1794, 1870
Brown, Mary Helen, 695
Brown, Paula M., 982
Brown, Rexford G., 519, 520, 584
Brown, Rosellen, 1472
Brown, Sam C., 1016
Brown, Stuart Cameron, 51
Brown-Williams, Jacqueline, 982
Browne, Charles Farrar, 1143
Browne, Sammy R., 1795
Browning, M. Curt, 1772
Bruce, Bertram, 103
Bruffee, Kenneth A., 187, 521
Brummett, Barry, 52
Bruner, Jerome, 53, 566
Brunner, Claire C., 235
Brunner, Diane D., 1399
Brunner, Hans, 904
Bryan, Alvenice H., 54
Bryne, Brian, 845
Bryson, Mary, 1463
Buchanan, Ronald Thomas, 359
Buckelew, Mary, 1400
Buehler, Mary Fran, 1709
Bularzik, Eileen M., 1401
Buley-Meissner, Mary Louise, 1405
Buller, David B., 1174
Bullis, Connie A., 200, 696
Bullock, Richard, 284
Bundy, Rosalee, 752
Burbules, Nicholas C., 55
Burchell, Graham, 1150
Burdette, Martha Bruner, 1199
Burgan, Mary, 1270
Burge, Penny L., 1425
Burke, Carolyn, 647
Burke, John G., 609
Burkholder, Thomas R., 360
Burks, Don M., 361
Burnett, Rebecca E., 1423, 1649
Burns, Richard A., 56
Burridge, Kate, 864
Bury, Mary J., 362
Bush, Don, 1650
Bushey, Barbara Carol, 1511
Bushman, Donald E., 522, 1353,
Butler, Marilyn S., 1584
Butler, Sidney J., 523
Butler, Susan Lowell, 1102
Butler-Pascoe, Mary Ellen, 1796
Butte, George, 1270
Buttny, N. R., 248
Bybee, Carl R., 1116
Bybee, Michael D., 57
Byrnes, Marie E., 1871

Caccamise, Frank, 982
Cadet, Lorraine Page, 1402
Cadman, Deborah, 1743
Cain, Mary Ann, 1403
Calderonello, Alice, 1376
Calfee, Robert, 584, 1463
Calkins, Lucy, 647
Calleros, Margie, 58
Calloway-Thomas, Carolyn, 1112
Cameron, John W., 1374
Campbell, JoAnn, 1488
Campbell, Karlyn Kohrs, 1103
Campbell, Kermit E., 1299
Campbell, Kim Sydow, 1651
Campbell, Lauren D., 363
Campbell, Patty Glover, 1585
Canapa, Sally Ann, 59
Cangarajah, Athelstan Suresh, 524
Canilao, Paz N. D. A., 1797
Cantor, Judy, 1017
Caplan, Richard, 1737

Capozuca, John Christopher, 878
Capps, Douglas, 879
Capron, Earl, 617
Cardona, Pablo, 614
Carelli, Maria Grazia, 268
Carey, John, 525
Carey-Webb, Allen, 753, 1715
Carino, Peter, 1300
Carlson, Helen L., 553
Carlson, Laura A., 823
Carpenter, Marlene, 1018
Carpenter, Thomas, 1463
Carr, Diane Rose, 1693
Carr, Janet H., 1848
Carr, Thomas H., 823
Carrell, David, 880
Carrell, Patricia L., 1798
Carroll, E. Ruth, 1586
Carroll, Jeffrey, 60
Carroll, Michael, 1404
Carroll, Rebecca, 364
Carson, Gatti, 1236
Carson, John Stanton, 1587
Carson, Rachel, 1173
Carter, Hodding, III., 365
Carter, Michael F., 285
Carver, Sharon M., 1463
Casady, Mona J., 1588
Cassady, David, 387
Castaldi, Teresa, 1841
Castel, Robert, 1150
Castellano, Marisa, 1520
Castellucci, Karen, 1301
Castle, Terry, 61
Castrey, Margaret, 1104
Catula, Richard, 1374
Cavalier, Todd, 526
Cavallaro, Joanne, 1872
Cavalli-Sforza, Luigi Luca, 881
Caverly, David C., 527
Cawsey, Alison, 528
Cayton, Mary Kupiec, 1237
Ceccio, Joseph F., 1589
Celce-Murcia, Marianne, 1799
Center, Candy, 739
Chall, Jeanne S., 1374
Chambers, Diane, 2
Chambers, J. K., 885
Chambers, Simone Evelyn, 63
Chandhok, Ravinder, 526
Chandler, Jean, 1097
Chang, Briankle G., 1151
Chapal, Scott, 1740
Chaplin, Miriam T., 133
Chapman, David W., 1574
Chapman, Raymond, 883
Chappell, Virginia A., 1405
Charney, Davida, 1488
Chase, Sharon, 529
Chastonay, P., 1238
Chee, C., 1492
Chelemer, Carol, 1463
Chen, Andrew, 1053
Chen, Rong, 884
Chenevat, Edward, 1907
Cheney, George, 697
Cheshire, Barbara W., 40
Cheshire, Jenny, 885
Chesin, Martin F., 1406
Chew, Joe, 506
Chiang, Johnson Chung Shing, 1800
Chick, J. Keith, 885
Chignell, Mark H., 681
Child, Robert D., 1353
Chinlen, Chris, 587
Chishimba, Maurice, 885
Chitty, Andrew, 1133
Christensen, Kimberly, 1857
Christensen, Mark Robert, 1019
Christensen, Norman, 1535
Christian, Barbara, 1210
Christiansen, Adrienne Elizabeth, 366
Christophersen, Paul, 886
Chuk, Denise D., 887
Cicognani, Elvira, 268
Cindoglu, Dilek, 754
Cintron, Ralph E., 888
Ciolli, Russ T., 1175
Cixous, Helene, 64
Clark, Carol Lea, 1536
Clark, Gregory, 65
Clark, Irene Lurkis, 1353
Clark, John, 1407
Clark, Matthew B., 260
Clark, Suzanne, 66, 530, 1200
Clarke, Ben, 1361
Clarke, Christopher Thomas, 531
Clarke, Sandra, 885
Classen, C. Joachim, 367
Clay, Marie M., 532, 825
Cleary, Linda Miller, 1020
Clemens, Herbert, 1249
Clemens, Samuel Langhorne, 1143
Clevenger, Theodore, Jr., 889
Clifford, John, 67, 68, 121, 187
Clifford, Margaret M., 1080

Clotfelter, Charles T., 1362
Cloutier, Richard Louis, 1873
Cochran, Cynthia, 579
Cochran-Smith, Marilyn, 533, 1239
Cohen, Elizabeh S., 286
Cohen, J. R., 248
Cohen, Nancy E., 506
Cohen, Roberta Parish, 1512
Coiner, Constance, 1759
Coldiron, A. E. B., 1537
Cole, Carole L., 755
Cole, Caroline, 69
Cole, Lucinda, 287
Cole, Suzanne C., 1363
Coles, N., 284
Collazo Bhakuni, Rosa, 1408
Collins, Allan, 1463
Collins, Deanne Margaret, 1201
Collis, Glyn M., 1021
Commins, Nancy L., 584
Comprone, Joseph J., 1202
Condit, Celeste Michelle, 368
Condravy, Jace, 1513
Connolly, Paula, 756
Connor, Jennifer J., 1652
Connor, Ulla, 1789
Connors, Robert J., 159, 284
Conover, Jerry N., 1016
Conquergood, Dwight, 757
Conroy, Sarah Booth, 369
Cooper, Allene, 1240
Cooper, Brenda Kay, 758
Cooper, Marilyn M., 70, 187, 536, 659
Corbeill, Anthony Thrower, 288
Corbett, Edward P. J., 1405
Corder, Jim W., 1409
Cortes, Carlos, 1410
Cosgrove, Cornelius, 1022
Coste, Tara G., 1116
Counihan, Timothy John, 1081
Coupland, Justine, 72, 248, 890
Coupland, Nikolas, 72, 248, 890
Courage, Richard Arthur, 1514, 1773
Cousin, P. T., 1492
Couture, Barbara, 1674
Covino, William A., 121
Cowan, Ruth Schwartz, 609
Cox, Carole, 103
Cox, J. Robert, 197
Cox, Susan, 963
Coxwell, Deborah L., 1538, 1911
Crafton, Linda K., 891
Craig, John S., 6
Creekmur, Corey Knox, 892
Crick, Francis, 1173
Crisp, Sally, 1302
Cronen, Vernon E., 111
Crook, Charles, 537
Crosby, Arthur, 538
Cross, Alice, 1716
Cross, Mary, 1590
Crowley, Ayn Elizabeth, 698
Crowley, Sharon, 121, 187
Csicsery-Ronay, Istvan, Jr., 770
Csikszentmihalyi, Mihaly, 566
Cullinan, Bernice E., 103
Cullinan, Mary, 1591
Cullum, Charles, 73
Culver, Steven M., 1425
Cummings, Katherine, 790
Cummings, Mary-Ellen, 74
Cummings, Selden William, 1874
Cummings, Victor, 1801
Cummins, Marsha Z., 1215
Cunningham, Mary Elizabeth, 1802
Currie, Gregory, 75
Curry, Jerome, 1592
Curtin, Thomas Duane, 1023
Curtis, Donnelyn, 1653
Cutts, Martin, 1738
Cutts-Dougherty, Katherine, 584

D'Souza, Dinesh, 1082
D'Souza, Patricia Veasey, 539
d'Ydewalle, Gery, 1070
Dahlgren, Richard, 1065
Daiker, Donald, 1875
Dalgish, Gerard M., 1803
Dallalfar, Arlene, 1759
Daly, Ann Marie, 1774
Daly, Bonita Law, 540
Damarin, Suzanne K., 541
Damisch, Jean Larson, 1912
Damon, William, 566
Damon-Moore, Helen, 598
Daneman, Meredyth, 824
Daniel, Brian Lewis, 370
Danis, M. Francine, 1411
Darsey, James, 371
Darsey, Nancy S., 701
Darwin, Charles, 1173
Dasenbrock, Reed Way, 76
Daston, Lorraine, 289
Datskovsky, Galina, 893
Dautermann, Jennie Parsons, 77
David, Yvonne Marie, 584

Davis, Candice, 1303
Davis, Gregson, 290
Davis, Kevin, 78, 1304
Davis, Lloyd Benjamin, 79
Davis, Lynne, 247
Davis, Robert Con, 1425
Davis, Ruth A., 542
Davis, Woody Lynn, 372
De Beaugrande, Robert, 80, 187, 1515
De Graaff, E., 1909
de la Luz Reyes, Maria, 584, 894
Deal, Nancy, 687
Dean, John Mark, 1740
Dear, Peter, 1176
DeBauche, Susan Clark, 1593
DeBower, Mark S., 1674
Debs, Mary Beth, 1654
DeCaro, James J., 982
Decker, Jeffrey L., 759
Declerck, Renaat, 895
Defert, Daniel, 1150
DeFina, Allan A., 1876
DeFord, Diane E., 825
DeGroot, Elizabeth J., 81
Deierl, Barbara Hardy, 1374
Dekker, Mary M., 1412
DeKlerk, Vivian., 82
Delahunty, Gerald P., 896
Delbanca, Nicholas, 1472
Demastes, William W., 1717
DeMatteo, Asa, 24
Deming, Mary P., 677, 1534
Dennie, Joseph, 1143
Dennis, Sarah, 1739
Dent, Thomas, 1377
Denzin, Norman K., 760
Depoe, Stephen P., 373
Derewianka, Beverly, 83
DeRidder, Mitchell Lee, 897
DeRose, Mimi, 1388
Dervin, Brenda, 111
Desan, Philippe, 1152
Dethier, Brock, 1203
DeVaney, Ann, 1083
Deverson, Tony, 898
Devet, Bonnie, 1305
Devine, Thomas G., 103
Devitt, Amy J., 38
Devonsih, Hubert, 885
Dey, Jim, 374
Diamond, Marian C., 1173
Dickinson, David K., 595, 617
Dickson, Marcia, 2
Diekema, David Anthony, 84
Dienes, Zoltan, 1024
Dillard, James Price, 1015
Dillon, George L., 85
Dimant, Rose J., 1025
Dinan, John, 1412
Dingwaney, Anuradha, 1488
Dinitz, Sue, 1443
Dirlek, Arif, 1210
Dittmer, Allan F., 1414
Dixon, Mimi Still, 1306
Djeddah, Richard, 699
Dobberstein, Michael, 543
Dobkin, Bethami A., 375
Dobos, Jean, 700
Dobrin, David, 544
Dobson, Ruth, 1353
Doheny-Farina, Stephen, 38, 65, 834
Dohrer, Gary, 1877
Dole, Janice, 103
Dombrowski, Paul M., 376
Donavan, T. R., 284
Donawerth, Jane, 7
Donlan, Dan, 1204
Donnelly, Nadine M., 377
Donzelot, Jacques, 1150
Dorenbusch, Saly J., 1412
Dorrell, Jean T., 701
Dorsey, Francis E., 378
Dorsey, Leroy, 398
Dorsey, Susan, 1317
Dortch, R. Neil, 729
Dossin, Mary M., 1307, 1415
Doty, Kathleen, 1405
Dow, Bonnie J., 379, 1105
Dowdey, Diane, 1488
Downing, Joseph G., 545
Doyle, Anne E., 900
Dragga, Sam, 1241, 1655
Draper, Stephen W., 1026
Draus, Julia, 1533
Dresden, Janna, 963
Droge, Edward F., Jr., 86
Droll, Linda, 1297
Dryden, Phyllis, 1416
Du Bartell, Deborah Ann, 546
DuBose, Philip B., 702
Dubrovsky, Vitaly J., 547
Duchan, Judith F., 222
Dudley-Marling, Curt, 647
Dufner, Donna, 586
Duin, Ann Hill, 548, 1674
Dulek, Ronald E., 1656

Duncan, Edwin, 1804
Duncan, Ralph Randolph, 87
Dunkeld, C., 825
Dunkle, Susan B., 1675
Dunn, Michelle Arlene, 901
Dunne, Finley Peter, 1143
Duppenthaler, Peter, 1775
Duran, Richard, 1053
Durfee, Patricia, 1215
During, Simon, 291
Durst, Russell K., 8, 1898
Dutkiewicz, Jody, 1661
Dyer, Patricia M., 1308
Dyson, Anne Haas, 103, 902, 903
Dziombak, Constance E., 1805
Dzuback, Mary Ann, 1084

Easthope, Anthony, 790
Ebert, Teresa L., 88
Ebisutani, Kay, 1204
Ede, Lisa, 159, 163, 187, 549, 1374
Edelman, Samuel M., 111
Edgerton, Russell, 1913
Edwards, Bruce L., 550
Edwards, Patricia A., 584
Eger, Henrick, 1027
Eggers, Ellen Kahan, 89
Egghe, L., 1417
Ehrenberg, Ronald G., 1362
Ehrhart, Margaret J., 1418
Ehri, Linnea, 845
Ehrlich, Heyward, 9
Eisenberg, Nora, 1215
Eisenhart, Margaret A., 584
Eisikovits, Edina, 885
Ekanger, Victoria Kill, 761
El Saffar, Ruth, 114
El-daly, Hosney Mostafa, 1806
el-Sakran, Tharwat Mohemed el-Sayed, 93
Elbow, Peter, 40, 90, 91, 1878
Elder, John, 1718
Eldred, Janet Carey, 551
Eldred, Janet M., 552
Eliades, Savvas Jack, 292
Elkin, Stanley, 1472
Elliot, David, 1419
Elliot, Norbert, 1657, 1918
Ellis, Donald G., 92
Ellis, P. M., 1178
Ellis, Rod, 1807
Elsley, Judith Helen, 94
Emerling, Fred, 1925
Emerson, Sheila, 770
Emmer, Carol, 584
Engelmann, Siegfried, 1250
Engle, Randall W., 1017
Englert, Carol Sue, 1420
Enos, Richard Leo, 114, 293
Enos, Theresa, 95
Entman, Robert M., 1106
Eribon, Didier, 1225
Erickson, Bette LaSere, 1539
Erickson, Frederick, 584
Erickson, Marianne, 1858
Erlwein, Bradley Raymond, 96
Erwin, T. Dary, 1424
Escure, Genevieve, 885
Eskenasy, Pauline Ellen, 294
Esling, John H., 885
Esposito, Dawn G., 762
Estice, R., 825
Etheridge, Chuck, 1242, 1364
Ethington, Corinna A., 253
Etsetty, C., 1492
Eubanks, Ilona M., 1422
Evans, Fred, 1028
Evans, Howard Ensign, 1173
Evans, John C., 1740
Evans, Martin G., 1107
Evans, Robert A., 505
Everson, Barbara J., 1029
Ewald, Francois, 1150
Ewald, Helen Rothschild, 1575

Fagen, Laurie, 1365
Fahnestock, Jeanne, 38, 1488
Faigley, Lester, 184, 187
Falk, Dennis R., 553
Falzer, Paul R., 295
Fandt, Patricia M., 1914
Fantine, Stephen Gary, 1776
Faraclas, Nicholas, 885
Faraday, Michael, 1173
Farkas, David K., 1674
Farnsworth, Rodney, 1205
Farr, Roger, 1879
Farrell, Amy E., 703
Farrell, Edmund J., 296
Farrell, James M., 380
Farrell, Thomas B., 97, 98
Farrell, Thomas J., 114
Farris, Christine R., 1405
Faulkenburg, Marilyn, 1594
Faust, Mark Andrew, 763
Faxon, Linda, 1108
Fearrien, Robert, 1215

Feder, Jens, 1173
Feinberg, Susan, 1682
Felch, Susan M., 764
Feldman, Tony, 554
Fennell, Barbara, 38
Fennema, Elizabeth, 1463
Ferdman, Bernardo M., 595
Ferguson, Eugene S., 609
Ferrara, Kathleen, 904
Ferriss, Suzanne E., 99
Ferro, Karen, 40
Fetterly, Judith, 135
Feynman, Richard P., 1173
Filppula, Markku, 885
Findler, Richard, 1153
Fine, E. S., 1492
Fineman, Martha Albertson, 381
Finlay, Linda Shaw, 905
Finnemore-Bello, Marilyn, 1579
Firment, Michael Joseph, 826
Fischer, Claude S., 609
Fischer, Susan D., 982
Fischer, Ute, 906
Fish, Stanley, 1085
Fishbein, Estelle A., 1271
Fisher, Charles W., 584
Fishman, A. R., 507
Fishman, Joshua, 907
Fishman, Stephen M., 1212
Fitzgerald, Sallyanne H., 1353
Fitzgerald, Sharyn, 555
Fitzsimmons, Denise A., 119
Five, Cora Lee, 647
Flander, Judy, 1109
Flanery, J. Michael, 679
Flannery, Kathryn T., 100
Flatley, Marie E., 1595
Fleckenstein, Kristie S., 101, 102
Fleming, Debryn R., 1215
Flesch, Lisa, 614
Fletcher, Ralph, 1388
Fletcher, Ronald, 1030
Flick, Carlos, 609
Floden, Robert, 1249
Flood, James, 103
Flora, Joseph M., 1272
Flores, Luis M., 1016
Flower, Linda, 831, 1423
Floyd, Lori, 1300
Flynn, Elizabeth A., 104, 187, 284, 827, 1425, 1658
Foertsch, Mary Mae, 105
Folly, Dennis Wilson, 908
Fontaine, Sheryl I., 40, 1919
Fontelar, Pilar Franche, 1206
Ford, Richard, 1472
Forehand, Garlie A., 1871
Forman, Janis, 582, 1596
Forrester, Michael A., 909
Foster, Philip, 595
Fotos, Sandra, 1807
Foucault, Michel, 342
Fowler, Roger, 1110
Fox, Dana Leigh, 1243
Fox, Helen, 1777
Fox, Jean, 1597
Fox, Mem, 1388
Foxworthy, Deb J., 10
France, Ilene M., 942
Frank, Jane, 1598
Frank, Robert L., 382
Frankinburger, Patricia, 11
Franklin, Benjamin, 1143
Franklin, Phyllis, 1085, 1286
Fraser, Kay Losey, 1520
Frazier, Hood, 1540
Freedle, Roy, 853
Freedman, Diane P., 1719
Freedman, Sarah Warshauer, 103
Freer, Kevin Joseph, 556
Freire, Paulo, 647
Freneau, Philip, 1143
Frese, Michael, 557
Frick, Jane, 1880
Friedheim, Jerry W., 1111
Friedman, Charles P., 1920
Frieds, M. D., 825
Fries, Sylvia D., 609
Frisch, Adam, 1599
Frodesen, Jan Marie, 106
Frohmann, Lisa, 1759
Fry, Maureen S., 1306
Frye, Barbara J., 1720
Fulk, Janet, 656
Fulkerson, Tahita, 1424
Fulmer, Hal W., 107
Fulton, Karen, 1880
Fulwiler, Toby, 284, 647
Funkhouser, Leslie, 647
Furnas, A., 1492
Fusfield, William D., 765

Gabriel, Susan L., 1425
Gaffney, Janet S., 584
Gaffney, Linda, 1065
Gage, John T., 159, 1249

Gajewski, Geoff, 1309
Galda, Lee, 103, 963
Gale, Fredric G., 1541
Gale, Irene, 187
Galindo, Rene, 647
Gallagher, Victoria J., 1207
Gamble, Kenneth R., 1049
Gamboa, Sylvia H., 1310
Gambrell, Linda B., 828
Gamoran, Adam, 1725
Gamow, George, 1173
Garcia, Georgia Earnest, 584
Garcia Duran, Sara Soledad, 1808
Gardener, S., 507
Gardiner, Ellen F., 558
Gardner, Howard, 566
Gardner, Phillip., 1426
Gardner, R. C., 1089
Garner, Thurmon, 1112
Garrison, Bruce, 387
Garrison, Douglas R., 1871
Garvey, Johanna X. K., 766
Gasarch, Pearl, 1600
Gates, Henry Louis, Jr., 1085, 1210
Gatherwall, Frances Mary, 1427
Gee, James Paul, 617, 982
Geisler, Cheryl, 38, 1576, 1733
Gengler, Charles Edward, 704
George, Diana, 40
Gere, Anne Ruggles, 285, 1405
Gergen, Constance A., 267
Gerrard, Lisa, 559
Getz, Malcolm, 1362
Giacobbe, Mary Ellen, 1388
Giarusso, Roseann, 1759
Gibbs, Raymond W., Jr., 175
Gibian, Jill L., 108
Gibson, Martin L., 560
Giddens, Elizabeth J., 1113
Gilbert, Pam, 109
Gilbert, Pamela K., 1428
Giles, Howard, 72, 248, 890
Gillam, Alice M., 1311, 1542, 1674
Gillespie, Marilyn Kay, 561
Gillespie, Tim, 647
Gillette, Barbara K., 1809
Gillis, Candida, 1429
Gilsdorf, Jeanette W., 1601
Gilstrap, Tracy A., 562
Girelli, Alan, 563
Girill, T. R., 1639
Giroux, Henry A., 790, 1085
Giuse, Nunzia B., 621
Glassman, Myron, 1641
Gleason, Maud Worcester, 297
Glendinning, Walter, 1036
Gless, Darryl J., 1085
Glick, Nancy Lea Parsons, 1273
Glossner, Alan Joseph, 1543
Glover, Carl W., 298
Godwin, Christine M., 1215
Godwin, Gail, 1472
Goetz, Ernest T., 849
Golbort, Robert C., 1721
Gold, R. Michael, 1544
Gold, Ruby, 110
Golden, James L., 1154
Golden, Louise, 1545
Goldfarb, Jeffrey C., 383
Goldin-Meadow, Susan, 982
Goldinger, Stephen D., 910
Goldstein, Norma W., 1722
Golub, Jeff, 133, 687
Gomez, Mary Louise, 582
Gonzalez, Andrew B., 885
Good, Howard, 1430
Goode, Gloria D., 384
Goodfield, June, 1173
Goodlett, Norma Claire, 911
Goodman, Irene F., 1097
Goodman, K. S., 1492
Goodman, Karen M., 1016
Goodman, Ken, 1388
Goodman, Kenneth, 647
Goodman, Michael B., 1778
Goodman, Yetta, 1388
Goodstein, Ronald C., 705
Goodwin, David, 1660
Gopen, George, 1179
Gorden, William I., 711
Gordon, Betsy, 981
Gordon, Colin, 1150
Gordon, Jon Clair, 385
Gordon, William I., 706
Goubil-Gambrell, Patricia, 1640
Gough, Philip, 845
Gould, Stephen J., 1173
Gourdine, Angeletta K. M., 1431
Gowen, Sheryl Greenwood, 564
Graeber, Janet Miller, 565
Graff, Gerald, 1085
Graham, Kenneth J. E., 767
Graham, Marguerite, 1388
Graham, Robert J., 1086
Gramsci, Antonio, 1114
Grant, Carl A., 1249

Grantham, Charles E., 1741
Graubard, Stephen R, 566
Gravely, Dan, 687
Graves, Dick, 1013
Graves, Donald H., 103, 647, 1432, 1492
Graves, Heather Brodie, 2
Gray, Chris Hables, 386
Greenberg, Karen Joy, 111
Greenberg, Karen L., 1881
Greenberg, Ruth B., 112
Greenberg, Seth N., 912, 931
Greenberg, Steven R., 1433
Greene, Beth G., 12
Greene, Kenneth R., 1778
Greene, Stuart, 113
Greenleaf, Cynthia, 1521
Greenway, William, 1859
Gregory, G. T., 507
Gregory, James B., 707
Gribbons, William M., 567
Grice, Roger A., 506, 1674
Gridley, Betty E., 837
Griffin, Elizabeth, 1871
Griffin, Robert J., 387
Griffith, Kevin, 1244
Grindstaff, Roy A., 388
Grisham, Therese, 913
Griswold, Charles L., Jr., 1155
Grogan, Nedra, 1875
Gronbeck, Bruce E., 114
Gross, Alan G., 1180, 1181
Grossen, Bonnie, 829
Grossman, Pamela L., 1245
Groswiler, Paul Ray, 1115
Grow, Shanna, 1516
Grudin, Jonathan, 568
Grundy, Peter, 1793
Grunst, Robert C., 115
Guilbert, J. J., 1238
Guindon, Raymonde, 569
Gullifor, Paul, 355
Guss, Donald L., 768
Guthrie, James W., 1366
Guthrie, John T., 570, 571
Guy, Gregory R., 885
Gyasi, Ibrahim K., 915

Haas, Christina, 585
Haber, Samuel, 1208
Hacker, Kenneth L., 1116
Hackett, Joseph, 687
Hacking, Ian, 1150
Hagen, Patricia, 769
Hahn, Dan F., 425
Haight, Robert, 1602
Haiman, Franklyn S., 1367
Hairston, Maxine C., 1546
Hajduk, Thomas, 1423
Hakuta, Kenyi, 1053
Halasek, Evonne Kay, 116
Haldane, J. B. S., 1173
Halford, Donna Allard, 299
Halford, Sarah A., 389
Halio, Marcia Peoples, 572
Halkowski, Timothy Robert, 390
Hall, B., 248
Hall, Bradford 'J', 691
Hall, Ernest, 1810
Hall, Mary Ann, 1603
Hall, Palmer, 573
Hall, Susan, 573
Halliday, M. A. K., 916
Halm, Ben Burnaby, 300
Halpern, Aaron, 965
Halstead, Kent, 1274
Halterman, Carroll, 1661
Halterman, Eve, 1661
Halverson, John, 574
Hambrick, Mary Margaret, 117, 391
Hamilton, George, 1017
Hamilton, Joan, 687
Hammond, Lynn, 40
Hammond, P. Brett, 1275
Hampton, Rosemary E., 118
Hampton, Sally B., 1915
Hanks, William, 1885
Hannafin, Michael J., 588
Hansen, Jane, 103
Harbaugh, Frederick W., 917
Harcourt, Jules, 708
Hardin, Garrett, 1173
Hardy, James K., 1046
Hardymon, Betsy L., 1222
Hare, Victoria Chou, 119
Harkin, Patricia, 120, 121
Harner, James L., 13
Harper, Dennis C., 1765
Harper, Mary Patricia, 918
Harrington, Susan Marie, 575
Harris, George Washington, 1143
Harris, Jeane, 1246
Harris, Joel Chandler, 1143
Harris, John, 885
Harris, Joseph, 133, 1434, 1517
Harris, Lois Ann, 1209
Harris, Muriel, 1276

Harris, R. Allen, 576, 1182
Harris, Randy, 919
Harris, Richard Jackson, 833
Harris, William V., 577
Harrison, Suzan, 1882
Harste, Jerome, 647
Hart, Roderick P., 1117
Hartley, Peter, 1662
Hartman, Geoffrey H., 578
Hartmann, Karen, 579
Hartstock, Nancy, 1210
Harvey, David R., 392
Harvill, Jerry G., 301
Hashim, Safaa H., 1604
Hashimoto, Takehiko, 1663
Haskell, Dale, 1547
Hasselriis, Peter, 920
Haswell, Richard H., 40, 122
Hatch, Gary, 123
Hatch, Richard A., 1626
Hatlen, Burton, 40
Haugen, Diane, 1664
Hausman, Carl R., 921
Haut, Jennifer Stempel, 1031
Haviland, Jeannette M., 1032
Hawisher, Gail E., 580, 581, 582, 687
Hawkes, Peter, 1435
Hawkins, David, 566
Hawkins, Jan, 1463
Hawkins, Katherine, 1033
Hayes, John R., 124, 1568
Hayles, N. Katherine, 770
Haynes, Douglas, 393
Haynes, Kathleen J. M., 1665
Hays, Janice N., 1488
Hayward, Malcolm, 1334
Hayward, Nancy M., 1436
Healy, Dave, 1312
Healy, David, 1313
Healy, Mary K., 103
Heath, Shirley Brice, 647
Hebert, Margaret, 1605
Heckel, David, 114
Heckman, Peter, 1156
Hedley, Jane, 1742
Heilbrun, Carolyn G., 1425
Heilke, Thomas Wolfgang, 394
Heilker, Paul, 1518
Heinbokel, Torsten, 557
Heine, Patricia Jean, 125
Heller, Carol, 126
Helmers, Marguerite H., 1412
Helms, Marilyn M., 721
Hemphill, Lowry, 1097
Henderson, Katherine Usher, 796
Henderson, Sarah, 1412
Hendrickson, Aletha, 1488
Henk, William, 1853
Henke, Linda, 647
Henley, Jessie L., 583
Henning, Barbara, 1519
Henry, David, 302
Henry, Dorothy, 1374
Henry, James, 1779
Henson, Kenneth T., 1118
Henwood, Karen, 72, 248
Herbert, Christopher, 303
Herman, Patricia A., 103
Herndl, Carl G., 38, 127
Herrington, Anne J., 1488, 1743
Herrman, Andrea W., 582
Herzberg, Bruce, 5, 121, 284
Hesse, Douglas, 771
Heuterman, Thomas, 387
Hever, Hannan, 1210
Heyn, John, 687
Hickey, James, 772
Hickman, Dixie Elise, 1674
Hicks, Deborah, 617
Hicks, Kim, 1548
Hickson, Mark, III, 1916
Hiebert, Elfrieda H., 584
Hightower, Paul, 1294
Hildebrandt, Herbert, 724
Hilgers, Thomas L., 40, 1870
Hill, Charles A., 585, 1549
Hill, Elizabeth Frances, 1811
Hill, James W., 1778
Hillocks, George, Jr., 103, 1249
Hiltz, Starr Roxanne, 586
Himley, Margaret, 128
Hinds, Lynn Boyd, 395
Hirsch, Linda, 1216
Hirschman, Albert O., 396
Hirst, Russel K., 397
Hlynka, Denis, 587
Hobbs, Jeffrey D., 709
Hobson, Eric H., 1437
Hodges, Richard E., 103
Hoefel, Roseanne Louise, 773
Hoffman, Barbara G., 922
Hogan, J. Michael, 398
Hogan, Mark Alan, 1247
Hohman, Jessica, 687
Holbrook, Sue Ellen, 129
Holland, K. E., 825

Holland, V. Melissa, 1488
Hollingsworth, Paul M., 843, 844
Hollis, Karyn L., 1353
Holman, Elizabeth Vanderventer, 1438
Holmes, Frederic L., 1176
Holmes, Janet, 885
Holmes, Michael, 586
Holton, Gerald, 1173
Holzman, Michael, 100, 284
Hooper, Susan, 588
Hopkins, Don, 657
Hoppe, Mary, 687
Horder, J., 1749
Horgan, John, 589
Horn, J. Kenneth, 710
Horn, John, 1119
Horner, Winifred Bryan, 14
Horning, Alice, 830
Horton, William, 1666
Houck, Davis W., 409
Houck, Karen, 1270
Houghton-Alico, Doann, 506
Houlette, Forrest, 590
Hourigan, Maureen M., 1883
House, Ernest R., 584
Houston, Marsha, 130
Houston, R. A., 591
Howard, George S., 1034
Howard, Nancy D., 1907
Howard, U., 507
Howell, Carles, 1668
Hoy, Suellen, 609
Hoye, Marj, 1314
Hoyt, L., 1492
Hubbard, Frank McKinney, 1143
Hubbard, Ruth, 647
Hubbard, Scott E., 506
Hubbuch, Susan, 1315
Huber, Bettina J., 1277
Huck, C. S., 825
Huckin, Thomas N., 38, 831
Huddle, David, 1472
Hudson, Judith A., 617, 1064
Hudson, Lucinda, 1317
Huettman, Elizabeth, 131
Hughes, Bradley T., 1316, 1354
Hughes, Geoffrey, 923
Hughes, Linda K., 770
Hughes, Ronald Elliott, 1884
Hughes-Wiener, Gail, 1216
Hughs, Linda Hazard, 1388
Hull, Glynda, 1520, 1521
Hull, Philip Veryan, 1035
Hult, Christine, 592
Hummer, T. R., 1472
Humphrey, C., 1749
Hunt, Bruce J., 1176
Hunt, Russell A., 1146
Hunter, Ian, 801
Hunter, Nancy, 832
Hunter, Susan, 132
Hupka, John Paul, 399
Hurlbert, C. Mark, 133
Hutchings, Patricia, 1913
Hutchinson, Leonard Carter, 593
Hutchinson, Susan R., 571
Hutton, Clark, 15
Huxley, Julian, 1173
Hyde, Richard B., 1157

Iandoli, Ce Ce, 1591
Impson, Beth, 1317
Infante, Dominic A., 706, 711
Ingham, Zita, 134, 135
Innes, D. C., 304
Irvin, James, 1712
Irvin, Sharon, 1712
Irving, John, 1472
Isenberg, Nancy Gale, 305
Ishak, Zuraidi B., 400
Isserlis, Janet, 1788
Italia, Paul G., 1318
Ivanic, Roz, 507
Ives, Nancy, 650
Ivie, Robert L., 433
Iyengar, Shanto, 1120

Jackson, Alan, 1439
Jackson, Janice Jaquenetta, 712
Jackson, Ronald, 1887
Jackson, S., 248
Jacob, Bernard E., 306
Jacobs, Barbara Vogel, 1849
Jacobs, S., 248
Jacoby, Jay, 1353
Jacques, Francis, 136
Jaggar, Angela M., 104
Jakobson, Roman, 925
Jamieson, Sandra, 137
Jamison, David L., 1158
Janangelo, Joseph, 594, 1278
JanMohamed, Abdul R., 1210
Jarratt, Susan C., 65, 121
Jarvis, Donald K., 1248
Javed, M. Latif, 1606
Jefferson, Thomas, 1173

Jeffrey, Alan John, 1885
Jenefsky, Cindy, 401
Jenkins, Keith B., 402
Jennings, Edward M., 595
Jensen, J. Vernon, 111
Jensen, Julie, 103
Jensen, Richard J., 302
Jensen-Cekalla, Susan K., 1215
Jenson, Julie, 103
Jessop, Ann, 1319
Jessup, Emily, 582
Jewett, John W., Jr., 1670
Jibril, Munsali, 885
Jobst, Jack, 596
Johanek, Cindy, 1320
Johansen, Robert, 1713
Johanyak, Michael, 1886
Johns, Ann M., 1813
Johnson, Gerald R., 597
Johnson, I., 1492
Johnson, Mark E., 1896
Johnson, Nan, 308
Johnson, Pamela R., 1671
Johnson, Philander Chase, 1143
Johnson, Ralph H., 1159
Johnson, Terry, 1865
Johnston, Anne, 1122
Johnston, Theodore E., 403
Johnstone, Henry W., Jr., 139
Johnstone, Sally M., 1321
Jones, Ann Rosalind, 774
Jones, Beau Fly, 1087
Jones, Elizabeth A., 687
Jones, Joan, 1887
Jones, Marjorie A., 1744
Jong, Erica, 1472
Jordan, Gillian, 1322
Jorn, Linda A., 1674
Jost, Walter, 140
Jou, Jerwen, 833
Joy, Robert O., 1607
Joyner, Michael, 1440
Joyrich, Lynne, 775
Judd, David Thomas, 141
Judy, Ronald A. Trent, 776
Julian, James Patrick, 1121
Juster, Susan Mary, 404
Justice, Donald, 1472

Kaestle, Carl F., 598
Kahaney, Phyllis S., 1745
Kahn, Jessica L., 533
Kaid, Linda Lee, 1122
Kalamaras, George, 1211
Kalb, Milton Larry, 405
Kaler, Ellen Redding, 599
Kallen, Jeffrey L., 885
Kameenui, Edward J., 103
Kamm, Daniel F., 1116
Kamphoefner, Kathleen R., 600
Kandiah, Thiru, 885
Kang, Jong Geun, 451
Kaniss, Phyllis, 1123
Kantrov, Ilene, 601
Kanyoro, Musimbi, 885
Kapinus, Barbara A., 828
Kaplan, Caren, 1210
Kaplan, Nancy, 582, 628
Karis, Bill, 1608, 1672
Karis, William M., 834, 1674
Karlson, Kathy J., 142
Kastely, James L., 309
Katz, Adam, 790
Katz, Steven B., 1488
Kaufer, David S., 1576
Kaye, Alan S., 926
Kecht, Maria-Regina, 1441
Kedzerski, Patricia, 2
Keehner, Mary F., 466
Keene, Michael L., 1641
Keene, Nadene A., 1353
Kehl, D. G., 1240
Keith, Philip, 143
Kell, Carl L., 107
Keller, Eve Miriam, 777
Keller, Ronald Edward, 602
Kelly, Priscilla, 1442
Kelman, Mark, 406
Kemmy, Anne M., 144
Kennedy, George A., 273, 1085
Kennedy, John M., 1641
Kennedy, Mary M., 1249
Kennedy, Rodney, 407
Kennedy, William J., 114
Kenny, Ed, 1388
Kent, Thomas, 145, 146, 187
Kepner, Christine Goring, 1888
Kern, Kathi L., 408
Kerr, Stephen T., 1088
Kess, Joseph F., 928
Khan, Farhat, 885
Kibby, Michael R., 604
Kidd, J., 1749
Kidder, Rushworth M., 1780
Kiedaisch, Jean, 1443
Kiefer, Kathleen, 582

Kienpointer, Manfred, 147
Kiesler, Sara, 547, 579, 664
Kiewe, Amos, 409
Kiewra, Kenneth, 1444
Kilduff, Margaret, 1657
Kim, Elaine H., 1210
Kim, Hyun Sook, 1814
Kim, Jong-Dae, 1815
Kinder, Rose Marie, 1522
King, Daniel W., 1232
King, Debra W., 148
King, Lynda A., 1232
Kinneavy, James L., 103
Kinsley, Michael, 410
Kintz, Linda, 778
Kirby, Dan, 1445
Kirkland, Margaret R., 1816
Kirsch, Gesa, 149
Kirsch, Irwin S., 627
Kirschner, Paul A., 1446
Kirton, Michael, 1036
Kissling, Elizabeth Arveda, 150
Kitchin, Deborah Ann, 1817
Kitzis, Stephen N., 1043
Kiyaani, D., 1492
Kiyaani, L., 1492
Klapp, Orrin Edgar, 1223
Klassen, C., 507
Kleimann, Susan D., 714
Klein, Helen D., 506
Klem, Elizabeth, 582
Klenk, Laura J., 1463
Kliegel, Reinhold, 1068
Klope, David C., 411
Klopf, Donald W., 929
Knapp, Michael S., 1463
Knezek, Gerald A., 679
Knight, Lee Ellen, 603
Knoblauch, C. H., 187, 1447
Knodt, Ellen Andrews, 1448
Knoespel, Kenneth J., 770
Knowles-Borishade, Adetokunbo F., 151
Knussen, Christina, 604
Koch, Tom, 605
Koenigsberg, Lisa M., 1224
Kogler, Susan E., 700
Kohut, Gary F., 655
Kolich, Eileen M., 606
Konishi, Toshiko, 930
Koriat, Asher, 912, 931
Kort, Melissa Sue, 1449
Korth, Philip A., 1523
Koskinen, Patricia S., 828
Kotecha, Piyushi, 1818
Kozma, Robert B., 607, 608
Kraemer, Don, 152
Kramarae, Cheris, 130, 1425
Kramer, Deirdre A., 1032
Krams, Dale S., 1920
Krasick, Carole Linda, 153
Krol, Tineke F., 154
Krug, Linda T., 412
Kryder, LeeAnne Giannone, 1609
Kubayanda, Josaphat B., 1210
Kuiper, Koenraad, 885
Kuklick, Bruce, 1085
Kumar, Amitava, 1450
Kuriloff, Peshe C., 1323, 1451
Kussrow, Paul G., 1324
Kutz, Eleanor, 1452
Kuykendall, Carol, 1445
Kuzmic, Jeffrey J., 155
Kwachka, Patricia, 932
Kwadwo, Anokwa, 1099

Laditka, James N., 1453
LaDuc, Linda, 715
Lafky, Sue A., 1124
LaFollette, Marcel C., 609
Laipson, Hannah Karp, 1215
Lake, Daniel, 663
Lamb, Catherine E., 1454
Lamb, Marvin R., 1059
Lamb, Maureen, 982
Lambert, Judith R., 1215
Lambert, Wallace, 1053
Landis-Groom, Eileen, 1551
Langer, Judith A., 156, 584
Lanham, Richard A., 1085
Lanoue, David J., 413
Lapp, Diane, 103
Larmouth, Donald W., 505
Larsen, Elizabeth, 1610
Larsen-Freeman, Diane, 1819
Larson, Richard L., 1374, 1921
Lassner, Phyllis, 156
Latona, John, 1455
Laurence, David, 1270, 1277, 1279
Lavelle, Ellen, 1889
Lawrence, LeeAnn Michelle, 310
Lawrence, Nancy, 584
Lawson, Anton E., 1249
Lay, Mary M., 1673, 1674
Lazere, Donald, 610
Lea, Sydney, 1472
Leahey, Margaret J., 933

Leahy, Richard, 1325, 1353
Lee, Donald Paul, 1183
Lee, Ronald E., 414
Lee, Sharon, 1257
Lee-Sammons, William H., 835
Leech, Nancy, 1215
Leeds, Bruce, 1456
Leeman, Richard W., 415
Leer, Mary N., 1463
LeGere, Adele, 1746
Leggo, Carl, 157
Lehman, Carol M., 1627, 1890
Leichty, Gregory B., 742
Leith, Philip, 114
Leki, Ilona, 158, 1820
Leland, Bruce H., 1250
Leland, Christopher M., 416
Lempereur, Alain, 417
Lennon, Paul, 934
Lenze, Lisa Firing, 1293
Leo, John, 1125
Leonard, C., 1492
Lerer, Seth, 779
Leroux, Neil R., 418
LeRoy, Patricia, 687
Lesgold, Sharon B., 1463
Leslie, Charles J., 1326
Lester, Charles Emory, 419
LeSueur, Laura Lynn, 1037
Leung, Constant H., 1822
Levenduski, Cristine, 780
Leverenz, Carrie Shively, 2
Levi-Strauss, Claude, 1225
Levin, Harry, 935
Levine, George, 1184
Levine, Linda, 1675
Levine, Marilyn M., 1126
Levine, Philip, 1472
Levine, Robert, 311
Lewis, Bernard, 420
Lewis, Charles Bertrand, 1143
Lewontin, R. C., 1185
Licklider, Patricia, 1850
Lieberman, Isabelle, 845
Lieberman, Jay, 506
Liebrandt, Thomas J., 1377
Liederman, Jacqueline, 832
Liggett, Sarah, 1457
Lightle, Marcia, 1300
Liljestrand, Petra, 421
Lillie, Richard George, 422
Limaye, Mohan, 1611
Limback, E. Rebecca, 1611
Linacre, John Michael, 1891
Lindemann, Erika, 159, 1272
Lindholm, Kathryn J., 1053
Lisowski, Marylin, 1458
Litke, Rebecca A., 1226
Litow, Ann B., 1327
Littlewood, Derek G., 160
Liu, Yameng, 312
Livingston-Weber, Joan, 1280
Llewellyn, John T., 716, 1117
Lloyd, David, 1143, 1210
Lloyd, Francis Bartow, 1143
Lloyd, M., 1749
Lloyd-Jones, Richard, 1405
Lobdell, James, 1368
Locke, David Ross, 1143
Lockhard, L., 1492
Lodtman, David Allen, 1038
Logan, Brian S., 161
Logan, Carole E., 1039
Logan, John S., 910
Lombardo, Sally, 1251
Lopez, Veronica, 2
Lotz, Roy Edward, 1127
Loughman, Tom, 1613
Lounsberry, Barbara, 1524
Lowell, James Russell, 1143
Lowenberg, Peter H., 885
Loxterman, Jane A., 822
Lu, Hsiao-peng, 162
Lu, Min-Zhan, 936
Lubart, Todd I., 237
Lucaites, John Louis, 368
Lucas, Michael A., 937
Lucas, Ruth, 1215
Lucas, Tamara, 1823
Lucht, Sandra, 687
Luckett, Sharon, 1552
Ludeman, Sandra Guth, 1459
Lund, Donna, 1614
Lund, Michael, 770
Lundman, John Peter, 781
Lunsford, Andrea A., 2, 159, 163, 187, 1328
Lutz, William, 16, 938, 939
Lux, Paul A., 164
Lyon, Arabella, 1160
Lyons, Carol, 825
Lyons, Greg, 1314, 1329
Lytle, Susan L., 611

Mabrito, Mark, 612
Macaruso, Victor Maurice, 165
MacCannell, Juliet Flower, 790

MacDonald, James C., 1330
MacDonald, Ross B., 1331
MacGowan-Gilhooly, Adele, 1824
Machann, Ginny Brown, 1281
Macintyre, Peter D., 1089
Mack, Nancy, 133
Mack, Phyllis, 423
Mackey-Kallis, Susan, 424, 425
MacRorie, Ken, 40
Madden, Frank, 613
Magnotto, Joyce N., 1215, 1252
Mahala, Daniel, 1253
Mahler, Karen, 940
Maimon, Elaine, 1748
Maitino, John R., 1723
Makau, Josina M., 111
Malikowski, Steve, 1332
Mallory, Loren Eugene, 1040
Malloy, Mary, 609
Malone, Elizabeth L., 1674
Maloney, Wendy Hall, 836
Mandelbaum, J., 248
Mangan, Katherine S., 1553, 1554
Mangelsdorf, Katherine Ward, 1525
Mani, Lata, 1210
Manly, Donna, 614
Mann, Dana J., 1041
Mann, Lian Hurst, 1227
Mann, Virginia, 845
Manusov, Valerie, 1042
Mar, Jean Olson, 1515
March, James G., 717
Marchalonis, Shirley, 782
Marchio, James David, 426
Marchman, Virginia, 869
Marcus, Stephen, 615, 687
Margulis, Lynn, 1173
Mariage, Troy V., 1420
Mariani, Paul, 1472
Marinara, Martha, 17
Mark, Robert, 609
Markel, Mike, 1676
Markley, Robert, 770
Markman, Stephanie, 1079
Marquis, Perry, 1143
Marsella, Joy, 40, 1870
Marshall, Gary Thomas, 783
Marshall, James D., 8
Marshall, Stewart, 1677
Marteau, T. M., 1749
Martens, David Bryan, 1161
Martin, Aida Ramsical, 1825
Martin, James E., 166
Martin, Judy L., 1460
Martinez, Miriam G., 103
Marting, Janet, 167
Martycz, Virginia K., 427
Marx, Michael Steven, 1333, 1555
Marzano, Robert J., 103
Masiello, Lea, 1334
Mason, Jana M., 103
Massaro, Dominic C., 1043
Masys, Daniel, 616
Mathie, Vonne, 1398
Mattern, William D., 1920
Matthews, Nancy A., 1759
Matthews, William, 1472
Mattoon, G., 1749
Maxwell, Madeline, 982
Maxwell, Martha, 1335
Mayberry, Rachel I., 982
Mayer, Elsie F., 784
Mayer, Kenneth R., 1615
Mayher, John S., 103
Mazuzan, George T., 609
McAndrew, Donald A., 168
McArthur, Tom, 941
McCabe, Allyssa, 617
McCabe-Juhnke, John E., 428
McCarron, Bill, 618, 1254
McCarthy, Lucille P., 38, 1212, 1750, 1766
McCarthy, Susan, 982
McCleary, Bill, 1336, 1369, 1461, 1526, 1556, 1892
McClish, Glen, 1462
McCollum, Pamela, 584
McComiskey, Bruce, 313
McCord, Elizabeth A., 1488, 1616, 1617
McCormick, Frank, 1851
McCreight, Thomas Dean, 169
McCutchen, Deborah, 942
McDaid, John, 582
McDiarmid, G. Williamson, 1249
McDonald, Fred Lochland, 1128
McDowell, Charles R., Jr., 1143
McDowell, Earl E., 1678
McEvoy, Sebastian T., 429
McFadden, Margaret, 1871
McFarland, Michael W., 430
McGarry, Richard G., 1129
McGaw, Dickinson, 431
McGrath, Dennis, 1215, 1751
McIntire, Marina L., 982
McIntosh, David, 837
McIntyre, Susan Ruth, 1852
McKain, Thomas Lee, 1044

McKeown, Margaret G., 822
McLain, K. Victoria Mayer, 837
McLaren, Peter, 790
McLellan, Hilary, 619
McLeod, Susan H., 170, 171, 1090, 1752, 1922
McLure, Pat, 647
McMath, William Thomas, III, 1045
McMillan, Jill J., 695
McNair, John R., 1680
McNamara, Timothy P., 1046
McNeill, William H., 1091
McTague, Mark J., 943
McVay, Freda, 388
Means, Barbara, 1463
Mear, Kimberly Matthews, 982
Mechling, Elizabeth Walker, 432
Mechling, Jay, 432
Medhurst, Martin J., 433
Medway, Frederic J., 1337
Meerhoff, Kees, 1162
Meester, Marthie, 1446
Meier, Cynthia M., 785
Meier, Kenneth J., 1092
Meier, Robert, 387
Melaver, Martin Edward, 786
Mellsop, G. W., 1178
Meloth, Michael S., 584
Merikle, Philip M., 1047
Merrell, Floyd, 944
Merrier, Patricia A., 1618
Mertesforf, Jane C., 1781
Merwin, Debra Davis, 1893
Mesch, Debra J., 1051
Mesfer, Al Beshr, 434
Mesner, David Earl, 435
Messer, Wayne Spencer, 1048
Mesthrie, Rajend, 885
Metcalf, Eric Nelson, 436
Mettauer, Patrice A., 172
Metz, Dale Evan, 982
Meyer, Paul R., 660
Meyers, Douglas G., 718, 1557
Meyers, Joyce S., 437, 438
Meyers, Renee A., 739
Meyers, Robin R., 439
Michael, Catherine, 1619
Michaels, Sarah, 617
Michaelson, Herbert B., 1130
Mickelson, Norma, 1865
Miholic, Vincent, 838
Milanes, Cecilia Rodriguez, 133
Mill, Michael, 173
Miller, Carlton Wayne, 1782
Miller, Carolyn R., 38
Miller, Chip E., 719
Miller, Emily P., 1894
Miller, Kathryn Elizabeth, 620
Miller, L. Dianne, 1753
Miller, Peter, 1150
Miller, Randolph A., 621
Miller, Richard E., 622
Miller, Rita Maria, 440
Miller, S., 284
Miller, Susan, 100, 1282
Miller, Suzanne, 1093
Miller, Thomas P., 314, 315
Milliken, Mark, 1388
Mills, Kay, 1136
Millsapps, Jan Leah, 787
Milroy, James, 885
Minnich, Elizabeth, 1410
Minnich, Elizabeth Kamarck, 1085
Minot, Walter S., 1049
Miramontes, Ofelia B., 584
Mirel, Barbara, 1681, 1682
Miriami, Djoudi, 1826
Mitoraj, Suzanne Ogorzalek, 1283
Moberg, Goran, 623
Moffat, Wendy, 788
Moffett, James, 103, 1464
Mohanan, Tara Warrier, 945
Mohr, Ellen, 1338
Molen, Dayle H., 387
Monaghan, E. Jennifer, 624
Monroe, Rick, 687
Monson, Dianne L., 103
Montgomery, Nancy Kathleen, 1255
Montgomery, Tracy T., 1683
Monty, Melissa Lee, 625
Monville-Burston, Monique, 925
Moore, Benetta, 1754
Moore, Dennis Duane, 316
Moore, Mark P., 441
Mooser, Christina, 557
Moran, Charles, 159, 582, 626
Morenberg, Max, 946
Morey, Ann-Janine, 789
Morgan, Harriet P., 1275
Morgan, Meg, 1674, 1685, 1686
Morics, Catherine, 687
Morris, Adalaide, 770
Morris, Robin Kay, 947
Morrow, Leslie Mandel, 103
Morton, Donald, 790
Morton, Johnnye L., 1256
Mosenthal, Peter B., 627

Moss, John Dietz, 1186
Moss, Malcom William, 1284
Moss, W., 507
Motley, Michael T., 174
Motto, Anna Lydia, 1407
Moulthrop, Stuart, 582, 628
Mounty, Judith L., 982
Moxey, Linda Mae, 948
Moye, Richard Hamilton, 317
Mueller-Lust, Rachel A. G., 175
Muharkey, James E., 614
Muhlhausler, Peter, 885
Mullen, William L., 442
Mullin, Anne E., 40
Mullin, Anne Johnson, 1724
Mulvihill, Peggy, 1353
Mumby, Dennis K., 720
Murdick, William, 1357, 1558
Murnane, Kevin, 949
Murphy, Christina, 1353
Murphy, James P., 1339
Murrain, Ethel P., 443
Murray, Bertha Flowers, 1465
Murray, Denise E., 629
Murray, Donald M., 100, 647, 1466, 1860
Murray, Heather, 790, 839
Murray, Mary, 1674
Musen, Gail, 1050
Mwachofi, Ngure Wa, 792
Myers, Greg, 38, 1187
Mylander, Carolyn, 982

Nadal, Joanne, 1215
Naficy, Hamid, 630
Nagel, Nicholas, 981
Nakayama, Thomas K., 1221
Narain, Mona, 1827
Nash, Cornelia Lynne, 1467
Nash, Jane Gradwohl, 176, 1063
Nass, Clifford, 177
Nathan, Ruth, 647
Nealy, Constance Jean, 178
Needham, Lawrence, 1488
Neel, Jasper, 187
Neff, Margaret Gentry, 2
Nehamas, Alexander, 1085
Nekvasil, Nancy P., 1755
Nellhaus, Tobin Benjamin, 631
Nelms, Ralph Gerald, 318
Nelson, Carlene H., 1884
Nelson, Chuck, 1669
Nelson, Elizabeth Jean, 444
Nelson, G. Lynn, 632
Nelson, Sally Furber, 1923
Nelson-Barber, Sharon, 584
Nern, Michael G., 1686
Nespor, Jan, 179
Neuleib, Janice W., 1353
Neuman, Michael, 1468
Neumann, Thomas, 687
Neuwirth, John, 579
Newell, Robert Henry, 1143
Newkirk, Thomas, 180, 284, 1388
Newlin, Maureen, 805
Newman, Diane, 633
Newton, Evangeline V., 1559
Ney, James W., 103, 950
Nichols, Patsy, 1620
Nicolescu, Nancy, 1131
Niehoff, Brian P., 1051
Nielson, H. Richard, Jr., 951
Nixon, Judy C., 721
Noda, Mari, 952
Noguchi, Rei R., 953
Nordling, John G., 181
Nordquist, Richard F., 182
Norman, G. R., 1909
Norris, Linda, 1423
North, Stephen M., 133
Norton, Mary Fenton, 319
Novak, Margaretta, 935
Nunnally, Thomas E., 1469
Nwogu, Kevin N., 1188
Nye, Emily F., 634
Nyhart, Lynn K., 1176
Nystrand, Martin, 183, 1725
Nystrand, Martin, 1725

Oates, Joyce Carol, 1472
O'Bannon, Patrick W., 609
O'Brian, Tim, 1472
O'Brien, Edward J., 821, 840
O'Connor, Michael E., Jr., 1783
O'Flaherty, Carol, 1340
O'Keefe, B. J., 248
O'Malley, Sharon, 722
Oaks, Dallin Dixon, 954
Ober, Josiah, 445
Ochsner, Robert, 1470
Odell, Lee, 1215
Odom, Keith C., 1471
Ogbu, John U., 566
Ohanian, Susan, 647
Ohmann, Richard, 284
Olawsky, Duane Evan, 955
Olds, Barbara M., 1687

Oliensis, Ellen S., 956
Olmsted, Wendy Raudenbush, 446
Olson, Gary A., 185, 186, 187
Olson, Gary M., 635
Olson, Gary R., 636
Olson, Gary, 184
Olson, James R., 1534
Olson, Judith S., 635
Olsson, Gunnar, 957
Oram, Andrew, 507
Oravec, Christine, 188
Orlinsky, Harry M., 447
Osborn, Susan, 189
Osborne, Kelly Thomas, 320
Osterhout, Lee Edward, 1052
Ostrander, Tammy M., 190
Otte, George, 637, 1560
Otter, Samuel, 793
Overmyer, Dwayne, 638
Owen, Diana, 448

Pack, Robert, 1472
Padden, Carol A., 982
Padilla, Amado M., 1053
Padmore, S., 507
Pagana, Michael P., 1756
Page, Miriam D., 191
Painter, Teresa, 1688
Paivio, Allan, 849
Palincsar, Annemarie Sullivan, 584, 1463
Palmer, William, 1412
Palmeri, Anthony J., 114
Palmquist, Michael, 579
Pandharipande, Rajeshwari, 959
Panetta, Clayann Gilliam, 639
Panici, Daniel A., 355
Paradis, James, 38
Parakrama, Arjujna, 960
Parenteau, Jean M., 640
Parini, Jay, 1472
Paris, Cynthia L., 533
Parker, Jo Ellen, 1742
Parker, Nancy Eliot, 1054
Parks, William, 1143
Parry, Robin, 1341
Parry, Sally E., 1473
Parsons, Lynn, 1388
Pascarella, Ernest T., 1861
Pasquino, Pasquale, 1150
Pastan, Linda, 1472
Patinkin, Mark, 961
Pattan, Stan, 1353
Patterson, Leslie, 1257
Paul, Marianne, 641
Pauley, Matthew Alfred, 449
Paulson, Lynn E., 1055
Paulson, William, 770
Payne, David, 114
Payne, Paula H., 794
Pearce, Frederick William, 795
Pearce, Glenn C., 642
Pearlman, Mickey, 796
Pearson, P. David, 584
Peck, George Wilbur, 1143
Peck, Wayne, 1423
Pedersen, Elray L. 687
Pederson, Lee, 962
Peirce, Roberta, 450
Pelligrini, A. D., 963
Pemberton, Michael A., 192, 580
Pena-Paez, Alberto, 1689
Penman, R., 248
Penn, William, 1143
Pennebaker, James W., 40
Pennino, Dorothy E., 797
Penti, Marsha, 1658
Peplow, P. V., 1895
Perdue, Virginia, 1285
Perelman, Les, 38
Perfetti, Charles A., 845, 942
Perkins, Sally J., 193
Perkinson, Henry J., 1132
Perrin, Robert, 1474, 1924
Perry, Devern, 643
Perry, Patricia Harris, 194
Persak, Christine, 321
Pery-Woodley, Marie-Paule, 1828
Pesante, Linda H., 1675
Peshkin, Alan, 1370
Peterson, B., 825
Peterson, Carole, 617
Peterson, Jane E., 1371
Peterson, Linda H., 1561
Peterson, Penelope L., 1463
Peterson-Gonzales, Meg Joanna, 1784
Petiprin, Gary L., 1896
Petkosh, David George, 644
Petraglia, Joseph, 195
Petrauskas, Bruno, 506
Peyton, Joy Kreeft, 1788
Pfau, Michael, 451
Pharness, Gary, 1788
Phelan, Anne Mary, 1258
Phelan, James, 1258, 1378
Phelps, Almira, 1173
Phelps, Louise Wetherbee, 196, 284, 1488

Philipson, Morris, 1077
Phinney, Marianne, 645
Pieper, Gail W., 1690
Piercy, Marge, 647
Pignattelli, Frank Charles, 1094
Pimple, Kenneth D., 452
Pinelli, Thomas E., 1641
Pinnell, Gay Su, 103, 825
Pinney, Denise, 1277
Pisoni, David B., 910
Plaisant, Catherine, 657
Plata, Maximino, 1918
Platt, John, 885
Pobo, Kenneth G., 1342
Pogoloff, Stephen Mark, 453
Pollard, Canstance, 1621
Pollard, Rita H., 1527
Polle, Sig T., 454
Pollock, Della, 197
Pomerance, Anita Humphreys, 1343
Pomerantz, A., 248
Pompian, Richard, 1611
Poole, Scott, 586
Popken, Randall, 1691
Popkin, Samuel L., 455
Porter, Frank Lee, 322
Porter, Kent, 964
Porush, David, 770
Posey, Evelyn, 1528
Possin, Kevin, 456
Poteet, Howard, 646
Potkay, Adam Stanley, 323
Potter, Jonathan, 1133
Poulakos, John, 324
Powell, Melissa L., 723
Power, Brenda Miller, 647
Powers, Suzanne, 1344
Pratt, Mary Louise, 1085
Pratt, Michael W., 198
Preece, Alison, 1865
Prentice, L., 1492
Prentice, Penelope, 1475
Price, Jody, 1726
Prineas, Julienne Swynny, 1829
Prior, Paul, 1785
Probst, Robert E., 103
Procacci, Giovanna, 1150
Proctor, Margaret B., 1476
Prose, Francine, 1472
Protherough, Robert, 1259
Prott, Lyndel V., 457
Pullman, George L., 199, 798
Pullum, Geoffrey K., 967
Purcell, William M., 325
Purdie, G. L., 1178
Purnell, Kenneth N., 1213
Pursell, Carroll W., 609
Purves, Alan C., 103, 595, 648, 649
Purvis-Smith, Virginia Louise, 458
Putnam, Linda L., 200
Pylkko, Pauli, 1228
Pytlik, Betty P., 201

Queenan, Margaret Lally, 1388
Quezada, Shelley, 1841
Quigley, Rooke Lee, 202
Quinlan, Kathleen, 1913
Quinn, Robert, 724

Raban, Birdie, 1477
Rabasa, Jose, 1210
Rada, Muriel M., 1056
Radhakrishnan, R., 790, 1210
Ragland, Cynthia Lee, 326
Raheim, Salome, 459
Rahman, Muhammed Asfah, 1830
Rahman, Tariz, 969
Raign, Kathrin Rossner, 1372
Raimes, Ann, 1831
Rajan, Gita, 327
Ramer, Mary Ann, 725
Randic, Jasna, 1562
Rank, Hugh, 726, 970
Rao, Arati, 460
Rau, Anita D., 1757
Rauenbusch, Frances, 841
Rawlins, W. K., 248
Ray, Ruth, 582
Raymond, Gino, 876
Reagan, Sally Barr, 1379, 1478
Reaves, Rita Reavis, 1479
Recchio, Thomas E., 842, 1758
Redd, Teresa M., 1135
Reed, Janine, 203
Reeves, Byron, 177
Reid, Allan Patrick, 799
Reid, Louann, 133
Reilley, Brian, 1521
Reilly, Judy Snitzer, 982
Reimers, Valerie Ann, 204
Reingold, Eyal M., 1047
Reinsch, Lamar, 727
Reinthaler, Bee, 971
Reither, James A., 205
Renaud, Judith, 1345
Resaldo, Renato, 1210

Resnick, Daniel P., 566
Resnick, Judith, 1786
Resnick, Lauren B., 1463
Reutzel, D. Ray, 843, 844
Reyes, Maria de la Luz, 584, 894
Reynolds, Mark, 1229
Reynolds, Nedra, 206
Rhodes, Barbara K., 650
Rhodes, Frances Gates, 1832
Rhodes, Lynn K., 647
Ricchiardi, Sherry, 1136
Rice, Donald Everett, 461
Rice, Myrtle W., 1871
Rice, Suzanne, 55
Richarde, R. Stephen, 1894
Richerson, Virginia, 708
Richlin-Klonsky, Judith, 1759
Ricker, Curtis E., 1353
Rickford, John R., 885
Rico, Gabriele Lusser, 1480
Riddell, Terence Joseph, 1163
Rider, Janine, 1714
Ridgeway, Lenore S., 506
Rieben, Laurence, 845
Rief, Linda, 647
Rieke, Richard D., 462
Riger, Stephanie, 1057
Riggenbach, Heidi, 1897
Rigsby, Enrique DuBois, 463
Riking, James, 1853
Riley, Kathryn, 1189
Riley-Nuss, Kerry K., 1164
Rind, Bruce Laurence, 1058
Risjord, Mark Winden, 207
Ritchie, Bill G., 260
Rivard, Stuart, 687
Rivers, Thomas R., 208
Rivers, William E., 1693
Roach, Timothy L., 464
Robbins, Bruce Wayne, 1260
Robert, Donald, 1143
Roberts, David H., 651
Roberts, Lissa, 1176
Roberts, Patricia Jenkins, 1481
Roberts, Patricia, 209
Robertson, Linda K., 1665
Robertson, Lynn C., 1059
Robins, Adrienne, 1346
Robins, Susan L., 198
Robinson, Douglas, 800
Robinson, K., 1492
Robinson, William S., 1380
Robinson-Armstrong, Abbie, 21
Rocklin, Edward, 1727
Rodman, Lilita, 1694
Rodriguez, Elizabeth, 1833
Roe, Mary, 566
Roemer, Marjorie Godlin, 1898, 1899
Rogers, Adair, 1143
Rogers, Glenn E., 1900
Rogers, Priscilla, 724
Rogers, Theresa, 846
Rogers, Trumbull, 847
Romaine, Suzanne, 885
Romano, T., 1492
Romano, Thomas S., 1862
Romano, Tony, 1249
Rondinone, Peter, 1529
Root, Robert L., Jr., 210, 1095, 1412
Rorty, Richard, 1085
Rose, L. A., 1492
Rose, Mike, 1520, 1521
Rosen, Jay, 133
Rosenberg, Roberta, 1622
Rosenblatt, Louise M., 647
Rosenn, Barbara Hemley, 1787
Rosenthal, Beverly Margaret, 652
Roser, Nancy L., 103
Roskelly, Hephzibah, 1452
Rosner, Lisa, 1176
Rosner, Mary, 1488
Rosnow, Ralph L., 1060
Ross, Donald, 582
Ross, James, 687
Ross, Philip E., 973
Ross, Susan, 1672
Rossetti, Jane, 728
Rothenbuhler, E. W., 248
Rougemont, A., 1238
Roulis, Eleni, 211
Round, Phillip H., 328
Rouse, Joy, 1137
Rowan, Katherine E., 1695
Roy, Alice M., 974
Roy, William G., 1759
Royer, Daniel J., 212
Ruberstein, Diane, 465
Rubin, David C., 255
Rudinow, Joel, 213
Rudnick, Kenneth Joseph, 214
Rueda, Robert, 584
Rule, Rebecca, 1482
Ruminski, Henry, 1885
Runciman, Lex, 215
Rundquist, Suellen Mae, 975
Runyan, M. Kay, 848

Russell, Bertrand, 1173
Russell, David R., 329
Russman, Linda deLaubenfels, 1138, 1139
Ruszkiewicz, John, 1563
Rutledge, J. Neal, 1072
Rutter, Russell, 1696
Ryan, Howard S., 216
Rymer, Jone, 1674
Rystrom, Kenneth, 387

Sadker, David, 1425
Sadker, Myra, 1425
Sadoski, Mark, 849
Sadowski, Vicki, 687
Sagan, Dorion, 1173
Sahgal, Anju, 885
Saito, Mioko, 653
Salyer, Monte Gale, 1834
Sams, Ed, 1347
Samson, Donald, 1353
Samson, Severine, 1061
Sanchez-Villamil, Olga Irene, 1835
Sanders, R. E., 248
Sandler, Bernice Resnick, 1261
Sangari, Kumkum, 1210
Sansom, Leslie, 1140, 1141
Santopietro, Kathleen, 1788
Sato, Charlene J., 885
Saunders, Anne P., 1816
Saunders, David, 801
Savage, Gerald, 1658
Sawadogo, Geremie, 976
Scardamalia, Marlene, 1463
Schaafsma, David W., 654
Schafer, William D., 571
Scharton, Maurice, 1353
Scheibal, William J., 655
Scheiber, H. J., 1623
Schenck, Mary Jane, 217
Schenkenberg, Mary, 687
Scheurer, Erika, 1483
Schiappa, Edward, 330, 331, 466
Schiefele, Ulrich, 1096
Schierhorn, Ann, 1624
Schiff, Peter, 1484
Schiffman, Byron C., 977
Schilb, John, 121, 187, 218
Schildgen, Brenda Deen, 1789
Schindley, Wanda B., 802
Schine, Rena, 1485
Schleiffenbaum, Erik, 557
Schmersahl, Carmen B., 1488
Schmied, Joseph J., 885
Schmitz, Joseph, 656
Schmudde, Carol, 1486
Schneider, Carolyn, 1625
Schneider, Kari, 2
Schneiderman, Ben, 657
Schneller, Beverly E., 1173
Schober, Michael F., 1062
Schoenfeld, Clay, 387
Scholes, Robert, 803, 1487
Schollmeier, Paul, 467
Schor, Sandra, 1530
Schramm, Mary Jane, 1348
Schramm, Robert M., 729
Schreffler, Peter Hans, 468
Schriver, Karen A., 219
Schroeder, Fred E. H., 609
Schrott, Peter R., 413
Schultz, Lucille M., 1898
Schultz, Robert, 1072
Schumacher, Gary M., 1063
Schuster, Charles I., 159, 284, 1405
Schwalm, David E., 658
Schwanenflugel, Paula J., 850
Schwartz, Jeffrey, 687
Schwartz, Roger, 1790
Schwartz, Sharon, 1472
Schwegler, R. A., 284
Schweickart, Patrocinio P., 1425
Scott, Izadora, 332
Scott, Joan M., 220
Scott, Patrick, 159
Scott, Paula J., 222
Scott, Robert L., 433
Scotton, James F., 387
Scriven, Jolene D., 1631, 1635
Seabury, Marcia Seabury, 1214
Sebasta, Sam L., 103
Sebastian, Daniel, 221
Sebastiani, Lee, 687
Sebeok, Thomas A., 978, 979
Secor, Marie, 38, 1488
Sedgwick, Eve Kosofsky, 1085
Segal, Erwin M., 222
Segan, Rosalie, 1558
Seimff, Dennis P., 114
Seitz, James E., 224
Seitz, James, 223, 980
Self, Burl, 1317
Selfe, Cynthia L., 506, 581, 582, 659, 660, 1488
Seltzer, Amy, 333
Selzer, Richard, 1190
Semple, Marlene C., 506
Sens, Alexander, 469

Sensebaugh, Roger, 22
Sessoms-Fennelly, Lois, 851
Sethna, Beheruz N., 547
Seward, Linda G., 470
Sewell, Marilyn J., 804
Seymor, Evan, 1215
Shakir, Abdullah, 1836
Shamonsky, Dorothy, 661
Shamoon, Linda K., 38
Shannon, Patrick, 647, 1388
Shapiro, Ann, 1697
Shapiro, Lauren R., 617, 1064
Shapiro, Lewis, P., 981
Shapiro, Michael A., 225
Sharratt, Peter, 1165
Shaw, Charles Stewart, 471
Shaw, Clara Seiler, 334
Shaw, Henry Wheeler, 1143
Shaw, Margaret L., 1564
Shaw, Philip, 1837
Shea, George Bernard, Jr., 1760
Shelby, Annette N., 730
Shenholm, Daisy E., 1
Shepard, Lorrie A., 584
Shepherd, G. J., 248
Shepherd, Michael A., 682
Sheridan, Daniel, 1489
Sherwood, Steve, 1349
Shiffrin, Richard, 949
Shipke, Rae C., 687
Shires, Nancy Patterson, 23
Shirk, Henrietta N., 506
Shirk, Henrietta Nickels, 582, 1674, 1698
Shohet, Linda, 1215
Short, Brant, 472
Short, Bryan C., 805
Short, Kathy G., 647, 825
Shrofel, Salina, 1262
Shumway, David R., 805
Shwegler, Robert A., 38
Siachitema, Alice K., 885
Sides, Charles H., 731
Sieber, Sharon, 1456
Siebers, Elizabeth, 1204
Siebert, Bradley Gene, 1565
Siegel, Jeff, 885
Siegfried, John J., 1362
Sills, Caryl K., 1761
Silva, Tony, 1838
Silverstone, Roger, 114
Simmons, Jay, 1901
Simmons, Lovie Sue, 335
Simons, Elizabeth Radin, 226
Simons, Herbert W., 227
Simpson, Jeanne, 1353
Simpson, Mark, 662
Sinatra, Gale M., 822
Singler, John Victor, 885
Singleton, Donna, 133
Sipiora, Phillip, 187
Siple, Patricia, 982
Siple, Patricia, 982
Sirc, Geoffrey, 1566
Sitko, Barbara M., 1488
Skoll, Geoffrey R., 983
Slagell, Amy R., 473
Slagle, Allogan, 1210
Slattery, Patrick J., 1567
Sledd, James, 133, 187, 228, 1287
Slevin, James F., 159, 184
Sloane, Sarah, 2
Sloane, Thomas O., 336
Smagorinsky, Peter, 229
Small, Samuel W., 1143
Smeltzer, Larry R., 732
Smit, David W., 230
Smith, Andrew Richard, 806
Smith, Barbara Herrnstein, 231, 1085
Smith, Brian D., 984
Smith, Carolena L., 1626
Smith, Catherine F., 582
Smith, Charles Henry, 1143
Smith, Craig R., 474
Smith, Frances Lee, 475
Smith, Louise Z., 1373
Smith, Maggy, 1531
Smith, Michael, 103, 1744
Smith, Nathaniel, 905
Smith, Peter Worthington, 733
Smith, Robert E., III., 1699
Smith, Seba, 1143
Smith, Susan Belasco, 1532
Smith-Howell, Deborah, 1117
Smitherman, Geneva, 875
Smithson, Isaiah, 1425
Smoke, Trudy, 1839
Smudde, Peter, 232
Snow, Catherine E., 595, 1097
Snowball, David, 476
Snyder, Benson R., 566
Snyder, Leslie B., 233
Sobnosky, Matthew J., 477
Sobota, Katharina, 478
Soh, Bee-Lay, 1840
Solman, Robert T., 1213
Solomon, Martha, 479

Soon, Yee-Ping, 1840
Sosnoski, James J., 121
Soukup, Paul A., 114
Sova, Ann, 1216
Soven, Margot, 1752, 1762
Sowers, Susan, 645
Spanos, George, 1841
Spatz, Elizabeth, 1412
Spaulding, Cheryl L., 663
Spear, Martin B., 1215, 1751
Speck, Bruce W., 1142
Spellmeyer, Kurt, 133, 1405
Spence, Sarah, 337
Spencer, Barbara, 1627
Spencer, Stacy Lee, 807
Sperling, Melanie, 234
Spinks, Nelda, 1633
Spitzberg, Brian H., 235
Spivey, Nancy Nelson, 236
Sproule, J. Michael, 111
Sproull, Lee, 579, 664
Spyridakis, Jan H., 1700
Squire, James R., 103
Sreherny-Mohmmadi, Annabelle, 114
Sridhar, Kamal K., 885
Stacks, Don W., 1916
Stadler, Harald Alfred, 808
Stafford, Janice Yvonne, 665
Stahl, Norman A., 1853
Stainton, Murray, 824
Stanley, Linda C., 1215, 1763
Stanley-Weigand, Pam, 1628
Stanovich, Keith E., 845, 852
Stansell, John C., 1257
Starr, Douglas P., 1902
Stasz, Bird B., 1790
Stay, Byron L., 1488
Stearns, S., 248
Steckfuss, Richard, 1490
Stedman, Lawrence C., 598
Steele, Meili, 985, 1166
Steelman, Jane Davis, 666
Steen, Lynn Arthur, 566
Steffensen, Margaret S., 885
Steinhoff, Carl R., 1900
Stensvold, Mark S., 1854
Stephens, Diane, 1491
Stephens, Irving E., 1701
Stepp-Bolling, Eric R., 1871
Stern, Leonard, 1065
Sternberg, Robert J., 237, 1046, 1903
Stevens, George E., 1914
Steward, Charles J., 480
Stewart, Ann Harleman, 38
Stewart, John, 238
Stewart, Joseph, Jr., 1092
Stewart, Robert A., 1033
Stewart, Susan, 239
Stewart, Veronica Jane, 809
Sticht, Thomas G., 667
Stine, Jeffrey K., 609
Stires, Susan, 647, 1492
Stiver, Margaret Farrell, 1904
Stock, Juanita K., 1702
Stoddard, Sally, 853
Stohl, Cynthia, 720
Stoicheff, Peter, 770
Stoker, Cheryl Lynn, 854
Stokes, Karina Nancilee, 1167
Stone, John Fred, 810
Stotsky, Sandra, 1066, 1374
Stout, Barbara R., 1215
Stover, Lois, 1791
Stowell, Hilton, 1067
Stratton, Charles R., 1264
Street, B. V., 507
Street, J. C., 507
Street, Richard L., Jr., 1174
Streeter, Edward, 1143
Strenski, Ellen, 1759
Strickland, James, 582
Strickland, Judy, 1350
Strickland, Kathleen, 1493
Strine, Mary S., 811
Strommer, Diane Weltner, 1539
Strong, Michael, 240
Stuart, Rory, 668
Stuckey, J. Elspeth, 133
Stuckin-Paprin, Jacqueline, 1215
Stygall, Gail, 38
Suchan, James E., 732
Sudol, Ronald A., 669
Sugg, Deborah, 671
Suhor, Charles, 1494
Suleri, Sara, 812
Sullivan, Dale L., 1191
Sullivan, Mary Margaret, 1495
Sullivan, Patricia, 241, 582, 1703
Sulzby, Elizabeth, 103, 617
Sun, Hsiao-yu Janet, 481
Sunstein, B. S., 1492
Surber, John R., 1689
Susman, Linda Santarelli, 242
Sutherland, Christine Mason, 338
Sutton, Jane, 339
Suwarno, Peter, 483

Suyama, Barbara, 614
Swan, Judith A., 1179
Swearingen, C. Jan, 114, 672
Sweigart, William, 243
Swilky, Jody, 1265
Swisher, M. Virginia, 982

Takayama, Machiko, 484
Tanner, Gary R., 604
Tanno, Dolores Valencia, 1192
Tate, Gary, 159
Tavakolian, Abdolhosain, 1216
Tay, Mary W. J., 885
Taylor, Bryan C, 485
Taylor, Charles A., 1193
Taylor, G. Stephen, 1890
Taylor, Hanni, 1496
Taylor, Larissa Juliet, 486
Taylor, Peter Leigh, 673
Taylor, Victoria Hyrka, 1905
Taylor, Welford Dunaway, 1143
Tchudi, Stephen, 1412
Tebbel, John, 1144
Tebeaux, Elizabeth, 340, 1674, 1704, 1705
Tebo-Messina, Margaret, 1412
Tedesco, Janis, 244
Teng, Chunghong, 1843
Teraoka, Arlene A., 1210
Terenzini, Patrick T, 1861
Tessmer, Marybeth, 1412
Thaiss, Chris, 1764
Thibeaux, Evelyn Rose, 488
Thiemann, Petra, 557
Thomas, Brook, 489
Thomas, Dene Kay, 104, 187, 674
Thomas, Gordon P., 674
Thomas, John C., 668
Thomas, Lewis, 1173
Thomas, Trudelle, 1288
Thompson, Edgar H, 1728, 1906
Thompson, Isabelle, 1706
Thompson, Laura A., 1068
Thompson, Michael, 724
Thompson, Pearl Monica, 1792
Thompson, William Tappan, 1143
Thralls, Charlotte, 1707
Throne, M. J., 1492
Tiffany, Gerald E., 1907
Tilevitz, Orrin, 989
Tindall, Mary Ellen, 1266
Tingle, Nick, 1497
Tinkler, Keith, 1173
Tinsley, Katherine, 598
Tirone, Patricia L., 245
Tittle, Carol Kehr, 1908
Tnmer, William, 845
Tobin, Lad, 1498
Todd, Judith A., 490
Tomlinsen, Rebecca Joy, 1069
Tompkins, Jane, 1499
Topham, Ronald William, 855
Torgovnick, Marianna, 1500
Touchton, Judith G., 247
Toulmin, Stephen, 1173
Tovey, Janice, 24
Townsend, Edward W., 1143
Tracey, Richard, 1405
Tracy, Karen, 248
Trauth, Gregory P., 990
Travitsky, Betty S., 813
Trebing, James D., 491
Treichler, Paula, 1425
Treiman, Rebecca, 845
Tremblath, Paul, 1217
Tremmel, Robert, 1501
Treweek, David John, 1708
Trimble, Deborah, 687
Trimbur, John, 284
Tritt, Michael, 1729
Troiano, Edna M., 1533
Trollinger, William Vance, Jr., 598
Trooien, Roberta Peirce, 492
Trout, Robert Edwin, 249
Troyan, Scott D., 814
Trufant, Laurel Warren, 250
Trummel, Paul, 675
Tryneski, John, 1267
Trzyna, Thomas, 1674
Tsosie, L., 1492
Tubbs, Gail Lewis, 991
Tucker, G. Richard, 1053
Tudjman, Miroslav, 1218
Tulin, Alexander, 341
Tuman, Myron C., 1375
Turoff, Murray, 676
Turow, Joseph, 251
Tyhurst, James J., 992

Ubbelohde, Michael D., 687
Ueta, Yamiko, 995
Ulmer, Gregory L., 790
Ulrich, Walter, 805
Urban, Greg, 1231

Valeri-Gold, Maria, 677, 1534
Valis, Noel, 114

Vamos, T., 678
Van Buren, Robert, 1709
Van der Vleuten, C. P. M., 1909
Van Dijk, Teun A., 1145
Van Hoeven, Shirley A., 200
Van Nortwick, Thomas, 1268
Van Pelt, William, 1674
van den Brink, Henk, 1446
VanDe Kopple, William J., 993
VanDeWeghe, Richard 1710
Vargas, Flavio O., 1788
Varnhagen, Connie K., 252
Varonis, Evangeline Marlos, 1488
Vassallo, Philip, 1629
Vaughan, David K., 1711
Vavra, Ed, 1351
Veglahn, Peter A., 702
Verlinden, Jay G., 493
Vetcher, Johanna Hester, 856
Vezdos, Tracy, 2
Villanueva, V., Jr., 284
Vipond, Douglas, 205, 1146
Vitanza, Victor J., 121, 342
Vivion, Michael J., 1502
Voight, Ellen Bryant, 1472
Von Koenigseck, Edward V., 1712

Wadsworth, John S., 1765
Wagner, Betty Jane, 103, 1464
Wagner, Daniel, 595
Wagner, Richard J., 734,
Wahlstrom, Billie, 596
Walberg, Herbert J., 253
Walker, Carolyn, 1352
Walker, J. Samuel, 609
Walker, Jeffrey, 994, 1488
Wall, S., 284
Wallace, David L., 254, 585, 1423, 1568
Wallace, F. Layne, 679
Wallace, Ray, 1353
Wallace, Robert K., 1503
Wallace, Wanda T., 255
Walmsley, Sean A., 595
Walsh, Christine M., 256
Walsh, Rosemary E., 494
Walther, Joseph B., 680
Walton, Douglas N., 1147
Walvoord, Barbara E., 1766
Walzer, Arthur E., 257
Wander, Philip, 433, 495
Wansart, W. L., 1492
Ward, Dean A., 1504,
Ward, Dorothy, 1528
Ward, Jay A., 1219
Ward, Steven Craig, 815
Warlaumont, Hazel G., 1630
Washington, Durthy A., 735
Watabe, Masakazu, 995
Watanabe, Suwako, 996
Waters, Gloria S., 982
Waterworth, John A., 681
Watke, Sarah, 1658
Watkins, Evan, 790
Watson, James, 1173
Watters, Carolyn, 682
Wattier, Mark J., 708
Waugh, Linda R., 925
Wayne, F. Stanford, 1631
Wayne, Stan, 1635
Weber, James R., 1674
Weber, Janet M., 496
Webster, Cameron Dale, 857
Webster, Janice Gohm, 1505
Wedell, Allen J., 1632
Weeden, Jared, 1790
Weedon, Chris, 790
Weekley, T., 1492
Weiland, William, 657
Weiler, Kathleen, 1506
Weiler, Marc, 1070
Weimer, Donna Schimeneck, 1194
Weinsheimer, Joel, 816
Weiss, Timothy, 1674
Weissert, Thomas P., 770
Weissmann, Katherine E., 1220
Welch, Kathleen E., 343
Weldon, Mary Susan, 1043
Wells, Barron, 1633
Wenger, Michael J., 1700
Wenner, Barbara, 1569
Wenzel, Gary Edwin, 1570
Wenzler, Ivo, 1289
Werckle, Gerard Joseph, Jr., 1071
Werckmeister, O. K., 737
Wergowske, Gilbert L., 1754
Wernick, Andrew, 738
Wershoven, Carol, 258
Wert-Gray, Stacia, 739
Wetherell, Margaret, 1133
Wetzel, Gloria Hipps, 1730
Wheeler, Phyllis, 1507
Whipple, Robert Dale, Jr., 259
Whitcher, Frances M., 1143
White, Calvin R., 850
White, Edward M., 1290, 1767
White, Eric Charles, 770

White, Fred D., 1571
White, Jan V., 1713
White, Linda, 1354
White, Robert A., 111
White, Ron, 1291
Whitehouse, C. R., 1768
Whitney, Paul, 260, 835
Whitney, Robert, 40
Whitson, Steve Earl, 344, 1168
Whittemore, Greg, 904
Whitworth, Richard, 997
Widiss, Alan, 1737
Wiegand, Richard, 1634
Wieland, Sharon, 1910
Wiemelt, Jeffrey, 183
Wiener, Harvey S., 1215
Wiener, Norbert, 1173
Wiesner, Marcus, 497
Wild, Peter, 135
Wildeson, Daniel L., 1169
Wiley, Karen B., 1687
Wiley, Terrence, 683
Wilkins, Harriet, 998
Williard, Nancy, 1472
Willerman, Lee, 1072
Willhite, R. Keith, 498
Williams, Angela W., 1310
Williams, Dana Nicole, 1215
Williams, David Cratis, 261
Williams, Mary R., 499
Williams, Paula, 1635
Williams, Sharon, 1355
Williams, William F., 684
Willinsky, John, 685, 817
Willis, Clyde Edward, 500
Willoughby, D. Michael, 506
Wilson, Allison, 1292
Wilson, Henry, 1353
Wilson, John T., 1854
Wilson, Paula, 501, 1635
Wilson, Rob, 818
Wilson, Suzanne M., 1249
Winders, James A., 262
Windham, Douglas M., 595
Windt, Theodore Otto, Jr., 395
Winford, Donald, 885
Winkelmann, Carol L., 999, 1572
Winn, William, 686
Winner, Emmanuel John, 345
Winterowd, Ross, 263
Wischner, Claudia M., 819
Wissing, Paula, 1225
Withrow, Mark Houston, 858
Witt, Nancy L., 1148
Witt, Stanley P., 1215
Wittrock, Merlin C., 103
Wiwcharuk, Tom, 264
Wodlinger-Cohen, Rhonda, 982
Wolff, William C., 25, 1353
Wolf, Maryanne, 859
Wolitzer, Hilma, 1472
Wollett, Eleanor L., 1412
Wolterbeck, Marc, 1356
Wongkhan, Siriporn, 1844
Wood, Julia T., 1293
Wood, Sarah Bane, 1073
Woods, Donald R., 1769
Woods, Ed, 1003
Woods, Howard B., 885
Woods, Marjorie Curry, 346
Woodward, Branson L., Jr., 1508
Woodward, Virginia, 647
Woolever, Kristin R., 1577
Woolsey, D. P., 825
Worley, Demetrice Anntia, 265
Worman, Dwight, 687
Worsham, Lynn, 121
Wresch, William, 558
Wright, Alan, 502
Wright, Alice A., 740
Wright, William W., 687, 1509
Wynter, Sylvia, 1210

Yahner, William, 1357
Yanos, Susan B., 1195
Yao, Lucy Chun-Kun, 1845
Yardas, Mark, 1358
Yates, Richard E., 1143
Yau, Ching-Mei Esther, 820
Yearwood, Stephanie, 1269
Yee, Marian, 133
Yeilding, Donnie Deverne Cook, 1573
Yoder, W. Barry, 860
Yohner, William A., 688
Youmans, Gilbert, 689
Youmans, Madeleine, 267
Young, Art, 40
Young, Candace Anne, 1074
Young, Lynne, 1000
Young, Richard, 347, 1405
Young, Thomas E., 1001
Young, Virginia, 1136
Yule, George, 1845

Zani, Bruna, 268
Zappen, James P., 40

Zatorre, Robert J., 1061
Zavarzadeh, Mas'ud, 790
Zebroski, James Thomas, 133
Zecker, Lilliano Barro, 617
Zeitz, Colleen Mary, 1075
Zelhart, Paul, 1918
Zelizer, Barbie, 1149
Zhao, Shanyang, 269
Ziarek, Krzysztof Marek, 1170
Zolliker, Susan, 1076
Zorn, Jeff, 503
Zorn, Theodore E., 741, 742
Zubrow, David, 579
Zuckerman, Mary Ellen, 1144
Zughoul, Muhammad Raji, 1002